ESS
TRANSLATION FRENCH

ESSAYS IN TRANSLATION FROM FRENCH

BY

R. L. GRÆME RITCHIE, D.Litt., LL.D.

AND

CLAUDINE I. SIMONS, Ph.D.

CAMBRIDGE
AT THE UNIVERSITY PRESS
1972

Published by the Syndics of the Cambridge University Press
Bentley House, 200 Euston Road, London NW1 2DB
American Branch: 32 East 57th Street, New York, N.Y.10022

ISBN: 0 521 09205 1

First edition 1941
Reprinted 1952 1957 1962
1965 1968 1972

Printed in Great Britain
at the University Printing House, Cambridge
(Brooke Crutchley, University Printer)

CONTENTS

Preface		*page* vii
I	Descriptive	1
II	Portraits	107
III	Historical and Narrative	135
IV	Characters	197
V	Conversational	227
VI	Literature and Art	253
VII	Philosophical and Reflective	285
VIII	Verse	333
Table of Passages		390
Index of Authors of Passages		391
Index of Titles of Passages		392
Index of First Words of Passages		394
Index of Words Mentioned or Discussed		396

PREFACE

'Translation' may mean many things, from loose inaccurate paraphrase upwards. The definition which we have adopted for our present (Academic) purposes is: 'Such a version as shall before all things make it plain that the translator: (1) has grasped the precise sense of each individual word or phrase as used in the original, (2) has selected, to render it, the nearest equivalent which English usage permits, and (3) has so arranged and welded together these equivalents that the whole becomes an exact counterpart of the French passage equally careful in diction, equally elegant in style.'[1]

The chief difficulties we have encountered in endeavouring to act up to this are discussed in the *Notes*. All the words and phrases concerned are collected in an Index (pp. 396–405).

The linguistic lore thus accumulated might no doubt have been presented in a connected form, or worked up into an ordered whole, as an Essay on Translation. But Essays *in* Translation seem more useful. Our own experience is that in actual practice theories of translation are not very helpful. In dealing with passages of varying style, each case has to be treated on its merits. Unless direct reference can be made to the context, discussion is difficult, and apt to be pointless. Moreover, no one can listen for long whether to undergraduate criticism or to the expostulations of colleagues without realizing that translation must always be largely subjective. What pleases one person of taste and judgment jars on another. The little the translator can do to secure general agreement or at least acquiescence is to put his cards on the table, draw attention to difficulties and offer possible solutions tentatively, with reasons or quotations in support.

---

[1] Ritchie and Moore, *Translation from French* (Camb. Univ. Press), 1918, which sets forth (pp. 1–97) the principles of which the present work is a practical application.

In translating from French, difficulties are apt to pass unnoticed. A French sentence seldom bears the meaning attributed to it by those English readers who assume that a French word has the same sense as its English homonym; or who neglect the context in which it occurs, the date of the passage, the idiosyncrasies of the author; or who overlook some literary reminiscence or are unfamiliar with some French attitude or practice or prejudice. The meaning they attach to a French sentence may be interesting, and the translation may 'make sense'. That it is *not* the meaning intended by the French author will become evident only on further consideration—for example, when in the rest of the passage a contradiction appears or something in the tone or the style arouses vague misgivings, or when somebody else queries the translation proposed.

We have adopted Notes as the best means both of dealing with difficulties as and when they occur and in their relation to a particular text, and of discussing the pros and cons of possible variants.

As regards the choice of English terms, we cannot claim to be consistent throughout. In general we have refrained from 'period' English, but endeavoured to avoid anachronisms, and made only occasional concessions to the apparently widespread belief that some words, e.g. 'glamour', have become inappropriate, even when one is translating, say, a French contemporary of Sir Walter Scott.

Some of the variants rejected are preferable in themselves. The tragedy of the translator's life is that he may hit upon a happy phrase, even upon *the* word, only to find it debarred by the proximity of certain other words or sounds. But we also quote (in *double* inverted commas) translations which are definitely erroneous, but which seem to be instructive. These errors are not at all imaginary; they have actually been made, at various times, some by our students, some also by ourselves.

In translating verse we should have preferred to use prose. But the result was always a hybrid *genre*, to which a verse rendering, with all its drawbacks, seemed in the end preferable. One drawback is that in English the choice of rime-words is much more restricted than in French

and normally the line is shorter; the translator of a French sonnet begins his task bound hand and foot, and some twenty-eight syllables short. In a verse rendering much is lost; in a prose rendering *too* much is lost. It is not of course suggested that verse should ever be used in examinations. Even in class exercises it demands more time and leisure than are usually available.

As to the principle on which the passages have been chosen, it is not primarily 'literature' or 'history of literature' or even interest of subject-matter; it is suitability for practice in translation. They are the siftings of a much larger number selected for class or examination purposes because of the translation 'points' which they contain. Teachers who may wish to use them for the same purposes will find the French text, without translation or notes, of seventy-eight in our *French Passages for Translation* (Cambridge University Press) and that of the remaining thirty-six in *Translation from French*. To both of these books (see Table, p. 390) the present volume will thus serve as a partial 'Key'.

While working at this book, we have constantly taken counsel of trusted friends, French and English, past or present colleagues and students. They are too numerous, not for grateful remembrance but for individual mention. We are particularly indebted, however, to Professor Thomas Bodkin, Mrs E. Duncan Jones, Dr Thomas Walton and Mr J. M. Milner, University of Birmingham; Mr J. H. Brown, King Edward VI School, Norwich; Professor F. C. Roe, University of Aberdeen; and to Miss Rosalind Barker, High School, Middlesbrough, and Monsieur A. Fréchet, Queen's University, Belfast, who, in addition to making valuable comments, have kindly and most carefully corrected the proofs.

R.L.G.R.
C.I.S.

July 1941

ABBREVIATIONS

Cent. Dict.: *The Century Dictionary.*

conj.: conjunction.

cp.: compare.

Dict. gén.: Hatzfeld, Darmesteter et Thomas, *Dictionnaire général de la langue française.*

Fr. Pr.: *French Prose from Calvin to Anatole France.*

H.B.V.: Jules Romains, *Les Hommes de bonne volonté.*

H.D.T.: See *Dict. gén.*

Harrap's: Harrap's *Standard French Dictionary*, vol. i, edited by J. E. Mansion.

Littré: Littré, *Dictionnaire de la langue française.*

Man. Ritchie and Moore, *Manual of French Composition.*

Mansion: see Harrap's.

N.M. *New Manual of French Composition.*

O.E.D.: *The Oxford English Dictionary.*

sb.: substantive.

s.v.: sub voce.

tr.: translate by.

Tr.: Ritchie and Moore, *Translation from French.*

vb.: verb.

=equals, means.

)(as contrasted with.

N.B. Double inverted commas indicate translations considered definitely erroneous.

A query (?) indicates doubt as to the meaning of the French.

I. DESCRIPTIVE

1. PAYSAGE D'AUTOMNE

Tournoël ne se fit pas répéter l'ordre: il engagea les avirons dans les tolets, poussa vivement au large.

Il dirigeait la barque vers la rive opposée. La forêt y dévale du sommet des collines en masses profondes; les chênes et les trembles font une large barre d'ombre sur l'eau qui baigne leurs pieds. Près de descendre dans cette mer de verdure, le soleil la nimbait d'une lumière cuivrée; ses rayons obliques rasaient les cimes des arbres, filtraient entre les dernières branches, allumaient des flammes roses sur la nappe où glissait le bateau. Il n'y avait ni vent ni haleine dans l'air léger, encore chaud à cette fin de jour; la nacre éparse dans l'atmosphère de septembre estompait en douceur toutes les lignes du paysage, arêtes brillantes de l'ardoise sur la silhouette grise du château, lointains boisés qui bleuissaient à l'horizon, nuages colorés de pourpre sur le pâle outremer du ciel. Quelques taches rousses annonçaient

CONTEXT. The scene is *une pièce d'eau* and the chapter is entitled *Sur l'Étang*. One lady has asked: 'M. de Tournoël embarque-t-il avec nous?' and another remarks: 'Je suis sûre que M. de Tournoël est excellent marin.'

1. **slipped his oars into the rowlocks**: *engager* is said of part of a mechanism fitting into another, e.g. of a cogwheel 'engaging'; *tolets* properly = tholepins, loosely = rowlocks.

2. **pulled**: var. *drew*, *put*, not "pushed" or "struck", which call attention to the effort of rowing, whereas *pousser* notes the result only; cp. Sully Prudhomme: 'Tantôt il [le cygne] pousse au large.'

3. **was making for.** The abrupt change of tense, *fit*... *engagea*...*poussa*...*dirigeait*, should be indicated in some way. To say 'made' might imply that the French was *dirigea* rather than *dirigeait*, which describes the course taken by the boat, an attendant circumstance, not a subsequent action.

6. **at their feet**: *l'eau qui baigne leurs pieds* is a case where English expresses the French relative clause more naturally by a preposition. We could say '*washing* up to their feet', but *baigne leurs pieds* is a stock expression which has lost much of its force.

7. **ruddy light**: *cuivré* properly = copper-coloured; the later reference to *flammes roses* supports 'ruddy'.

1. AN AUTUMN LANDSCAPE

Tournoël did not need a second bidding; he slipped his oars into the rowlocks, and pulled quickly out.

He was making for the opposite bank, where the forest comes sweeping down in dense masses from the hills and the oaks and aspens cast a broad bar of shadow over the water 5 at their feet. The sun which was about to sink into that sea of verdure haloed it with a ruddy light; its slanting rays skimmed over the tree-tops, filtered through the last of the branches and kindled rosy flames on the lake with its gliding boat. There was not a breath of wind in the buoyant air, still 10 warm in the late afternoon; the pearly shimmer abroad in the September atmosphere softened all the lines of the landscape: the gleaming edges of the slates on the grey silhouette of the Château, the wooded distances turning to blue on the horizon, and the clouds tinged with crimson against the pale 15 ultramarine of the sky. A few russet patches heralded the

8. Var. *the topmost branches.*

9. **the lake:** *une nappe* is 'a smooth expanse of water', 'a sheet of water'; but these phrases are cumbrous and the normal English for *nappe* is often 'lake'.

with its gliding boat: *où* + verb is often best rendered by 'with'.

13. **edges of the slates.** This Château (de Jossé, en Berri) is described as: 'admirable spécimen de l'art franco-italien de la toute première Renaissance...situé au cœur d'une vaste forêt dans une clairière en contre-haut d'un étang. Un porche féodal donne accès dans une cour carrée, ouverte au regard du couchant sur la nappe d'eau qu'elle domine. Deux corps de bâtiments... se développent au nord et au levant, l'aile du midi, accotée à la cour qui surplombe l'étang....' Looking up at the château from the lake, one might see the *arêtes* of the two wings silhouetted on the main building or, more probably, against the sky; *arête* = any sharp point or edge; *l'ardoise* may be 'the slated roof' rather than 'the slates'.

15. **the pale ultramarine.** The contradiction in *le pâle outremer* is only apparent: 'ultra-' refers not to the shade, but to the fact that the substance from which the colour was obtained was originally brought from 'beyond the sea'. The colour of the sky is described as closer to ultramarine than to any other, and yet lighter in shade. Var. *faded, fading.*

l'arrière-saison, dans le feuillage des arbustes où elle choisit ses premières victimes. On était à cette limite indécise des beaux jours qui change de nom avec les dispositions de chacun : l'été encore, pour les natures exubérantes, sourdes aux pas furtifs du temps ; déjà l'automne pour les complexions intuitives, sensibles aux nuances des choses qui déclinent et finissent. Il en est de nous comme des arbres de la forêt : tous ne sentent pas à la même heure l'éveil du printemps, l'alanguissement de l'automne; les espèces plus délicates devancent la saison des autres.

E.-M. DE VOGÜÉ, *Le Maître de la Mer*.

17. **in the foliage:** *dans* goes with *taches* rather than with *annonçaient*, i.e. in certain shrubs patches of red were beginning to appear.
18. **indeterminate borderline:** for '*cette limite indécise*' cp. No. 13: 'L'Aventin...c'est un lieu indécis', etc., and No. 62: 'cette frontière indécise, où le Limousin', etc.
19. **the fine weather season:** not "summertime", because the name of the season is just what is being discussed; cp. *les derniers*

AN AUTUMN LANDSCAPE 5

fall of the year, in the foliage of the shrubs where it singles out its first victims. That indeterminate borderline of the fine weather season had been reached whose name varies with our own individual moods—still summer, for exuberant natures deaf to the stealthy tread of time; already autumn, for intuitive temperaments alive to the subtle changes at work in things which are declining to their end. It is with us as with the trees of the forest: all do not feel in the self-same hour the awakening of Spring or the approach of Autumn's languor; the more delicate species are the first to feel the change of season.

beaux jours, a common expression for the last fine days of the year, not of the summer; so Lamartine, *L'Automne*:
   'Salut! bois couronnés d'un reste de verdure!
   Feuillages jaunissants sur les gazons épars,
   Salut, *derniers beaux jours*.'
Cp. No. 86: 'quand revient la belle saison.'
 21. **deaf**: var. *insensitive*.

2. PAYSAGE DU SOIR

Puis, il longeait la petite mare à côté, enfermant une eau fauve dans sa cuvette de pierre blanche, à la marge mamelonnée, ondulante et rongée. Il s'asseyait quelques minutes au petit café de Franchart, repartait, retrouvait les arbres, retraversait encore une fois le Bas-Bréau.

Il se faisait, à cette heure, une magie dans la forêt. Des brumes de verdure se levaient doucement des massifs où s'éteignait la molle clarté des écorces, où les formes à demi flottantes des arbres paraissaient se déraidir et se pencher avec les paresses nocturnes de la végétation. Dans le haut des cimes, entre les interstices des feuilles, le couchant de soleil en fusion remuait et faisait scintiller les feux de pierreries d'un lustre de cristal de roche. Le bleuissement, l'estompage vaporeux du soir montait insensiblement: des lueurs d'eau mouillaient les fonds; des raies de lumière d'une pâleur électrique et d'une légèreté de rayons de lune, jouaient entre les fourrés. Des allées, du sable envolé sous les voitures, il se levait peu à peu un petit brouillard aérien, une fumée de rêve suspendue dans l'air, et que perçait le soleil rond, tout blanc de chaleur, dardant sur les arbres toutes les

CONTEXT. Coriolis, a painter suffering from overwork, is recuperating at Barbizon in the Forest of Fontainebleau: 'Coriolis passait ses journées dans la forêt, sans dessiner, laissant se faire en lui ces croquis inconscients....Une émotion...presque religieuse le prenait chaque fois, quand, au bout d'un quart d'heure, il arrivait à l'avenue du Bas-Bréau....'

1–4. The *mare de Franchart* is a small irregularly shaped pool. The path goes past the narrower end. Round the sides are large rounded rocks or boulders. See illustration in Larousse, *Paris Atlas*, p. 229. Visits to the spot (in April) showed that *eau fauve* and *pierre blanche* are not strictly accurate descriptions.

5. **back to**: *re-* in *retrouver* retains some of its original force here, but often means 'duly' rather than 'again', e.g. 'J'ai *re*trouvé mon chapeau', and it is sometimes doubtful whether English requires to express the *re-*, e.g. in No. 14: 'Il ne retrouvait aucune des impressions', etc.

2. AN EVENING SCENE

Then he used to walk past the little pool near by, which contains brownish water in its white stone basin and has a hummocky, undulating, eroded shore. He would sit a few minutes at the little café at Franchart, start off again, get back to the trees, and go through the Bas-Bréau once more. 5
At that hour, in the forest, there was witchery afoot. Mists of green were slowly rising from the clumps where the gentle radiance of the bark was dying away and the trees' half-floating forms seemed to be relaxing, drooping with the listlessness of plant-life at night. High up in the tree-tops, 10 through the fret-work of the foliage, the molten sunset stirred and set flashing the jewelled lights in a crystal lustre. The blue, the misty blur, of evening, was creeping imperceptibly higher; watery glimmers softened the depths; streaks of light, electric-pale and insubstantial as moonbeams, played 15 among the thickets. Rising slowly from the drives, from the sand flying after the carriages, there was a faint ethereal haze, a dream-vapour floating in mid-air and pierced by a round,

---

7. **clumps**: not a very beautiful word, but there seems to be no other = *massifs*.

8. **dying away**: var. *dulling*; cp. O.E.D. s.v.: 'A white mist, gradually *dulling* to a faint red'; 'A sort of mist *dulling* the rich colours of the glen.'

11. **the fret-work of the foliage**: quoted from de Quincey, *The Spanish Military Nun*; var. *between the interlacing leaves*.

12. Cp. Meredith, *Rhoda Fleming*: 'A really fine opal, coquetting with the *lights* of every gem...shot succinct red *flashes*.'

Var. *a lustre of rock crystal*: cp. Lady M. W. Montagu (O.E.D.): 'in almost every room large *lustres* of rock crystal.' The metaphor comes readily after a visit to the Palace at Fontainebleau, where lustres are very conspicuous.

15. **electric-pale**: ? *lightning-pale*. Perhaps *d'une pâleur électrique* is an allusion to electric lighting in its early days, *c.* 1867, when *Manette Salomon* was published. Cp. the '*reflets lunaires* des fanaux électriques' in No. 16, and Kingsley, *Yeast*: 'The kingfisher darted from the hole in the bank like a blue spark of electric light.'

18. Var. *The sun, round*. For a somewhat similar use of *rond* cp. Goncourt (Tr. p. 102) and Flaubert (Tr. p. 103).

flammes d'un écrin céleste. La fenêtre de Rembrandt, où il y a un prisme, et où jouerait la Titania de Shakespeare dans une toile d'araignée d'argent—c'était ce paysage du soir.

E. ET J. DE GONCOURT, *Manette Salomon* (Fasquelle).

20. **Rembrandt's window**: in 'The Philosopher' (Louvre).
21. **were Titania**, etc.: the tense in *il y a* denotes fact, in *jouerait* fancy. Reference to *A Midsummer Night's Dream* does

AN EVENING SCENE

white-hot sun, which was flinging on the trees all the flaming radiance of a celestial jewel-box. Rembrandt's window with a prism, were Shakespeare's Titania sporting in it upon a silvery cobweb—such was that evening scene.

not elucidate the author's meaning, but at least suggests 'cobweb' in preference to 'gossamer', etc.

3. PER AMICA SILENTIA LUNAE

La lune pleine, rayonnante, victorieuse, s'était tout à fait levée dans le ciel irradié d'une lumière de nacre et de neige, inondé d'une sérénité argentée, irisé, plein de nuages d'écume qui faisaient comme une mer profonde et claire d'eau de perles; et sur cette splendeur laiteuse, suspendue partout, les mille aiguilles des arbres dépouillés mettaient comme des arborisations d'agate sur un fond d'opale.

Les massifs serrés et maigres du Bois commençaient à s'étendre. Le ruban blanchissant des allées s'enfonçait très loin dans des taches de noir. Une voiture qui riait passa; puis un pas.

Anatole prit à gauche, entra dans un fourré, marcha cinq minutes, s'arrêta comme un homme qui a trouvé: il était dans une petite clairière. L'éclaircie était mélancolique, douce, hospitalière. La lune y tombait en plein. Il y avait dans ce coin le jour caressant, enseveli, presque angélique de la nuit. Des écorces de bouleaux pâlissaient çà et là, des clartés molles coulaient par terre; des cimes, des couronnes de ramures fines et poussiéreuses, paraissaient des bouquets de marabouts. Une légèreté vaporeuse, le sommeil sacré de

CONTEXT. Anatole, an artist, has gone to bury a pet monkey, Vermillon, in the Bois de Boulogne. 'Anatole se trouvait au milieu de l'avenue de l'Impératrice, quand un morceau de la lune jaillit du nuage déchiré. "Bravo l'effet! fit Anatole....Mais, regarde donc, Vermillon, vois-tu?...Tu as le ciel à ton convoi... la lune, rien que ça! Première classe, franges d'argent...."' Then the author, not Anatole, describes the scene: 'La lune pleine', etc.

1. Var. *was now riding clear*.

2. **opal**: the possible variants for *de nacre* are not very easily worked into the sentence, e.g. *opalescent* [='having a milky iridescence', O.E.D.], *iridescent, nacreous, mother-of-pearl*. The alliteration and the repetition of sounds (*nacre, neige; mille aiguilles, dépouillés, arborisations d'agate*, etc.) should be noted.

3. **a kind of**: a useful translation of *comme* in the sense of 'as it were'.

pearly water. The meaning of *eau de perles* is not clear.

6. **as of agate**. Transposing *comme* is another useful method of avoiding a clumsy 'as it were'.

3. PER AMICA SILENTIA LUNAE

The moon, full, radiant, triumphant, had now risen clear in a sky flooded with snowy, opal light, steeped in silvery calm, iridescent and full of foamy clouds which formed a kind of deep limpid sea of pearly water; and on the milky radiance overhead the myriad twigs of the leafless trees made branching traceries as of agate on an opal ground.

The cramped, meagre clumps of the Bois were beginning to open out. The whitening ribbon of the drives went plunging deep into patches of black. A carriage, and sounds of laughter, passed; then—footsteps.

Anatole turned off to the left, entered a thicket, walked on for five minutes, then stopped like a man who has found his quest. He was standing now in a little clearing. A wistful, gentle, hospitable glade, with the moonlight falling full upon it. Night's caressing, shrouded, almost seraphic light was in that spot. Here and there the bark of birch-trees showing pale; soft lights flowing along the ground; tree-tops, crowns of fine, powdery twigs, looking like tufts of marabou; a vapoury lightness; the sacred slumber of trees in the calm of

---

agate. Cp. 'tree-agate: a variety of agate with tree-like markings', and also 'opal-agate' (O.E.D.).

7. **cramped, meagre clumps**: the reference is perhaps not so much to the *massifs* = clumps as to the trees in them, which are *serrés* = close-set and *maigres* = spindly.

8. **drives**: var. *avenues*.

9. The French sentence is a characteristic effort of Impressionist style, conveying the undifferentiated impression which the senses receive and which the brain afterwards analyses; cp. Mme de Sévigné's similar phrase: 'C'est joli, une feuille qui chante!'

15. **caressing**: var. *soothing, fond, kindly*.

For the boldness of *le jour...de la nuit* cp. Chateaubriand (No. 6), *le jour...de la lune* and Herrick, 'the noon of night'. 'The soothing...*light* of *night*' is not necessarily cacophonous: cp. Genesis i, 16: 'the lesser *light* to rule the *night*.'

16. **the bark of birch-trees**: *des* is not 'the' and 'bark' does not render the plural form of *écorces*. But here the choice is between inaccuracy and bad English.

la paix nocturne des arbres, ce qui dort de blanc, ce qui semble passer de la robe d'une ombre sous la lune, entre les branches, un peu de cette âme antique qu'a un bois de Corot, faisaient songer devant cela à des Champs-Élysées d'âmes d'enfants.

Rien ne déchirait le silence qu'un appel de canards de loin en loin, et le bruissement de la nappe d'eau du lac, frissonnante, à l'horizon.

E. ET J. DE GONCOURT, *Manette Salomon* (Fasquelle).

21. Cp. Ruskin, *Modern Painters*, v: 'these tremulous streets, that filled, or fell, *beneath the moon.*'

night; whiteness asleep; the fancied glimpse of a shadow's 20
robe fleeting beneath the moon, between the branches; something of the soul of Antiquity which broods over a wood by
Corot—it all called up the thought of Elysian Fields for
souls of children.

Nothing broke the silence but a fitful cry of duck and 25
the ripple of the Lake, whose smooth expanse shimmered
on the sky-line.

26. **smooth expanse**: for *nappe* see No. 1, note 9.

Var. *the whispering of the Lake, a sheet of rippling water on the horizon.*

4. CLAIR DE LUNE

La lune était à son plein.... Cet astre qui semble si souvent en France écorné, aminci par l'avarice et l'esprit économe, jamais Bardini ne l'avait vu, non seulement aussi rond, mais aussi bombé. La lune semblait vraiment pleine, sur le point de donner à la nuit la nouvelle jeune lune.... Jamais aussi lumineuse.... Tout le parc s'amusait à jouer, à dix heures du soir, le jeu de l'ombre et de l'éclat.... Seule, au centre du tertre flanqué sur sa droite du grand cormier, la dalle de marbre blanc, entourée à distance de sa chaîne, étincelait sans contraste. Pas un morceau de nuit, pas une poussière même, tant l'air était pur, entre cette dalle et la lune. Bardini se rappelait le jour où elle avait été placée, dans une cérémonie qui ressemblait moins à un enterrement qu'à la pose d'une première pierre. Tout l'édifice ce soir était construit. Bardini admira ses murailles lumineuses, son plafond infini. Autour de cette tombe, plus aucun changement à apporter au monde. Jamais Bardini ne l'avait trouvé à ce point fini, à ce point terminé. Plus rien à changer au cri de la chouette, à ce mutisme des bois que nul vent n'atteignait. L'évolution mourait aux pieds froids de Bella. Le langage de la nuit, le contour des collines étaient à leur sommet classique. Les groupes de bouleaux, les bosquets de hêtres, les touffes de pins parsemées dans le parc, grâce à ce cercle

---

1. **planet**: var. **orb**; *astre* is a general term for the heavenly bodies—sun, moon, planets and stars.

2. **the spirit of thrift**: var. *the thrifty mind*. Cp. Browning, *Men and Women, One Word More*:

'Now, a piece of her old self, impoverished,
   Hard to greet, she [the moon] traverses the house roofs,
   Hurries with unhandsome thrift of silver.'

5. **infant moon**: for *jeune lune* cp. Paul-Hyacinthe Loyson, *Elégie funèbre*:

   'Mais que la jeune lune en un ciel nébuleux
   Te soit une lueur d'elle, suave et triste.'

7. **light and shadow**: var. (if *éclat* seems inadequately accounted for by 'light') *chiaroscuro* = 'the treatment of the light and shade, or *brighter* and darker masses in a picture', O.E.D.

4. MOONLIGHT

The moon was at its full.... The planet which in France so often seems clipped, worn thin by meanness and the spirit of thrift—never had Bardini seen it not merely so round, but so plump. The moon seemed literally full, on the point of giving the infant moon to the night.... Never had it been so luminous. Ten o'clock at night, and the whole park was indulging in the game of light and shadow. Alone—in the centre of the knoll which has the great service-tree on its right—the slab of white marble, loosely girdled by its chain, glittered without contrast. No patch of darkness, no faintest mote, so clear was the air between stone and moon. Bardini remembered the day it had been set in place, at a ceremony less like a funeral than the laying of a foundation stone. The whole monument, to-night, stood completed. Bardini marvelled at its walls of light, its infinite canopy. Around that grave, there should no more change be made upon the world. Never had the world seemed to him so *finished*, so complete. Nothing to alter now in the cry of the owl, or in this hush of the woods unstirred by any wind. Evolution died away at Bella's lifeless feet. The language of the night, the ordered line of the hills, were at their classic pitch. The groups of birches, the groves of beech, the clusters of pine scattered about the park, had rounded out since the

---

10. **no faintest mote:** cp. for the use of *poussière*: Giraudoux, *op. cit.*: 'Un rayon de soleil... chargé de *poussières*, dont chacune était reconnaissable', and Jacques Chardonne, in *Tableau de la litt. fr.* (Gallimard), 1939, p. 127: 'De tous les romans de ce temps, un seul a survécu. Il est venu jusqu'à nous *sans une poussière*.... C'est la *Princesse de Clèves*.'

15. **marvelled:** the change of tense from *se rappelait* to *admira*, when memories gave way to admiration, almost requires 'turned to admire'.

23. **rounded out:** the metaphor—the *cercles* or 'rings' in the growth of trees—is one to which Giraudoux is partial; e.g. *Siegfried*, III, vii: 'Tu peux remettre tes complets français, Siegfried. Tu ne te débarrasseras pas plus qu'un arbre des sept *cercles* que tes années allemandes ont passés autour de toi. Celui

qu'ils avaient pris depuis la mort de Bella avaient atteint la perfection. On sentait à chaque élément sa densité suprême. Le fer de la chaîne était pesant, la terre opaque, l'air lumineux. Aucun bruit du monde qui parvînt là autrement que par l'écho.

    JEAN GIRAUDOUX, *Aventures de Jérôme Bardini*.

que notre vieil hiver a gelé sept fois...est désormais d'une matière insensible aux sentiments et aux climats tempérés.' Cp.

death of Bella, and attained to perfection. One could feel each element had achieved its final density. The iron in the chain was ponderous, the earth opaque, the air luminous. No sound of the world came in but by way of echo.

also Jules Romains, H.B.V. VII (*Province*), p. 96: 'Mareil-en-France.... Le paysage n'avait rien d'extraordinaire.... Il y avait alentour, comme les *cercles* d'un vieil arbre, les pays de France.'

5. COUCHER DE SOLEIL EN AMÉRIQUE

Le soleil tomba derrière le rideau d'arbres de la plaine; à mesure qu'il descendait, les mouvements de l'ombre et de la lumière répandaient quelque chose de magique sur le tableau: là, un rayon se glissait à travers le dôme d'une futaie, et brillait comme une escarboucle enchâssée dans le feuillage sombre; ici, la lumière divergeait entre les troncs et les branches, et projetait sur les gazons des colonnes croissantes et des treillages mobiles. Dans les cieux, c'étaient des nuages de toutes les couleurs, les uns fixes, imitant de gros promontoires ou de vieilles tours près d'un torrent; les autres flottant en fumée de rose ou en flocons de soie blanche. Un moment suffisait pour changer la scène aérienne: on voyait alors des gueules de four enflammées, de grands tas de braise, des rivières de laves, des paysages ardents. Les mêmes teintes se répétaient sans se confondre; le feu se détachait du feu, le jaune pâle du jaune pâle, le violet du violet: tout était éclatant, tout était enveloppé, saturé de lumière.

Mais la nature se joue du pinceau des hommes: lorsqu'on croit qu'elle a atteint sa plus grande beauté, elle sourit et s'embellit encore.

A notre droite étaient les ruines indiennes; à notre gauche, notre camp de chasseurs: l'île déroulait devant nous ses paysages gravés ou modelés dans les ondes. A l'orient, la lune touchant l'horizon, semblait reposer immobile sur les côtes lointaines; à l'occident, la voûte du ciel paraissait fondue en une mer de diamants et de saphirs, dans laquelle le soleil, à demi plongé, avait l'air de se dissoudre.

CHATEAUBRIAND, *Voyage en Amérique.*

4. **pillared grove**: *une futaie* is a wood or plantation in which trees are allowed to grow to their full height.

8. **were to be seen**: *c'étaient des nuages* represents a usage which is rather subtle, where *ce* refers to something not yet expressed, to the state of matters just about to be described. *C'est, ce sont,* etc., thus take the place of verbs like *apercevoir,*

5. SUNSET IN AMERICA

The sun dropped behind the screen of trees in the plain; as it sank lower and lower, the play of light and shadow spread a glamour over the scene: there, a sunbeam stole through the dome of a pillared grove and shone like a ruby set in the dark foliage; here, the light diverged between the trunks and the branches, and cast lengthening columns and shimmering trellis-work upon the grass. In the heavens clouds of every hue were to be seen, some stationary, simulating huge headlands or ancient towers by mountain streams, others drifting like rose-coloured smoke or flocks of white silk. A moment sufficed to alter the scene overhead, and then the eye beheld fierce furnace-mouths, great heaps of red-hot cinders, rivers of lava, landscapes ablaze. The same tints recurred, yet never mingled; flame stood out from flame, pale yellow from pale yellow, purple from purple; all was brilliant, all was surrounded and saturated with light.

But Nature makes sport of the artist's brush; when we fondly think she has attained her greatest beauty, she smiles and grows fairer still.

On our right were the Indian ruins; on the left, our hunters' camp; before us the island unfolded its landscapes etched or modelled in the waters. In the East, the moon, touching the sky-line, appeared to rest motionless on the distant hillsides; in the West, the vault of heaven seemed to have melted into a sea of diamonds and sapphires, in which the sun, half-sunken, looked as if it were dissolving.

sentir, entendre, voir, and must be translated as such, and carefully distinguished from *Il y a, Il y avait*, etc., which have not quite the same sense.

9. **ancient**: var. *hoary*.

mountain streams: *torrent* usually has this special sense.

16. **saturated with**: var. *steeped in*.

21. Var. *the island spread out before us* (*unfolded to our eyes*) *its landscapes*, etc.

6. UNE NUIT DANS LE NOUVEAU-MONDE

Une heure après le coucher du soleil, la lune se montra au-dessus des arbres, à l'horizon opposé. Une brise embaumée, que cette reine des nuits amenait de l'orient avec elle, semblait la précéder dans les forêts comme sa fraîche haleine. L'astre solitaire monta peu à peu dans le ciel: tantôt il suivait paisiblement sa course azurée; tantôt il reposait sur des groupes de nues qui ressemblaient à la cime de hautes montagnes couronnées de neige. Ces nues, ployant et déployant leurs voiles, se déroulaient en zones diaphanes de satin blanc, se dispersaient en légers flocons d'écume, ou formaient dans les cieux des bancs d'une ouate éblouissante, si doux à l'œil qu'il croyait ressentir leur mollesse et leur élasticité.

La scène sur la terre n'était pas moins ravissante: le jour bleuâtre et velouté de la lune descendait dans les intervalles des arbres, et poussait des gerbes de lumière jusque dans l'épaisseur des plus profondes ténèbres. La rivière qui coulait à mes pieds tour à tour se perdait dans le bois, tour à tour reparaissait brillante des constellations de la nuit, qu'elle répétait dans son sein. Dans une savane, de l'autre côté de a rivière, la clarté de la lune dormait sans mouvement sur les gazons; des bouleaux agités par des brises et dispersés çà et là formaient des îles d'ombres flottantes sur cette mer immobile de lumière. Auprès, tout aurait été silence et repos, sans la chute de quelques feuilles, le passage d'un vent subit, le gémissement de la hulotte; au loin, par intervalles, on entendait les sourds mugissements de la cataracte du Niagara, qui, dans le calme de la nuit, se prolongeaient de désert en désert et expiraient à travers les forêts solitaires

CHATEAUBRIAND, *Génie du Christianisme*.

5. **planet**: var. for *astre*, see No. 4, note 1.
8. **folding and unfolding**: cp. G. Moore, *The Lake*, p. 4: 'and the clouds continued to *fold and unfold*, so that neither the colours nor the lines were ever the same.' For the sense of *voiles* here = veils, cp. Larousse, s.v. DÉPLOYER: 'La nuit déploie ses voiles.'
9. **girdles**: cp. Shelley, *The Cloud*:
   'I bind the Sun's Throne with a burning zone
   And the Moon's with a *girdle* of pearl.'

6. A NIGHT IN THE NEW WORLD

An hour after sundown, the moon showed above the trees on the horizon opposite. A fragrant breeze, which that Queen of Night brought with her out of the East, seemed to go before her into the forests like her own cool breath. The lonely planet slowly mounted in the sky, now peacefully following her azure course, now resting on groups of clouds like the summits of lofty snow-capped mountains. These clouds, folding and unfolding their veils, unfurled into filmy girdles of white satin, dissolved into feathery flakes of foam, or high in the heavens formed into banks of dazzling fleece, so grateful to the eye that it seemed to *feel* their softness and their elasticity.

The scene on earth was no less entrancing: the blue, velvety sheen of the moon came down into the gaps among the trees, driving shafts of light into the depths of thickest darkness. The river flowing at my feet now lost itself in the wood, now came into view again, resplendent with the constellations of the night, which it mirrored upon its bosom. In a savannah across the river, the moonlight slept motionless upon the swards; birch-trees, wind-stirred and sparsely set, formed isles of floating shadows on that still sea of light. Close at hand, all had been peace and silence but for the fall of a stray leaf, the passing of a sudden gust, the hooting of the wood-owl; far off, at intervals, could be heard the dull roar of the Niagara Falls, which, in the stillness of the night, was wafted on from wild to wild and died away through the lonely forests.

11. **grateful**: both *doux* and *mollesse* call for 'soft' and 'softness'. For *doux*, possible variants are 'downy' and 'fleecy', and for *mollesse* the corresponding nouns. See also No. 15, note 2.

14. **sheen**: var. *light*, which, however, recurs very frequently.

17. **resplendent**: *brillante* (and *flottantes* further on) are adjectives since they agree. But the rule is not strictly observed, and they may be participial in meaning, in which case the translation may be 'shining' and 'shadows floating.'

23. **hooting**: cp. W. Irving, *Legend of Sleepy Hollow*: 'the dreary *hooting* of the screech-owl'; var. *hoot*.

26. Var. *went echoing on*.

7. LA TOMBE DE CHATEAUBRIAND

En face des remparts, à cent pas de la ville, l'îlot du Grand-Bay se lève au milieu des flots. Là se trouve la tombe de Chateaubriand; ce point blanc taillé dans le rocher est la place qu'il a destinée à son cadavre....

L'île est déserte; une herbe rare y pousse où se mêlent de petites touffes de fleurs violettes et de grandes orties. Il y a sur le sommet une casemate délabrée avec une cour dont les vieux murs s'écroulent. En dessous de ce débris, à mi-côte, on a coupé, à même la pente, un espace de quelque

---

1. **Facing**: not "in front of", which would apply to every place within a few miles' radius of circular walls. *En face de* means that the islet *faces* (is over against, slopes towards) the town; cp. a preceding sentence: '*En face de* la ville...s'étend le quartier de Saint-Servan.'

walls: not "ramparts"; *un rempart* = 'muraille *en maçonnerie pleine*, servant à entourer et à protéger une ville ou un château', Littré; 'rampart' = 'mound of *earth* raised for the defence of a place and usually surmounted by a stone parapet', O.E.D.

a few hundred yards: *à cent pas*, a general phrase, is not to be taken literally. The distance is considerably beyond *cent pas*.
Var. *Facing the walls, a few hundred yards from the town.*

Grand-Bay. The spelling *Grand-Bey* found in the Conard edition (1910) of *Par les Champs et par les Grèves* is the local, and the correct, form. There is another islet, *le Petit-Bey*.

2. **rises out of**: var. *rises straight (sheer) from*. The distinction between *se lève* here and *s'élève* farther on is as between '*Le vent se lève*' (after a dead calm) and '*Le vent s'élève*' (=begins to blow harder). The islet rises straight out of the sea without any intermediary stage, gently rising ground or preparatory rocks, whereas the granite block is placed on a high ledge overlooking the sea; the eye notes, first the ledge and then something superimposed on it. But it is also possible that *s'élève* is accounted for merely by considerations of style.

tomb. The distinction between *tombe* = burial-place (cp. 'Je suis allé prier sur sa tombe') and *tombeau* = funeral monument will be sufficiently noted by using 'tomb' here and 'tombstone' or 'monument' in line 11.

3. **the**: var. *that*: as opposed to 'this' (line 14); here the point of view is from the walls, later it is from the islet itself.

7. THE TOMB OF CHATEAUBRIAND

Facing the city walls, a few hundred yards off, the Grand-Bay islet rises out of the waves. There stands the tomb of Chateaubriand; the white speck notched in the rock is the place he has appointed for his body....

The island is a desert one, with thin-growing grass and a sprinkling of small tufts of purple flowers and tall nettles. On the summit there is a dilapidated fort, with a courtyard surrounded by crumbling old walls. Below these ruins, half-way down, they have cut out in the slope a space of

speck: cp. Fromentin, *Sahara*, p. 266: 'On voit de loin entre la ville et la montagne *un point blanc de maçonnerie.*' N.B. *un point* = a speck)(*une pointe* = a sharp point; cp. No. 80, line 5 and No. 86, note 31.

notched: "cut" is rarely sufficient for *tailler*, which means to cut into a certain shape; cp. tailler *un crayon*, 'to sharpen a pencil' and *un tailleur*, a tailor. Var. *cut out, hewn*.

4. **has appointed**: var. *has intended*; 'has' is necessitated by the facts: the tomb was prepared in Chateaubriand's lifetime at his own request, between 1836 and May 1839; Flaubert's visit took place in July 1847; Chateaubriand died, in Paris, on July 4, 1848, and was buried at St Malo on July 19.

5. For 'thin' cp. *des cheveux rares*. Var. *scanty grass grows on it, mingled with*, etc., cp. No. 87, line 8. The sense of *rare* may be 'sparse', but "sparse grass" is not harmonious. A visit to the spot did not show that the grass was particularly "*rare*"— nor noticeably mingled with "*touffes*". But *rare* is a favourite epithet with Flaubert in this connection: cp. (at Combourg): 'Le silex sort ses pointes de la terre battue où se montre *une herbe rare.*'

9. **half-way down**: "half-way up" would be illogical—or perverse.

they have cut: not quite "has been cut". Flaubert generally prefers the active form, and a subject: *on, ils* [= *les bourgeois*], etc., and may be assumed to be thinking here of human agency = the workmen, the municipal authorities, etc.

in the slope: for *à même* see No. 27, note 6. It is used as in *boire à même la bouteille* (= straight from the bottle, without an intermediary cup or glass, or in *porter un tricot à meme la peau*). The ground in fact slopes gently from the summit of the islet to the tomb, after which it falls sharply to the sea.

dix pieds carrés, au milieu duquel s'élève une dalle de granit surmontée d'une croix latine. Le tombeau est fait de trois morceaux, un pour le socle, un pour la dalle, un pour la croix.

Il dormira là-dessous, la tête tournée vers la mer; dans ce sépulcre bâti sur un écueil, son immortalité sera comme fut sa vie, déserte des autres et tout entourée d'orages. Les vagues avec les siècles murmureront longtemps autour de ce grand souvenir; dans les tempêtes elles bondiront jusqu'à ses pieds, ou les matins d'été, quand les voiles blanches se déploient et que l'hirondelle arrive d'au delà des mers, longues et douces, elles lui apporteront la volupté mélancolique des horizons et la caresse des larges brises. Et les jours ainsi s'écoulant, pendant que les flots de la grève natale iront se balançant toujours entre son berceau et son tombeau, le cœur de René devenu froid, lentement, s'éparpillera dans le néant, au rythme sans fin de cette musique éternelle.

FLAUBERT, *Par les Champs et par les Grèves*.

10. **ten feet square**: strictly speaking, *dix pieds carrés* = ten square feet (= rather more than three feet each way) and seems an inadvertence; for the correct (and cumbrous) formula = ten feet square, see Mansion, vol. II, s.v. SQUARE.

11. **block**: usually *une dalle* = 'slab'. But Flaubert's words suggest some little height above the ground and the cross actually is placed on what we should call a 'block' rather than a slab. So also perhaps *dalle* in No. 4.

12. **base**: var. *plinth*, *socle* (imported from French, 1704, O.E.D.).

14. **beneath**: var. *thereunder*.

face: not "head", which would imply that the body was turned *away* from the sea; *tête* is not generally the back of the head; cp. e.g. 'Il a une bonne tête' = He has a nice face; 'Elle fait la *tête* [= sulks'], 'Il fallait voir sa *tête*'; 'Il en fit une *tête*', 'Quelle *tête*!' etc. See also No. 36, note 3.

14–15. **shall**. The latent idea that it is right, that it is in accordance with the fitness of things, that René should lie for ever by the sea, makes the prophetic 'shall' preferable to 'will'.

20. **unfurl....comes in.** The tense in *se déploient* and *arrive* should be noted. By changing from the future to the present tense Flaubert keeps two ideas distinct: In summer mornings,

THE TOMB OF CHATEAUBRIAND

some ten feet square, in the middle of which stands a 10
granite block, surmounted by a Latin Cross. The monument
is composed of three stones, one for the base, one for the
block and one for the cross.

He shall sleep beneath, with his face to the sea. In this
sepulchre built upon a lonely rock, his immortality shall be 15
as was his life, remote from other men, encompassed about
with storms. The waves, as ages pass, will whisper long
around that mighty memory; in the tempests they will dash
up to his feet, or in the summer mornings when the white
sails unfurl and the swallow comes in from over the seas, 20
long and softly rolling they will bring to him the wistful
charm of far horizons and the kiss of the ranging breeze.
And the days thus gliding by, while the waves of his native
shore swing ever to and fro between his cradle and his tomb,
the heart of René, grown cold, shall slowly crumble away, 25
to the ceaseless rhythm of that everlasting music.

(1) the waves *will* bring certain consolations to the dead,
(2) white sails *do* unfurl, and swallows *are* seen, off the Breton
coast, (1) being a poetical prediction, and (2) an observed fact.

21. **the wistful charm.** As there is no English noun quite
corresponding to *volupté*, paraphrase is unavoidable: var. *the
sad delight, the melancholy consolation.*

22. **the kiss of the ranging breeze.** Here also some latitude
is necessary. In *des larges brises* the epithet *large* connotes
expressions like *prendre le large*, to put out to sea; *au large de
Saint-Malo*, off St Malo. Thus *les larges brises = les brises du
large* = the winds of the open sea. The sense is not far from that
of 'ranging', or of 'free' in 'the wind is blowing free'; cp.
Ruskin, *Modern Painters*, v: 'Above, *free winds* and fiery clouds
ranging at their will.'

23. **gliding by.** Cp. Conrad, *The Mirror of the Sea*, p. 17: 'and
so the *days glide by*.'

24. **cradle...tomb.** The usual collocation 'cradle...grave'
is best avoided; cp. Washington Irving: 'From the *birth-place*
of Shakespeare, a few paces brought me to his grave.' Here
'cradle' is required, *berceau* having probably been suggested by
se balançant. Chateaubriand was born at St Malo.

25. **crumble away:** Flaubert is not speaking only of the
physical heart. We must choose words that are not too material
(like 'moulder') and phrases that are not too vague (like 'be
diffused in the infinite').

26. Var. *to the endless rhythm of that eternal harmony (lullaby).*

8. LES VENTS DU LARGE

Le vaste trouble des solitudes a une gamme; crescendo redoutable: le grain, la rafale, la bourrasque, l'orage, la tourmente, la tempête, la trombe; les sept cordes de la lyre des vents, les sept notes de l'abîme. Le ciel est une largeur, la mer est une rondeur; une haleine passe, il n'y a plus rien de tout cela, tout est furie et pêle-mêle.

Tels sont ces lieux sévères.

Les vents courent, volent, s'abattent, finissent, recommencent, planent, sifflent, mugissent, rient; frénétiques, lascifs, effrénés, prenant leurs aises sur la vague irascible. Ces hurleurs ont une harmonie. Ils font tout le ciel sonore. Ils soufflent dans la nuée comme dans un cuivre, ils embouchent l'espace, et ils chantent dans l'infini, avec toutes les voix amalgamées des clairons, des buccins, des olifants, des bugles et des trompettes, une sorte de fanfare prométhéenne. Qui les entend écoute Pan. Ce qu'il y a d'effroyable, c'est qu'ils jouent. Ils ont une colossale joie composée d'ombre. Ils font dans les solitudes la battue des navires. Sans trêve, jour et nuit, en toute saison, au tropique comme au pôle, en sonnant dans leur trompe éperdue, ils

1. **torment**: var. *turmoil, tumult*.

1–3. **gamut**: *gamme* is used of any gradation = series, range, scale; here it means the musical scale, a series of notes differentiated by pitch; *crescendo* adds the idea of differentiation by intensity; *les sept cordes* returns to the notion of pitch. The lyre has traditionally seven strings; cp. the title of George Sand's work, *Les Sept Cordes de la lyre*.

2. **scud**: O.E.D. s.v. Sense 2*c*: 'a sudden gust of wind.'

le grain is accompanied by rain or hail; *la rafale* = 'un coup de vent court et violent', *une bourrasque* = 'un coup de vent violent', H.D.T.; *la tourmente* = 'une tempête passagère'; cp. Leconte de Lisle, No. 109: 'Ceux qu'a brisés l'assaut sans frein de la *tourmente*.'

5. Var. *one perfect (unbroken) curve*.

6. Var. *Such are these grim wastes*.

14. **blending**; var. *combined*; *amalgamées* comes perilously near the ridiculous = massed bands.

Roman horn; *le buccin* = Lat. *bucina* = a crooked horn (as opposed to *tuba*). The *bucina* was used to give the signal for

8. THE OCEAN WINDS

The mighty torment of the wastes has a gamut of its own, a dread crescendo: scud, gust, squall, storm-wind, whole gale, tempest, tornado—the seven strings of the Lyre of the Winds, the seven notes of the deep. The sky is one wide expanse, the sea one perfect round; there comes a blast, and of all this naught remains; all is frenzy and chaos.

Such these grim waters are.

The winds run, fly, drop, cease to blow, rise again, hover, whistle, roar or laugh; frantic, wanton, unrestrained or riding at ease upon the fretful wave. There is harmony in the howling winds. They make the heavens ring, blow into the thunder-cloud as into an instrument of brass; they set their lips to space, they resound through the infinite with all the blending voices of bugle, Roman horn, oliphant, cornet, trumpet—a sort of Promethean fanfare. Whoso hears them, hears the God Pan. The terrifying fact is that they are at play. Theirs is a monstrous glee, a thing of darkness. In the watery wastes they hunt down the ships. Unrelenting, day and night, in all seasons, at Tropic and Pole alike, sounding their wild horn, they lead, through the tangle of

changing the night-watches (and in Virgil it gives a signal for table); in such contexts it is usually translated by 'trumpet'. Cp. No. 102: 'Au fracas des *buccins* qui sonnaient leur fanfare.'

15. Promethean. The allusion is obscure. Loud noise—in the spirit of Prometheus' defiance of Zeus? Or vaguely = fiery, because Prometheus stole fire from heaven? Or merely = titanic, gigantic?

hears...hears.[1] "Who hears them listens to Pan" would seem odd. The distinction between *entendre* and *écouter* is not always as between 'hear' and 'listen to'; *écouter* may take the place of *entendre*, e.g. to avoid cacophony, as here: 'Qui les entend entend Pan!'

16. fact; var. *truth, thought, thing.* Var. *What is terrifying is that they are merely at play.*

18. hunt down; properly 'beat up', which despite its modern associations is still the technical equivalent of *faire la battue* = to drive game, e.g. grouse, towards the guns.

mènent, à travers les enchevêtrements de la nuée et de la vague, la grande chasse noire des naufrages. Ils sont des maîtres de meutes. Ils s'amusent. Ils font aboyer après les roches les flots, ces chiens. Ils combinent les nuages, et les désagrègent. Ils pétrissent, comme avec des millions de mains, la souplesse de l'eau immense.

VICTOR HUGO, *Les Travailleurs de la Mer*.

the storm-cloud and the wave, the great dark chase of shipwreck. In that chase they are huntsmen. They are at sport, setting the waves, their hounds, to bay at the rocks. They gather the clouds together, and scatter them again. They knead, as with myriad hands, the plastic substance of the boundless waters.

9. LA TEMPÊTE

Depuis deux jours, la grande voix sinistre gémissait autour de nous. Le ciel était très noir; il était comme dans ce tableau où le Poussin a voulu peindre le déluge; seulement toutes les nuées remuaient, tourmentées par un vent qui faisait peur.

Et cette grande voix s'enflait toujours, se faisait profonde, incessante: c'était comme une fureur qui s'exaspérait. Nous nous heurtions dans notre marche à d'énormes masses d'eau, qui s'enroulaient en volutes à crêtes blanches et qui passaient avec des airs de se poursuivre; elles se ruaient sur nous de toutes leurs forces: alors c'étaient des secousses terribles et de grands bruits sourds.

Quelquefois la *Médée* se cabrait, leur montait dessus, comme prise, elle aussi, de fureur contre elles. Et puis elle retombait toujours, la tête en avant, dans des creux traîtres qui étaient derrière; elle touchait le fond de ces espèces de vallées qu'on voyait s'ouvrir rapides, entre de hautes parois d'eau; et on avait hâte de remonter encore, de sortir d'entre ces parois courbes, luisantes, verdâtres, prêtes à se refermer.

Une pluie glacée rayait l'air en longues flèches blanches, fouettait, cuisait comme des coups de lanières. Nous nous étions rapprochés du nord, en nous élevant le long de la côte chinoise, et ce froid inattendu nous saisissait.

En haut, dans la mâture, on essayait de serrer les huniers, déjà au bas ris; la *cape* était déjà dure à tenir, et maintenant il fallait, coûte que coûte, marcher droit contre le vent, à cause de terres douteuses qui pouvaient être là, derrière nous.

3. of: probably the normal English: var. *representing*; "endeavoured to", "tried to" or "attempted to" is fainter praise than *a voulu*. Var. *the picture in which Poussin took the Flood as his subject*.

4. were in motion: var. *were racking*. But the tone of the whole passage is colloquial.

harried: var. *tossed about*.

10. there was: this is a case where *c'étaient* (see No. 5, note 8) is hardly distinguishable from *il y avait*.

17. sheer: we take *rapides* as = steep; cp. *une pente rapide*.

9. THE STORM

Two days now had that mighty voice of doom been moaning round us. The sky was very dark—like what it is in Poussin's picture of the Flood; but the whole of the cloud-masses were in motion, harried by a wind which was terrifying.

And that mighty voice was still gaining volume, growing deep, and continuous—like fury rising into frenzy. As we ploughed onwards we crashed into huge seas, which swirled up into curling white crests and swept by, seemingly in pursuit of each other; they came rushing at us with all their force, and every time there was a terrific shudder and a great dull roar.

Sometimes the *Medea* would rear up and fling herself on to them as though she too were infuriated with them. Then always she dropped down again, with her head still to the wind, into treacherous hollows which lay behind them —into the trough of those species of valleys which opened up sheer before us, between two high enclosing walls; and we felt impatient to come up again, from between those concave, shining, greeny walls which were ready to close in.

Icy rain slashed through the air in long white shafts, flogging and stinging like the strokes of a lash. We had come farther north while beating up the China coast, and the unexpected cold had us in its grip.

Up aloft in the rigging they were trying to furl the topsails, which were already close-reefed; as things were, it was difficult enough to keep her lying to, and now there was nothing for it but to make some headway in the wind's eye, at all costs, because of uncertain land which might be there, astern.

18. **we:** *on* is vague, referring here to the people on board, including Loti, and, further on, to *les gabiers*.

21. **flogging and stinging.** Difficulty is caused by the fact that *fouettait* is transitive and *cuisait* intransitive.

the strokes of a lash: *des coups de lanières* are 'strokes' and not "*the* strokes", but some concession must be made to English usage; see also No. 12, note 4.

25. **as things were:** "already", besides having just been used, is better avoided here. It is apt to give an exotic tone to an English sentence; see for example No. 31, note 16.

Il y avait deux heures que les gabiers étaient à ce travail, aveuglés, cinglés, brûlés par tout ce qui leur tombait dessus, gerbes d'écume lancées de la mer, pluie et grêle lancées du ciel; essayant, avec leurs mains crispées de froid qui saignaient, de crocher dans cette toile raide et mouillée qui ballonnait sous le vent furieux.

Mais on ne se voyait plus, on ne s'entendait plus.

PIERRE LOTI, *Mon frère Yves.*

31. **was battering at:** *leur tombait dessus* is familiar, almost = was being dumped on them.

THE STORM

For two hours the topmen had been on the job, blinded, lashed and seared by what was battering at them—masses of spray hurled from the sea, rain and hail pelting from the sky; trying with their numbed and bleeding hands to get a grip on that stiff soaking canvas which kept flying out in the raging wind.

But they could not see each other now, nor hear each other speaking.

33. **to get a grip on**: *crocher = saisir la toile d'une voile à plusieurs mains pour la ferler* = technically, 'to hand in'.
36. **hear each other**: ? *hear themselves*.

10. SOUS L'ÉQUATEUR

De la hune où Yves habitait, en regardant en bas, on voyait que ce monde bleu était sans limite, c'étaient des profondeurs limpides qui ne finissaient plus; on sentait combien c'était loin, cet horizon, cette dernière ligne des eaux, bien que ce fût toujours la même chose que de près, toujours la même netteté, toujours la même couleur, toujours le même poli de miroir. Et on avait conscience alors de la *courbure* de la terre, qui seule empêchait de voir au delà.

Aux heures où se couchait le soleil, il y avait en l'air des espèces de voûtes formées par des successions de tout petits nuages d'or; leurs perspectives fuyantes s'en allaient, s'en allaient en diminuant se perdre dans les lointains du vide; on les suivait jusqu'au vertige; c'étaient comme des nefs de temples apocalyptiques n'ayant pas de fin. Et tout était si pur, qu'il fallait l'horizon de la mer pour arrêter la vue de ces profondeurs du ciel; les derniers petits nuages d'or venaient *tangenter* la ligne des eaux et semblaient, dans l'éloignement, aussi minces que des hachures.

Ou bien quelquefois c'étaient simplement de longues bandes qui traversaient l'air, or sur or: les nuages d'un or clair et comme incandescent, sur un fond byzantin d'or mat et terni. La mer prenait là-dessous une certaine nuance bleu paon avec des reflets de métal chaud. Ensuite tout cela s'éteignait très vite dans des limpidités profondes, dans des couleurs d'ombre auxquelles on ne savait plus donner de nom.

Et les nuits qui venaient après, les nuits mêmes étaient

NOTE. The frequent repetitions (*s'en allaient, s'en allaient*, etc.), abstract plurals (*immobilités lourdes*) and purely stylistic distinctions (*profondeurs limpides*)(*limpidités profondes*) are very characteristic of Loti, and hardly translatable.

Title; var. *Crossing the Line = Nous passons l'équateur.*

1. **lived.** Yves did 'live' up aloft, with his belongings round him.

3. **crystal depths;** for the force of *c'étaient* here and below, which are to be distinguished from *il y avait*, see No. 5, note 8.

10. Var. *During (the) sunset hours.*

10. AT THE EQUATOR

From the crow's nest where Yves lived up aloft, you could see, looking downward, that this blue world was boundless— crystal depths without end. You could feel how very far away was the horizon, that uttermost line of the waters, though everything was still the same as when seen from close at hand, had still the same sharpness, still the same colour, still the same mirror-like polish. And then you realized the Curvature of the Earth, the only thing preventing a further view.

At sun-down, every day, there were airy archways formed by a series of tiny little golden clouds; their retreating vistas grew fainter and fainter till lost to sight in the distances of empty space; the eye continued along them till giddiness supervened; the impression was of naves in temples of the Apocalypse which had no end. And all was so perfectly clear that only the sea-line could intercept the view into those celestial depths; the last little golden clouds took the water-line at a tangent and seemed, with the effect of distance, as slender as hachures.

Or else sometimes you saw just long streamers floating through the air, gold upon gold—the clouds, of a light and apparently incandescent gold, on a Byzantine ground of gold which was dulled and lustreless. The sea beneath them assumed a certain peacock-blue shade, with glints of heated metal. Then the whole faded away very quickly into limpid depths, into shadowy colours no longer possible to name.

And the nights which followed on—the very nights them-

airy archways; cp. the parallel passage from H. Melville, given on next page.

13. Var. *you traced them out.*

15. **Apocalypse**; var. *Book of Revelations.* Var. *in some visionary temple.*

18. Var. *met the water's rim.*

22. **apparently**; *comme* = as it were. But this English phrase is heavier than *comme* and cannot be repeated many times in one passage as *comme* is, notably in Loti's prose.

26. Var. *into shadow shades which one could no longer name.*

lumineuses. Quand tout s'était endormi dans des immobilités lourdes, dans des silences morts, les étoiles apparaissaient en haut plus éclatantes que dans aucune autre région du monde.

Et la mer aussi éclairait par en dessous. Il y avait une sorte d'immense lueur diffuse dans les eaux. Les mouvements les plus légers, le navire dans sa marche lente, le requin en se retournant derrière, dégageaient dans les remous tièdes des clartés couleur de ver-luisant. Et puis, sur le grand miroir phosphorescent de la mer, il y avait des milliers de flammes folles; c'étaient comme des petites lampes qui s'allumaient d'elles-mêmes partout, mystérieuses, brûlaient quelques secondes et puis mouraient. Ces nuits étaient pâmées de chaleur, pleines de phosphore, et toute cette immensité éteinte couvait de la lumière, et toutes ces eaux enfermaient de la vie latente à l'état rudimentaire, comme jadis les eaux mornes du monde primitif.

PIERRE LOTI, *Mon frère Yves*.

31. **gave out light**: *éclairait* is intransitive here.

37. **like tiny lamps**: 'like' condenses the whole expression *c'étaient comme*.

41. **generated**: var. *smouldered with*.

Ch. I (end). ...I went aloft one day, to stand my allotted two hours at the masthead. It was toward the close of a day, serene and beautiful. There I stood, high upon the mast, and away, away, illimitably rolled the ocean beneath. Where we then were was perhaps the most unfrequented and least known portion of these seas....

I cast my eyes downward to the brown planks of the dull, plodding ship, silent from stem to stern; then abroad.

In the distance what visions were spread. The entire western horizon high piled with gold and crimson clouds; airy arches, domes and minarets; as if the yellow, Moorish sun were setting

selves had light in them. When all things lay sunk in heavy
stupor, in deathly silence, the stars shone out above, brighter
than in any other part of the world.

And the sea too gave out light, from underneath. There
was a sort of immense glow diffused through the waters.
The faintest movements—the ship plodding onwards, the
shark turning over in the wake—brought out lights like
glow-worms in the warm eddies. Also, on the great phosphorescent mirror of the sea, there were thousands of
flickering flames, like tiny lamps lighting up everywhere
of their own accord, mysteriously, burning for a few seconds
and then dying out. Those nights were a-swoon with heat,
teeming with phosphorus; the whole of that vast darkened
expanse generated light, and all those waters held latent
within them life in its rudimentary forms, as did of old the
watery wastes of the primæval world.

behind some vast Alhambra. Vistas seemed leading to worlds
beyond. To and fro, and all over the towers of this Nineveh in
the sky, flew troops of birds. Watching them long, one crossed
my sight, flew through a low arch, and was lost to view....

Ch. xxxviii. Starting, we beheld the ocean of a pallid white
colour, coruscating all over with tiny sparkles. But the pervading
hue of the water cast a cadaverous gleam upon the boat, so
that we looked to each other like ghosts. For many rods astern
our wake was revealed in a line of rushing illuminated foam;
while here and there beneath the surface, the tracks of sharks
were denoted by vivid, greenish trails, crossing and recrossing
each other in every direction. Farther away, and distributed
in clusters, floated on the sea, like constellations in the heavens,
innumerable Medusae....   HERMAN MELVILLE, *Mardi.*

11. CARTHAGE

Mais une barre lumineuse s'éleva du côté de l'Orient. A gauche, tout en bas, les canaux de Mégara commençaient à rayer de leurs sinuosités blanches les verdures des jardins. Les toits coniques des temples heptagones, les escaliers, les terrasses, les remparts, peu à peu, se découpaient sur la pâleur de l'aube; et tout autour de la péninsule carthaginoise une ceinture d'écume blanche oscillait tandis que la mer couleur d'émeraude semblait comme figée dans la fraîcheur du matin. Puis à mesure que le ciel rose allait s'élargissant, les hautes maisons inclinées sur les pentes du terrain se haussaient, se tassaient, telles qu'un troupeau de chèvres noires qui descend des montagnes. Les rues désertes s'allongeaient: les palmiers, çà et là sortant des murs, ne bougeaient pas; les citernes remplies avaient l'air de boucliers d'argent perdus dans les cours, le phare au promontoire Hermæum commençait à pâlir. Tout au haut de l'Acropole, dans le bois de cyprès, les chevaux d'Eschmoûn, sentant venir la lumière, posaient leurs sabots sur le parapet de marbre et hennissaient du côté du soleil.

Il parut; Spendius, levant les bras, poussa un cri.

Tout s'agitait dans une rougeur épandue, car le Dieu, comme se déchirant, versait à pleins rayons sur Carthage la pluie d'or de ses veines. Les éperons des galères étincelaient, le toit de Khamon paraissait tout en flammes, et l'on apercevait des lueurs au fond des temples dont les portes s'ouvraient. Les grands chariots arrivant de la campagne faisaient tourner leurs roues sur les dalles des rues. Des dromadaires chargés de bagages descendaient les rampes. Les changeurs dans les carrefours relevaient les auvents de leurs boutiques. Des cigognes s'envolèrent, des voiles blanches palpitaient.   FLAUBERT, *Salammbô* (Fasquelle).

1. **in**: *du côté de*, properly = 'in the direction of', is often simply 'in'.

4. **city walls**: for *remparts* see No. 7, note 1.

6. **surf**: *écume* here is hardly "foam"; cp. 'There is a *belt of surf* along the African coast and ships land their passengers in surf-boats' (*Encycl. Brit.*).

19. **throwing up**: var. *raising*, if it is an act of adoration.

21. **was now astir.** The abrupt changes of tense *posaient*...

11. CARTHAGE

But a bar of light arose in the East. Below, on the left, the water-ways of Megara began to show their white curves streaking the greenery of the gardens. The conical roofs of the seven-sided temples, the stairways, terraces, city walls, little by little stood out against the pallor of the dawn; and all round the Carthaginian peninsula a belt of white surf swung to and fro, while the emerald sea looked as though it were frozen in the chill of the morning. Then, as the rosy sky widened out, the tall houses sloping with the ground towered up, and bunched together like a herd of black goats coming down from the mountains. The empty streets lengthened out; the palm-trees, rising from the walls here and there, stirred not a leaf; the brimming cisterns looked like silver bucklers left lying in the courtyards; the beacon on the Hermæum headland was beginning to pale. At the very top of the Acropolis, in the cypress grove, the horses of Eshmun, feeling the light approaching, set their hoofs upon the marble parapet and whinnied towards the sun.

The sun appeared; Spendius, throwing up his arms, uttered a cry.

All was now astir in streaming crimson, for the Sun-God, as if rending himself, was pouring freely over Carthage the golden glory of his veins. The beaks of the galleys glittered, Khamon's roof seemed all in flames and lights could be perceived glimmering in the depths of the temples through their opening doors. The great wains from the country were coming in, rumbling over the flagstones in the streets. Dromedaries laden with baggage stalked down the steep lanes. The money-changers in the crossways were setting up the awnings of their booths. Storks rose on the wing; and there were white sails fluttering.

hennissaient (descriptive)...*parut* (narrative)...*s'agitait* (descriptive) should be noted.

22. **freely**: for *à pleins rayons* cp. *à pleines mains*.

the golden glory: this rendering, though free, may be justifiable as a stock expression and it avoids the jingle 'rain...veins'.

26. **wains**: N.B. *un chariot* = a cart; a 'chariot' = *un char*.

27. **rumbling**: var. *lumbering*.

12. LE CAMPO VACCINO

C'était le *Campo Vaccino*: des portiques survivant à des temples écroulés, des colonnades isolées qui ne s'appuyaient plus qu'au ciel, des colonnes foudroyées soutenant des entablements où des graminées rongeaient des noms d'empereurs, des arcs de triomphe enterrés de vingt pieds et de vingt siècles, des fosses encombrées de fragments et de miettes d'édifices, d'énormes voûtes de basiliques, aux caissons effondrés, repercées par le bleu du jour—au bout de la Voie sacrée, de grandes dalles gisantes, des quartiers de lave, pavés de feu refroidi, usés par le pas enchaîné des Nations, creusés par les ornières de la Victoire—ici, la vieillesse d'or des pierres; là, au devant d'églises, le marbre païen pourri, les troncs de cipolin dépolis, exfoliés, usés du temps, blessés de coups, ayant des entailles comme des armures et de grands trous comme de vieux arbres—partout des débris formidables, religieux et superbes, sur lesquels semblait avoir

CONTEXT. Mme Gervaisais is a Frenchwoman who has come to live in Rome and is brought back from philosophic doubt to the Catholic faith by contact with the grandeur of the Holy City. On her first outing she was being driven to the Forum when the carriage stopped before an open space and she looked up in wonder. It was the Campo Vaccino....

1. Var. *porticos surviving fallen temples* (*surviving from temples that had crumbled away*).

3. **splintered**: var. *blasted*.
upholding: var. *supporting, bearing aloft*.
entablatures: that part of an order which is above the column, including the architrave, the frieze and the cornice.

4. **fretted away**: var. *gnawed, ate away, eroded*.
the names of Emperors: *des noms d'empereurs* = properly 'names', not '*the* names' but see No. 9, note 21.

7. **basilicas**: *une basilique* is a long building with double columns and a semicircular apse at the end.
coffered panels: *caisson* means a sunken panel in ceilings, vaults and cupolas.

9. **slabs**: possibly rather 'blocks'; on *dalles* see No. 7, note 11.

12. THE CAMPO VACCINO

It was the *Campo Vaccino*: porches which had outlasted their
fallen temples, severed colonnades abutting now on nothing
but sky, splintered pillars upholding entablatures where wild
grasses fretted away the names of Emperors, triumphal
arches buried twenty feet and twenty centuries deep, pits 5
encumbered with shards and fragments of masonry, wide-
spanned vaultings of basilicas, their coffered panels fallen
in—now penetrated again by the blue of daylight—at the
end of the Via Sacra, great slabs lying on the ground, blocks
of lava—causeways of fire extinct and cold, worn by the 10
fettered feet of the Nations, rutted by Victory's chariot-
wheels—here the mellow old age of stones; there, on the fronts
of churches, the pagan marble in decay, the column-shafts of
cipolin, sheenless and flaking, worn by time, dinted by blows,
gashed like plates of armour and riddled with great holes, 15
like old trees; everywhere ruins, stupendous, awesome,

lying on the ground: var. *prostrate*; cp. Scott, *Ivanhoe* (ch. 1),
Man., No. XLIX.

10. **causeways:** it seems best for translation purposes to
interpret freely and take *pavés* in its secondary sense = causeways;
but the construction without *des* shows that *pavés* further defines
quartiers and has its primary sense = paving-stones. Cp. also
Mme de Staël, *Corinne* (Littré): 'Les larges pavés blancs de
Naples, ces *pavés de lave*.'

13. **column-shafts:** perhaps *les troncs* were only 'stumps' or
'drums'.

14. **sheenless:** cp. W. de la Mare:
    'Dim-berried is the mistletoe
    With globes of *sheenless* grey.'
dépolis means 'that had lost their polish'; var. *dulled*; cp. *verre
dépoli* = non-transparent (frosted) glass.

flaking: var. *exfoliated, scaling*; cipolin [Italian *cipolla* =
onion] is a marble of foliated structure like the coats of an
onion.

16. **awesome, proud:** *religieux* and *superbes* have here their
full Latin sense (*religiosus* = awe-inspiring, *superbus* = proud.

passé la rouille de l'eau et le noir de la flamme, un incendie et un déluge, toutes les colères de l'homme et du ciel—telle fut, dans sa grandeur invaincue, la première apparition de Rome antique à Mme Gervaisais.

E. ET J. DE GONCOURT, *Madame Gervaisais* (Fasquelle).

proud, over which seemed to have passed the rust of water and the smirch of flame—fire and flood, the whole wrath of man and of heaven—such was, in its unvanquished grandeur, the first vision of ancient Rome as it broke on Mme Gervaisais.

13. L'AVENTIN

J'aime le mélancolique Aventin; c'est un lieu indécis couvert de vignes et de jardins, de couvents et d'églises....La dernière fois que je me promenai sur ces pentes, c'était au commencement d'un après-midi d'Avril. Tout respirait le désordre tumultueux du Printemps. La terre et le ciel étaient aussi encombrés l'un que l'autre. De gros nuages noirs et déchiquetés pendaient sur les ruines du Palatin, qui leur répondaient par des masses presque aussi informes. La lumière jaune tombait par plaques sur le paysage; une église disparaissait dans l'ombre d'un nuage; une autre, frappée d'un rayon, prenait une importance momentanée; çà et là, le rose violacé des arbres de Judée alternait avec le mauve pâle des glycines, des boutons d'or éclairaient l'herbe à mes pieds, et, dans cette incertitude où se bousculaient la nature, la religion, l'art et l'histoire, sans qu'aucune prédominance s'établît, il n'était pas jusqu'à la petite fleur éclose près de moi qui, secouant sa tête folle, ne se vantât d'être la reine de l'instant.

Redescendu dans Rome, j'oubliai le ciel. Je ne le revis qu'après le soleil couché. Toutes les choses de la terre s'étaient massées et durcies. Sur un fond d'espace limpide, les nuages s'entassaient des deux côtés de Saint-Pierre, ils montaient à des hauteurs vertigineuses, et, dessinant, en plein ciel, d'énormes gestes d'architecture, ils rivalisaient avec la coupole. Mais elle ne leur cédait nullement. Fermement établie parmi eux, dans sa compacte rondeur, rien

1. **melancholy...indeterminate**: '*mélancolique*' here seems to border on 'forlorn', 'disconsolate', and *indécis* on 'undecided', 'haphazard'. For *indécis* cp. No. 1, note 18.

6. **encumbered**: var. *heavy-laden, overcrowded*; cp. *une rue encombrée*.

8. **formless**: var. *amorphous*; cp. No. 94, note 2.
   in patches: var. *patchily*.

9. **was lost**: var. *was dim, lay dim*; not "disappeared into". In descriptions *disparaître dans le brouillard*, etc., usually means to be *dimly* seen, but seen all the same; cp. No. 20, note 10.

10. Var. *took momentary bulk*; *bulked largely for a moment* (*importance* often refers to size).

13. THE AVENTINE

I love the melancholy Aventine; it is an indeterminate sort of spot, covered with vineyards and gardens, with convents and churches.... The last time I walked these slopes was early one April afternoon, when everything suggested the riotous confusion of Spring. Earth and sky were equally encumbered. Great black jagged clouds hung over the ruins on the Palatine, which responded with masses well-nigh as formless. The yellow light fell in patches on the landscape; one church was lost in the shadow of a cloud; another, caught by a ray of sunshine, came into momentary prominence; here and there the pink and purple of the Judas trees alternated with the pale mauve of the wistarias, the grass at my feet was lit with buttercups and in that atmosphere of uncertainty, with nature, religion, art and history jostling each other and none attaining predominance, even the tiny flower abloom beside me, tossing her daft head, vaunted herself queen of the hour.

Down in Rome once more, I forgot about the sky and did not see it again till after sunset. Then all things on earth had massed and hardened. Against a background of limpid space, the clouds piled themselves up on either side of St Peter's; they climbed to dizzy heights and, tracing out in the heavens vast architectural flourishes, vied with the cupola. But it yielded not one whit. Firmly set among them,

---

15. **predominance**: var. *mastery*.

Var. *the very floweret*.

16. **daft**: var. (if the Northern flavour seems too pronounced) *crazy, silly, wanton*.

Var. *boasted to be*.

19. **on earth**: var. *terrestrial*.

20. Var. *had grown tenser and harder; had drawn together and hardened in outline*.

"clear space" would be ambiguous.

21. **piled themselves up**: var. *were banking up (gathering)*.

22. Var. *in mid-heaven, in the open sky*.

23. **flourishes**: var. *designs, schemes*.

24. Var. *fully held its own*.

qu'en étant fixement la même, elle dominait leurs prestiges. Ces nuages ressemblaient à tout parce qu'ils n'étaient rien. Ébauches, rêves, projets, on voyait en eux toutes les formes ambitieuses de l'impuissance. Mais le Dôme, lui, c'était l'Œuvre. ABEL BONNARD, *Rome.*

25. Var. *simply by remaining its own solid self.*
27. Var. *First drafts, Adumbrations, Attempts, Essays.*

in its compact roundness, merely by being steadfastly the same, it outdid their splendours. Those clouds seemed to be all things because they were nothing. Sketches, dreams, plans—in them you could see all the ambitious forms of impotence. But the Dome—the Dome was Achievement.

28. **forms:** var. *shapes.*
29. **impotence:** var. *futility, failure.* Var. *you could see in them impotence in all its ambitious forms.*

14. LES TOMBEAUX DES KHALIFES

Assemblage unique des plus gracieux bijoux de pierre que des architectes joailliers aient jamais ciselés. Égrenés sur la plaine, ils sortaient de l'écrin de sable dont ils ont la teinte de grisaille jaunâtre, au point qu'on les pourrait croire modelés par le vent du désert avec la poussière ambiante. Mieux que le plein jour, la lumière de la lune découpait chaque relief des mosquées funéraires: coupoles en forme de mitres, dômes cannelés, minarets où une dentelle d'arabesques s'enroule sous les balcons ajourés. Les deux coupoles conjuguées de Sultan Barkouk et le minaret élancé de Kaït bey dominaient la cité des tombes charmantes. Délabrées et croulantes pour la plupart, ces merveilles ont la séduction des choses frêles, trop fines pour vivre longtemps, et qu'il faut admirer vite parce qu'on les sent qui meurent. Un enchantement de rêve, c'était le seul sentiment qu'éprouvât Tournoël. Devant les sépultures sarrasines, il ne retrouvait aucune des impressions que lui avait laissées sa soirée à Saqqarah; l'immémoriale et sérieuse nécropole de Memphis lui avait parlé d'éternité; ici, tout était songe d'ombres légères, jeux des génies aériens, roses effeuillées, dentelles déchirées dans un bal de la Mort, chez les princes élégants

1. **unique**: var. *peerless, unmatched, matchless*; **assemblage**: not quite "collection"; cp. Proust, *Du Côté de chez Swann*, II, p. 185: 'Ainsi, c'était la saison où le Bois de Boulogne trahit le plus d'essences diverses et juxtapose le plus de parties distinctes en un *assemblage* composite.'

2. Var. *dotted*: *égrener* (from *é-* and *grain* was used originally of grapes, e.g. '*égrener* une grappe de raisins' = to pick the grapes from the bunch; and is frequently transferred to similar cases, particularly to the beads (*les grains*) of a rosary, also to musical notes, e.g. in No. 99.

7. **the tomb mosques**: near Cairo, 'erroneously known to Europeans as the Tombs of the Caliphs....The chief tomb mosques are those of Sultan Barkuk (1410) and Kaït Bey (*c.* 1470) with a slender minaret 135 feet high' (*Encycl. Brit.*).

9. **twining**: var. *twisting and twining*.

10. **twin cupolas**: cp. *canons conjugués* = paired guns.

11. **towered above**: var. *rose over* (*above*).

14. THE TOMBS OF THE CALIPHS

A unique assemblage of the daintiest trinkets of stone-work
ever wrought by jeweller-architects, they lay strung out over
the plain, spilled from their sandy casket, whose tinge of
yellowish grisaille they share—so much so that one might
fancy they had been fashioned by the desert wind from the 5
dust around. More clearly than broad daylight, the light of
the moon showed up every bit of relief on the tomb mosques:
mitre-shaped cupolas, fluted domes, minarets with a tracery
of arabesques twining under the fretted balconies. Sultan
Barkuk's twin cupolas and Kaït Bey's slender minaret 10
towered above the city of lovely tombs. Dilapidated and
ruinous, most of them, these marvels have the fascination
of things fragile, too delicate to last, things which we must
hasten to admire because we feel they are dying. Dream-
like enchantment was the only feeling Tournoël experienced. 15
Looking at the Saracen burial-places, he did not feel this
time any of the impressions left with him by his evening at
Sakkara; the solemn age-old necropolis at Memphis had
spoken of eternity; here, all was a dream of flitting shadows,
frolics of the genies of the air, rose-leaves scattered, lace 20
torn at a Dance of Death in the halls of the dashing princes

city of lovely tombs: ? *the*; cp. city of *the* dead, city of *the* dreaming spires, but *la cité des livres* = the city of books; *tombes charmantes*: cp. Baudelaire, *Le Flacon*, No. 111, stanza 5: 'charmant et sépulcral.'

16. **Looking at:** var. *Standing before.*

feel this time: var. *recover, recapture.* For the use of *retrouver* see No. 2, note 5.

18. **Sakkara:** opposite Memphis, which was the ancient capital of Egypt, fourteen miles south of Cairo.

had spoken. English perhaps hardly requires 'to him'; e.g. 'Je *lui* ai répondu' is often simply 'I replied'. It is also doubtful whether 'had spoken' would not be better expressed simply as 'spoke'. In such cases French throws the action farther back than English usually does, e.g. 'Tiens, je ne vous *avais* pas *reconnu*'; 'Je ne vous *avais* pas *entendu* sonner.'

19. **flitting:** var. *fickle.*

des Mille et une Nuits. Ces mausolées n'avaient de triste que leur abandon dans le désert et le regret qu'ils donnaient de leur fin prochaine; des rayons de lune filtraient entre les grandes lézardes, plongeaient dans les plaies béantes des dômes; sur les carcasses des plus mutilés, on découvrait à peine quelques vestiges des anciennes rosaces; de la face des vieux squelettes le plâtre était tombé comme un fard.

E.-M. DE VOGÜÉ, *Le Maître de la Mer*.

23. **forlornness**: var. *loneliness*.
25. **end**: var. *doom*.
26. **shell**: *la carcasse* is quite different from "the carcass"; it denotes the bony framework; cp. No. 24: 'la carcasse d'un

of the Arabian Nights. These mausoleums had nothing mournful about them but their forlornness in the desert and the feeling of regret which they gave for their approaching end; moonbeams came stealing through the long cracks, probed the gaping wounds in the domes; on the empty shell of the most damaged among them, one could barely make out some traces of the former rose-windows; from the face of these old skeletons the plaster had come off like make-up.

châtaignier mort'; No. 94 (*Léviathan*): 'Un grand cachalot mort à *carcasse* de fer' (of a wrecked ship = iron-ribbed). Cp. also the carving of a chicken (*ailes, cuisses* and *la carcasse,* the remainder).

27. **damaged**: var. *ravaged.*

15. PARIS: SUR LES QUAIS

J'aime à regarder de ma fenêtre la Seine et ses quais par ces matins d'un gris tendre qui donnent aux choses une douceur infinie. J'ai contemplé le ciel d'azur qui répand sur la baie de Naples sa sérénité lumineuse. Mais notre ciel de Paris est plus animé, plus bienveillant et plus spirituel. Il sourit, menace, caresse, s'attriste et s'égaie comme un regard humain. Il verse en ce moment une molle clarté sur les hommes et les bêtes de la ville, qui accomplissent leur tâche quotidienne. Là-bas, sur l'autre berge, les forts du port Saint-Nicolas déchargent des cargaisons de cornes de bœuf, et des coltineurs posés sur une passerelle volante font sauter lestement, de bras en bras, des pains de sucre jusque dans la cale du bateau à vapeur. Sur le quai du nord, les chevaux de fiacre, alignés à l'ombre des platanes, la tête dans leur musette, mâchent tranquillement leur avoine, tandis que les cochers rubiconds vident leur verre devant le comptoir du marchand de vin, en guettant du coin de l'œil le bourgeois matinal.

Les bouquinistes déposent leurs boîtes sur le parapet. Ces braves marchands d'esprit, qui vivent sans cesse dehors, la blouse au vent, sont si bien travaillés par l'air, les pluies, les gelées, les neiges, les brouillards et le grand soleil, qu'ils finissent par ressembler aux vieilles statues des cathédrales. Ils sont tous mes amis et je ne passe guère devant leurs boîtes sans en tirer quelque bouquin qui me manquait jusque-là, sans que j'eusse le moindre soupçon qu'il me manquait.

ANATOLE FRANCE, *Le Crime de Sylvestre Bonnard.*

2. **embankments:** var. *quay-side.*

soft...mellowness. There is the same difficulty as in No. 6 (note 11), 'soft' and 'softness' being both called for in one sentence. For *tendre* 'delicate' is just possible; for *douceur* 'mildness' would tend to suggest temperature more than tone.

5. **animated:** var. *animate, living, alive.* The analogy of *une rue animée*='a (busy) animated street (full of life)' points to *animated.*

6. **sprightly.** Anatole France uses *spirituel* peculiarly, somewhat in the sense of 'sprightly', 'expressive', 'appealing to the mind', 'human'; cp. *Le Lys rouge,* p. 92: 'Oui, à Venise le ciel est coloriste. A Florence il est *spirituel.* Un vieil auteur a dit: Le ciel de Florence, léger et *subtil,* nourrit les belles idées des hommes.' On 'notre ciel de Paris' cp. J. Romains, H.B.V. VIII (*Province*): 'Au sommet des collines la ligne des maisons s'enlève sur un ciel plus *subtil* que jamais.'

15. PARIS: ON THE EMBANKMENT

I love to look out of my window over the Seine and the embankments on one of these soft grey mornings which give everything an infinite mellowness of tone. I have gazed upon the azure sky which sheds its quiet sheen over the Bay of Naples. But our own Paris sky is more animated, more genial, more sprightly. It can smile, threaten, caress, look grave or gay, just like a human face. At this moment it is casting a gentle light on man and beast throughout the city, at their daily task. Over on the other bank, the dockers of St Nicholas' Wharf are unloading cargoes of ox-horns, and stevedores on a gangway are deftly passing along sugar-loaves all the way down into the steamer's hold. On the northern embankment, the cab-horses, lined up in the shade of the plane-trees, with their heads in their nose-bags, are peacefully munching their oats whilst the red-faced drivers empty their glasses at the local bar, watching with the tail of their eye for the early 'fare'.

The second-hand booksellers are setting down their cases on the parapet. These worthy purveyors of enlightenment, living, as they do, constantly in the open, their overalls floating in the breeze, are so well-seasoned by exposure to wind, rain, frost, snow, fog and the full blaze of the sun that they come to look like the venerable statues on cathedrals. They are all of them friends of mine, and I seldom pass their cases but I take out some old book which had hitherto been wanting in my collection, without my feeling the slightest sense of wanting it.

8. **casting:** var. *diffusing*.

9. **at:** var. *about, in the performance of*; var. *as they perform (accomplish, go about, pursue)*. Var. *performing throughout the city their daily task*.

10. **St Nicholas' Wharf:** on the right bank of the Seine, directly opposite the Quai Malaquais, where 'Sylvestre Bonnard' lived.

11. **on a gangway:** *posés* = set, poised, can be safely omitted. French prepositions stand less strain than English and often require to be reinforced by a past participle. In such cases the participle is best left untranslated; see No. 51, note 23.

18. **setting down:** var. *depositing*.

19. **enlightenment:** *intellectual fare* is unfortunately debarred by 'the early fare'.

25–27. Var. *which had been wanting without my feeling until then the slightest lack of it*.

16. LE RHIN

Son seul ami, le confident de ses pensées, était le fleuve qui traversait la ville—le même fleuve puissant et paternel, qui là-haut, dans le nord, baignait sa ville natale. Christophe retrouvait auprès de lui les souvenirs de ses rêves d'enfance.... Mais dans le deuil qui l'enveloppait, ils prenaient, comme le Rhin lui-même, une teinte funèbre. A la tombée du jour, appuyé sur le parapet d'un quai, il regardait le fleuve fiévreux, cette masse en fusion, lourde, opaque, et hâtive, qui était toujours passée, où l'on ne distinguait rien que de grands crêpes mouvants, des milliers de ruisseaux, de courants, de tourbillons, qui se dessinaient, s'effaçaient: tel, un chaos d'images dans une pensée hallucinée: éternellement, elles s'ébauchent, et se fondent éternellement. Sur ce songe crépusculaire glissaient comme des cercueils des bacs fantomatiques, sans une forme humaine. La nuit s'épaississait. Le fleuve devenait de bronze. Les lumières de la rive faisaient luire son armure d'un noir d'encre, qui jetait des éclairs sombres. Reflets cuivrés du gaz, reflets lunaires des fanaux électriques, reflets sanglants des bougies derrière les vitres des maisons. Le murmure du fleuve remplissait les ténèbres. Éternel bruissement, plus triste que la mer par sa monotonie....

ROMAIN ROLLAND, *Jean-Christophe*.

2. **fatherly**: cp. 'Father Rhine'.
3. **place**: to avoid repeating 'town' at the end of the sentence.
5. Var. *in his overshadowing sense of bereavement*.
9. **opaque**: the word is less natural in English (so also *opacité*, see No. 29, note 4); but cp. Ruskin, *Stones of Venice*: 'The Brenta flows slowly, but strongly: a muddy volume of yellowish-grey water that neither hastens nor slackens, but glides heavily... with here and there a short babbling eddy twisted for an instant into its *opaque* surface and vanishing....'

always gone by: cp. Ruskin, *Praeterita*, II (Man., p. 238): 'Waves are always coming or gone.'

11. *crêpes* = crape is no doubt suggested by *le deuil qui l'enveloppait* and is in keeping with *des cercueils*. If *crêpes* were

16. THE RHINE

His one friend, the confidant of his thoughts, was the river which ran through the town—the same strong, fatherly river which, away in the North, flowed by his own native place. With it for company, Christopher could recall the memories of his childhood dreams.... But in the atmosphere of be- 5
reavement around him, these, like the Rhine itself, assumed a funereal tinge. At nightfall, on the embankment, leaning over the parapet, he would gaze at the restless river—that mass in a state of fusion, ponderous, opaque, hurrying on, always gone by, in which nothing was to be discerned but great moving 10
lengths of crape, innumerable trickles, currents, eddies, taking shape and vanishing; it was like a jumble of visions in a disordered brain, ever essaying a form and ever melting away. Over that twilight-dream glided, like coffins, ghostly ferry-boats, without one human figure. As darkness deepened, 15
the river turned to bronze. The lights along the bank gave a lustre to its ink-black armour, which threw off dull gleams. Reflections, like copper, from the gas; reflections, like moonlight, from the electric lamps; reflections, like blood, from the candles behind the window-panes. The murmur 20
of the river filled the darkness. An unceasing wash, wearier than the sea, because of its monotony!

to be taken as = 'crimpings', the rendering might be: *great moving sheets of crimping (crinkled) water*.

12. Var. *visions in a hallucinated mind; ever they take form, ever they melt away*.

15. Var. *The night grew darker*.

17. **threw off**: cp. D. H. Lawrence, *The Plumed Serpent*, p. 118: 'the water gleaming and *throwing off* a dense light'; for *éclairs sombres*, cp. Charles Morgan, *The Fountain*: 'the dark glitter of evergreens.'

20. 'in the houses' seems unnecessary, being implied in 'window-panes'.

17. A AMSTERDAM

Tout en rêvant mille choses de lui [Descartes], je m'amusais là-bas à voir de ma fenêtre les passants trotter dans la neige toute fraîche, les mariniers emmitouflés manœuvrer sur l'eau blanche et noire, à demi prise, à demi rompue, déplacer avec une adresse incroyable leurs péniches lourdes et longues, si pressées et engagées quelquefois les unes entre les autres qu'il faut s'y prendre comme au jeu de dames, opérer par substitutions réfléchies, créer devant soi le lieu où l'on va se mettre, en trouver un pour la coque que l'on déloge, attendre, pousser, gouverner, gagner enfin l'entrée de quelque tunnel étroit et sombre où l'on disparaît au bruit sourd du moteur, l'homme à la barre ployant la tête au moment juste qu'elle va heurter le sommet de la voûte. Les mouettes innombrables dissipaient mon attention, la ravissaient et renouvelaient dans l'espace. Leurs corps lisses et purs, bien placés contre le vent, glissaient, filaient sur d'invisibles pentes, effleuraient le balcon, viraient, rompaient le vol et s'abattaient sur les gros glaçons, où les blanches bêtes posées se disputaient entre elles les ordures tremblantes et les débris affreux de poisson rejetés à l'eau.

Entre deux oiseaux instantanés je revenais à ma première pensée.   PAUL VALÉRY, *Le Retour de Hollande.*

CONTEXT. 'Je viens d'Amsterdam où Descartes et Rembrandt ont coexisté. On y voit leurs maisons. On ne peut s'empêcher d'essayer de leurs songes. On se place naïvement dans leur personnage, au bord des canaux, sur les passerelles de l'Amstel, ou sur quelque point animé de ce labyrinthe d'eaux tout encombré de barques, de pontons', etc. (p. 29) [Tout en rêvant, etc.... à ma première pensée] 'Reprenant distraitement une rêverie quasi cartésienne, j'imaginais à ma façon les sensations de ce grand homme. J'accordais, j'arrangeais à ma guise ce que je voyais avec une vague idée de sa philosophie....'

2. **to enjoy:** *amuser* generally means to interest the mind; so *amusant*, as opposed to *drôle*.

3. **padding:** var. *bustling, scurrying.*

6. Var. (continuing the sentence) *displaying uncanny skill in shifting.*

7–8. Var. *so crowded and sometimes wedged together* (*interlocked*).

9. Var. *as a draughts-player would.*

11. **boat:** *la coque* = hull, which is hardly used absolutely.

15. **tiller:** *la barre* = *la barre du gouvernail* = tiller; *l'homme*

17. AT AMSTERDAM

When I was there, I used, while turning over all sorts of
thoughts about him [Descartes] in my mind, to enjoy
looking out of my window at the passers-by padding along
in the freshly fallen snow and the heavily muffled lighter-
men handling their craft on the black and white river, half
ice-bound, half freed. They displayed extraordinary skill in
shifting their long lumbering barges—so crowded together
and sometimes so dove-tailing into each other that the men
have to go about the business as one would at draughts,
proceed by a series of carefully thought-out moves, make
a space ahead to get into and find one for the boat which has
to be dislodged, wait about, push, give a touch of the rudder,
work out to the entrance of some dark narrow tunnel and
vanish within, to the dull throb of the motor, while the man
at the tiller ducks his head at the very moment it is going
to bump against the crown of the arch. My attention was
distracted by the numberless sea-gulls, and swept away into
space and given a new turn. Their smooth clean-cut bodies,
set well into the wind, glided over invisible slopes, skimmed
past my balcony, wheeled round, broke flight and dropped
on to the blocks of floating ice, where these white creatures
stood squabbling over the quivering refuse and the horrible
fish-guts cast back into the water.

In the intervals between the sudden swoops of the gulls,
I came back to my train of thought.

à la barre = the man at the tiller)(*l'homme de la barre* = the steersman, the man at the wheel.

15–16. Var. *just in time to avoid a collision with*; *a fraction of a second before it banged against.*

16–18. Var. *The innumerable sea-gulls distracted my attention, carried it away to new interests up aloft.*

18. **clean-cut:** *pur* is not "spotless"; cp. *un front pur* = a noble brow.

24. **in the intervals:** for *entre* (and *effleuraient*) cp. P. Valéry, op. cit. p. 27 (Night express from Amsterdam): 'Il naît et meurt des feux terrestres, postes soudains, signaux aigus, éclats subits de vies inconnues *effleurées*....*Entre deux lueurs*, mes yeux... cessaient de voir.' N.B. *deux* is usually omitted in English; *entre deux trains* = between trains, not "between two trains". Cp. No. 54, note 10.

Var. *lightning swoops.*

18. BOULOGNE

Boulogne-sur-mer, en novembre, le matin. Une transparente brume blanche naissait à terre et devenait opaque à fleur de toit. Pas de ciel. Les vols, en accents circonflexes, des mouettes gris perle, montaient s'engloutir dans ces ténèbres blafardes. Des édifices de la ville, les silhouettes seules subsistaient, foncées, sur écran blanc. Ce temps mou ôtait sa sonorité à la vie de la terre. Les charrettes des mareyeurs, rendues prudentes par la route invisible, roulaient à petite allure.

La marée basse donnait au port une profondeur d'abîme. Contre la paroi gluante, ornée de grappes de moules, les nombreuses barques de la flotte de pêche se calaient l'une l'autre. La *Notre-Dame* de Boulogne, basse sous sa charge lourde, accostait avec seize cents mesures de harengs. Des tas argentés luisaient sur le pont. Aux secousses, des poissons, glissant du haut, passaient le bordage, et flottaient, ventre en l'air, pour les mouettes. Le bateau, halant sur l'amarre cravatée au col d'un pieu de fonte, s'élargissait une place entre deux barques. Pouce à pouce, la *Notre-Dame* avança, un coin émoussé dans du bois dur. Enfin, du tranchant de sa proue, elle toucha le quai.

Le panneau ouvert creusait, au milieu du pont noir, un puits de lumière. Au fond, deux hommes, les bottes dans la glace pilée, triaient le poisson de la cale. Gelés sous leur

3. Var. *Not a vestige of sky.*
For *circonflexes* cp. Jules Lemaître:
> 'La mouette
> Qui s'ébat
> Sur le mât
> Le complète,
>
> Simulant
> D'un vol lent
> Et perplexe
>
> *Un accent
> Circonflexe*
> En passant.'

4. **pallid**: var. *livid.*

18. BOULOGNE

Boulogne on a November morning. A transparent white mist, rising from the ground, becoming opaque at roof-level. No sky. Like circumflex accents on the wing, the pearl-grey sea-gulls rose and vanished into the pallid gloom. Of the buildings in the town, only the outlines subsisted—dark against a white screen. The muggy weather deadened the sounds of life on shore. The fish-salesmen's carts, taking no risks on an invisible road, were going slowly.

Low tide gave the harbour abysmal depths. Up against the slimy wall, which was hung with clusters of mussels, the many boats of the fishing-fleet lay wedged together. The *Notre-Dame* of Boulogne, low in the water with her heavy load, was coming alongside with 200 crans of herring. Silvery heaps glistened on the deck and at every jolt, fish slithered down over the gunwale and floated, belly uppermost, food for the gulls. The boat, straining on the mooring-rope which was looped round the neck of an iron bollard, widened out a berth for herself between two fishing-smacks. Inch by inch the *Notre-Dame* worked her way in, like a blunt wedge going into hard wood. At length, with her cutwater, she touched the quay.

The open hatch, in the middle of the black deck, made a yawning well of light. Down below, two men, their sea-boots crunching the pounded ice, were sorting the fish in

---

5. **subsisted**: var. *came through*.

8. Var. (*driven*) *cautiously because of the low visibility, came along at a quiet pace* (*at a snail's pace*).

10. **hung**: "adorned" would be ironical, which *ornée* is not; *ornée* could be safely omitted; see No. 15, note 11.

Var. *clustered over* ('*barnacled*') *with mussels*.

13. **200 crans.** The exact relationship between 'a cran' and *une mesure* we have been unable to ascertain. A cran is equivalent to three baskets (of hamper size), and an abnormally large catch might be 200 crans, certainly not 1600.

19. **worked her way in**: var. *drew in*.

24. The ice used on trawlers is roughly pounded.

falot rond comme la lune, ils se réchauffaient en battant des bras, selon le rite populaire, et se claquaient dans le dos leurs rudes mains mouillées.

Un autre, penché sur leur trou, en tirait les paniers pleins. Ils avaient de l'ouvrage. Outre sa pêche, le bateau rapportait les filets pleins du *Bon Vent*, un Boulonnais perdu dans la Mer du Nord avec onze hommes et deux mousses. Par gros temps ses filets avaient pris un banc de harengs haut comme une maison. Le bateau pencha sur son filet trop lourd. Le patron hésitait à le couper. La bourrasque n'hésita pas et chavira le pêcheur sur sa pêche. La *Notre-Dame* rencontra les flotteurs à la dérive: il vint autant de poissons que de mailles.... PIERRE HAMP, *Marée fraîche*.

26. Var. *They were warming themselves up by swinging their arms, in the time-honoured way.*

34. Cp. No. 20: 'hauts comme des édifices.'

36. **hesitated whether**: *hésiter à* means 'to hesitate about', 'to consider the advisability of', 'to be reluctant to', e.g. 'Il *hésita à* prendre un fiacre, mais il n'en prit pas et s'en fut à pied par les rues'; 'Quand ils arrivèrent au Parc vers huit heures du matin,

the hold. Half-frozen beneath their round moon of a lantern, they went through the popular ritual of warming themselves by swinging their arms and slapping themselves in the back with their rough dripping hands.

Another man, leaning over their well, drew up the full baskets. The men had plenty of work to do. Over and above her own catch, the *Notre-Dame* was bringing in the full nets of the *Bon Vent*, a Boulogne boat lost in the North Sea with eleven men and two boys. In heavy weather her nets had struck a shoal of herring as high as a house. The boat listed over on her net, which was too heavy for her—the skipper hesitated whether to cut loose— the gale had no hesitation—and capsized the fisher on top of his fish. The *Notre-Dame* ran across the drifting floats—as many fish came up as there were meshes in the nets.

ils y trouvèrent quelques milliers de patriotes qui n'avaient pas *hésité à* coucher sur place'—at the Revue du 14 juillet (1938).

19. FALAISE

Au jour où je l'ai vue, Falaise baignait dans la tendre clarté d'une somptueuse journée de soleil. Dans l'air lavé par les pluies récentes, sur les étages des jardins, sur les bois que varient des hêtres pourpres, c'était un rayonnement doux. Je retrouvais la fine lumière de Vermeer de Delft, lumière sans éclat mais si nette que l'on apercevait au bord des fenêtres lointaines la pourpre des géraniums. Et quel silence !...

La ville, cependant active, ne laisse monter jusqu'à la haute terrasse aucun bruit. Dans les rues, jadis habitées par les gens de noblesse et de justice, les marchands œuvrent sans rumeur. Les tuiles rouges des toits ont pris sous le soleil des tons de rose sèche. Une lumière digne de l'aube dessine des festons sur les murs qui se donnent des airs d'enceintes crénelées. On dirait, à juger d'ici, que toute vie s'est retirée, car on n'aperçoit âme humaine, les rues et les venelles formant tranchée entre les maisons à encorbellement ; sur le nu d'une place on s'attend à voir passer un moine blanc de Saint-Augustin. La vie semble d'ici toute souterraine. La nappe de lumière s'épand du mont Mirat jusqu'à la colline couronnée de sapins où, jadis, on allait prendre les oiseaux de proie et passagers, tiercelets et faucons, émerillons et éperviers, et aussi des aigles, toute bête tant

---

1. Var. *the day I saw it, Falaise*, etc., but the repetition 'day' =*jour* and 'day'=*journée* would be regrettable.

4. **flecked**: var. *splashed*.

purple beech: there are several sorts of beech, including the 'purple beech' and the 'copper beech'. Presumably the first is intended here. But *le hêtre rouge*, usually translated the 'copper beech', is the *Fagus purpurea* and may be synonymous with *le hêtre pourpre*; see also note 7, below.

reminded: for the value of *re-* in *retrouver* see No. 2, note 5.

5. **Vermeer**: Jan Van der Meer or Vermeer (1632–75), whose figures seem to move in light and air.

7. **scarlet**: *pourpre* generally=red, not purple [French *violet* or (modern) *mauve*], except in *la pourpre romaine*, e.g. No. 102: 'Sous la pourpre flottante.'

7–8. Var. *And all was silence!*...

19. FALAISE

Falaise, when I saw it, was steeped in the mellow light of
a glorious sunny day. In the air purified by the recent
showers, a soft radiance shimmered on the terraced gardens
and the woods flecked with purple beech. It reminded me
of Vermeer van Delft's subtle light. It was light without 5
brilliancy, but so clear that on the window-sills far away
you could make out the scarlet of the geraniums. And such
silence!...

From the town, busy though it is, not a sound rises to the
high-perched terrace. In the streets which were inhabited 10
in the old days by the nobility and the law the tradespeople
are going about their business noiselessly. The red tiles on
the roofs have been sunned into tints of dry rose. Light
worthy of early dawn is setting festoons on the walls, which
put on an air of being battlemented circuit-walls. You would 15
think, from up here, that all life had ebbed away, for not
a soul can you see, the streets and vennels forming trenches
between the corbelled houses; on the blank space left by
a square you expect to see an Austin friar going by. Life
seems from here wholly subterraneous. The expanse of light 20
ranges from Mont Mirat right away to the fir-crested hill
where in olden days men would go to capture birds of prey,
passage hawks, tercels, falcons, merlins and sparrow-hawks,

11. **the law:** var. *the legal profession (fraternity)*; *la justice*
includes judges, magistrates and police; *les gens de justice* are
legal officials of all sorts.

11–12. Var. *the shop-keepers carry on a noiseless trade.*

13. **dry rose:** cp. Huysmans, *La Cathédrale*, p. 193: 'Puis, il
y avait encore une couleur charmante qui continue d'ailleurs
à figurer dans la gamme du rit Romain, mais que presque partout
les églises omettent, la teinte dite "*de la rose sèche*", tenant le
milieu entre le violet et le pourpre, entre la tristesse et la joie,
une sorte de compromis, de nuance diminutive, dont l'Église se
servait le troisième dimanche de l'Avent et le quatrième de
Carême.'

14. **early dawn:** 'early' is implied in *aube* [Lat. *alba* = white]
as opposed to *aurore* = dawn in its later stages (of *golden* light).

17. **trenches:** var. *cuttings*; cp. for *formant tranchée* No. 27,
note 6. Var. *on the open space of a square.*

de poing que de leurre. Elle baigne les vieux faubourgs, les fontaines où se lavaient les toiles, ce qui reste des anciens moulins à foulon et à tan. Les chroniqueurs comparaient Falaise à une nef longue et étroite, avec son château à la poupe. Cette nef, aujourd'hui, toutes voiles abaissées, semble immobile dans la lumière.

ÉDOUARD HERRIOT, *Dans la Forêt normande*.

24. **fist...lure.** Hawks are divided by falconers into two classes: (1) falcons, i.e. long-winged hawks or *hawks of the lure*, such as merlins, and (2) hawks, i.e. short-winged hawks or *hawks of the fist*; 'lure' and 'fist' refer to different methods of training the hawk to return to its master.

25. **outskirts:** *faubourgs* are seldom 'suburbs' in our understanding of the term. Etymologically *fors-bourg* (i.e. outside the town proper, hence by a misapprehension *faux-bourgs*) they are usually working-class districts lying on the outskirts of a town.

eagles too—all manner of birds, whether of fist or of lure; it
bathes the old buildings on the outskirts, the water-tanks
where the linen cloth was washed, the remnants of the former
fulling mills and tan-yards. The mediæval chroniclers used
to liken Falaise to a long narrow ship, with her castle at the
poop. To-day the ship, all sails down, seems becalmed in the
sunlight.

25. **water-tanks:** *fontaine* has many senses = well, spring, fountain, tank, etc.

27. **tan-yard:** var. *tanneries*. At Falaise tanning was in mediæval times one of the chief local industries. Arlette, the mother of the most illustrious native, William the Conqueror, was the daughter of a tanner.

28. **castle:** the raised deck or 'castle' of mediæval ships: hence 'foc'sle'.

20. LE PORT DE MARSEILLE

Afin de ne pas être bloqués à tout instant par l'embarras des attelages et des marchandises, ils prirent l'escalier de la jetée qui domine, d'un côté, toute la longueur des quais, et, de l'autre, les rangées des brise-lames.

Parvenu au sommet, Jaubert s'arrêta brusquement, pour regarder. L'immensité, l'étrangeté de la vue lui causaient une véritable stupeur.

Tout le ciel, d'un bleu pâle crêpelé de petites nuées grises, était encore enveloppé de brumes. Marseille, la Joliette disparaissaient sous un voile de brouillard jaune, où scintillaient comme des gouttes de pluie lumineuses. D'abord, le jeune homme, à travers ce brouillard, ne distingua rien que des mâtures-fantômes. Puis, l'abside de la Major, la tour de Notre-Dame de la Garde s'accusèrent en masses plus sombres sur le fond transparent des vapeurs matinales. Un rais diamantin dessina en lignes brillantes les renflements bulbeux des coupoles. Au-dessus, parmi les moutonnements des nuées couleur de perle, le disque bleuâtre du soleil montait dans un cerne d'or. Et tout un ruissellement de flammes, un torrent d'or et d'acier, se précipitait dans les eaux molles des bassins, dont les vaguelettes frissonnaient à la fraîcheur du vent de mer.

6. Var. *to look around*.

8. **crinkled**: *curly*; *crêpelé* is said properly of the hair = crimped.

9. **La Joliette**: a dock for large ships.

10. **almost hidden**: for this sense of *disparaissaient* see No. 13, note 9.

11. **comme** = as it were; but the English phrase is more cumbrous and cannot be readily worked in here. In fact *comme* in this sense often owes its presence in a sentence to the French fear of saying anything which could be pilloried as 'not French' or considered too bold. In such cases it can be safely left untranslated. Unless this precautionary *comme* is ignored, a page of translated French is apt to present an alarming number of 'as it were's' or 'so to speak's'.

12. **forest of masts**: *mâtures*, as compared with *mâts*, is collective = masts and spars; hence 'forest of'.

20. MARSEILLES HARBOUR

So as not to be held up every minute by the block of drays and heavy goods, they went on to the steps of the jetty which, on one side, commands the whole length of the wharves and, on the other, the rows of breakwaters.

When he reached the top, Jaubert stopped abruptly to have a look. The vastness, the strangeness of the view literally astounded him.

The entire sky, pale blue with crinkled little grey clouds, was still shrouded in mist. Marseilles and La Joliette were almost hidden by a veil of yellow fog, glistening with what looked like shining rain-drops. At first, through the fog, the young man could make out nothing but a forest of phantom masts. Then the apse of St Mary Major and the Tower of Notre-Dame de la Garde showed up as darker masses against the light background of the morning haze. A diamond ray picked out the swelling curves of the domes in brilliant outline. Overhead, among the fleecy folds of the pearl-coloured clouds, the bluish disc of the sun was mounting in a golden halo. And a whole rush of flames, a torrent of gold and steely light streamed down on the torpid waters of the docks and the wavelets shivering in the cool sea-breeze.

13. **la Major:** the modern Cathedral of Marseilles, dedicated to Sainte-Marie-Majeure (St Mary Major).

14. **Notre-Dame de la Garde:** a church which, standing high above the sea and surmounted by a gilded statue of the Virgin, is a prominent landmark.

as darker masses: evidently not "*in* darker masses".

15. **light:** "a transparent background" might seem odd. Like *comme* above, *fond* is a short convenient word which is apt to be over-translated by the longer, more explicit, corresponding terms in English.

16. **swelling curves:** var. *the bulbous swelling*; *renflement* is in technical English *entasis* = a gentle swelling out, O.E.D.

19. **halo:** var. *ring*: cp. Longfellow, *Wreck of the Hesperus*:
   'Last night the moon had a golden *ring*.'

rush: var. *river*; but *ruissellement* has become a stock word and may not have much image value left. Cp., however, No. 94, note 16.

La ville restait toujours invisible derrière la ligne blanchâtre des quais, les tulles opaques des lourdes vapeurs, les bouillonnements fuligineux qui s'élevaient au-dessus des bateaux en partance. Seuls, émergeaient les profils gigantesques des grues en fonte, les colonnes des lampadaires électriques, et, çà et là, des tas de charbon, hauts comme des édifices, dont le faîte s'effaçait sous un tourbillon perpétuel de poussières noires.

Ce vaste paysage, qui semblait sur le point de se dissoudre et de s'évanouir dans les brumes, vivait d'une vie monstrueuse par l'énormité de ses bruits, la continuité hallucinante de sa rumeur. Mugissements prolongés des sirènes, claquements des fouets, grincements des ancres, sifflets des machines, tintements des coques de fer sous les marteaux des radoubeurs, et, par-dessus tout, la clameur confuse du demi-million d'hommes pressés entre les collines et les rivages—c'était du tumulte dans de la fumée!...

LOUIS BERTRAND, *L'Invasion*.

27. Cp. No. 18: *haut comme une maison*.
28. **obscured**: var. *obliterated*.

swirls: the very frequent plurals (*vapeurs*, etc.) have to be rendered by singulars, but *poussières* (cp. No. 4, note 10) at least can be 'swirls' instead of 'swirl'.

The town still remained invisible, screened by the grey-white line of the wharves, the thick veil of heavy mist and the seething eddies of sooty smoke rising over the ships stoking up for departure. Alone emerged from the mist the gigantic 25 outlines of the iron cranes, the electric lamp standards and, here and there, as high as buildings, coal dumps with their tops obscured by perpetual swirls of black dust.

The immense panorama, which seemed on the point of dissolving and fading away into the mist, was given life, 30 uncanny life, by the vastness of its various sounds, the nightmare continuity of its dull roar. Sirens wailing loud and long; whips cracking; anchors grating; engines whistling; iron hulls clanking to the fitters' hammers; and over all, the confused hum from the half-million men packed in 35 between the hills and the shore—Smoke over Tumult!

34. **clanking**: for the root sense of *tintement* see No. 85, note 18. Var. *the clangour of riveters' hammers on iron hulls*; cp. G. Blake, *Shipbuilders*, p. 74: 'people could hardly hear themselves speak for the *clangour* of metal upon metal that filled the valley, from Old Kirkpatrick up to Govan.'

21. LA GORGE DE PIERREFITTE

De lourds nuages montaient dans le ciel, et l'horizon terni s'encaissait entre deux rangs de montagnes décharnées, tachées de broussailles maigres, fendues de ravines; un jour pâle tombait sur les sommets tronqués et dans les crevasses grises....

On entra dans la gorge de Pierrefitte. Les nuages avaient gagné et noircissaient tout le ciel; le vent s'engouffrait par saccades et fouettait la poussière en tourbillons. La voiture roulait entre deux murailles immenses de roches sombres, tailladées et déchiquetées comme par la hache d'un géant désespéré: sillons abrupts, labourés d'entailles béantes, plaies rougeâtres, déchirées et traversées par d'autres plaies pâlies, blessure sur blessure; le flanc perpendiculaire saigne encore de ses coups multipliés.

Des masses bleuâtres, demi-tranchées, pendaient en pointes aiguës sur nos têtes; mille pieds plus haut, des étages de bloc s'avançaient en surplombant. A une hauteur prodigieuse, les cimes noires crénelées s'enfonçaient dans la vapeur. Le défilé semblait à chaque pas se fermer; l'obscurité croissait, et, sous les reflets menaçants d'une lumière livide, on croyait voir ces saillies monstrueuses s'ébranler pour tout engloutir. Les arbres pliaient et tournoyaient, froissés contre la pierre. Le vent se lamentait en longues plaintes aiguës, et, sous tous ces bruits douloureux, on entendait le grondement rauque du Gave, qui se brise furieux contre les roches invincibles, et gémit lugubrement comme une âme en peine, impuissant et obstiné comme son tourment.

1. **now gloomy** = *terni* as opposed to *terne*; so *pâlies* = *pâles* farther on. The participles raise considerable difficulties in this passage.

3. **light scrub**: for *broussailles maigres*, cp. No. 3: 'les massifs serrés et *maigres* du Bois.'

ravines: *une ravine* = (1) *un torrent*, (2) as here, *un ravin*.

9. **went on**: var. *proceeded*. Not "rolled" or "bowled along"; *rouler* does not connote speed or rotatory movement; cp. the *agent* on traffic duty, *Roulez!* = Go!

10. **precipices**: cp. Macaulay, describing Glencoe: 'Huge precipices of naked stone frown on both sides...'; *un précipice* is a chasm, a void, whereas 'precipice' means the steep rock-face, *la muraille*; var. *towering walls*.

21. THE PIERREFITTE GORGE

Heavy clouds were mounting in the sky and the now gloomy horizon seemed boxed in between two lines of gaunt hills dotted with light scrub and split up by ravines; a pallid light was falling on the truncated summits and into the grey crevasses....

We entered the Pierrefitte gorge. The clouds had been gaining ground and were now making the whole sky black; sudden gusts of wind kept sweeping into the gorge, whipping up columns of swirling dust. Our carriage went on between huge precipices of dark rock hacked and slashed as though a demented giant with his axe had opened up deep furrows scored by gaping clefts, angry scars torn and criss-crossed by other paler scars, new wounds upon old wounds,—as though the perpendicular mountain-side were still bleeding from his oft-repeated blows.

Masses of bluish stone, half lopped off, hung in jagged points over our heads; a thousand feet higher up, jutted out ledges of solid rock. Aloft, at a stupendous height, the black serrated summits thrust into the mist. With every foot we advanced, the pass seemed to close in on us; the gloom increased, and in the ominous gleams of a livid light these monstrous protrusions seemed to be tottering and about to engulf everything in their fall. The trees twisted and writhed, scraping against the stone. The wind wailed out long piercing lamentations and we could hear, like a burden to all these dolorous sounds, the hoarse rumbling of the Gave, which breaks in fury on the indomitable rocks and, like a lost soul, moans dismally, powerless yet persistent as the torment it endures.

12. **angry**: var. *reddish*.

13. **scars...wounds**: N.B. *une plaie* is the mark left by the injury; *une blessure* is the injury inflicted.

19. Var. *At every moment*; "*At every step*" seems inexact in reference to 'Our carriage'.

21. **ominous gleams**: var. *lowering glimmer*.

24. Var. *crumples against the rocks*.

28. **lost soul**: var. *soul in torment*, if 'torment' were not required in the next line. Var. *unavailing yet unrelenting*.

La pluie vint et brouilla les objets. Au bout d'une heure, les nuages dégonflés traînaient à mi-côte; les roches dégouttantes luisaient d'un vernis sombre, comme des blocs d'acajou bruni. L'eau troublée bouillonnait en cascades grossies; les profondeurs de la gorge étaient encore noircies par l'orage; mais une lumière jeune jouait sur les cimes humides, comme un sourire trempé de larmes. La gorge s'ouvrait; les arches des ponts de marbre s'élançaient dans l'air limpide, et, dans une nappe de lumière, on voyait Luz assise entre des prairies étincelantes et des champs de millet en fleur.

TAINE, *Voyage aux Pyrénées.*

30. **The rain arrived**: we had originally 'came', and then 'came on', but afterwards noticed that 'arrived' is commonly used in this sense.

31. Var. *were straggling down the slopes.*

35. **fresh**: var. *new-born.* In another description (*Voyage aux*

The rain arrived, and obscured everything. An hour later the spent clouds hung trailing half-way down the mountain-side; the dripping rocks shone with a dull glaze like blocks of polished mahogany. The troubled water seethed in swollen torrents; the deep-lying parts of the gorge were still black with the storm, but a fresh light was playing on the rain-washed summits, like a smile through tears. The gorge widened out; the arches of the marble bridges rose high into the limpid air and, away in a sheet of light, we could see Luz ensconced among shining meadows and fields of millet in flower.

Pyrénées, p. 215) Taine says: 'rien ne peut donner l'idée de cette lumière si *jeune*.'

39. **shining**: cp. Tennyson's
> 'Go not, happy day,
> From the *shining* fields.'

22. COUCHER DE SOLEIL SUR LA JUNGFRAU

Un nuage allongé, aux extrémités apointies, pareil à un projectile lancé par quelque artillerie de géants, prenait en travers le flanc de la montagne, séparant la base du sommet; tandis que les assises perdaient peu à peu leurs contours et leurs couleurs jusqu'à se confondre avec les vapeurs amassées au fond de la vallée, la cime se détachait, en tons de cuivre et d'or, sur un fond plus clair où se mêlaient les plus délicates nuances des mauves, des gris, des roses. A mesure que la tache livide de la base montait, s'étendait, l'entamait au-dessus des nuages, elle devenait plus transparente et aérienne: sans attaches avec le sol, elle flottait dans l'éther, à des hauteurs incalculables. Le nuage disparut presque tout à coup, disloqué par une rafale. Pendant que ses lambeaux s'étiraient, s'effilaient, s'enfuyaient, se fondaient, l'ombre précipita sa montée. Il n'y eut bientôt plus qu'une flamme légère à l'extrême sommet, un peu pareille à la coulée de lave d'un volcan qui s'émeut; puis cette flamme elle-même s'éteignit, comme au souffle d'une bouche toute-puissante. La montagne entière, frileusement enveloppée dans ce manteau d'ombre, reprit sa teinte uniforme, sa teinte d'opale sans reflets, qui s'abaissa peu à peu jusqu'à la lividité de la mort; en sorte qu'elle ne fut plus qu'un cadavre, marqué pour la décomposition prochaine.

ÉDOUARD ROD, *L'Ombre s'étend sur la Montagne*
(Fasquelle).

1. **pointed:** *apointi*, usually spelled *appointi* = sharpened into a point (cp. *appointir une aiguille*), as opposed to *pointu* = pointed = sharp.

2. **launched:** var. *cast, hurled*.

of the Giants: "some giants' artillery" seems less clear.

3. Var. *struck across the mountain, dividing (off)* etc.

4. **lower slopes:** *assises* = the foundations of the mountain (on which *elle est assise*); normally, 'base' would be a good enough translation, but here *la base* also occurs.

6. **crest:** var. *peak*.

9. **greys.** There is often some dubiety as to the exact shade of colour indicated by *gris*; here "grey" seems too neutral to be

22. A SUNSET ON THE JUNGFRAU

A cloud, long drawn out, with pointed ends, suggesting a projectile launched by some artillery of the Giants, caught the mountain on the flank, separating the base from the summit. While the lower slopes were gradually losing outline and colour till finally they were indistinguishable from the mists which had gathered down in the valley, the crest stood out, in copper and gold tints, from a lighter background of the most delicate intermingling shades of mauves, greys and pinks. As the livid patch from the base went spreading upwards, encroaching upon it above the clouds, the crest became more transparent, more ethereal; unconnected with the ground, it was floating in the upper air, at incalculable heights. Suddenly almost, the cloud vanished, broken up by a gust of wind. Whilst the shreds of it were still lengthening out, tapering off, fleeing, melting away, the shade quickened its ascent. Soon there was nothing left but a faint flicker at the topmost summit, not unlike the trickle of lava from an awakening volcano; then the flicker itself went out, as at the breath of mighty lips. The entire mountain, wrapt shivering in that mantle of shade, took on its uniform tint again, its tint of sheenless opal, which gradually faded to the livid hue of death; so that the mountain was now but a corpse, consigned to speedy decay.

convincing between 'mauve' and 'pink'; perhaps = blue-grey. But the plural saves the situation by giving a choice of shades.

livid patch: var. *leaden(-coloured) shadow*; *pallid blur*.

9–10. Var. *As the pale bank of mist drifted up and outwards.*

11. **unconnected with:** var. *severed from*. Var. *Bound by no earth-fetters, it was floating in*, etc.; *away from the ground, it was floating loose*, etc.

14–16. *While its last shreds, lengthening and tapering, stole away to merge into space, the shadowy form pressed on its heavenward climb.*

17. Var. *at the very tip.*

21. **sheenless opal:** var. *dull opal*, i.e. a bluish colour without the usual reflection of green, yellow and red. Cp. Balzac, *Le Colonel Chabert*: 'Vous eussiez dit *de la nacre sale* dont les reflets *bleuâtres* chatoyaient à la lueur des bougies.'

23. LES VOIX DE LA CAMPAGNE

Je couchais dans une salle paysanne, meublée comme au temps de Greuze, et dont la porte ouvrait au ras de l'herbe. Des espaliers l'enserraient et le grenier était bondé de foin. Au petit jour, j'entendais des foulées de sabots, des chocs de seaux à lait, les pas de la jument, des trilles d'oiseaux, bruits espacés dans le silence, qui me tiraient du sommeil et semblaient m'appeler. Bientôt je partais à l'aventure, je prétendais chasser, pêcher, collectionner. Mes poursuites me menaient dans les futaies, sur les pentes glissantes d'aiguilles ou couvertes de myrtil, au bord de l'étang encombré de roseaux, sur les pierres de la rivière où je cherchais les écrevisses et les anguilles.

Quand je restais à l'affût, j'entendais toutes les voix de la campagne; à côté de moi, le pépiement d'un roitelet dans les ronces; sur un noisetier, le cri de rat d'un écureuil; à la cime d'un hêtre, le choc des ailes puis le roucoulement d'un ramier. Le croassement des corbeaux accentuait la grandeur sauvage et sombre des sapins; les vallées résonnaient sans cesse du meuglement des vaches et de l'appel aigu des taureaux; et, comme j'étais toujours suivi d'un chien, un halètement continuel m'accompagnait, comme la respiration même de la nature. C'est en ces jours que je découvris les libellules des eaux, qui sont de toutes les couleurs; l'œil d'or des grenouilles laquées émergeant de la verte canetille des mares; le papillon morio aux ailes de velours noir et le grand

1. **living-room.** *La salle* (in the East of France, *le poêle*) is the "room" par excellence—in smaller houses the living-room or parlour, in larger houses a reception-room; cp. Flaubert, *Un Cœur simple*: 'Un vestibule étroit séparait la cuisine de la *salle*, où Mme Aubain se tenait tout le long du jour, assise près de la croisée, dans un fauteuil de paille.'

2. **Greuze:** cp. his picture 'L'Accordée de village', where there is a staircase from *la salle* to *le grenier*, which appears to be *bondé de foin*.

3. **trained on:** *l'enserraient* properly = clasped it (*la salle*).

5. **tramping of clogs:** ? *trampling of hoofs*: *foulées* usually means the trace of a horse's foot, but is said of human beings as well; so also is *sabots*.

23. VOICES OF THE COUNTRYSIDE

I used to sleep in a rustic living-room, furnished as in Greuze's day, and with the door opening straight on to the grass. There were espaliers trained on the walls and the loft was stuffed full of hay. At break of day I could hear a tramping of clogs and a clanking of milk-pails, the mare clattering past, birds twittering. These sounds, interspersed in the silence, roused me from my sleep and seemed to be calling me. Before long I was off, bound for nowhere in particular. I had notions of going shooting or fishing, or adding to my collections. My hunts took me in among the tall forest trees, on to the slopes slippery with pine-needles or the bilberry-clad hill-sides, along the reedy pond, or on to the stones in the river to look for crayfish and eels.

While on the watch, I could hear all the voices of the countryside; close by, the chirping of a wren in the brambles; from a hazel-bush, the rat-like squeak of a squirrel; at the top of a beech, the flap of wings and then a wood-pigeon cooing. The cawing of the rooks seemed to intensify the wild dark majesty of the firs; the valleys unceasingly echoed with the lowing of the cows and the high-pitched call of the bulls and, as I always had a dog at my heels, a continual panting kept me company, which seemed the very breathing of nature itself. It was during those days that I discovered the water dragon-flies—all colours they are; the golden gleam in the eyes of the lacquered frogs as they come out from the green duckweed on the ponds; the red admiral with the black velvet wings, and the great peacock butter-

6. **twittering**: var. (more exact) *trilling*.

10. **hunts**: *poursuites* does not have the sense of English 'pursuits' = occupations, recreations.

11. **tall forest trees**: for *futaie* see No. 5, note 4.

27. **duckweed.** We have failed to find *canetille* in the Dictionaries and merely hazard a guess at the meaning; *cannetille* = braid, but it might possibly = fringe here.

the red admiral: *morio* is the general name of the *Vanessa* species of butterfly; *Vanessa atalanta* = red admiral; *Vanessa io* = peacock butterfly. For *morio*, Mansion gives 'Camberwell Beauty'.

paon incarnat, si beau avec ses taches de topaze et de saphir que j'en rêvais. Je rentrais, accablé d'images et de sons, la tête lourde d'odeurs de foin, de menthe, de résine et de chèvrefeuille. Et quand, la nuit venue, dans le silence et les ténèbres, au fond de mon lit de plume, je sombrais dans le sommeil, je sentais les buissons qui, tout le jour, m'avaient griffé, les plantes qui m'avaient embaumé, les bêtes qui m'avaient fui et les oiseaux qui m'avaient émerveillé, me soutenir au-dessus de l'abîme, comme des bras fraternels.

JEAN GALLOTTI, *Le règne de l'inerte.*

29. Var. *splashes.*
37. Var. *had fled at my approach.*

fly, rosy pink, so splendid with its markings of topaz and
sapphire that it left me dreaming. I would come home
overwhelmed with sights seen and sounds heard, dizzy with
scents of hay and mint and resin and honeysuckle. And
when night came round again and in the silence and the
darkness, down in the depths of my feather-bed, I was
dropping off to sleep, I could feel the bushes which all
day long had been scratching me, the plants which had
imparted their perfume, the creatures that had scuttled
away and the birds that had filled me with wonder—I could
feel them bearing me up above the abyss, as on the arms of
friends.

38. Var. *had won my admiration.*

24. DANS LA FORÊT

Un grand nuage de pluie passa sur la forêt; les bouleaux s'enlevèrent plus blancs sur le gris de plomb du ciel, une flamme rosée modela la carcasse d'un châtaignier mort. Il regardait tout cela, et la fraîcheur de l'air lui caressait la figure et la fraîcheur de la terre lui montait aux jambes.

'Ah! disait-il en s'en allant, quand il faudra mourir!... Les arbres morts restent debout!... Il semble même qu'ils continuent à se sentir des arbres!... Mais ne plus voir, ne plus entendre!... enfin!... J'ai bien encore, je suppose, vingt ans à vivre!... Ai-je bien encore vingt ans à vivre?'...

Il montait par un chemin creux, pierreux, fauve comme les loups, bordé de ces arbres de coupe dont les puissantes racines ongulaires font corps avec le talus. Il marchait tout doucement, en faisant sonner ses semelles sur les escaliers de roc. Les longs et souples genêts, aux gousses noires, le frôlaient, et lui-même frôlait les souches, creuses, éventrées, que la nuit habite, frôlait les troncs déchaussés, pleins de suies humides et de déchiquetures poreuses. Autour de lui se multipliaient les gibbosités en profil de sanglier, les exostoses en contours de bêtes étranges, les rondeurs en silhouettes d'épaules humaines.

1. **showed up**: for *s'enlevèrent* cp. *un portrait bien enlevé* = boldly drawn; see also the quotation in No. 15, note 6.
3. Var. *picked out in relief*.
   skeleton: var. *shell*. For the sense of *carcasse*, see No. 14, note 26.
4. Var. *He took in the whole scene*.
12. **sunken lane**: var. simply *lane*; *hollow way* is exact, but the term is antiquated; *hill path*. For *chemin creux* (occurring also in No. 62), cp. Edmond Picard, in *A la Gloire de la Belgique*: 'La plaine flamande prend fin. Les premières collines restreignent l'horizon. Dans leurs flancs sont découpés les premiers *chemins creux*, aux berges abruptes et ombragées, aux ornières profondes.'
13. **timber-trees**: var. *felling-trees*.
14. The text has *ongulaires*: ? a coined word based on *ongle*; or a misprint?
15. **taking it easy**: cp. *Doucement!* = Easy! Steady!
19. Var. *trunks with their roots laid bare (exposed)*. For

24. IN THE FOREST

A large rain-cloud drifted over the forest; the birches showed up whiter against the leaden-grey of the sky; a rosy flame modelled in the round the skeleton of a dead chestnut tree. He stood looking at it all, the coolness of the air playing on his face and the coolness of the earth creeping up his legs.

"Ah," he said, moving off, "and when it's my turn to die! Trees remain standing when they're dead!... Indeed, it looks as though they still feel they are trees!... But when you can't see, can't hear any more!... Well, well! I suppose I am good for twenty years yet. But *am* I really good for twenty years?"

He turned up into a sunken lane, which was stony, sandy like the colour of wolves, and lined by those timber-trees which have strong, clawing roots forming part of the bank itself. As he walked on, taking it easy, his boots made a clatter on the rocky steps. The long pliant broom with black seed-pods brushed lightly against him, as he himself brushed past the hollow, gutted stumps, abodes of darkness, past the bare tree-roots full of damp blight and spongy notches. Around him was an endless array of gibbosities recalling boars' heads seen in profile, exostoses with the outlines of strange beasts, humpy silhouettes like human shoulders.

déchaussés cp. *Ses dents se déchaussent* = His gums are receding (shrinking).

blight: *suie* = 'maladie de plantes diverses... appelée encore *noir* ou fumagine.' Larousse du XXe siècle; var. *smut* = 'a disease of cereal plants caused by a parasitic fungus breaking out into masses of brownish black spores resembling soot' (O.E.D.). Var. *full of damp blight and rotting cracks* (*full of damp rot and spongy slits*).

20. **gibbosities,** etc. These technical words are as unpleasing in French as in English, but are no doubt helpful in creating the requisite atmosphere of corruption and decay.

21. 'Exostosis, a diseased condition in plants, in which hard masses of wood are produced, projecting like warts or tumours from the main stem or root' (O.E.D.).

20–22. Var. *Around him gathered the outlines of hump-backed*

Une belette traversa le chemin; Lirot fit un bond.

— Hé! Lirot, tu n'as droit qu'aux champignons, tu oublies!

Il le retenait par son collier, le laissant aboyer, donnait à la petite bête le temps de s'enfouir dans un creux du talus. Puis il reprit sa route, car maintenant, au haut de la montée, dans l'ovale des frondaisons, s'embrunissait la perle humide et dorée du soir.

A. DE CHÂTEAUBRIANT, *Monsieur des Lourdines*.

boars, the contours of strange deformed beasts, the silhouettes of round human shoulders.

24. **sprang forward**: var. *made a dart at it.*
25. Var. *Mustn't touch anything but mushrooms, remember!*
avoir droit à = to be entitled to.

IN THE FOREST

A weasel ran across the path. Lirot sprang forward.
"Hi, Lirot! Nothing but mushrooms for you, you know!"
He held the dog back by his collar, letting him bark away, and so gave the little creature time to scuttle into a hole in the bank. Then he started off again, for now at the top of the hill, in the oval of the leafy branches, the watery golden pearl of evening was deepening into dusk.

26. Var. *regardless of his barking.*
29. **the oval**: i.e. the leafy branches meeting overhead made an oval setting for the sunset sky seen at the top of the lane; the sky is thus like a pearl, in shape as well as in colour.

Var. *a dusky hue was spreading over the watery golden,* etc.

25. DEMI-TOUR

J'avais dix-huit ans. J'étais heureuse. J'habitais avec mon tuteur une maison toute en longueur dont chaque porte-fenêtre donnait sur la ville, chaque fenêtre sur un pays à ruisseaux et à collines, avec des champs et des châtaigneraies comme des rapiéçages... car c'était une terre qui avait beaucoup servi déjà, c'était le Limousin. Les jours de foire, je n'avais qu'à tourner sur ma chaise pour ne plus voir le marché et retrouver, vide de ses troupeaux, la campagne. J'avais pris l'habitude de faire ce demi-tour à tout propos, cherchant à tout passant, au curé, au sous-préfet, son contrepoids de vide et de silence entre des collines; et pour changer le royaume des sons, c'était à peine plus difficile, il fallait changer de fenêtre. Du côté de la rue, des enfants, jouant au train, un phonographe, la trompe des journaux, et les chevreaux et canards qu'on portait aux cuisines poussant

CONTEXT. Suzanne is giving (1921) reminiscences of her younger days, and an occasional lapse into schoolgirl English would be not inappropriate. The bold imagery in the passage need not be weakened by inserting "as if", "as though", or by expanding metaphors and similes to make them explicit.

1. **happy**: var. (to make the context clear) *a happy girl*.

2. **a long, narrow house**: *une maison toute en longueur* shows that the length of the house was its important feature. It was, for its length, narrow (the rooms on the ground-floor had a window on either side), but it was not necessarily "straggling", or "rambling". Var. *a house running all to length, a house that was all length*.

4. **all patched up**: not "patch-work" which, though it seems at first sight = *des rapiéçages*, suggests the sewing together of pieces of material *in good condition* to make a quilt or cushion. What is meant here is the insertion of patches to mend a garment which has already seen much service. Var. *with fields and chestnut woods like patches upon it*. Cp. Gerard Manley Hopkins, *Pied Beauty*:

Glory be to God for dappled things—
...Landscape plotted and pieced—fold, fallow and plough.

6. **the Limousin**: the old Province; capital Limoges. 'The' seems appropriate to Limousin, but not, for example, to

25. ABOUT-TURN

I was eighteen, and I was happy. I lived with my guardian in a long, narrow house, in which every french-window opened on the town and every ordinary window on a landscape of hills and streams, all patched up with fields and chestnut-woods, for it was land which had already seen much service— it was the Limousin. On Fair days I had only to swing round on my chair to shut out the market and be back again in the country void of its flocks and herds. I had formed the habit of doing this about-turn on the slightest provocation, trying to find, for any passer-by—the priest, the sous-préfet —his counterpoise of void and silence in the space between hills; and when I wanted to alter the realm of sounds, it was scarcely more difficult. I had only to change windows. On the street side, children playing at trains, a gramophone, the news-boy's trumpet, the kids and ducks being borne

Périgord; in French *Limousin* is felt to retain some of its original adjectival force (*Lemovicensis ager*).

Fair days: not "market days"; in French towns there may be *marché* twice a week, but *foire* only once a month.

7. **market**: ? *market-place*.

8. **flocks and herds.** The word *troupeau* includes sheep and oxen, and allusion to both is made later on, in *meuglement* and *bêlement*.

9. **about-turn.** *Demi-tour* is properly a military term and keeps its military flavour; *faire demi-tour* is part of the drill-ground sequence: halt, face about and march in the opposite direction, whereas "half-turn" is only a partial turn, to the right or the left.

11. **his counterpoise.** Before translating, we must visualize the author's implied image of scales, with a passer-by in one pan and silence in the other.

12. **when I wanted to alter.** Some such expansion is required to bring out the force of *pour*. Otherwise the rendering would imply that the French was *et changer...c'était*.

15. **the news-boy's trumpet.** In country towns the *marchand de journaux* announces by means of a 'penny trumpet' that the daily paper has been deposited in the letter-box: 'boy' does not necessarily indicate age; cp. 'cow-boy'.

un cri de plus en plus métallique à mesure qu'il devenait leur cri de mort. Du côté de la montagne, le vrai train, des meuglements, des bêlements que l'hiver on devinait d'avance au nuage autour des museaux. C'est là que nous dînions l'été, sur une terrasse. C'était parfois la semaine où les acacias embaument, et nous les mangions dans des beignets; où les alouettes criblaient le ciel, et nous les mangions dans des pâtés; parfois le jour où le seigle devient tout doré et a son jour de triomphe, unique, sur le froment; nous mangions des crêpes de seigle. Un coup de feu dans un taillis: c'est que les bécasses passaient, allant en un jour, expliquait mon tuteur, à l'Afrique centrale. Une bergère qui faisait claquer ses deux sabots l'un contre l'autre: c'était voilà vingt ans l'appel contre les loups, il servait maintenant contre les renards, dans vingt ans il ne servirait plus que contre les fouines. Puis le soleil se couchait, de biais, ne voulant blesser mon vieux pays qu'en séton. On le voyait à demi une minute, abrité par la colline comme un acteur. Il eût suffi de l'applaudir pour qu'il revînt. Mais tout restait silencieux....Illuminés de dos, toutes les branches et les

17. **turned**: var. *hardened*.
18. Not "the mountain"; cp. '*passer les vacances* à la montagne *ou* à la mer' = in the hills (among the mountains).

lowings. Distinguish *le meuglement* = lowing from *le beuglement* = bellowing.

19. **beforehand**: var. *before you heard them*.
21. **dine.** In the country *dîner* is constantly used for *déjeuner* and *souper* for *dîner*; here the reference is to lunch, on the *terrasse* at the back of the house looking towards the hills.
22. **are fragrant**: var. *perfume the air*.

had: var. *ate*. The allusion is to *beignets d'acacia*; acacia blossoms are put into the batter of which these fritters are made.

23. **were dotted.** The change of tense, from *embaument* to *criblaient*, should be noted.
27. **that meant.** *c'est que* gives, as usual, an explanation; var. *and we knew*.
29. **herd-girl:** "shepherdess" would suggest, perhaps unjustifiably, the daintiness of Little Bo-Peep or Marie Antoinette and *une bergère* may herd cows or goats as well as sheep.

kitchenwards, with screamings and screechings growing more
and more metallic as they turned into death-cries. On the
side facing the hills, real trains, and lowings and bleatings
which in winter-time you divined beforehand, from the
vapour around the animals' mouths. It was there we used 20
to dine in summer, out on a terrace. Sometimes it was the
week when the acacias are fragrant, and then we had them
in fritters; or when the larks were dotted over the sky, and
then we had them in pies; sometimes it was the day the rye
turns all golden, and has its one and only day of triumph 25
over the wheat, and we had rye pancakes. A shot in a
coppice—that meant the woodcock were passing overhead,
flying in a single day (so my guardian would explain) to
Central Africa. A herd-girl knocking her clogs together;
that, twenty years before, used to be the alarm for wolves; 30
now it served for foxes; in twenty years' time it would only
mean weasels. Then the sun would set slant-wise, anxious not
to wound but only to graze my old homeland. You could see
half of him for a moment, screened by the hill like an actor.
A round of applause would have sufficed to bring him back. 35
But everything kept mum. Illuminated from behind, all the

30. **the alarm for wolves:** var. *the call to keep off wolves*;
perhaps "against wolves" would be too strong, implying a *levée
en masse* of the whole countryside and a general onslaught on
the wolves. The call is no doubt to the flock, to gather, and be
protected.

32. **weasels:** properly *fouines* = martens; but cp. *à figure de
fouine* = weasel-faced.

33. Var. *give my old district only a flesh-wound. Un séton*
is a seton, a thread drawn through a fold of skin so as to main-
tain an issue or opening for discharges, or to act as a counter-
irritant. *Une blessure en séton* is the ordinary phrase for a wound
that is only skin-deep, made by a rapier passing under the skin
without affecting the muscles. The allusion here is to the slanting
wound inflicted by the sun's declining rays; hence 'slant-wise'
seems better than 'aslant', as more explicitly describing a
glancing blow.

see half of him: not "half-see him".

35. **to bring him back:** the idea is that the actor was still on
the stage, not even in the wings, waiting to 'take his curtain'.

36. **kept mum:** var. *kept quiet, remained silent.*

moindres rameaux semblaient se lever, tous les arbres se rendre à merci....On les rassurait....On faisait malgré soi un demi-geste pour les rassurer.

JEAN GIRAUDOUX, *Suzanne et le Pacifique.*

37. **to go up**: var. *to be put up*. The allusion is to hands going up. The trees, so to speak, threw up their hands as if to surrender.

branches and the tiniest twigs seemed to go up, all the trees seemed to be making unconditional surrender. You reassured them; you involuntarily made a half-gesture to reassure them. 40

38. **unconditional**: *merci* is here used in its old meaning of 'good pleasure', 'discretion'.

26. LA PETITE VILLE: VUE D'ENSEMBLE

Au milieu de terrains vagues, des maisons neuves isolées, l'air emprunté comme d'avoir grandi trop vite, et qui tendent leurs pierres d'attente avec l'air de vouloir amorcer une conversation, se faire des amis, fonder une rue—comme on fonde une famille.

Des maisons humbles et petites, qui s'appuient l'une sur l'autre, se gênent, se supportent, des maisons en robes pauvres et barbouillées, qui ont beaucoup d'enfants devant la porte.

Des maisons en robes claires et nettes qui s'isolent avec orgueil et qui en ont les moyens, prennent leurs aises, s'étalent dans leurs jardins; des maisons riches, qui n'ont qu'un bel enfant tout brodé, ou deux, et qu'on met dans les allées, ou dans la serre selon le temps.

Quelques maisons encore, vieilles, usées, en loques, des maisons du XVIe siècle, c'est écrit dessus, et, comme elles—trop vivantes pour être des mortes, trop mortes pour être des vivantes—des vieilles de la même époque.

Des rues qui aboutissent à la campagne, lointainement verte aux yeux des 'enfermés', comme l'espoir de leur promenade du dimanche. D'autres rues qui se jettent dans les places comme dans des lacs tranquilles et toutes pleines du bruit des maisons. Chant des pendules annonçant: 'Nous

1. **waste ground**: var. *building-sites*, '*undeveloped*' *land*.
2. Var. *ill at ease (awkward) as if from having grown too quickly.*
3. **toothing-stones**: var. *toothings*, i.e. stones left projecting from a wall to form a bond for additional work to be built on.
7. Var. *putting up with each other*; *se supportent* can hardly mean "hold each other up"; that idea has already been expressed in *s'appuient*, and the contrast seems to be with *se gênent*. Cp. 'Je ne peux pas le *supporter*' = I cannot bear ("abide") him.
9. Var. *standing proudly aloof; in splendid isolation.*
10. **taking their ease**: var. *sprawling.*
12. **embroidered all over**: *tout brodé* may refer to a baby in a perambulator and also to a second and older child 'all dressed up'.
14. Var. *as weather permits.*

26. THE SMALL TOWN: GENERAL VIEW

In the midst of waste ground, new houses, all by themselves, looking self-conscious, as though they had shot up too fast, and putting out their toothing-stones with an air of wanting to strike up a conversation, make friends, have a street— as people have a family. 5

Humble little houses, leaning one on the other, inconveniencing but bearing with each other, houses in mean soiled dresses, with lots of children on the door-step.

Houses in clean light frocks which keep themselves to themselves, proudly, and can afford it; taking their ease, 10 spreading themselves out in their gardens; rich houses, with just one pretty child, embroidered all over—or two, maybe —put out on to the garden paths or into the conservatory, according to the state of the weather.

A few more houses, old, the worse for wear, out-at-elbows— 15 sixteenth-century houses they are, it's written up on them, and—just like the houses, too much alive to count as dead and too nearly dead to count as living—a few old ladies, of the same period.

Streets ending up in the country, which to the eyes of 20 those 'in city pent' is faraway and verdant—like the hopes of their Sunday walk. More streets, flowing into the squares as though into quiet lakes and brimful of sound from the houses: the chime of the clocks singing out: 'We've again

16. Var. *says the inscription* (*tablet*).

21. *comme* can be interpreted as either (1) introducing the second term of the comparison = the country (as) green *as* the hope, or (2) explaining *why* the *enfermés* look at the country = *as being* the hope. The allusion is to green as the colour of hope.

Var. (if the allusion to Milton, *Par. Lost*, IX, 441: 'As one who long in populous city pent...' or to Keats: 'To one who has been long in city pent' is inappropriate) *the people cooped up indoors*.

22. **flowing**: var. *falling*.

24. A clever example of the contemporary *précieux* metaphor: when the clock strikes the hour, the minute hand has gone completely round the face.

avons encore pondu un œuf plat comme la lune et rond comme notre cadran'; bruit du hachoir dans une cuisine et bruit du piano que dans le salon une jeune fille picore.

JEANNE RAMEL CALS, in *La Revue de France*, IV, 1924.

27. **is picking out**: *picorer* is said of a hen 'dabbing' at its food, pecking here and there, especially among growing

laid an egg as flat as the moon and round as our faces'; 25
thuds of the chopping-knife from a kitchen; the tinkle of
a piano from the drawing-room where a young miss is picking
out a tune.

vegetables. Here the girl is playing notes one at a time, here
and there, on the piano. Cp. No. 99, note 16.

27. ODEURS

Son appartement particulier donnait sur la rue Saint-Jacques qui aboutissait beaucoup plus loin au Grand-Pré (par opposition au Petit-Pré, verdoyant au milieu de la ville, entre trois rues) et qui, unie, grisâtre, avec les trois hautes marches de grès presque devant chaque porte, semblait comme un défilé pratiqué par un tailleur d'images gothiques à même la pierre où il eût sculpté une crèche ou un calvaire. Ma tante n'habitait plus effectivement que deux chambres contiguës, restant l'après-midi dans l'une pendant qu'on aérait l'autre. C'étaient de ces chambres de province qui—de même qu'en certains pays des parties entières de l'air ou de la mer sont

2. **farther on**: "Up", "down" and even "along" *may* be correct, but there is no evidence in the French text that they are.

4. **uniform and grey**: *uni* refers not to colour but to shape = smooth, smooth-faced, unbroken in outline, and not to the roadway, but to the house-walls: *grisâtre* need not be rendered by 'greyish', the slightly depreciatory sense of *-âtre* being almost inherent in 'grey'. Var. *in its grey uniformity*.

5. In *presque devant chaque porte* the order of the words is not to be retained in English; cp. Littré, s.v. PRESQUE: 'Il faut... éviter les équivoques et ne pas imiter cette phrase d'Arnaud: C'est une faute qui se trouve presque dans toutes les éditions de Cicéron.' But, Littré adds, 'Cette prescription n'est plus observée.'

6. **like a defile**, etc. *Défilé* might have two senses: (1) = mountain-pass, gorge; (2) = march-past or procession. *Pratiquer* might = (1) to make an opening for, let in, e.g. 'pratiquer *une porte dans un mur*', or (2) to use up (stone), utilize it fully, e.g. pratiquer *la pierre* = 'en tirer un bon parti, de façon qu'il y ait le moins de déchet possible'. Taken together, *défilé* and *pratiqué* suggest sense (1) of both words. *Images* are not "images", but include statues and all ornamental sculpture in a cathedral, done by *l'imagier*. Proust brings in the mediæval simile very abruptly. Perhaps he began by comparing the street with a narrow pass or cutting between precipitous hill-sides and then had the idea of a deep channel or groove chiselled out by a mediæval stone-cutter, the line of steps along the street suggesting a line of

27. FRAGRANCES

Her own rooms overlooked the rue St Jacques, which ended, much farther on, in the Grand-Pré (as opposed to the Petit-Pré, a bit of green in the middle of the town, bounded by three streets). The rue St Jacques, uniform and grey, with the three high sandstone steps in front of almost every 5 door, seemed like a defile hewn out by some sculptor of Gothic statuary in the stone he had used for a Nativity or a Calvary. My aunt was now in actual occupation of only two rooms, adjoining ones, and spent the afternoon in one while the other was being aired. They were rooms such as 10 you find in provincial towns, rooms which—just as in certain

partially chipped stone left at the base of the walls of the channel. Cp. the use of *tranchée* in No. 19; also Elizabeth Bowen, *The House in Paris* (1935): 'They swerved right...then engaged in a complex of deep streets, *fissures* in the craggy gloomy height.'

For the sense of *à même* cp. Flaubert: 'habits-vestes dont les pans semblaient avoir été coupés *à même* un seul bloc par la hache du charpentier', and Amicis, *La Hollande*: 'De quelque côté qu'on regarde, on ne voit que du rouge...comme si la ville avait été taillée *à même* une montagne de jaspe sanguin.' Examples quoted by Robert, *Questions de langue*. See also No. 7, note 9.

7. **had used**: probably not "might have used"; *eût* is sufficiently accounted for by the simile and as = *aurait*. N.B. In similes the conditional tense is regular, e.g. Buffon: 'Le zèbre paraît comme s'il était environné partout de bandelettes qu'on *aurait* pris plaisir à disposer régulièrement sur toutes les parties de son corps.'

7–8. Var. *for a Christmas crib or a wayside Cross.*

8. Var. *Actually my aunt was now occupying only two rooms.* For the sense of *effectivement* cp. *effectif* = real as opposed to nominal, e.g. in *Le règne* effectif *de Louis XV*, i.e. the period which began when Louis XV, who acceded in 1715, attained his legal majority in 1723.

10. **rooms such as**: the *de* in *C'étaient de ces chambres* is partitive. Cp. Vigny, *Le Cor*:

'Car je croyais ouïr *de ces* bruits prophétiques
Qui précédaient la mort des Paladins antiques.'

illuminées ou parfumées par des myriades de protozoaires que nous ne voyons pas—nous enchantent des mille odeurs qu'y dégagent les vertus, la sagesse, les habitudes, toute une vie secrète, invisible, surabondante et morale que l'atmosphère y tient en suspens; odeurs naturelles encore, certes, et couleur du temps comme celles de la campagne voisine, mais déjà casanières, humaines et renfermées, gelée exquise industrieuse et limpide, de tous les fruits de l'année qui ont quitté le verger pour l'armoire; saisonnières, mais mobilières et domestiques, corrigeant le piquant de la gelée blanche par la douceur du pain chaud, oisives et ponctuelles comme une horloge de village, flâneuses et rangées, insoucieuses et prévoyantes, lingères, matinales, dévotes, heureuses d'une paix qui n'apporte qu'un surcroît d'anxiété et d'un prosaïsme qui sert de grand réservoir de poésie à celui qui la traverse sans y avoir vécu.

15. **the virtues**, etc. The use of the definite article in *la sagesse* and *les habitudes* might be generic, but in *les vertus* it seems to be specific = *the* (well-known) virtues, *the* seven virtues or = *the* virtues practised in the abodes described. The natural assumption therefore is that the specific sense is intended in all three cases.

respectability: var. *rectitude*; *sagesse* = here, not so much "wisdom" as 'good conduct'; cp. *le prix de sagesse* = the Good Conduct prize.

15–16. Var. *a whole secret life, unseen, superabundant and with a moral value* (*and in the moral sphere*); *a whole teeming moral life, hidden away and unseen*.

18. **still of Nature.** The contrast is between the scents of nature outside and the same scents indoors.

In *couleur du temps*, *le temps* = the clear sky; 'le temps est couvert'; 'le temps se dégage'; hence *couleur du temps* = sky-blue; e.g. in Mme d'Aulnoy's fairy story *L'oiseau bleu* is called also *oiseau couleur du temps*. This usage must not be confused with the figurative one: *la couleur du temps* = the complexion of the time, the nature of the circumstances.

21. **jelly.** The unexpected appearance of *gelée* is only slightly less startling in French; var. *confection, compound*.

22. **seasonal**: var. *changing with the seasons*.

23. **mitigating**: var. *counteracting, tempering*.

24. **hoar-frost.** It is odd that Proust should have used *gelée*

countries whole tracts of air or sea receive light or perfume from myriads of protozoa which we cannot see—fascinate us with the thousand and one odours emanating from the virtues practised in them, the respectability, the settled habits: a whole secret life, unseen, abounding, and of moral significance, which their atmosphere holds in suspension; fragrances which indeed are still of Nature and blue sky, like those of the neighbouring countryside, but are becoming indoor, humanized, confined—an exquisite, cunningly blended, clear jelly of all the fruits of the year which have left the orchard for the store cupboard; fragrances seasonal, yet of the furniture and of the home, mitigating the nip of the hoar-frost outside with the warmth of the newly baked bread, leisurely and unfailing as a village clock, vagrant and ordered, heedless and provident, redolent of household linen, early rising and piety, of contentment in a peacefulness which is only an added source of anxiety and in a prosaic matter-of-factness which is as a great fount of poetry to him who passes through without having lived amongst it all.

in apparently different senses at so close an interval; he may have had in mind some play on the word and not developed it further, or *gelée* may have lost its identity in the expression *gelée blanche*.

25. **leisurely and unfailing**: var. *slow and steady* (*ponderous and punctilious*). N.B. *Ponctuel* is not "punctual" in reference to time, but rather 'punctilious'; cp. '*s'acquitter* ponctuellement *de son devoir*', to discharge one's duty point by point, i.e. scrupulously. The idea here is that the clock in the village steeple had little to do between the hours, yet never failed to strike them.

If the personification of *odeurs* is felt excessive in English, it can be toned down from this point by expanding, thus: [*odours which suggest a life*] *both leisurely* (*indolent*) *and precise, carefree and cautious*, etc.

26. Var. *scents of household linen, early morning or hour of prayer*.

27. **contentment in**: var. *contentment with, glorying in, rejoicing in*.

29. **to him who passes through.** In *celui qui la traverse*, is *celui* (as so often) general = one who? Or does it refer to the person speaking? The question need not be answered; 'him' will bear either interpretation. Grammatically *la* can refer only to *paix*. But the connexion is loose. Proust was notoriously careless in correcting his proofs.

L'air y était saturé de la fine fleur d'un silence si nourricier, si succulent que je ne m'y avançais qu'avec une sorte de gourmandise, surtout par ces premiers matins encore froids de la semaine de Pâques où je le goûtais mieux parce que je venais seulement d'arriver à Combray.

MARCEL PROUST, *Du Côté de chez Swann.*

31. **steeped in**: var. *permeated by.*

quintessence: *la fine fleur* is a stock phrase = the very best, the pink. It has been in use since the Middle Ages (la fine fleur

The air in these rooms was steeped in the quintessence of a silence so nourishing, so succulent that I could not enter into it without a sort of greedy relish, particularly on those first, still chilly mornings in Easter Week when I appreciated it better because I had only just arrived at Combray. 35

de la chevalerie), and both the epithet and the noun have lost any very definite meaning. Var. *rare essence.*
  32. **nourishing**: var. *nutritive, nutritious.*
  34. Var. *I was more sensitive to it because,* etc.

28. LE JARDIN DES TREMBLES

Vous auriez beau connaître les Trembles aussi bien que moi, je n'en aurais pas moins beaucoup de peine à vous faire comprendre ce que j'y trouvais de délicieux. Et pourtant tout y était délicieux, tout, jusqu'au jardin, qui, vous le savez cependant, est bien modeste. Il y avait des arbres, chose rare dans notre pays, et beaucoup d'oiseaux, qui aiment les arbres et qui n'auraient pu se loger ailleurs. Il y avait de l'ordre et du désordre, des allées sablées faisant suite à des perrons, menant à des grilles, et qui flattaient un certain goût que j'ai toujours eu pour les lieux où l'on se promène avec quelque apparat, où les femmes d'une autre époque auraient pu déployer des robes de cérémonie. Puis des coins obscurs, des carrefours humides où le soleil n'arrivait qu'à peine, où toute l'année des mousses verdâtres poussaient dans une terre spongieuse, des retraites visitées de moi seul, avaient des airs de vétusté, d'abandon, et sous une autre forme me rappelaient le passé, impression qui dès lors ne me déplaisait pas.

FROMENTIN, *Dominique*.

1. **Even though.** The construction *auriez...aurais* is the double conditional found, for example, in the popular type of phrase: 'Vous *prendriez* l'autobus, vous y *seriez* dans dix minutes' = '*If* you took', etc. Using *avoir beau* in the same type of sentence, we should have, for example, 'Vous *auriez beau* prendre l'autobus, vous n'arriveriez pas à temps' = '*Even though* you did take', etc.

2. Var. *in conveying what I found delightful about the place. And yet...was delightful.*

7. **roosted**: var. *found a roosting-place*, a more accurate rendering of *se loger* than 'made a home', 'settled', the presence of the birds in the garden being only temporary—for the night or for the summer.

8. **regularity...irregularity**: var. *symmetry...lack of symmetry, order...disorder* (cp. 'A sweet disorder in the dress'). The distinction is between the severe regularity of the formal French garden (cp. No. 96), and the unstudied naturalness of the English garden, e.g. the 'jardin anglais' in the Luxembourg; cp. Jusserand, *Litt. angl.* II, p. 865: 'Classique dans l'âme il

28. THE GARDEN AT 'LES TREMBLES'

Even though you knew 'Les Trembles' as well as I do, I should nevertheless have great difficulty in conveying the peculiar charm I found in the place. And yet everything about it had charm, everything, even the garden, which (as you know, however) is quite unpretentious. There were trees, an unusual thing in our part of the country, and plenty of birds, which are fond of trees and could not have roosted anywhere else. There was regularity, and irregularity—gravelled walks following on from flights of stone steps and leading to wrought-iron gates, and humouring a certain fancy I have always had for places where folk may walk abroad in some state, and ladies of other days might have flaunted Court gowns. Then, shady nooks, dank crossways where the sun only just won through and, all the year round, there were green mosses growing in a spongy soil, secluded spots where nobody went but me—all these had an olden-time, forlorn air and, in another form, reminded me of the past, an impression which consequently was not unpleasing to me.

[Bacon] dispose son jardin à la française, avec des allées au cordeau, des charmilles, des fantaisies et des haies taillées en pyramides; il laisse à son ami, l'ambassadeur Wotton, le soin de célébrer dans le même temps, puisque tel était son goût, "ces jardins irréguliers ou du moins d'une régularité très sauvage" qu'on devait appeler plus tard jardins à l'anglaise.'

9. **flights...gates.** Some expansion is necessary unless we use the French, *perrons* and *grilles*, as is sometimes done in English, though generally 'terraces' and 'garden gates' are loosely used; *grille* is usually an ornamental iron gate, at the entrance to a park, gardens, etc.

13. **flaunted**, etc. The allusion to spreading the train of state robes or Court dresses would perhaps be sufficiently indicated by 'flaunted' alone or 'flaunted their finery'; cp. 'the *flaunting* peacock', 'the peacock's *train*', etc.

Court gowns: var. *train-gowns.* Var. *spread their stately trains.*

15. **green:** var. *green-tinted,* but the suffix *-âtre* has often little force; the mosses were 'green', as opposed to 'brown', because of the moisture.

29. DANS LA CATHÉDRALE DE CHARTRES

Cette basilique, elle était le suprême effort de la matière cherchant à s'alléger, rejetant, tel qu'un lest, le poids aminci de ses murs, les remplaçant par une substance moins pesante et plus lucide, substituant à l'opacité de ses pierres l'épiderme diaphane des vitres....

Elle stupéfiait avec l'essor éperdu de ses voûtes et la folle splendeur de ses vitres. Le temps était couvert et cependant toute une fournaise de pierreries brûlait dans les lames des ogives, dans les sphères embrasées des roses.

Là-haut, dans l'espace, tels que des salamandres, des êtres humains, avec des visages en ignition et des robes en braises vivaient dans un firmament de feu; mais ces incendies étaient circonscrits, limités par un cadre incombustible de verres plus foncés qui refoulait la joie jeune et claire des flammes, par cette espèce de mélancolie, par cette apparence de côté plus sérieux et plus âgé que dégagent les couleurs sombres. L'hallali des rouges, la sécurité limpide des blancs, l'alleluia

1. **basilica**: *pile*. *Une basilique* is properly (1) a building in a certain architectural form (see No. 12, note 7) and (2) the church in a diocese which ranks next to the Cathedral. But it is also used generically = fane, pile, church, etc. Var. *This basilica —it was....*

2. **diminished**: var. *thinned down, lightened, attenuated, lessened.*

4. **opaqueness**: for French *opaque* see No. 16, note 9.

5. Var. *masonry...glass-work.*

transparent: var. *diaphanous.*

film: var. *shell.* Cp. Huysmans, describing a river (Le Drac) as a serpent: 'plus loin il déroulait ses anneaux et disparaissait, en pelant, laissant après lui sur le sol *un épiderme* blanc et grenelé de cailloux, *une peau* de sable sec.'

7. **wild splendour**: var. *reckless (riotous) glory.*

8. **burned**: cp. Ruskin, *Stones of Venice*: 'a courtyard paved with pebbles all *burning* in the thick glow of the feverish sunshine.'

lancets. See *Cent. Dict.* s.v. 'Lancet-window', and cp. Tennyson, *Aylmer's Field*:

'The church—one night except
For greenish glimmerings thro' the *lancets*.'

29. IN THE CATHEDRAL OF CHARTRES

This basilica was the crowning effort of matter striving for lightness, casting off, like ballast, the diminished weight of its walls, replacing them by a substance less ponderous, more translucent, and substituting for the opaqueness of its stonework the transparent film of windows.... 5

It had a dazing effect with the dizzy soaring of its vaults and the wild splendour of its windows. The day was overcast, and yet a whole furnace of jewels burned in the lancets of the ogives and the blazing spheres of the roses.

Up aloft, in space, human creatures, with faces alight 10 and robes of glowing embers, lived salamander-like in a firmament of fire; but these conflagrations were circumscribed, bounded by a fire-proof frame of deeper-tinted panes, which curbed the bright youthful glee of the flames by that species of melancholy, that more sober, more mature 15 effect which dark colours produce. The triumphal blare of the reds, the limpid serenity of the whites, the pealing

---

Huysmans contrasts the two shapes of window at Chartres, the Western rose and the lancets under it.

10. **Up aloft**: var. *Overhead.*
11. **robes**: var. *vestments.* Cp. A. E. Housman, *Last Poems* (*Hell Gate*):

> 'Trim and burning, to and fro,
>   One for women to admire
>   In his finery of fire.'

13. **bounded**: var. *marked off, curtailed.*
fire-proof: var. *fire-resisting.*
14. **curbed**: var. *checked.*
15. **species**: var. *semblance.*
16. **the triumphal blare**: *l'hallali* is the flourish of trumpets sounded when the stag is dying, in the ritual of the chase; cp. F. Thompson, *Ode to the Setting Sun*: 'I *see* the *crimson blaring of thy shawms*', and Huysmans (passage quoted in note 5, above): 'Le train...descendait dans les tunnels...puis il sortait *dans un hallali* de lumière.'
17. **pealing**: var. *repeated, reiterated.*

répété des jaunes, la gloire virginale des bleus, tout le foyer trépidant des verrières s'éteignait quand il s'approchait de cette bordure teinte avec des rouilles de fer, des roux de sauces, des violets rudes de grès, des verts de bouteille, des bruns d'amadou, des noirs de fuligine, des gris de cendre.

J.-K. HUYSMANS, *La Cathédrale*.

18. hosannah. This seems a legitimate substitute for *alleluia* [now usually *alléluia*]; cp. Goncourt, *Madame Gervaisais*: 'Tout à coup éclata...un *hosanna* qui déchirait l'air de notes argentines, montant et se perdant à la hauteur des voûtes.'

19. flame. Properly '*foyer*'='focus' [cp. 'le foyer d'un incendie'], here 'foci'; but this is too technical.

great: *verrières* gives the idea of great size, not necessarily given by the word 'windows'.

20. sauce-browns: *roux* is the culinary term=browning; cp. *beurre roux*=browned butter.

hosannah of the yellows, the virgin glory of the blues, all the quivering flame in the great windows dulled down as it drew near that border stained with rust-coloured reds, sauce- browns, crude, stone-ware purples, bottle-greens, amadou-browns, soot-blacks, ash-greys.

21. **amadou**: var. *tinder*, *touchwood* (which is snuff-coloured).
22. **ash-greys**: cp. Ruskin, *Modern Painters*, II: 'The broad and sunlike glory about the head of the Redeemer has become wan and *of the colour of ashes*.'

Cp. with this passage, W. J. Locke, *The Usurper*, p. 70: 'The man sang colour. He intoxicated you with the swirl of luminous reds, woke you with the ripple of blues, made you tremulous with the frosty shiver of whites, and then drowned you in tumultuous seas of purple.'

II. PORTRAITS

30. SAINT-JUST

Les paroles de Saint-Just, lentes et mesurées, tombaient d'un poids singulier, et laissaient de l'ébranlement, comme le lourd couteau de la guillotine. Par un contraste choquant, elles sortaient, ces paroles froidement impitoyables, d'une bouche qui semblait féminine. Sans ses yeux bleus fixes et durs, ses sourcils fortement barrés, Saint-Just eût pu passer pour une femme. Était-ce la vierge de Tauride? Non, ni les yeux, ni la peau, quoique fine et blanche, ne portaient un sentiment de pureté. Cette peau, très aristocratique, avec un caractère singulier d'éclat et de transparence, paraissait trop belle, et laissait alors douter s'il était sain. L'énorme cravate serrée, que seul il portait alors, fit dire à ses ennemis, peut-être sans cause, qu'il cachait des humeurs froides. Le col était comme supprimé par la cravate, par le collet raide et haut; effet d'autant plus bizarre que sa taille longue ne faisait point du tout attendre cet accourcissement du col. Il avait le front très bas, le haut de la tête comme déprimé, de sorte que les cheveux, sans être longs, touchaient presque aux yeux. Mais le plus étrange était son allure, d'une roideur automatique qui n'était qu'à lui. La roideur de Robespierre n'était rien auprès. Tenait-elle à une singularité physique, à son excessif orgueil, à une dignité calculée? peu importe. Elle intimidait plus qu'elle ne semblait ridicule. On sentait qu'un être tellement inflexible de mouvement devait l'être aussi de cœur. Ainsi lorsque, dans son discours, passant du roi à la Gironde et laissant là Louis XVI, il se tourna d'une pièce vers la droite, et dirigea sur elle, avec la parole, sa personne tout entière, son dur et meurtrier regard, il n'y avait personne qui ne sentît le froid de l'acier.

MICHELET, *Histoire de la Révolution française.*

1. **Saint Just:** The hyphen in this name is usually dropped in English. The Revolutionary leader (1767–94) made his first speech (Nov. 13, 1792) on the condemnation of Louis XVI.

fell: var. *came down.*

5. Var. *But for the stony stare of his blue eyes.*

7. **the Virgin of Tauris:** Iphigeneia, the maiden whom Artemis carried away to be her priestess in the Tauric Chersonese [Crimea], where it was her duty to sacrifice all strangers to the goddess.

30. SAINT JUST

Saint Just's slow measured words fell with a strange thud and lingering vibration, like the heavy knife of the guillotine. By a disconcerting contrast, they came, these coldly pitiless words, out of a mouth which seemed feminine. But for his hard, staring blue eyes and his strongly marked eyebrows, Saint Just might have passed for a woman. Was this the Virgin of Tauris? No, neither the eyes nor the skin, white and delicate though it was, conveyed any notion of purity. Such a skin, highly aristocratic and with a strange quality of brilliance and transparency, looked *too* beautiful, and thus raised doubts as to whether he was healthy. The large closely-fitting cravat, which he was the only man to wear at that time, made his enemies say, possibly without any grounds for this, that he was concealing cold humours. The neck seemed cut short by the cravat and the high stiff coat-collar—an effect all the odder because his lank figure made this abbreviation of the neck quite unexpected. He had a very low forehead, the top of the head being depressed as it were, so that the hair, though not long, reached almost to the eyes. But strangest of all was his gait, which had an automaton-like rigidity peculiar to himself. Robespierre's rigidity was nothing to his. Was it due to some physical peculiarity, or to his overweening pride, or to studied dignity? No matter. It instilled fear rather than aroused ridicule. The feeling was that a being so inflexible in movement must be equally so in heart. When, accordingly, in the middle of his speech, passing on from the King to the Gironde and dropping the subject of Louis XVI without more ado, he turned on the Right bodily and levelled at them, not only his words, but his entire person, his grim, deadly stare, there was not a man among them but felt the chill of steel.

11. Var. *led one to doubt whether*.
13. Var. *prompted his opponents to say, though perhaps without reason (justification)*.
15. **cut short**: var. *extinguished*.
20. **gait**: var. *way of walking*.
24. Var. *One felt*; *One had the feeling*, unless 'One' implies that Michelet was an eye-witness.

31. LE MÉDECIN DE CAMPAGNE

Benassis était un homme de taille ordinaire, mais large des épaules et large de poitrine. Une ample redingote verte, boutonnée jusqu'au cou, empêcha l'officier de saisir les détails si caractéristiques de ce personnage ou de son maintien; mais l'ombre et l'immobilité dans laquelle resta le corps servirent à faire ressortir la figure, alors fortement éclairée par un reflet des flammes. Cet homme avait un visage semblable à celui d'un satyre : même front légèrement cambré, mais plein de proéminences toutes plus ou moins significatives; même nez retroussé, spirituellement fendu dans le bout; mêmes pommettes saillantes. La bouche était sinueuse, les lèvres étaient épaisses et rouges. Le menton se relevait brusquement. Les yeux bruns et animés par un regard vif auquel la couleur nacrée du blanc de l'œil donnait un grand éclat, exprimaient des passions amorties. Les cheveux jadis noirs et maintenant gris, les rides profondes de son visage et ses gros sourcils déjà blanchis, son nez devenu bulbeux et veiné, son teint jaune et marbré par des taches rouges, tout annonçait en lui l'âge de cinquante ans et les rudes travaux de sa profession. L'officier ne put que présumer la capacité de la tête, alors couverte d'une casquette; mais, quoique cachée par cette coiffure, elle lui parut être une de ces têtes proverbialement nommées *têtes carrées*. Habitué par les rapports qu'il avait eus avec les hommes d'énergie que rechercha Napoléon, à distinguer les traits des personnes

CONTEXT. Major Genestas (see No. 59) has gone out to intercept the doctor on his round; he sees him, for the first time, visiting a patient in a cottage. Like Balzac, Genestas dabbled in the then popular 'science' of phrenology, founded by Doctor Franz-Joseph Gall (1750–1828), who practised in Paris from 1802: 'Le médecin...se retourna vers le malade sans se croire l'objet d'un examen aussi sérieux que le fut celui du militaire....'

1. **ordinary**: var. *middle, normal, average*.
2. **broad-chested**: cp. O.E.D. 1662, Fuller, *Worthies, Rutlandshire*: 'A very proper man, broad shouldered and chested.'
3. **observing**: var. *taking in*.

31. THE COUNTRY DOCTOR

Benassis was a man of ordinary height, but broad-shouldered and broad-chested. A roomy green frock-coat, buttoned up to the chin, prevented the officer from observing the very characteristic details of the person or of his bearing; but as the body remained motionless and in shadow, this helped 5 to give prominence to the face, at that moment vividly lit up by a flicker from the firelight. The man had features like a satyr's: there was the same forehead, slightly bulging, but full of bumps, all of them more or less significant; the same turned-up nose, with the groove at the tip denoting wit; the 10 same high cheek-bones. The mouth was sinuous, the lips thick and red, the chin sharply tilted. The brown eyes, animated by a keen glance, and made very bright by the pearl-colour of the 'whites', expressed passions subdued. The hair, once black and now grey; the deep lines on his 15 face, and his bushy eyebrows, gone white; his nose, become bulbous and veined; his sallow complexion blotched with red—all evidenced his age (fifty) and the strenuous labours of his profession. The officer could only guess at the dimensions of the head, it being then covered by a cap; but, 20 though thus concealed, it looked to him like one of those heads proverbially known as 'level'. Accustomed as he was, from his dealings with the men of action whom Napoleon

---

7. **features**: var. *a face*, if the repetition is not unpleasant.

9. Var. *all of more or less phrenological significance.*

11. Cp. O.E.D. 1822: 'The mouth was widely sinuous.'

16. **gone white.** This is a case (see also No. 33, note 30) where 'already' = *déjà* seems peculiar in English. Var. *prematurely white.*

18. Var. *all pointed to the age of fifty, and revealed the hard grind of his profession.*

19. **guess at**: var. *surmise.*

22. 'level': *tête carrée* = 'homme d'un jugement juste et solide, ou d'un caractère opiniâtre' (Littré)—what we should call 'level-headed', though this does not necessarily include *opiniâtre*.

Var. *one of those square-shaped heads which are proverbially screwed on the right way.*

destinées aux grandes choses, Genestas devina quelque mystère dans cette vie obscure, et se dit en voyant ce visage extraordinaire: — Par quel hasard est-il resté médecin de campagne? BALZAC, *Le Médecin de campagne.*

24. **features**: *traits* may not mean only 'features'; ? *discern the characteristics.*

sought out, to recognize the features of people destined to do great things, Genestas felt there was some mystery about this man's obscure life, and said to himself when he saw that remarkable face: 'By what strange chance is he still a country doctor?'

32. LE COUSIN PONS

Sous ce chapeau, qui paraissait près de tomber, s'étendait une de ces figures falotes et drolatiques comme les Chinois seuls en savent inventer pour leurs magots.

Ce vaste visage percé comme une écumoire, où les trous produisaient des ombres, et refouillé comme un masque romain, démentait toutes les lois de l'anatomie. Le regard n'y sentait point de charpente. Là où le dessin voulait des os, la chair offrait des méplats gélatineux, et là où les figures présentent ordinairement des creux, celle-là se contournait en bosses flasques. Cette face grotesque, écrasée en forme de potiron, attristée par des yeux gris surmontés de deux lignes rouges au lieu de sourcils, était commandée par un nez à la Don Quichotte, comme une plaine est dominée par un bloc erratique. Ce nez exprime, ainsi que Cervantes avait dû le remarquer, une disposition native à ce dévouement aux grandes choses qui dégénère en duperie. Cette laideur, poussée tout au comique, n'excitait cependant point le rire. La mélancolie excessive qui débordait par les yeux pâles de

1. Var. *as if it might fall off at any moment.*
2. **quaint**: var. *queer*; cp. Th. Botrel, *Les Deux Gosses*:
    'Ils ont des allures *falotes*
    D'attendrissants petits *magots*.'
falot properly = *cocasse*, but is often used with some notion of *douloureux*.
3. **magots**: 'small grotesque figures of porcelain, etc., of Chinese or Japanese workmanship' (O.E.D.); var. *dolls*.
4. **countenance**: the various words used for 'face' in this passage have not the same connotations: *figure* is a general word (and means in addition 'figure'); *face* is often depreciatory = a blank expanse of face; *visage* has some reference to facial expression.
5. **holes**: i.e. pock-marks.
6. **mask**: 'a likeness of a person's face in clay, wax, etc.' (O.E.D.).
7. Var. *Looking at it, one had no impression of any underlying framework (any understructure).*
8. **design**: var. *pattern*.
planes: *méplats* 'planes that build up the face'. Mansion.

32. COUSIN PONS

Underneath that hat, which looked as if it were about to topple off, spread one of these quaint, droll faces such as only the Chinese have the knack of devising for their magots.

This expansive countenance, filled, like a skimming-ladle, with holes which made shadows on it, and as deep-chiselled 5 as a Roman mask, gave the lie to all the laws of anatomy. A glance at it suggested no framework underneath. Where the design called for bones, the flesh offered gelatinous planes, and where faces usually have hollows, this face swelled out into flabby protuberances. This grotesque physiognomy, 10 squashed into the shape of a pumpkin and saddened by grey eyes with two red lines above for eyebrows, was commanded by a nose of the Don Quixote sort, as a plain is dominated by an 'erratic block'. Such a nose expresses, as Cervantes must have noticed, a natural aptitude for that 15 devotion to things of great moment which degenerates into mere credulity. This ugliness, though its whole tendency was towards the comical, did not, however, excite laughter. The extreme melancholy welling out in the poor man's pale

The word occurs again in No. 37, line 13. French technical artistic vocabulary is fuller than English and much more freely used.

9. Var. *where faces usually go in, this one bulged out.*

10. **physiognomy**: var. (if the depreciatory sense of *face* is insufficiently given) *phiz*, which has been in literary use since 1688 (O.E.D.).

12. Var. *set beneath two red lines in lieu of eyebrows.*

14. **erratic block**: the technical term. It has certainly a semi-humorous effect, even when toned down by the addition of inverted commas. But Balzac and also his English contemporaries loved these scientific terms and the variant 'isolated boulder' is no better.

15. **must have noticed**: *avait dû* throws the action back into the remoter past = 'as Cervantes of old', etc., in distinction to *a dû*, e.g. 'Baedeker *a dû* se tromper'.

Var. *a natural (native) tendency to take up great causes.*

17. **credulity**: var. *gullibility.*

18. **laughter**: var. *merriment.*

19. **pale eyes**: cp. G. Moore, *Ave atque Vale*, p. 35: 'looking into his *pale eyes* I often wondered', etc.

ce pauvre homme atteignait le moqueur et lui glaçait la plaisanterie sur les lèvres. On pensait aussitôt que la nature avait interdit à ce bonhomme d'exprimer la tendresse, sous peine de faire rire une femme ou de l'affliger. Le Français se tait devant ce malheur qui lui paraît le plus cruel de tous les malheurs: ne pouvoir plaire!

BALZAC, Le Cousin Pons.

22. **under penalty**: var. *on pain.*
23. Var. *causing a woman amusement or pain.*

eyes came home to the scoffer and froze the jest upon his lips. The thought at once arose that nature had debarred this man from ever voicing a tender thought, under penalty of making a woman laugh or distressing her. Your Frenchman is silent in the presence of this misfortune which to him seems cruellest of all: inability to charm!

25. **to charm:** var. *to attract; plaire* often almost = *plaire aux femmes.*

33. BALZAC

Au commencement de cette étude, nous avons raconté les velléités de dandyisme manifestées par Balzac; nous avons dit son habit bleu à boutons d'or massif, sa canne monstrueuse surmontée d'un pavé de turquoises, ses apparitions dans le monde et dans la loge infernale; ces magnificences n'eurent qu'un temps, et Balzac reconnut qu'il n'était pas propre à jouer ce rôle d'Alcibiade ou de Brummel. Chacun a pu le rencontrer, surtout le matin, lorsqu'il courait aux imprimeries porter la copie et chercher les épreuves, dans un costume infiniment moins splendide. L'on se rappelle la veste de chasse verte, à boutons de cuivre représentant des têtes de renard, le pantalon à pied quadrillé noir et gris, enfoncé dans de gros souliers à oreilles, le foulard rouge tortillé en corde autour du col, et le chapeau à la fois hérissé et glabre, à coiffe bleue déteinte par la sueur, qui couvraient plutôt qu'ils n'habillaient 'le plus fécond de nos romanciers'. Mais malgré le désordre et la pauvreté de cet accoutrement, personne n'eût été tenté de prendre pour un inconnu vulgaire ce gros homme aux yeux de flamme, aux narines mobiles, aux joues martelées de tons violents, tout illuminé de génie, qui passait emporté par son rêve comme par un tourbillon! A son aspect, la raillerie s'arrêtait sur les lèvres du gamin, et l'homme sérieux n'achevait

1. Essay: var. *Study*.

4. Var. *with turquoises in a 'pavé' setting*. A *pavé* is a setting of jewels 'placed closed together like the stones of a pavement, so that no metal is visible', *Westminister Gazette*, Dec. 1903. 'The *pavé* setting makes a mosaic of the stones' (O.E.D.). Cp. A. Billy, *Honoré de Balzac*, 1944, p. 265: '...la fameuse canne au pommeau incrusté de myosotis en turquoises...et agrémenté d'une chaîne d'or: la propre chaîne et les propres myosotis que Mme Hanska jeune fille avait portés au cou'.

5. Var. *loge infernale*. Cp. Edmond Texier, *Tableau de Paris*, p. 107: '...messieurs les abonnés de la *loge infernale*, composée de la fleur des pois des élégances...du boulevard, de lions à tous crins, de spéculateurs enrichis...vieux jeunes gens pour la plupart.' An engraving accompanying the text shows four of these *abonnés* in the left-hand stage box, i.e. the ground-floor box nearest the proscenium, of the *Opéra*. According to A. Billy, *op. cit.* p. 137, the legendary *loge infernale* 'n'a jamais existé'.

33. BALZAC

At the beginning of this Essay we gave some account of Balzac's leanings towards dandyism, and we mentioned his blue coat with solid gold buttons, his prodigious walking stick, headed with a mosaic of turquoises, his appearances in society and at the Opera, in the Pandæmonium Box. These splendours had their day. Balzac realized that he was not cut out for the part of Alcibiades or Beau Brummell. Any of us may have come across him—particularly in the morning, hurrying away to his printers with 'copy' or for proofs—in far less splendid array. We can remember the green shooting-jacket, with brass buttons representing foxes' masks, the footed shepherd's-tartan trousers, tucked into heavy boots with flaps, the red scarf twisted ropewise round the neck, and the top-hat, all tufts and bare patches, with a blue lining discoloured by perspiration—the whole rather clothing than dressing 'the most prolific of our novelists'. But, despite the untidiness and shabbiness of the get-up, it would not have occurred to anyone to take for a mere nobody this stout man with the blazing eyes, the sensitive nostrils, the high-coloured cheeks, who went on his way with the light of genius round him, swept along by his inward vision as by a whirlwind! At the look of him, the jest died away on the street-boy's lips and the grown man checked an incipient smile. You

---

8. **Brummell**: usually *Brummel* in French: 1778–1840, *arbiter elegantiarum* in England from about 1800 till 1816, when he fled from his creditors to France.

13. **heavy**: see No. 35, note 3.

boots: *souliers* = boots as well as shoes, see No. 39, note 16.

flaps: i.e. as in snow-boots or house-boots.

14. **ropewise**: cp. Balzac's own description of M. Poiret's '*jabot*...qui s'unissait imparfaitement à la cravate *cordée* autour de son cou de dindon'.

Var. *at the same time shaggy and napless*; for *glabre* = glabrous see No. 37, note 5. The allusion is to a dilapidated silk hat 'brushed the wrong way'.

24. **grown**: perhaps sufficient, since it implies *sérieux* =

pas le sourire ébauché.—L'on devinait un des rois de la pensée....

Cette rude vie de travail nocturne avait, malgré sa forte constitution, imprimé des traces sur la physionomie de Balzac, et nous trouvons dans *Albert Savarus* un portrait de lui, tracé par lui-même, et qui le représente tel qu'il était à cette époque (1842) avec un léger arrangement.

'...Une tête superbe: cheveux noirs mélangés déjà de quelques cheveux blancs, des cheveux comme en ont les saint Pierre et les saint Paul de nos tableaux, à boucles touffues et luisantes, des cheveux durs comme des crins, un col blanc et rond comme celui d'une femme, un front magnifique, séparé par ce sillon puissant que les grands projets, les grandes pensées, les fortes méditations inscrivent au front des grands hommes: un teint olivâtre marbré de taches rouges, un nez carré, des yeux de feu, puis les joues creusées, marquées de deux longues rides pleines de souffrances, une bouche à sourire sarde et un petit menton mince et trop court, la patte d'oie aux tempes, les yeux caves, roulant sous les arcades sourcilières comme deux globes ardents; mais malgré tous ces indices de passions violentes, un air calme, profondément résigné, la voix d'une douceur pénétrante et qui m'a surpris par sa facilité, la vraie voix de l'orateur, tantôt pure et rusée, tantôt insinuante, et tonnant quand il le faut, puis se pliant au sarcasme, et devenant alors incisive. M. Albert Savarus est de moyenne taille, ni gras ni maigre; enfin, il a des mains de prélat.'

THÉOPHILE GAUTIER, *Portraits contemporains*:
Honoré de Balzac.

serious-minded = come to years of discretion. Cp. No. 29: 'plus sérieux et plus âgé.' Var. *sober elders*.

Var. *You felt that here was a prince*, etc.

28. Var. *We possess a self-portrait of Balzac, namely, Albert Savarus.*

31. **premature grey**: 'hair' is called for so often in the sentence that it is better to avoid 'a few grey hairs' or 'white hairs'. Var. *with some white in it already*. But *déjà* is often over-translated by 'already', cp. No. 31, note 16; 'premature' seems the normal English. Balzac (1799–1849) was forty-three at this time.

felt this must be one of the princes in the realms of thought....

That hard life, all night-work, had, in spite of his powerful constitution, left traces on his face. We have a portrait of Balzac by himself, in *Albert Savarus*, which depicts him as he was at that time (1842), with a few slight embellishments:

'...A superb head; black hair, with some premature grey in it—hair like that of St Peter and St Paul in the picture-galleries, with lustrous thick curls—rough as horsehair; a neck as white and rounded as a woman's; a magnificent forehead cleft by that strong furrow which great projects, great thoughts, deep meditation drive across great men's brows; an olive complexion with markings of red; a square-shaped nose, and eyes of fire; and the sunken cheeks, seamed by two long wrinkles suggestive of much suffering; a mouth with a Sardinian smile; a small, slender, abbreviated chin; crows'-feet about the temples; eyes deep-set, rolling beneath the ridges of the brows like two globes of fire; but, despite all such indications of strong passions, a quiet air of profound resignation, a voice of penetrating sweetness which surprised me by its easy modulation, the true voice of the orator, now clear and cunning, now insinuating, and rising to thunder on occasion, then taking on the note of sarcasm and becoming, in that event, incisive. M. Albert Savarus is of medium height, neither stout nor thin; and he has the hands of a prelate.'

36. **deep**: var. *profound, intense*.

drive across: var. *trace upon*.

40. **Sardinian**: var. *sardonic*, but Balzac has preferred to the usual *sardonique* the form *sarde*=Sardinian; cp. Johnson, *Rambler*: 'what the Latins call *Sardinian* Laughter, a distortion of the face without gladness of heart.' Cp. Du Bellay, *Les Regrez*, LXXVII: 'Car je ry, comme on dit, d'un riz Sardonien.'

41. **eyes**: are mentioned twice—perhaps inadvertently.

46. **cunning**: *rusée* seems to indicate making a skilful or a wily use of a voice which was naturally clear (French: *pure*) and sounded guileless. For *pure* cp. Loti, *Prime Jeunesse*, p. 169: 'C'était la chère voix de ma mère, si *pure* jadis, mais où je percevais pour la première fois quelque chose comme une imperceptible fêlure dans un son de cristal.'

47. Var. *adapting itself (sinking) to sarcasm; se pliant* has a notion of 'lending itself to'.

34. TAINE

Le philosophe avait alors cinquante-six ans. Enveloppé d'un pardessus de fourrure grise, avec ses lunettes, sa barbe grisonnante, il semblait un personnage du vieux temps, un alchimiste hollandais. Ses cheveux étaient collés, serrés sur sa tête, sans une ondulation. Sa figure creuse et sans teint avait des tons de bois. Il portait sa barbe à peu près comme Alfred de Musset qu'il avait tant aimé, et sa bouche eût été aisément sensuelle. Le nez était busqué, la voûte du front belle, les tempes bien renflées, encore que serrées aux approches du front, et l'arcade sourcilière nette, vive, arrêtée finement. Du fond de ces douces cavernes, le regard venait, à la fois impatient et réservé, retardé par le savoir, semblait-il, et pressé par la curiosité ! Et ce caractère, avec la lenteur des gestes, contribuait beaucoup à la dignité d'un ensemble qui aurait pu paraître un peu chétif et universitaire dans certains détails, car M. Taine, par exemple, portait cette après-midi une étroite cravate noire, en satin, comme celle que l'on met le soir.

Le jeune carabin démêla très vite que ces yeux gris de M. Taine, remarquables de douceur, de lumière et de profondeur, étaient inégaux et voyaient un peu de travers; exactement, il était bigle. Ce regard singulier, avec quelque chose de retourné en dedans, pas très net, un peu brouillé, vraiment d'un homme qui voit des abstractions et qui doit se réveiller pour saisir la réalité, contribuait à lui donner, quand il causait idées, un air de surveiller sa pensée et non son interlocuteur, et ce défaut devenait une espèce de beauté morale.   MAURICE BARRÈS, *Les Déracinés*.

CONTEXT. A medical student, Roemerspacher, a fictitious character representing no doubt Barrès himself, is supposed to have written an article on Taine, published in a Paris paper. Taine's interest is aroused and he calls on the author, who here describes, unflatteringly, the person who came into his room.

3. **Dutch alchemist:** no doubt one of Rembrandt's 'Philosophers', see No. 2, note 20. There are two in the Louvre.

5. **colourless:** var. *complexionless*, which is exactly *sans teint* and has excellent authority in O.E.D.

7. **had:** the date of the interview is about 1884. Musset died in 1857.

34. TAINE

The philosopher was at that time fifty-six. Muffled up in a grey fur coat, he looked, with his spectacles and his iron-grey beard, like some character of olden days, like a Dutch alchemist. His hair was firmly plastered down on his head, without the trace of a wave, and his gaunt, colourless face had tints of wood. He wore his beard after the manner of Alfred de Musset, whom he had so much admired, and his mouth would have easily seemed a sensual one. The nose was Roman, the dome of the brow well-shaped, the temples full, though narrowing in towards the forehead, and the arch of the eyebrows clear-cut, bold and finely chiselled. From the quiet depths of these caverns the glance came eager and at the same time reserved, seeming to be checked by learning and quickened by curiosity! And that peculiarity, along with the deliberate gestures, considerably enhanced the dignity of a general appearance which might have seemed somewhat unimpressive and scholastic in certain details; for instance, that afternoon M. Taine was wearing a narrow black satin tie, of the sort for evening wear.

The budding medical very quickly diagnosed the fact that those grey eyes of M. Taine's, noteworthy for their softness, for the light in them and for their depth, were not equal and that their vision was slightly oblique; to be accurate, he had a squint. That peculiar glance, with something introspective in it, not very clear, a little blurred—the glance, in fact, of a man who sees abstractions and has to rouse himself before he can come to grips with reality—helped to give him, when talking philosophy, an air of watching his own thoughts and not the listener, and this defect became a sort of moral beauty.

9. **well-shaped:** var. '*noble*'.

11. Said of paintings at least, *arrêté* means 'finished'.

12. **quiet:** *douces* may be, like the surrounding details, physical='smooth-shelving'.

17. **scholastic:** *l'Université* comprises Universities and schools and *un universitaire* means as often a secondary schoolmaster as a university teacher.

23. Var. *looked slightly cross-ways.*

25. **blurred:** var. *hazy.*

28. Var. *when discussing ideas.*

35. LA VIEILLE SERVANTE

Alors on vit s'avancer sur l'estrade une petite vieille femme de maintien craintif, et qui paraissait se ratatiner dans ses pauvres vêtements. Elle avait aux pieds de grosses galoches de bois, et, le long des hanches, un grand tablier bleu. Son visage maigre, entouré d'un béguin sans bordure, était plus plissé de rides qu'une pomme de reinette flétrie, et des manches de sa camisole rouge dépassaient deux longues mains à articulations noueuses. La poussière des granges, la potasse des lessives et le suint des laines les avaient si bien encroûtées, éraillées, durcies, qu'elles semblaient sales, quoiqu'elles fussent rincées d'eau claire; et, à force d'avoir servi, elles restaient entr'ouvertes, comme pour présenter d'elles-mêmes l'humble témoignage de tant de souffrances subies. Quelque chose d'une rigidité monacale relevait l'expression de sa figure. Rien de triste ou d'attendri n'amollissait ce regard pâle. Dans la fréquentation des animaux, elle avait pris leur mutisme et leur placidité. C'était la première fois qu'elle se voyait au milieu d'une compagnie si nombreuse, et intérieurement effarouchée par les drapeaux, par

CONTEXT. The second part of *Madame Bovary* contains a description of the local *comices agricoles* or cattle show. After prizes have been given for fat hogs, etc., someone calls out the name of "Catherine-Nicaise-Élisabeth Leroux...pour cinquante-quatre ans de service dans la même ferme, une médaille d'argent—du prix de vingt-cinq francs!" Catherine comes forward.

N.B. A full discussion of this passage will be found in M. Roustan, *Précis d'explication française* (Delagrave), pp. 396–424.

1. Var. *making her nervous way across the platform a little old woman who*, etc.
2. **shrivel up**: var. *shrink into*.
3. **great**: var. *heavy* (cp. *de gros souliers* in No. 33); grosses = '*épaisses, grossières, surtout bruyantes*' (Roustan); *galoches*, as contrasted with *sabots*, are ornamental wooden shoes with leather uppers, for Sunday wear, i.e. clogs.
8. **the lye of wash-tubs.** Flaubert, when he said *la potasse*, probably had in mind not so much the precise chemical substance, potash, as the country practice of putting ashes in the wash-tub to give the correct colour to linen; *les lessives* = washing, is

35. THE OLD SERVANT

Then was seen coming forward on the platform a little old woman of timorous bearing who seemed to shrivel up inside her humble garments. On her feet she had great wooden clogs, and from her waist hung a big blue apron. Her thin face, framed in a peasant cap with no edging, was more puckered with wrinkles than a withered russet apple, and from the sleeves of her red jacket emerged two long horny-knuckled hands. The dust of barns, the lye of wash-tubs, the grease of sheep's wool had so coated, so scored and hardened them that they looked dirty, though they had been rinsed in water; and, being long accustomed to serving others, they remained half open, as if to offer of their own accord humble evidence of the many hardships she had endured. A touch of monastic austerity ennobled the expression on her face. Nothing sad, nothing tender softened that colourless gaze. Living amongst animals, she had acquired their dumb stolidity. It was the first time she had seen herself in such numerous company and, inwardly scared by the flags

properly lye-washing, and also = washing water; a wash-tub is *un cuvier* or *un baquet* (*à lessive*).

9. **scored**: var. *seamed*; *éraillé* describes the texture of linen which has become disintegrated by wear and tear.

11. **water**: var. *simply in water*; *eau claire* means 'nothing but water', 'water and nothing more': in this instance = 'without soap in it', in other cases, 'without wine in it', or 'without anything to eat with it'.

14. **monastic**: *monacale* is probably suggested by *béguin* = the peasant woman's cap (the Scottish 'mutch'), but also the head-dress of several religious orders; var. *nun-like*. For '*rigidité monacale*' cp. Huysmans, *La Cathédrale*: (of a servant), '*De face, la rigidité du profil s'émoussait dans une mansuétude de* placide nonne'.

15. **colourless**: for *pâle*, said of eyes, see No. 32, note 19.

17. **seen herself...company**: *se voyait, compagnie* (cp. Salut, la compagnie!) and perhaps *les messieurs* may be to some extent reported speech, i.e. terms such as Catherine herself would afterwards use in relating the incident.

les tambours, par les messieurs en habit noir et par la croix d'honneur du Conseiller, elle demeurait tout immobile, ne sachant s'il fallait s'avancer ou s'enfuir, ni pourquoi la foule la poussait et pourquoi les examinateurs lui souriaient. Ainsi se tenait, devant ces bourgeois épanouis, ce demi-siècle de servitude. FLAUBERT, *Madame Bovary*.

19. **in black coats**: *habit noir*, here probably = frock-coat, is to be distinguished from *l'habit* = evening dress, which is worn in France at official ceremonies at any hour of the day.

20. **Councillor.** The Préfet himself, unable to preside, had sent a high official of the *Préfecture*.

24. **half-century**: Flaubert is fond of *un demi-siècle*; cp. the

and the drums, the gentlemen in black coats and the Cross
of the Legion of Honour worn by the Councillor, she stood
stock still, not knowing whether she should go forward or
turn and flee, nor why the crowd was urging her on and the
judges smiling to her. So stood, before these beaming
bourgeois, that half-century of bondage.

beginning of *Un Cœur simple*: '*Pendant un demi-siècle*, les
bourgeoises de Pont-l'Évêque envièrent à Madame Aubain sa
servante Félicité.' Here 'half-century' comes naturally in
English, but in other cases, e.g. in No. 45, 'fifty years' seems
a better translation.

86. LA POLKA

Reprenant vivement sa polka, elle se mit à la danser sur son tabouret, en ne tenant à terre que par la pointe des pieds. Elle jouait sans regarder, la tête retournée vers le salon, animée, souriante, le feu de la danse dans les yeux et sur les joues, ainsi qu'une petite fille qui fait danser les autres, et, tout en jouant, les suit et s'agite avec eux. Elle balançait les épaules. Son corps ondulait comme sous un enlacement, sa taille marquait le rythme. Il y avait dans sa tournure la molle indication d'un pas ébauché. Puis elle se retourna vers le piano; sa tête se mit à battre doucement la mesure; ses yeux coururent avec ses mains sur les touches noires et blanches. Penchée sur la musique qu'elle faisait, elle semblait battre les notes ou les caresser, leur parler, les gronder, leur sourire, les bercer, les endormir. Elle appuyait sur le tapage; elle jouait avec la mélodie; elle avait de petits mouvements tendres et de petits gestes passionnés; elle se baissait et se relevait, et le haut de son peigne d'écaille à tout moment entrait dans la lumière, puis aussitôt s'éteignait dans le noir de ses cheveux. Les deux bougies du piano, frémissantes au bruit, jetaient un éclair sur son profil ou bien croisaient

---

CONTEXT. Renée Mauperin is playing to her father's guests after dinner, and her attempt to get them to dance has been met by his stolid 'Laissez-nous fumer tranquillement'. Her eager youthful gaiety is in contrast with the staidness of the elders.

1. The force of *vivement* seems sufficiently given by 'Striking up'.

Var. *Resuming her polka with renewed vigour, she began*, etc.

3. Var. *without the music; without looking at the piano (at what she was doing)*.

Var. *facing round to the drawing-room (to the company)*; for *tête* see No. 7, note 14.

5. Var. *her eyes and cheeks glowing with the excitement of the dance*.

6. **watches**: the sense of *suit* is as in *suivre des yeux*.

8. The movement denoted by *ondulait* is that which the Gon-

36. THE POLKA

Striking up her polka again, she started dancing it out on her piano-stool, with only the tips of her toes touching the floor. She played without looking, with her face turned towards the room, full of animation, smiling, the spirit of the dance ablaze in her eyes and on her cheeks—like a little 5 girl who is playing for the others to dance and watches them all the time and jigs about with them. She swung her shoulders; she seemed to sink into a partner's arms; her waist marked the rhythm. There was something in the way she held herself that suggested yielding to the temptation 10 of breaking into a dance-step. Then she turned round again to the piano; her head began gently beating time; her eyes raced with her hands up and down the black and white keys. Bending over the music she was making, she seemed to be beating the notes, or patting them, talking to them, scolding 15 them, smiling to them, lulling them to sleep. She emphasized the fortes, played pranks with the melody, gave way to affectionate little movements, vehement little gestures; she stooped and straightened up again, and the tip of her tortoise-shell comb at every moment flashed into the light and 20 was quenched immediately in the darkness of her hair. The

courts' Victorian contemporaries described when they wrote 'She sank into her partner's arms and, taking up the step, waltzing divinely', etc.

10–11. The idea of a dance-step latent in the girl's attitude as she plays is expressed with great subtlety in '*la molle indication d'un pas ébauché*'. The *indication*, 'hint', does not materialize and the dance-step remains a mere adumbration; *molle* suggests a suppleness of bearing, unresisting, yielding; cp. No. 85: 'elle se sentit *molle*.'

16. **emphasized**: var. *dwelt upon, stressed*; var. *the forte passages*.

17. Var. *played tricks with* (*made free with*).

In *avait des mouvements* the sense is as in: 'Il *eut* un geste de découragement' = *made* a discouraged gesture. The insistence on *petits* suggests very slight involuntary movements betraying inward feelings: hence the rendering '*gave way to*'.

leurs flammes sur son front, ses joues, son menton. L'ombre de ses boucles d'oreille, deux boules de corail, tremblait sans cesse sur la peau de son cou, et les doigts de la jeune fille couraient si vite sur le piano qu'on voyait seulement je ne sais quoi de rose qui volait.

E. ET J. DE GONCOURT, *Renée Mauperin.*

two piano candles, set a-quiver by the noise, would light up her profile or cross flames upon her forehead, her cheeks, her chin. The shadow from her ear-rings, two coral balls, trembled unceasingly on her neck, while her girlish fingers ran so fast over the key-board that all one could see was a flutter of pink.

37. UN QUINQUAGÉNAIRE

Cet homme pouvait avoir cinquante ans. Grand, massif, le torse long, les membres musculeux et courts, il était là d'aplomb, solide, les jambes un peu écartées, comme s'il avait défié le vent.

Entièrement glabre, sa face lourde était marquée d'un singulier caractère de hardiesse et de force. Le visage carré s'élargissait vers le bas, en un puissant maxillaire pesant, légèrement projeté en avant: un menton de statue romaine. La grande bouche fermée, mal dessinée, aux lèvres minces. se marquait, aux commissures, d'un pli énergique. Le nez était large, dilaté. Les narines mobiles humaient l'air. Les joues maigres, tendues, sans graisse, dessinaient en relief les méplats vigoureux des pommettes et des muscles de la mâchoire. Des sourcils mal formés, mal plantés, perpétuellement contractés, ombrageaient des yeux petits, ardents et sombres, aux sclérotiques d'un jaune brun filigrané de sang. Le front, soucieux, très lourd aussi, carré, bossué, vaste, montait haut, sous des cheveux noirs et gris, abondants, rejetés en arrière et retombant sur les oreilles, d'une façon quelque peu médiévale. Cette raide chevelure trop longue, ronde sur le front, coiffant la tête d'une sorte de casque, et brutalement coupée à hauteur des oreilles, ce pli vertical et dur des sourcils, ce regard droit, ces narines ouvertes aspirant la bataille, faisaient penser à ces têtes du XIIIe siècle en bois polychrome, images d'hommes de guerre ou de barons croisés. MAXENCE VAN DER MEERSCH, *L'Élu*.

CONTEXT. Siméon has just gone to the door of his house to show the doctor out. He watches him get into his car and drive away. 'Siméon resta encore une minute sur le seuil, haute silhouette tourmentée, dans la bourrasque.'

1. Var. *The man looked about fifty.*

5. **clean-shaven**: need not be taken literally; *glabre* means 'hairless', 'without beard or moustache', and applies to a man who, to appear 'clean-shaven', does not require to shave.

5–6. **face...face.** The repetition seems unavoidable; for the distinction between *la face* and *le visage* see No. 32, note 4.

37. A MAN OF FIFTY

The man might have been fifty. A tall burly figure, long in the body, short and muscular of limb, there he stood, four-square, firm on his feet, legs a little apart, as though he had challenged the wind.

His heavy clean-shaven face bore a strange character of daring and strength. It was a square-cut face, the lower part broadening out into a powerful, massive, slightly protruding jaw, a chin worthy of a Roman statue. The large firmly closed mouth, irregular and thin-lipped, puckered up at the corners into an expression of determination. The nose was broad; the dilated, twitching nostrils seemed to be sniffing the air. The pinched cheeks, taut and lean, brought into relief the surfaces of the strong cheek-bones and jaw muscles. Ill-shapen, ill-set eyebrows, knitted in a perpetual frown, overshadowed small glowing, sombre eyes, with 'whites' of a brownish-yellow shade and blood-shot. The forehead, anxious, very heavy like the rest of the face, square, rugged, wide, rose high, into plentiful iron-grey hair, which was swept back and fell over the ears, somewhat in mediæval fashion.

The shock of coarse hair worn too long, curving out over the forehead, helmeting the head and abruptly cropped level with the ears; the hard vertical groove between the eye-brows; the straight glance; the dilated nostrils scenting the fray—all brought to mind one of those thirteenth-century heads in polychrome wood which represent warriors or crusading barons.

17. **anxious**: hardly "care-worn". The anxiety seems momentary.
22. **abruptly.** N.B. *brutal (brutalement)* is rarely = 'brutal' or 'brutish'; it has a notion of stark simplicity, lack of subtlety. Cp. the remark made by the inventor of the original gear-box of motor-cars [vulgarly 'the old crash gear-box']: 'C'est *brutal.* Mais ça marche.' Often = rough-and-ready, unsophisticated, etc.

III. HISTORICAL AND NARRATIVE

38. LES PARLEMENTS

Depuis les temps de la Fronde, la monarchie avait eu à compter avec cette magistrature indépendante, sa propre création, presque aussi vieille qu'elle-même et qui, peu à peu, lui avait échappé. Louis XIV avait résolu la difficulté par la méthode autoritaire et grâce à son prestige. Pendant son règne, les Parlements avaient été soumis. Ranimés par la Régence, ils s'étaient enhardis peu à peu, et leur opposition, fondée sur le respect des droits acquis, était devenue plus nuisible à mesure que l'État et l'administration s'étaient développés, avaient eu besoin d'organiser et de rendre moderne une France constituée pièce à pièce, reprise, pièce à pièce aussi, sur le vieux chaos de l'Europe féodale. Les ministres du dix-huitième siècle, jusqu'au malheureux Calonne, ne tarissent pas sur la difficulté de gouverner un pays qui avait mis huit cents ans à former son territoire, à réunir des villes et des provinces dans les circonstances et aux conditions les plus diverses, où l'on se heurtait, dès que l'on voulait changer, simplifier, améliorer quelque chose, à des exceptions, à des franchises, à des privilèges stipulés par contrat. A la fin du règne de Louis XV, il apparut que les Parlements, en s'opposant aux changements, par conséquent aux réformes et aux progrès, mettaient la monarchie dans l'impossibilité d'administrer, l'immobilisaient dans la routine, et, par un attachement aveugle et intéressé aux coutumes, la menaient à une catastrophe, car il faudrait alors tout briser pour satisfaire aux besoins du temps. La résistance que la monarchie avait toujours rencontrée dans son œuvre

7. **by the Regency.** After the death of Louis XIV in 1715 the Regent, Philippe d'Orléans, restored some of the Parlement's lost rights.

11. **coordinate:** *organiser* is perhaps hardly quite "organize", which, moreover, would cause a jingle with 'modernize'. Bainville avoids this by using *rendre moderne* in preference to the usual *moderniser*.

13. **inveterate:** var. *long-standing*.

15. **Calonne:** (1734–1802) the Finance Minister who failed to win the approval of the Notables and resigned April 9, 1787.

38. THE PARLEMENTS

Ever since the days of the Fronde, the monarchy had had to reckon with this independent judicial body, which was its own creation and almost as time-honoured as itself, and which had gradually escaped from its control. Louis XIV had solved the difficulty by authoritarian methods and by his own prestige. During his reign the Parlements had been submissive. Given fresh life by the Regency, they had gradually grown bolder, and opposition from them, based on preservation of vested rights, had become more pernicious with the development of the State and the central administration and with their increasing need to coordinate and modernize a France which had been built up bit by bit, reclaimed—also bit by bit—from the inveterate chaos of feudal Europe. The eighteenth-century ministers, down to the ill-starred Calonne, never tire of expatiating on the difficulty of governing a country which had taken eight hundred years to form its territory, to bring in towns and provinces in circumstances, and upon conditions, of the most varied character, a country in which anyone who endeavoured to alter, simplify or improve on anything, at once came up against a blank wall of exceptions, immunities and privileges fixed by charter.

At the end of Louis XV's reign, it became apparent that the Parlements, by standing out against any change, and consequently against progress and reform, were making it impossible for the monarchy to carry on the government, tying it up in red tape and, by a blind, self-interested adherence to Custom, leading the monarchy on to a catastrophe; for, when reform did come, a clean sweep would have to be made, in order to satisfy the requirements of the age. The resistance the monarchy had always encountered

19–21. Var. (more literal) *the moment one endeavoured to alter...one was confronted with exceptions*, etc.

28. **Custom**: not so much general use and wont, tradition, etc., as the special usages of different provinces and districts in pre-Revolution France which had grown into a local body of law = *la coutume* = Customary Law.

politique et administrative, résistance qui avait pris la forme féodale jusqu'au temps de Richelieu, prenait alors une forme juridique et légale, plus dangereuse peut-être, parce que, n'étant pas armée, elle n'avait pas le caractère évident et brutal d'une sédition.

JACQUES BAINVILLE, *Histoire de France.*

THE PARLEMENTS

in its political and administrative action, resistance which until Richelieu's time had clothed itself in feudal forms, was now assuming a juridical and legal form, more dangerous perhaps, because, not being armed action, it had not the obvious and uncompromising character of revolt.

35. **uncompromising**: var. *violent*; for *brutal* see No. 37, note 22.

39. LE CAMP DES ÉMIGRÉS

Après être tombée toute la nuit, le 26 août au matin, la pluie cessa un moment. Un violent vent d'ouest chassait dans le ciel d'opaques nuées couleur de suie. Bien que, par intervalles, de brèves et pâles soleillées courussent sur les chemins défoncés, sur les prairies semées de flaques miroitantes, on pressentait que l'accalmie serait de peu de durée, et que l'averse recommencerait avant la fin du jour. Néanmoins, profitant de cette embellie, de nombreux groupes d'officiers et de soldats stationnaient sur la petite place rectangulaire formée par l'église, l'auberge du village, et les bâtiments de la poste. Crottés et trempés, des chevaliers de Saint-Louis conduisaient eux-mêmes leurs chevaux à l'abreuvoir ou regagnaient le camp, pliés sous le poids d'une botte de foin. Un vieux noble à la mine hautaine, l'habit en loques, les souliers troués, traînait péniblement un seau rempli à la fontaine publique, tandis que, penché sur le bord de l'auge dont l'eau troublée lui servait de miroir, un officier supérieur en bras de chemise se faisait la barbe en plein air. Devant l'église, un peloton de jeunes soldats, presque des enfants, ayant suivi leurs pères à l'étranger, s'exerçaient au maniement d'armes sous la direction d'un gentilhomme au poil gris, à la voix rude, à la face rébarbative.

CONTEXT. These nobles were preparing to join the Prussians in an attempt to overthrow the French Republic. The scene is their camp in Luxembourg, a month before their defeat at Valmy, September 26, 1792.

1–3. Alteration in the order of words avoids absurdity in the first section and improves the rendering of the second. Var. *Rain had been falling all night, but in the morning, on the twenty-sixth of August, it stopped for a little.*

4. **churned up**: for *défoncé* cp. Châteaubriant, *Monsieur des Lourdines*: 'un rond-point herbeux, *défoncé* par les passages du bétail.'

6. Var. *One had a feeling*: *One felt a premonition*.

10. **quadrangle**: var. *square*; *rectangulaire* is included in both of the English words.

12. **the Order of Saint Louis**: instituted by Louis XIV in 1693 for distinguished military or naval service; abolished

89. THE ÉMIGRÉS' CAMP

On the morning of August 26 the rain, which had been falling all night, stopped for a little. Thick sooty clouds were scudding across the sky before a strong westerly gale. Though brief glints of pale sunshine fitfully traversed the churned-up roads and the meadows dotted over with glistening pools, there was a feeling that the respite would be of brief duration and the downpour would begin again before the close of day. Nevertheless, making the most of this fair interval, numbers of officers and men were standing about in knots on the little quadrangle formed by the Church, the village inn and the Posting Establishment. Mud-stained and rain-soaked, Knights of the Order of Saint Louis were leading their own horses to the watering-place, or returning to camp, bent double beneath the weight of a bundle of hay. One elderly noble of haughty mien, with his coat in tatters and holes in his boots, was laboriously lugging a bucket filled at the village pump, whilst, stooping over the trough whose troubled water did for a mirror, a field-officer in his shirt-sleeves was shaving in the open air. In front of the Church, a squad of recruits, mere boys who had followed their fathers abroad, were doing musketry drill under the command of a grizzled nobleman with a harsh voice and forbidding countenance. While

by the Revolution; revived at the Restoration; abolished in 1830.

own: more normal English than 'themselves'; cp. 'Elle fait son ménage *elle-même*', 'She does her *own* house-work'.

13. **bent double**: '*pliés*' is more than "bending" or "bowed".
14. **bundle**: var. *truss*.
16. **boots**: *souliers* means 'boots' as well as 'shoes'; cp. Roger Martin du Gard, *L'été* 1914, p. 70: 'Les boutiques de chaussures arboraient sous des bandes de carton...des enseignes improvisées....Les plus timides annonçaient: *Souliers de chasse*, ou: *Souliers de marche*. Quelques audacieux affichaient: *Godillots*; et même: *Brodequins militaires*. Les femmes soupesaient les brodequins cloutés.'

the village pump: possibly *the village well*, since *fontaine* (see No. 19, note 26) may have this sense.

Pendant les repos, on voyait ces adolescents tirer de leur poche un morceau de pain noir qu'ils grignotaient dédaigneusement, après en avoir enlevé la mie dont ils se jetaient des boulettes au nez.

ANDRÉ THEURIET, *La Chanoinesse.*

THE ÉMIGRÉS' CAMP 143

'standing easy', these young fellows produced a bit of black bread from their pockets now and again and nibbled at it disdainfully, having first removed the crumb to make pellets which they threw in each other's faces.

24. **now and again**: *on voyait* is a convenient phrase in French and not always to be rendered by 'you could see', 'could be seen', etc.

40. LES CHEFS DES PUISSANCES COALISÉES

Frédéric-Guillaume et François, l'un fougueux et fantasque, l'autre empesé et entêté, bornés tous les deux, sont livrés fatalement aux conseillers. Ils n'en trouvent que de médiocres dans l'armée aussi bien que dans la chancellerie, et parmi les médiocres, ils n'écoutent que les serviles et les subalternes. A cette éruption véhémente du génie militaire et conquérant de la France, ils n'opposent que des négociateurs à recettes et des stratégistes à formules.... Avec eux, de bons divisionnaires, corrects, instruits, rompus au métier, braves, précautionneux, capables de donner à leurs adversaires improvisés de beaux exemples de tenue au feu et de rudes leçons de tactique, mais perplexes, déroutés, sans invention, sans flamme, sans génie....

Quant aux ministres, ils sont médiocres.... En réalité, ce sont des commis qui mènent les affaires: décrépits, secondaires, subordonnés, expéditionnaires de cour plutôt que conseillers d'État; derrière eux, les manœuvres de second plan et les machinistes du théâtre, les confidents et les courtiers d'intrigue.... Enfin, pour tout avenir prochain dans ces conseils où Marie-Thérèse et Frédéric disposaient naguère de l'Europe, un Thugut et un Haugwitz, deux épaves de l'ancien régime; l'un parti de très-bas et parvenu à force d'artifice, par les chemins tortueux de la diplomatie secrète; l'autre gentilhomme libertin, frotté de théosophie, arrivé à la faveur par les rose-croix et les maîtresses.

ALBERT SOREL, L'Europe et la Révolution.

1. **Frederick William**: II (1744–97), King of Prussia; defeated at Valmy.

Francis: II (1768–1835), the last Roman Emperor and, as Francis I, first Emperor of Austria. Sorel, in a preceding passage (II, p. 373), describes him as: 'd'un esprit peu étendu, mais non sans clarté, médiocre dans les vues d'ensemble, judicieux et sensé dans le détail, entêté, mais capable d'élever l'entêtement jusqu'à la constance.'

8. **put forward**: var. *set*, but 'setting' is required soon after.

40. THE LEADERS OF THE COALITION POWERS

Frederick William and Francis—one hot-headed and freakish, the other starchy and obstinate, both of them narrow in their outlook—are, of necessity, entirely in the hands of advisers. They can find only second-rate ones in the Army, as in the Chancellery, and among the second-rate they give ear only to the servile and to the men in inferior positions. Against this volcanic outburst of the military and conquering genius of France, they can put forward only rule-of-thumb negotiators and text-book strategists.... With these there are good divisional commanders, unexceptionable, well-informed, thoroughly experienced, brave, cautious, and capable of setting their improvised adversaries splendid examples of conduct under fire and teaching them sharp lessons in tactics, but easily confused, nonplussed, and devoid of originality, fire or genius....

As for the ministers, they are second-rate.... In reality they are clerks put at the head of affairs; men past their best, seconds-in-command, subordinates, court secretaries rather than councillors of state; behind these there are the workers in the back-ground and the stage-hands of the political theatre, the confidants and the go-betweens.... Lastly—sole hope for the immediate future in the council-chambers where but lately Frederick and Maria Theresa could settle the fate of Europe—a Thugut and a Haugwitz, two survivors from the old order. One, from very humble beginnings, had schemed his way to success by the tortuous paths of secret diplomacy; the other was a libertine nobleman with a smattering of theosophy, who had risen to favour by the help of the Rosicrucians and of his mistresses.

  only: the repetition of 'only', like that of *ne...que* in the French, seems inevitable.

  11. **cautious**: var. *determined to take no risks*.

  19. **workers**: *manœuvres* is pejorative: var. *hacks, drudges*.

  21. **confidants**: *confidents* has no doubt its technical theatrical sense = secondary characters of the *théâtre classique*.

41. LE CRIME DE NAPOLÉON

Les conjurés ayant tous déclaré qu'un prince devait les rejoindre, le Premier Consul résolut de faire un exemple. Quoiqu'il eût en toute occasion marqué son horreur pour l'exécution de Louis XVI, c'est à l'équivalent d'un régicide qu'il recourut à son tour pour donner à son trône un sanglant baptême républicain. Le prince annoncé par les conspirateurs royalistes ne paraissant pas, Napoléon ne voulut pas abandonner le plan qu'il avait formé. Il fit enlever de force le jeune prince de Condé, duc d'Enghien, qui se trouvait à Ettenheim, en territoire badois, et qui fut passé par les armes après un simulacre de jugement.

Ce crime était-il nécessaire pour que Napoléon devînt empereur? Même pas. La monarchie héréditaire lui venait naturellement, pour les raisons qui lui avaient déjà donné le consulat à vie. Mais la machine infernale avait aidé au succès du premier plébiscite. Le dernier pas se fit grâce à la conspiration de Georges et de Pichegru. Observant le réveil général de l'idée monarchique en France, les royalistes avaient pensé que la personne du Premier Consul était le seul obstacle à une restauration. Pour que la place fût libre aux Bourbons, il devait suffire de l'abattre. Le Premier Consul ayant échappé aux conjurés, le péril qu'il avait couru servit sa cause. On pensa que le consulat à vie était fragile et qu'une forme de gouvernement exposée à périr avec son

CONTEXT. The duc d'Enghien (1772–1804), only son of the Prince de Condé, "emigrated" in 1789 and remained in exile, seeking to raise forces for the invasion of France. On March 15, 1804, Bonaparte, then First Consul, suspecting him of complicity in the Cadoudal conspiracy, had him seized at Ettenheim in Baden and brought to the fortress at Vincennes, where he was hastily tried by a commission of colonels and shot.

1. **conspirators**: var. *confederates*. For *conjurés = conspirateurs* cp. Bainville, *Napoléon*, p. 222 (on the Georges and Pichegru affair): 'C'est plus qu'un *complot*. C'est une *conspiration*, au sens le plus vrai et le plus fort, car elle rassemble des hommes très divers qu'anime la même haine, celle de Bonaparte, qui veulent tous ensemble cette même chose, qu'il *disparaisse*.' N.B.

41. NAPOLEON'S CRIME

As the conspirators had all declared that a Prince was going to join them, the First Consul resolved to make an example. Though he had at all times manifested his abhorrence for the execution of Louis XVI, he, too, resorted to what was virtually regicide, in order to give his throne a Republican baptism of blood. The Prince announced by the Royalist conspirators failing to appear, Napoleon would not give up the plan he had formed. He caused the young Prince de Condé, Duc d'Enghien, who was living at Ettenheim, on Baden territory, to be seized and carried off, and after a mock trial he was shot.

Was this crime necessary that Napoleon might become Emperor? We cannot even say it was. The hereditary monarchy was, in the natural course of things, devolving on him, for the very reasons which already had made him Consul for life. But the bomb incident had contributed to the success of the first plebiscite, and similarly the final step was taken on the opportunity offered by the Georges and Pichegru conspiracy. Observing the revival of the monarchical principle everywhere in France, the Royalists had come to think that the sole obstacle to a Restoration was the First Consul's person and that his removal should suffice to clear the way for the Bourbons. The First Consul having escaped the conspirators, the risk he had run furthered his cause. People concluded that the life Consulship was a precarious affair and that a form of government liable to perish along

disparaître = to die, not merely "to disappear"; cp. *Il faut que je disparaisse* = 'I must commit suicide' (make away with myself).

11. **a mock trial**: var. *a semblance of trial*.

16. **bomb**: var. *machine infernale*—with which an attempt was made on Bonaparte's life, in the rue Saint-Nicaise, December 24, 1800.

17. **and similarly**: without this addition the connexion between the sentences might be obscure.

18. **Georges**: the Chouan leader, Georges Cadoudal, popularly known as Georges, who in 1803 conspired with General Pichegru to overthrow Bonaparte.

chef n'était pas assez sûre. Du jour au lendemain, Bonaparte pouvait disparaître tandis que la dynastie de Napoléon lui survivrait et le continuerait. Alors, cet homme que ses ennemis, qui étaient les ennemis de la Révolution, voulaient détruire, "il fallait, dit Thiers, le faire roi ou empereur pour que l'hérédité ajoutée à son pouvoir lui assurât des successeurs naturels et immédiats, et que, le crime commis en sa personne devenant inutile, on fût moins tenté de le commettre". JACQUES BAINVILLE, *Histoire de France*.

28. die: for *disparaître* see above, note 1.

with its Head, gave insufficient security. Bonaparte might die at any moment, whereas a Napoleonic dynasty would outlive him and carry on his tradition. That being so, the man whom his enemies (who were also the enemies of the Revolution) were anxious to destroy had, as Thiers says, 'to be made King or Emperor so that his power might be reinforced by heredity, which would ensure him natural and direct successors, and so that, attempts on his life being thus rendered futile, there should be less inducement to make any'.

29. Var. *carry on his work, continue his régime.*
33. **ensure**, etc.: *lui assurer des successeurs* = to assure successors to him (not "to assure him of successors")

42. UNE AGENCE D'ESPIONNAGE SOUS LE CONSULAT

A cet admirable roman—*Une ténébreuse affaire*—il manque un personnage que Balzac n'a pas connu et que lui seul aurait pu peindre: *l'ami*. Il en eût fait ce que *l'ami* était en réalité, une sorte de Gobseck politique, machiniste monstrueux qui a sa place marquée dans les coulisses de la *Comédie humaine*.

Je me figure ce vieux commis de province, obséquieux, cafard, âpre à la curée, infatigable à la besogne, périphrasant, important, à prétentions d'éminence grise et à mine de cuistre, le sachant et en profitant pour faire le bonhomme et se recroqueviller devant les chefs et capter le maître même par la docilité silencieuse de son travail, sa mémoire toujours dispose, sa plume toujours servile, son esprit inépuisable en arguments, avide, captieux, impénétrable. Il abhorre Bonaparte pour l'hypocrisie qu'il s'impose, pour la trahison qu'il consomme, pour la peur mortelle qu'il en ressent et qui le talonne jour et nuit.

Quand il revient chez lui, le sang échauffé par la contrainte et l'effort, congestionné, bourru, il trouve cependant le courage et le temps d'écrire à d'Antraigues, puis de chiffrer à l'encre sympathique d'interminables lettres. C'est qu'il y épanche sa bile et sa colère rentrée....

ALBERT SOREL, *Lectures historiques*.

CONTEXT. The Comte d'Antraigues, an *émigré* prominent among the agents of the counter-Revolution, conducted a spy agency for Austria (1797–9) and for Russia (1800–6). During the latter period his principal agent was known as *l'ami de Paris*. The occasion of Sorel's study, *Une Agence d'espionnage*, was the publication of Léonce Pingaud's *Le Comte d'Antraigues*, 2nd ed. 1894.

1. **Une ténébreuse affaire:** Balzac's novel, sub-title, *Le Député d'Arcès*, comes under Section 4 (Scènes de la vie politique) of *La Comédie humaine*.

5. **Gobseck:** chief character in Balzac's novel of that name (1830), type of the moneylender.

11. **power behind the throne:** var. *Hidden Hand*; *l'éminence grise* was Richelieu's right-hand man, Father Joseph, partly

42. A SPY AGENCY IN THE TIME OF THE CONSULATE

In that admirable novel, 'A Mysterious Case', there is one character lacking whom Balzac did not know and whom none but he could have painted: 'the friend'. He would have made of him what 'the friend' actually was, a sort of Gobseck turned politician, a prodigious scene-shifter with his place marked out for him in the wings of the 'Comédie humaine'.

I can picture that old provincial clerk—cringing, sanctimonious, greedy for a share in the spoils, indefatigable at routine work, full of circumlocution and self-importance, with claims to being a power behind the throne and with the look of an ignorant fellow; he is quite aware of all this and takes advantage of it to play the simple soul, to bend double before his superiors and curry favour with the Chief himself by the silent docile way he goes about his work, by his memory ever ready, his pen ever servile, his mind never at a loss for an argument to suggest—grasping, plausible, inscrutable. He detests Bonaparte for his own self-imposed hypocrisy, for the treachery he is perpetrating, and the mortal terror which it is causing him and which dogs him night and day.

When he comes home, with his blood heated by constraint and hard work, apoplectic, surly, he yet finds the time and the courage to write to d'Antraigues, and then to cypher interminable letters in sympathetic ink. For that provides an outlet for his venom and pent-up wrath.

friar and partly secret diplomatic agent. Cp. Trahard, *La sensibilité révolutionnaire*, p. 219: 'Les historiens ne voient que le rôle officieux, sinon officiel, de Mme Roland, lorsque son mari est au pouvoir, et ce rôle *d'Éminence grise* n'est pas négligeable.'
    12. Var. *with a half-educated air.*
    13. Var. *Honest John.*
    14. **curry favour:** var. *ingratiate himself.*
    23. **apoplectic:** var. *red in the face, flushed.*
    25. **sympathetic ink:** var. *invisible ink.*

43. WATERLOO

De toutes les batailles que Napoléon a livrées, la plus célèbre est celle qu'il a perdue. Waterloo apporte à son histoire la catastrophe, qui est l'événement dernier et principal des tragédies. Un désastre soudain, total, retentissant, tant de victoires, d'exploits stratégiques qui s'achèvent par un effondrement militaire....Encore un élément de légende et d'épopée qui manquait à la vie de Bonaparte. Elle se surpassera par le martyre, et le martyre ne tardera plus.

Refaisant en idée la bataille de Waterloo, mille historiens, et l'empereur le premier, ont montré qu'elle aurait pu être gagnée, qu'elle aurait dû l'être, sans se demander ce qui serait arrivé le lendemain. Napoléon, battu, s'écroula d'un coup. Wellington et Blucher en retraite, la guerre continuait, la même guerre qui durait depuis vingt-trois ans. Et l'empereur risquait encore, dans cette plaine belge, la partie dont la Belgique avait été l'essentiel enjeu. Il venait finir, avec la vague mourante de la Révolution belliqueuse, près de Fleurus et de Jemmapes, aux portes de Bruxelles, pour les lieux que la République avait conquis et qu'elle s'était acharnée, jusqu'à se renier elle-même, à conserver malgré l'Europe.

3. **catastrophe:** the end of a play, following the *dénouement*.
4. Var. *A disaster, sudden, complete and resounding.*
5. Var. *strategic feats, feats of strategy.*
6. Var. *Yet another element.*
9. **was not to be long in coming.** The future *ne tardera plus* is due to the practice, popular with French historians, of putting oneself back to the point of time described and then looking forward from it and treating subsequent events as still to come. Such 'vivid' futures are apt to be very confusing in English and are better rendered by a past.

Var. *was already imminent, was now at hand.*

10. Var. *Fighting the battle...over again.*
11. **innumerable:** var. *scores of, large numbers of.*
13. Var. *that it could...have been won by him; that it could have been won—and indeed should have been—by the French*; *gagnée* looks at the result from the French side and therefore requires expansion in English.
15. **utterly:** var. *at a blow.*
16. **would have gone on:** '*continuait*' is (as also, further on,

43. WATERLOO

Of all the battles Napoleon fought, the most famous was the one he lost. Waterloo provides in the drama of his life the 'catastrophe', that last and principal event in any tragedy. A sudden, a complete, a resounding disaster—so many victories and so many strategic achievements ending only in a military collapse!...One more element of legend and epic grandeur, lacking till then in Bonaparte's life! That life was to transcend itself through martyrdom, and now martyrdom was not to be long in coming.

Reconstructing the battle of Waterloo in imagination, innumerable historians, and first among them the Emperor himself, have shown that the victory could, and should, have been ours. But they have never asked themselves what would have happened in the sequel. Napoleon, once beaten, collapsed utterly. With Wellington and Blücher in retreat, the war would have gone on, the same war which had been in progress for twenty-three years. And again, the Emperor would, on those Belgian plains, have risked his fortunes in the game in which Belgium had been the real stake. He was coming to meet his doom, with the expiring wave of Revolution militant, near Fleurus and Jemmapes, at the gates of Brussels, fighting for the territory which the Republic had conquered and had stubbornly endeavoured— even to the point of disavowing its own principles—to hold against Europe.

---

risquait, but not *venait*) the vivid imperfect = *aurait continué*; cp. 'Si je bougeais *j'étais* mort'. It is dependent on the hypothesis *Wellington et Blucher en retraite* (= 'If...'). Bainville is showing Napoleon's career as an episode in the Revolutionary Wars. They began in Belgium, with the victories over the Austrians at Jemmapes (1792) and Fleurus (1794), and were bound to finish in Belgium, whether at Waterloo or somewhere else in the same region.

20. **venait finir...pour:** *make a final bid...for*, etc.
24. Var. *betraying, disowning*.

Le dénouement se trouve au point de départ. Il apporte le dernier résultat et l'explication d'aventures inouïes, pourtant si bien liées. La résonance lugubre de Waterloo ne tient pas seulement à la chute d'un homme. Elle signifie, pour les Français, la fin d'un rêve par un dur contact avec le monde extérieur. C'est le principe d'un renoncement et d'un repliement sur eux-mêmes, pour tout dire une humiliation plus cruelle que la bataille, du moins perdue avec honneur et avec éclat. JACQUES BAINVILLE, *Napoléon*.

32. **beginning**: *principe* = 'origin' or 'beginning' = *commence-*

The end takes place where the drama began. It brings the final outcome, and the explanation, of adventures unprecedented, yet perfectly interdependent. The mournful reverberations of Waterloo are not simply due to the downfall of one man. They mean for Frenchmen the ending of a dream by rude contact with the outer world. They mark the beginning of a renunciation and a drawing-in—in a word, a humiliation more cruel than the battle, which at any rate was honourably and gloriously lost.

ment, which word Bainville probably avoided because it would have jingled with *renoncement*.

34. Var. *was lost with honour and glory.*

44. LA FRANCE DE 1820

Ce qui m'a frappé le plus, à mon premier retour d'Amérique, dans la situation de cette France à laquelle j'ai toujours été si filialement attaché, et pour laquelle je saignais jusque sous l'étole durant les années envahies, c'est qu'après l'Empire et l'excès de la force militaire qui y avait prévalu, on était subitement passé à l'excès de la parole, à la prodigalité et à l'enflure des déclamations, des images, des promesses, et à une confiance également aveugle en ces armes nouvelles. Je n'entends parler ici, vous me comprenez bien, que de la disposition morale de la société, de cette facilité d'illusion et de revirement qui nous caractérise; les restrictions peu intelligentes du pouvoir n'ont fait et ne font que l'augmenter.

Cette fougue presque universelle des esprits, si je n'avais déjà été mis depuis maintes années sur mes gardes, à commencer par les conseils de mon ami M. Hamon, cette fougue crédule d'alentour aurait suffi pour m'y mettre, et m'aurait fait rentrer encore plus avant dans mon silence. Il n'est de plus en plus question que de découvertes sociales, chaque matin, et de continuelles lumières; il doit y avoir, dans cette nouvelle forme d'entraînement, de graves mécomptes pour l'avenir.

J'ai la douleur de me figurer souvent, par une moins flatteuse image, que l'ensemble matériel de la société est assez semblable à un chariot depuis longtemps très embourbé, et que, passé un certain moment d'ardeur et un certain âge, la plupart des hommes désespèrent de le voir avancer et même ne le désirent plus: mais chaque génération nouvelle arrive, jurant Dieu qu'il n'est rien de plus facile,

N.B. Sainte-Beuve's hero Amaury is referring to France under the *Restauration*, about 1820.

1–4. "On my first return" would suggest several visits to America—which does not seem to be meant. "I bled" is too literal. Amaury never actually shed his blood for his country.

17. **M. Hamon**: the seventeenth-century Port-Royal character. Amaury had profited by reading his letters. For *Monsieur* cp. '*les messieurs de Port-Royal*'.

44. FRANCE IN 1820

What struck me most, when I first came back from America, about the state of affairs in this France of ours for which I have always had such filial affection—and for which my heart bled even while I wore the priestly stole, during the years of invasion—was that after the Empire and the excess of military force prevalent then, people had suddenly gone over to excess in words, to copious, high-falutin declamation, metaphors and promises, and to equally blind confidence in these new weapons. I am only referring now, you understand, to the moral tendency of society, that proneness to illusions and to sudden swings of the pendulum which is so characteristically French and which the Government's unintelligent restrictions have merely increased and are still increasing.

This wild enthusiasm, well nigh universal in men's minds —had I not been made wary many years ago, primarily by my friend M. Hamon's counsellings—this credulous enthusiasm around us would have been sufficient warning to me and made me sink yet deeper into silence. More and more, to the exclusion of all else, the talk is of social discoveries, every morning, and of continual enlightenment; this new form of mental excitement must be laying up serious disappointments for the future.

I am often distressed by the thought—and it is a less flattering simile—that the whole material structure of society is not unlike a cart which has for long been stuck fast in the mud. After a certain period of zeal and after a certain time of life, most men lose all hope of ever seeing the cart move and even any desire that it should. But each new generation, as it comes up, calls God to witness that there

19. Var. *withdraw yet farther.*
24. **less flattering**: i.e. than a simile used in a preceding passage, in which life was represented as progress towards higher things.
30. Var. *swears by all the gods.*

et elle se met à l'œuvre avec une inexpérience généreuse, s'attelant de toutes parts à droite, à gauche, en travers (les places de devant étant prises), les bras dans les roues, faisant crier le pauvre vieux char par mille côtés, et risquant mainte fois de le rompre. On se lasse vite à ce jeu; les plus ardents sont bientôt écorchés et hors de combat; les meilleurs ne reparaissent jamais, et si quelques-uns, plus tard, arrivent à s'atteler en ambitieux sur le devant de la machine, ils tirent en réalité très peu, et laissent de nouveaux venus s'y prendre aussi maladroitement qu'eux d'abord, et s'y épuiser de même.

En un mot, à part une certaine générosité première, le grand nombre des hommes dans les affaires de ce monde ne suivent d'autres mobiles que les faux principes d'une expérience cauteleuse qu'ils appliquent à l'intérêt de leur nom, de leur pouvoir ou de leur bien-être.

SAINTE-BEUVE, *Volupté* (Fasquelle).

31. **the courage of inexperience:** 'generous' in the sense of *généreux* = 'noble', 'high-spirited' may be somewhat archaic. So 'generosity' further down.

is nothing easier. They set to, with the courage of inexperience, and harness themselves all round, right, left, crossways (the positions in front being taken), trying to twist the wheels round, making the wretched old cart rattle and squeak all over and running the risk, many a time, of smashing it up. They tire quickly of this game; the most eager soon bark their shins and are out of action; the best never come back, and, though a few, later on, manage to harness themselves, being ambitious, to the front of the cart, they really do very little pulling and let newcomers tackle the job as clumsily as they did at first, and wear themselves out in the same way.

In short, save for a certain high-heartedness in the early stages, most men, where the affairs of this world are concerned, have no other guiding motives than the unsound principles derived from over-cautious experience and these they apply in the interests of their own reputation, influence or comfort.

35. **squeak**: var. *creak, groan.*
39. **being ambitious**: var. *ambitiously.*

45. LA FRANCE SOUS LOUIS-PHILIPPE

Jamais conjonctures plus propices à toutes les mascarades sociales. Dix régimes en cinquante ans. On avait vécu comme on avait pu sous des gouvernements de vie courte et rude, tous anxieux de sonder les cœurs, aucun ennemi de la fraude. On avait assisté aux mues et aux reprises fort brusques des personnages les plus graves, aux vives substitutions de cocardes, à la fantasmagorie de la puissance, aux sorties et aux rentrées de la légitimité, de la liberté, des aigles, de Dieu même; à l'étonnant spectacle d'hommes égarés entre leurs serments, disputés par leurs souvenirs, leurs passions, leurs intérêts, leurs rancunes, leurs pronostics. Quelques-uns se sentaient confusément sur la tête tout un échafaud de coiffures, une perruque, une calotte, un bonnet rouge, un chapeau à plume tricolore, un chapeau à cornes, un chapeau bourgeois. Parfois surpris, parfois justifiés par l'événement; et tantôt par le rapatriement des lys, tantôt par le retour de flamme de 1815, tantôt par la duperie de 1830, toujours suspendus à l'instant, presque dressés à se changer du soir au matin de proscripteurs en proscrits, de suspects en magistrats, de ministres en fugitifs, ils vivaient une farce plus ou moins dangereuse, et finissaient pour la plupart, dans tous les partis et sous tous les visages, par ne

---

STYLE. An exact English rendering of Valéry's very terse style can hardly avoid being unpleasantly terse and may be barely intelligible. Some concessions must be made, but they should be limited to those which English usage renders inevitable.

6. Var. *Men had watched quick-change doffing and donning of coats*. Through all this long sentence there is some doubt as to whether *les* does really mean 'the' or is generic; *mue* = properly moulting, change of plumage; *reprise* = resumption, starting again.

8. Var. *the most dignified public figures*.

9. **party ribbons**: var. *party favours*; *cocardes* = properly cockades.

phantasmagoria: var. *kaleidoscope, shifting scene*.

45. FRANCE UNDER LOUIS-PHILIPPE

Never had there been a combination of circumstances more favourable to every sort of social masquerade. Ten different forms of government in fifty years! Men had lived as best they might under governments of brief and troubled existence, all of them anxious to sound popular feeling and none of them opposed to fraudulent practices. Men had stood by and watched very sudden changings of coats, and resumptions thereof, by the gravest of personages, quick-change substitutions of party ribbons, the phantasmagoria of Power, the exits and re-entrances of Legitimacy, of Liberty, of the Imperial Eagles, even of Religion, the astonishing spectacle of people all at sea about their allegiances, torn this way and that between their memories, passions, interests, hatreds, anticipations.... Some had a confused sensation of wearing a whole pile of varied headgear—periwig, clerical skull-cap, red cap of liberty, hat with tricolour plume, cocked hat, bourgeois hat. Sometimes taken unawares, sometimes vindicated by the turn of events; now by the restoration of the fleur-de-lys, now by the meteoric return in 1815, now by the deception of 1830—for ever waiting upon the moment, almost expert at changing overnight from proscribers into proscribed, suspects into office-holders, ministers into fugitives, they lived a life which was more or less a dangerous farce and came in the end, most of them, in all parties and under all outward forms, to believe in nothing but money.

11. **Imperial eagles.** Napoleon's emblem: exit 1814, re-entrance 1815.

12. Var. *bewildered* (*erring and straying*) *among their pledges* (*solemn promises*).

18. **restoration**: i.e. *La Restauration*, the return of the Bourbons in 1814.

19. **meteoric return**: i.e. of Napoleon from Elba: *retour de flamme* may retain here some of its literal meaning, 'back-flash'.

22. **office-holders**: var. *holders of public office, dignitaries*; *un magistrat* is not at all what we mean by 'a magistrate', but anyone holding judicial or administrative functions.

23–24. **they...they.** The reference of *ils* is vague.

plus croire qu'à l'argent. Ce caractère *positif* s'accusa sous Louis-Philippe, où l'on vit enfin l'enrichissement se proposer sans vergogne et sans fard comme suprême leçon, vérité dernière, moralité définitive d'un demi-siècle d'expériences politiques et sociales.

PAUL VALÉRY, *Variété: Stendhal.*

26. **Positivist.** The allusion in *positif* is to the 'Positivist' philosophy of Auguste Comte, whose earlier works, 1839 onwards, appeared in the reign of Louis-Philippe (1830–48).

28. openly: *sans fard* = without meretricious ornament, undisguisedly, unblushingly; var. *naked and unashamed*. Cp. No. 83, note 13.

FRANCE UNDER LOUIS-PHILIPPE

That Positivist trait became marked under Louis-Philippe, when money-making was at length put forward shamelessly and openly as chief lesson, last truth, final moral, of fifty years' political and social experiment.

last truth: cp. *les vérités dernières* = the Four Last Truths; var. *ultimate truth*.

28. **fifty years**: seems to come more naturally here than 'a half-century' or 'half-a-century', for which see No. 35, note 24.

46. PARIS BRÛLANT

Jean, plein d'angoisse, se retourna vers Paris. A cette fin si claire d'un beau dimanche, le soleil oblique, au ras de l'horizon, éclairait la ville immense d'une ardente lueur rouge. On aurait dit un soleil de sang, sur une mer sans borne. Les vitres des milliers de fenêtres braisillaient, comme attisées sous des soufflets invisibles; les toitures s'embrasaient, telles que des lits de charbons; les pans de murailles jaunes, les hauts monuments, couleur de rouille, flambaient avec les pétillements de brusques feux de fagots, dans l'air du soir. Et n'était-ce pas la gerbe finale, le gigantesque bouquet de pourpre, Paris entier brûlant ainsi qu'une fascine géante, une antique forêt sèche, s'envolant au ciel d'un coup, en un vol de flammèches et d'étincelles? Les incendies continuaient, de grosses fumées rousses montaient toujours, on entendait une rumeur énorme, peut-être les derniers râles des fusillés, à la caserne Lobau, peut-être la joie des femmes et le rire des enfants, dînant dehors après

CONTEXT. The scene is Paris on the Sunday (May 28, 1871) when, after a week of horrors, the Commune came to an end. 'Lorsque Jean monta le sombre escalier de la maison, rue des Orties, un affreux pressentiment lui serrait le cœur. Il entra, et tout de suite il vit l'inévitable fin, Maurice mort sur le petit lit.... Jean s'était approché du corps de Maurice.... Au dernier jour, sous les derniers débris de la Commune expirante, il avait donc fallu cette victime de plus! Jean, plein d'angoisse', etc.

STYLE. The effects of the sunset and of other flames which were only too real are so blended together that we have to allow ourselves more latitude than usual in translating and insert a word here and there.

1. **sick at heart**: *angoisse* is seldom "anguish"; the idea is rather 'mortal anxiety'.

10. **gerbe.** 'Gerbes are choked cases, not unlike Roman candles, but often of much larger size. Their fire spreads like a sheaf of wheat' (O.E.D.).

crowning-piece: *le bouquet* (which takes the actual shape of a bouquet) is traditionally the last and best item in a display of fireworks.

46. PARIS BURNING

Sick at heart, Jean turned away and looked out over Paris.
At that glorious Sunday's radiant close, the slanting sun
low on the horizon lit up the whole vast city with a glow of
fiery red. It seemed a sun of blood over a boundless sea.
The panes of the multitudinous windows were glowing like
red-hot cinders fanned by invisible bellows; the roofs were
breaking into flame like beds of live coal; the expanses of
yellow wall and the high public buildings, now rust-coloured,
blazed in the evening air with the crackle of briskly burning
firewood. And the final *gerbe*, the gigantic crowning-piece
in crimson—was it not all Paris burning like a monster
fascine, like an old forest, tinder-dry, flaring up to heaven
in one swirl of fiery flakes and sparks? The fires still continued; huge clouds of lurid smoke kept rising; a dull far-
spreading murmur could be heard, it might be the dying
groans of the people shot in the Lobau Barracks, it might be
the merry laughter of the women and children who, after

12. **fascine**: 'a long cylindrical faggot of brush or other small
wood, firmly bound together at short intervals, used in filling
up ditches, etc.' (O.E.D.): var. *wood-pile*.

flaring up: sufficiently accounts for '*d'un coup*' = 'suddenly'.

13. **The fires**, etc.: *un incendie* often gives the translator
some trouble. In some contexts (e.g. *un incendie et un déluge*,
in No. 12), 'fire' is quite clear; 'conflagration' may not be easily
worked in. The point here is that the fires already started
continued—not that new conflagrations broke out; cp. *La
Débâcle*, p. 298: 'Toute la journée d'ailleurs les incendies de
la veille avaient continué... le ministère des Finances fumait
à gros tourbillons.' But perhaps 'the fires still continued' is
unambiguous.

16. **Lobau Barracks**: called after Marshal Lobau (1770–1838):
'On traînait les condamnés jusqu'à la caserne Lobau, où des
pelotons en permanence les fusillaient, dans la cour intérieure,
presque à bout portant. Ce fut là surtout que la boucherie devint
effroyable: *des hommes, des enfants*...' (p. 301). '...Pendant
tout ce beau dimanche, les feux de peloton ne cessèrent pas, dans
la cour de la caserne Lobau, pleine de râles, de sang et de fumée'
(p. 306).

l'heureuse promenade, assis aux portes des marchands de vin. Des maisons et des édifices saccagés, des rues éventrées, de tant de ruines et de tant de souffrances, la vie grondait encore, au milieu du flamboiement de ce royal coucher d'astre, dans lequel Paris achevait de se consumer en braise.

ÉMILE ZOLA, *La Débâcle* (Fasquelle).

18. **a pleasing walk**: the definite article is often to be rendered by 'a' when it expresses something very general, almost = 'the very well-known', 'the regular', as here *l'heureuse promenade* = *a* Sunday walk. The irony in *heureuse* would hardly be given by "pleasant"; var. *enjoyable*. A preceding passage has: 'Une foule énorme encombrait les rues reconquises, des promeneurs allaient

a pleasing walk, were having dinner in the open, at the tables outside the restaurants. From the looted houses and buildings, the torn-up streets and all the destruction and suffering still came the hum of life while, in the flaming glory of that regal sunset, Paris was burning down to red-hot ash.

d'un air de flânerie *heureuse* voir les décombres fumants des incendies, des mères tenaient à la main des enfants rieurs, s'arrêtaient, écoutaient un instant avec intérêt les fusillades assourdies de la caserne Lobau' (p. 307).

21. **hum**: var. *plaint*.

22. **burning down**: *achevait de* = was finishing off, can seldom be rendered literally.

47. TRAJET SANS ARRÊT

Un sifflet strident retentit, et le train apparut au fond du sombre entonnoir. Vrai train royal, rapide et court, chargé de drapeaux français et tunisiens, et dont la locomotive mugissante et fumante, un énorme bouquet de roses sur le poitrail, semblait la demoiselle d'honneur d'une noce de Léviathans.

Lancée à toute volée, elle ralentissait sa marche en approchant. Les fonctionnaires se groupèrent, se redressant, assurant les épées, ajustant les faux-cols, tandis que le Nabab allait au-devant du train, le long de la voie, le sourire obséquieux aux lèvres et le dos arrondi déjà. Le convoi continuait très lentement. Jansoulet crut qu'il s'arrêtait et mit la main sur la portière du wagon royal étincelant d'or sous le noir du ciel; mais l'élan était trop fort sans doute, le train avançait toujours, le Nabab marchant à côté, essayant d'ouvrir cette maudite portière qui tenait ferme, et de l'autre main faisant un signe de commandement à la machine. La machine n'obéissait pas. 'Arrêtez donc!' Elle n'arrêtait pas. Impatienté, il sauta sur le marchepied garni de velours et avec sa fougue un peu impudente qui plaisait tant à l'ancien bey, il cria, sa grosse tête crépue à la portière:

'Station de Saint-Romans, Altesse.'

ALPHONSE DAUDET, Le Nabab.

CONTEXT. The distinguished visitor was expected to break his journey and visit the Nabob's [Jansoulet's] château, as the previous Bey had done. But Jansoulet had meantime fallen from Royal favour and the train did not stop.

2. **little valley:** *un entonnoir* is a funnel, here a funnel-shaped valley or cutting. The approach to St Romans was this: 'Sur la droite, du côté par où le train allait venir, deux grands coteaux chargés de vignes formaient *un entonnoir* dans lequel la voie s'enfonçait, disparaissait comme engloutie.'

3. **an express:** *rapide* is of course the adjective here, not the noun = a long distance express.

47. A NON-STOP RUN

A shrill whistle sounded, and the train appeared at the far end of the dark little valley. A proper Royal train it was, an express with very few coaches and heavily draped with French and Tunisian flags; its roaring and steaming engine, with a huge bouquet of roses on its bosom, looked like the bridesmaid at a Brobdingnagian marriage-feast.

It had been running at full speed, but began to slow down as it approached. The officials formed into groups, throwing back their shoulders, feeling for their swords, adjusting their collars, while the Nabob stepped out to meet the train, walking alongside the permanent way, an ingratiating smile on his lips, his back already bent. The train went on very slowly. Jansoulet thought it was coming to a stop and put his hand on the door of the Royal coach, which sparkled with gold beneath the blackness of the sky; but the momentum was too great, no doubt, and the train was still moving, the Nabob walking beside it, trying to open that confounded door which would *not* open, and with the other hand waving orders to the engine. The engine was taking no notice. 'Stop, will you!'—It was not stopping. Losing patience, he jumped on to the velvet-covered foot-board and with that dashing, rather cheeky manner of his, which used to appeal so much to the former Bey, he called out, with his great woolly head at the window, 'Saint-Romans Halt, Your Highness!'

4. **steaming**: *fumant* perhaps suggests this rather than *smoking* (*belching out smoke*), so also No. 49: 'la Lison soufflait, *fumante*.'
5. **bosom**: *poitrail*, properly = boiler-front, boiler-plate. Cp. No. 50: 'la Lison...buta du *poitrail*.'
7. Var. *From full speed it slowed down*, etc.
8. Var. *The official party took up their positions*.
20. Var. *Hi! Stop!*

48. SA DERNIÈRE ESPÉRANCE

Dans le couloir, Jansoulet entendait des garçons qui parlaient:

'A-t-on des nouvelles de Mora? Il paraît qu'il est très malade.... — Laisse donc, va. Il s'en tirera encore.... Il n'y a de chance que pour ceux-là....'

Il suffit de ces quelques mots... pour lui rendre le courage. Après tout, on en avait vu revenir d'aussi loin.... 'Si j'allais voir....' Il revint vers l'hôtel, plein d'illusion.... Vraiment l'aspect de la princière demeure avait de quoi fortifier son espoir. C'était la physionomie rassurante et tranquille des soirs ordinaires, depuis l'avenue éclairée de loin en loin, majestueuse et déserte, jusqu'au perron au pied duquel un vaste carrosse de forme antique attendait.

Dans l'antichambre, paisible aussi, brûlaient deux énormes lampes. Un valet de pied dormait dans un coin, le suisse lisait devant la cheminée. Il regarda le nouvel arrivant par-dessus ses lunettes, ne lui dit rien, et Jansoulet n'osa rien demander. Des piles de journaux gisant sur la table avec leurs bandes au nom du duc semblaient avoir été jetées là comme inutiles. Le Nabab en ouvrit un, essaya de lire; mais une marche rapide et glissante, un chuchotement de mélopée lui firent lever les yeux sur un vieillard blanc et courbé, paré de guipures comme un autel, et qui priait en s'en allant à grands pas de prêtre, sa longue soutane rouge déployée en traîne sur les tapis. C'était l'archevêque de Paris, accompagné de deux assistants. La vision avec son murmure de bise glacée passa vite devant Jansoulet, s'engouffra dans le grand carrosse et disparut emportant sa dernière espérance. ALPHONSE DAUDET, *Le Nabab*.

2. Mora, i.e. the Duc de Mora, Jansoulet's patron.
8. Var. *misplaced optimism*; *false hopes* is better, but 'hopes' ends the next sentence.

48. HIS LAST HOPE

In the passage, Jansoulet overheard some waiters talking: 'Any news of Mora? They say he's in a bad way.'—'Oh! don't you bother about him. He'll pull through all right. They've always the devil's own luck, these sort of folk.'

Those few words... were enough to make Jansoulet take heart again. After all, other people had been as far gone, and got over it.... 'Let's go and see....' He turned back towards the mansion, full of vague optimism. And indeed the appearance of the Ducal establishment was such as to revive his hopes. Everything wore the quiet reassuring look of normal evenings, from the stately, deserted avenue, with its lamps set at wide intervals, to the steps in front of the house, where a big coach of old-fashioned make stood waiting.

In the hall, which was just as peaceful, there were two huge lamps burning. A footman dozed in one corner; the porter was reading by the fire. He glanced at the new arrival over the top of his glasses, but said nothing, nor did Jansoulet venture to make any inquiry. Bundles of newspapers, lying anyhow on the table and still in their wrappers addressed to the Duke, seemed to have been tossed on to it, as though not required. The Nabob opened one and tried to read: but a sound of quick shuffling steps and *sotto voce* intoning made him look up, and he saw a pallid old man with a stoop, all hung about with lace like an altar, who was repeating a prayer, as he departed with a long priestly stride, his full red cassock trailing out behind him on the carpet. It was the Archbishop of Paris, attended by two acolytes. The apparition swept past Jansoulet with the sough of a bleak wind, sank into the depths of the great coach and vanished, bearing away with it his last hope.

9. Var. *that princely residence.*
26. repeating: var. *saying.*

49. DÉPART DE LA 'LISON'

Déjà, sous la halle couverte, la Lison soufflait, fumante, attelée à un train de sept wagons, trois de deuxième classe et quatre de première. Lorsque, vers cinq heures et demie, Jacques et Pecqueux étaient arrivés au Dépôt, pour la visite, ils avaient eu un grognement d'inquiétude, devant cette neige entêtée, dont crevait le ciel noir. Et, maintenant, à leur poste, ils attendaient le coup de sifflet, les yeux au loin, au delà du porche béant de la marquise, regardant la tombée muette et sans fin des flocons rayer les ténèbres d'un frisson livide.

Le mécanicien murmura:

— Le diable m'emporte si l'on voit un signal!

— Encore si l'on peut passer! dit le chauffeur...

Des voyageurs arrivèrent, emmitouflés, chargés de valises, toute une bousculade dans le froid terrible du matin. La neige des chaussures ne se fondait même pas; et les portières se refermaient aussitôt, chacun se barricadait, le quai restait désert, mal éclairé par les lueurs louches de quelques becs de gaz; tandis que le fanal de la machine, accroché à la base de la cheminée, flambait seul, comme un œil géant, élargissant au loin, dans l'obscurité, sa nappe d'incendie.

TITLE: **The 'Lison'**: var. '*Lizzie*', but the name, though exactly =*La Lison*, is unconvincing as the name of a railway engine, and has inappropriate motoring associations.

2. Var. *stood snorting, under steam*: for *fumante* see No. 47 note 4.

5. **given**: for this sense of *avoir* see No. 36, note 17; just as we can say 'il *eut* un geste', we can say 'il *eut* un grognement'.

13. Var. *Supposing we can get through!* The fireman means that even if the signals are clear, the snow may stop the train. But his sentence is not easily completed: ?*il ne faudra pas se plaindre*.

16. For *bousculade*=jostling, crowding on a station platform, cp. a later passage in Zola: 'Il y avait une vraie *bousculade*.... A

49. THE 'LISON' STARTS

By this time, in the covered-in part of the station, the 'Lison' stood puffing and steaming, coupled to a train with seven coaches, three second-class and four first. About 5.30, Jacques and Pecqueux had gone round to the running sheds for the inspection—and given an uneasy grunt at the sight 5 of the persistent snow and the black sky full to bursting. And now at their posts they were waiting for the whistle to go, their eyes far away, beyond the wide, open porch where the glazed roof came to an end—watching the silent, ceaseless flakes fluttering down through the darkness in livid 10 streaks.

The driver muttered: 'I'll be blowed if you can see a signal!' 'We'll have enough to do to get through, anyway!' said the fireman...

Travellers arrived on the scene, all wrapped up, carrying 15 bags—a regular scramble for seats it was, in the dreadful cold of the early morning. The snow on their boots showed no sign of melting. The doors slammed to, everybody barricading himself in, and the platform was left deserted, ill-lit by the furtive gleams of a few gas-jets, while the engine- 20 lamp on the base of the funnel blazed alone, like a giant's eye, the flame from it broadening out far into the darkness as from a house on fire.

cause des fêtes du Havre la foule était énorme.... Nous avons été obligés de défendre notre compartiment contre des voyageurs....'

21. **lamp:** seems the normal English both for *fanal* here = engine-lamp and for *lanterne* = station-master's lamp further on.

on: *accrochée à* means 'hooked on', but this is a case where English (see No. 15, note 11) dispenses with a participle.

like a giant's eye: var. *like a gigantic eye*; for the reminiscence, more or less unconscious, of Polyphemus see No. 70, note 22.

23. **house on fire:** for *un incendie* see No. 46, note 13. Zola says later on: 'Ce fut la machine qui en jaillit [du tunnel] avec l'éblouissement de son gros œil rond, la lanterne d'avant, dont *l'incendie* troua la campagne, allumant au loin les rails d'une double ligne de flammes.'

Mais Roubaud éleva sa lanterne, donnant le signal. Le conducteur-chef siffla, et Jacques répondit, après avoir ouvert le régulateur et mis en avant le petit volant du changement de marche. On partait. Pendant une minute encore, le sous-chef suivit tranquillement du regard le train qui s'éloignait sous la tempête.

ÉMILE ZOLA, *La Bête humaine* (Fasquelle).

THE 'LISON' STARTS

But Roubaud held up his lamp to give the signal. The guard blew his whistle, and Jacques responded, after opening 25 the regulator and winding forward the small gear handle. They were off. For one minute more, the assistant stationmaster stood quietly watching the train draw away into the storm.

24. **But:** *Mais* is used, as often, to put an end to a description and announce action. It marks also the change of tense = 'But Roubaud was now holding up', etc.

50. LA 'LISON' BLOQUÉE DANS LES NEIGES

Jacques remarquait que la cause de l'arrêt, l'empâtement dans la neige, ne provenait pas des roues: celles-ci coupaient les couches les plus épaisses; c'était le cendrier, placé entre elles, qui faisait obstacle, roulant la neige, la durcissant en paquets énormes. Et une idée lui vint.

— Il faut dévisser le cendrier.

D'abord, le conducteur-chef s'y opposa. Le mécanicien était sous ses ordres, il ne voulait pas l'autoriser à toucher à la machine. Puis, il se laissa convaincre.

— Vous en prenez la responsabilité, c'est bon!

Seulement, ce fut une dure besogne. Allongés sous la machine, le dos dans la neige qui fondait, Jacques et Pecqueux durent travailler pendant près d'une demi-heure. Heureusement que, dans le coffre à outils, ils avaient des tournevis de rechange. Enfin, au risque de se brûler et de s'écraser vingt fois, ils parvinrent à détacher le cendrier. Mais ils ne l'avaient pas encore, il s'agissait de le sortir de là-dessous. D'un poids énorme, il s'embarrassait dans les roues et les cylindres. Pourtant, à quatre, ils le tirèrent, le traînèrent en dehors de la voie, jusqu'au talus.

— Maintenant, achevons de déblayer, dit le conducteur...

— Non, non, c'est assez déblayé, déclara Jacques. Montez, je me charge du reste.

Il était de nouveau à son poste, avec Pecqueux, et lorsque

---

2. **sticking in the snow**: a preceding passage has: 'il sembla qu'elle allait s'immobiliser, ainsi qu'un navire qui a touché un banc de sable...elle s'engluait, prise par toutes ses roues.'

the cause had nothing to do with: *la cause ne provenait pas de* is odd; one would expect either *la cause...n'était pas* or *l'empâtement ne provenait pas de*.

3. **would**: var. *could*. The force of the Imperfect in *coupaient* is somewhat as in '*Je les voyais venir*'='I *could* see them coming'.

6. **take off**: var. *screw off, shift*.

9. **interfere with**: var. *meddle with*. For the sense of *toucher à* cp. *touche-à-tout*.

13. Var. *additional* (*extra*) *spanners*, but though 'spanners'

50. THE 'LISON' SNOWED UP

Jacques noticed that the cause of the stoppage, namely this sticking in the snow, had nothing to do with the wheels; these would cut through the deepest of layers; the obstacle was the ash-box between the wheels, which was pushing the snow along and caking it up into huge lumps. He had an 5 idea: 'We've got to take off the ash-box', he said.

The guard objected at first, for, the driver being under his orders, he was unwilling to give permission for him to interfere with the engine. Eventually he was talked over; '*You*'re taking the responsibility', he said. 'Carry on!' 10

But it was a tough job. Jacques and Pecqueux had to work nearly half an hour underneath the engine, flat on their backs in the slush. Luckily they had spare screw-drivers in the tool-box. At length, after they had run the risk of getting burnt and crushed a score of times, they 15 managed to screw off the ash-box. But they hadn't got it yet; the point was how to work it out from underneath the engine; it was an enormous weight and fouled the wheels and cylinders. None the less, the four of them together tugged and hauled it free of the line, up to the bank. 20

'Now let's finish off that clearing job', said the guard...

'No, no, it's cleared away enough', Jacques declared. 'You get in. I'll do the rest.'

Back he was at his place, with Pecqueux, and once the

---

comes more naturally to us, it may not denote the instrument intended here. Its French name (*une clef anglaise*) suggests that the spanner is in France of fairly recent introduction; *tournevis* may have done duty for both 'spanner' and 'screw-driver' till 1890, the date of *La Bête humaine*. The earliest reference (1790) in O.E.D. is: 'Spanner: a nut *screw-driver*.'

16. Var. *they hadn't done the trick yet.* Cp. *On les aura* = 'We'll *get* them'.

20. **free**: var. *clear*, but it is wanted immediately after.
bank: var. *embankment*.

21. **finish off**: for *achever de* see No. 46, note 23.

23. Var. '*Get on board. Leave the rest to me.*'

les deux conducteurs eurent regagné leurs fourgons, il tourna lui-même le robinet du purgeur. Le jet de vapeur brûlante, assourdi, acheva de fondre les paquets qui adhéraient encore aux rails. Puis, la main au volant, il fit machine arrière. Lentement, il recula d'environ trois cents mètres, pour prendre du champ. Et, ayant poussé au feu, dépassant même la pression permise, il revint contre le mur qui barrait la voie, il y jeta la Lison, de toute sa masse, de tout le poids du train qu'elle traînait. Elle eut un han! terrible de bûcheron qui enfonce la cognée, sa forte charpente de fer et de fonte en craqua. Mais elle ne put passer encore, elle s'était arrêtée, fumante, toute vibrante du choc. Alors, à deux autres reprises, il dut recommencer la manœuvre, recula, fonça sur la neige, pour l'emporter; et, chaque fois, la Lison, raidissant les reins, buta du poitrail, avec son souffle enragé de géante. Enfin, elle parut reprendre haleine, elle banda ses muscles de métal en un suprême effort, et elle passa, et lourdement le train la suivit, entre les deux murs de la neige éventrée.

ÉMILE ZOLA, *La Bête humaine* (Fasquelle).

34. gave: see No. 49, note 5.

two guards were into their vans again, he turned on the 25
steam-hose tap himself; the jet of scalding steam, with its
screech damped down, melted away the last lumps of snow
still adhering to the rails. Then, with a touch on the wheel,
he reversed the engine. He backed slowly for about three
hundred yards to get a run, and having turned on the 30
blower, exceeding indeed the authorized pressure, he charged
at the drift blocking the line, flung 'Lison' on to it, the
whole mass of her and the whole weight of the train she
was pulling. She gave a terrific grunt like a woodman
driving in his axe, and her powerful steel and iron frame 35
rattled and shook. But she failed to get through yet, and
there she was, brought to a standstill, steaming, quivering
all over with the shock.

Then, twice again, Jacques had to repeat the operation;
he backed, and bore down on the drift, to batter it out 40
of the way; and each time 'Lison', girding her loins,
struck hard with the boiler-front, snorting like a giantess
in a fury. At length, she seemed to get her second wind,
braced her iron muscles for one final effort, and crashed
through, and the train came lumbering on behind, between 45
the two walls of the ploughed up snow.

42. **boiler-front:** for *poitrail* see No. 47, note 5.

51. L'EXPANSION DE PARIS (I)

Ainsi l'enceinte de 1846, après lui avoir servi de protection avancée, était devenue la forme même de la ville. Et voilà qu'à son tour elle pesait sur Paris, l'empêchait de se développer naturellement. Une fois de plus il devait renoncer à trouver sa forme par lui-même. Le rempart émoussait l'élan des quartiers neufs, arrêtait les avenues, les coupait de leurs prolongements, maintenant beaucoup de rues de l'extrême périphérie à l'état de culs-de-sac ou de coupe-gorge, y laissait fermenter les voyous et les ordures. De proche en proche, la pression se communiquait jusqu'au centre. Les rues des vieux quartiers renonçaient à s'élargir. Les anciennes maisons bourgeoises ou marchandes qu'on n'abattait plus dégénéraient sur place en taudis purulents. Les logements noircissaient dans un air mal remué qui finissait par vieillir comme eux. C'était l'enceinte qui, de loin, y comprimait les familles, couchait les gens les uns contre les autres sur des lits pliants, sur des matelas à même le sol, dans des salles à manger au plafond bas, dans des cuisines, des couloirs, des réduits sans fenêtre. C'était elle qui obligeait les bâtisseurs à dresser des maisons étroites sur des bouts de terrains taillés de travers: elle qui, peu à peu, par

CONTEXT. 'Paris, la ville du fleuve et des collines, n'avait pas eu seulement affaire au sol. Il demeurait depuis ses origines une place guerrière et murée. L'imagination de défense, qui va juste à l'encontre de l'imagination de croissance, avait toujours contribué à lui dicter ses contours. Tant qu'une enceinte subsistait, Paris poussait et pressait sur lui-même' (p. 197). 'La dernière enceinte, celle de Thiers, la plus ample et la plus épaisse de toutes, avec son talus, son glacis et les 500 mètres de zone militaire qui la couvraient...n'enveloppait qu'à distance le Paris de 1846....Elle avait été d'abord, et jusqu'à la fin du siècle, quelque chose qu'il faut remplir. En 1908, elle était remplie.'
1. Var. *an advanced protective belt*.
3. Var. *preventing it from following*, etc.
8. **as**: *à l'état de* = *in the condition of*; cp. No. 62: *à l'état fruste*.

51. THE EXPANSION OF PARIS (I)

Thus the fortified zone of 1846, after serving as an advanced cover, had become the actual outline of the city and now in its turn was pressing in on Paris and hindering its natural development. Once again Paris had to give up the attempt to take shape in its own way. The walls checked the expan- 5 sion of the newer suburbs, brought the avenues to a standstill, cut them off from their extensions, so that many streets on the outer circle were kept on as blind alleys or Cut-Throat Lanes and left to fester with refuse and roughs. From point to point the pressure spread right through to the centre. 10 The streets in the older parts were not being widened. The houses formerly occupied for residential or business purposes were no longer being pulled down, but deteriorating as they stood into foul slums. Tenements were turning grimy in a stagnant atmosphere which was coming to be as musty as 15 themselves. It was the distant pressure of the fortifications that was squeezing families together in such places, huddling people up against each other on folding-beds or on mattresses laid out on the floor, in low-ceilinged living-rooms, kitchens, passages, windowless cubby holes. The fortifications, too, 20 were forcing speculative builders to run up narrow houses on oddments of sites; gradually crushing out back-gardens

---

14. **Tenements**: *logements* means simply places where people live, dwellings, not necessarily tenements, though that is probably the meaning here.

17. **in such places**: merely to render *y*, perhaps unnecessarily.

18. **folding-beds**: var. *turn-up bedsteads*; not "camp-beds", which suggests temporary accommodation for a visitor; these *lits pliants* were kept in the room and became some other piece of furniture during the day.

19. **living-rooms**: var. *parlours*; "dining-rooms" is much too grand for these *salles à manger*.

20. **cubby holes**: var. *recesses, box-rooms*.

21. **speculative builders**: *bâtisseurs* is uncomplimentary, almost = jerry builders.

22. **back-gardens**, i.e. garden-plots enclosed by blocks of flats.

écrasement, éliminait les jardins intérieurs, les cours plantées d'arbustes; qui augmentait l'épaisseur de la circulation et commençait à la ralentir; qui, jusque sur les grands boulevards, serrait les files de voitures, rapprochait les moyeux.

JULES ROMAINS, *Les Hommes de bonne volonté.*

23. **courtyards with shrubberies**: in phrases like *cours plantées d'arbustes* English leaves *plantées* to the imagination; see also No. 15, note 11 and No. 62, note 18.

and courtyards with shrubberies; increasing the congestion of the traffic and beginning to slow it down; and, right away into the great central boulevards, closing up the lines of vehicles and reducing the space between them. 25

25. *serrait* indicates longitudinal pressure (cp. *serrer les rangs*); *rapprochait* means lateral pressure, resulting in reduction of space between two lines of traffic. Var. exactly: *reducing hub-clearance,* but this is almost *too* exact—too reminiscent of Manuals 'How to drive a car', etc.; *giving less clearance, giving them less room.*

52. L'EXPANSION DE PARIS (II)

Quant aux Villages, elle en avait bien happé quelques-uns, qu'elle condamnait ainsi à se dissoudre plus ou moins vite. Mais les autres, ceux qui étaient restés en dehors, se trouvaient protégés, et remis pour trois quarts de siècle à leur aise. Aucune expansion brusque de Paris ne pouvait plus les atteindre. Ils eurent le temps de grossir: les hameaux de devenir des bourgs, et les bourgs, de grandes villes. Ils ramassèrent la terre d'alentour, l'organisèrent à leur façon, pour leurs besoins, avec de courtes vues villageoises, des ambitions bornées de petits pays. Ils avaient employé ces trois quarts de siècle à tordre et à embrouiller des rues, des ruelles, des impasses, que personne n'arriverait jamais plus à détordre et à débrouiller. Ils firent des boulevards de trois cents mètres de long qui finissaient sur un mur d'usine. Ils lancèrent vers la campagne des avenues plantées d'échalas, qui se perdaient un peu plus loin dans un bas-fond de choux et de mâchefer. Pourtant ils éprouvaient le voisinage de Paris. Ils faisaient avec lui un échange d'hommes qui, d'une année à l'autre, devenait un va-et-vient plus rapide et plus compliqué. L'enceinte empêchait Paris de passer, mais laissait fuir les Parisiens. Ils allaient chercher le gîte dans cet espace d'alentour, où ils s'étaient promenés le dimanche, et que, rentrés au milieu de Paris, ils se représentaient comme une suite inépuisable de demeures rustiques, de bois, de vallons, de jardins. Pour la

1. **the Villages**, i.e. those which have been referred to before—'les villages capturés, qui portaient de si beaux noms: Clignancourt, Charonne, Grenelle....'

2. Var. *a certain number*.

10. **small-town ambitions**: *pays* often means 'part of the country', e.g. *dans mon pays* = in my part of the country and particularly a small locality, frequently a hamlet: cp. *Ralentissez à l'entrée du pays* = 'Little Puddlington: Please drive slowly'. *Petit pays* means 'a small town', with some of the contemptuous flavour noticeable in the English phrase. But cp. Ivor Brown, *Manchester Guardian*, July 1939: 'Largely through American influence, the two words "small town" have become a single

52. THE EXPANSION OF PARIS (II)

As for the Villages, they [the fortifications] had of course snapped up some and thus doomed these to more or less rapid dissolution. But the rest, those that had remained without, found themselves protected, and set at ease again for three-quarters of a century. No more could any sudden expansion of Paris affect them. They obtained time to fill out; the hamlets, to grow into large villages and the large villages into big towns. They took in the land round about, developed it in their own way, for their own requirements, with village short-sightedness, with limited small-town ambitions. They had devoted these three-quarters of a century to contorting and entangling streets, lanes, blind alleys, which no one now would ever manage to disentangle and straighten out. They made boulevards three hundred yards in length which came to a dead end at a factory wall. They threw out towards the country avenues planted with tree-props, which petered out a little way farther on in a hollow among cabbages and clinkers. Yet they were affected by the proximity of Paris, and carried on an exchange of men which year by year developed into faster and more complex to-and-fro traffic. The fortifications prevented Paris from breaking out, but let the Parisians through. They went seeking for quarters in the hinterland which had been the scene of their Sunday outings and which, once they were home again in central Paris, they visualized as an inexhaustible series of rural dwellings, of woods and dales and gardens. For the first time there were hundreds of

adjective.... The "small town" atmosphere can provide ambitious spirits and aspiring minds....'

16. **planted**: necessary here; see No. 51, note 23.

17. **tree-props**: *échalas*, usually = vine-props, are the guards put round young trees.

20. **complex**: var. *intricate*.

22. Var. *allowed a leakage of Parisians*; with *fuir* = to escape cp. *une fuite de gaz*.

23. **hinterland**: var. *the outlying places*.

première fois on vit des centaines de milliers d'hommes travailler tout le jour dans une ville qu'ils n'habitaient plus. Mais la ville les reprenait de maintes façons. Leurs femmes, dépaysées, venaient faire des achats dans les magasins du centre, et réchauffer aux devantures illuminées leurs yeux qui avaient contemplé toute la semaine une ruelle boueuse où la nuit tombe vite. JULES ROMAINS (*suite*).

29. Var. *recaptured them; regained its hold (grip) on them in many a way.*

thousands of men working all day in a city where they had ceased to be residents. But the city caught them again in numerous ways. Their women-folk, being out of their element, 30 would come in to shop at the big stores in town and feast their eyes on the brightly-lit shop windows—eyes which all the week had been looking out on a muddy lane where darkness sets in early.

30. **women-folk:** *leurs femmes* are not necessarily 'their wives' (*leurs épouses*).

out of their element: var. *feeling lost (strange); in strange surroundings.*

53. RÉFLEXIONS SUR L'AFFAIRE DREYFUS

Ce qui se mobilisait chez moi en toute ardeur dans cette affaire, c'était mon culte de la méthode, tel que me l'avaient inculqué la mathématique et la discipline historique, et ma haine du littérateur avec ses chants de ténor qu'il prend pour des raisons et son mépris de la patiente recherche dont il est, par essence, entièrement incapable. Quant à ceux qui invoquaient la raison d'État, je ne le leur reprochais nullement. Elle me parut toujours une doctrine fort soutenable et j'eus toujours pour elle, avec ce goût qu'une autre partie de moi-même a pour l'autorité, une certaine sympathie. Ce que je leur reprochais, c'est qu'ils ne l'invoquaient pas franchement mais voulaient nous faire croire qu'ils respectaient la vérité, alors qu'ils ne cessaient de bassement l'estropier.

Comme je devais l'écrire trente ans plus tard, je crois que si l'État m'eût dit: 'La condamnation de Dreyfus est parfaitement injuste; mais, pour des raisons d'ordre social, je la maintiens', j'eusse répondu: 'Dès que vous ne proclamez plus que deux et deux font cinq et ne violez plus les lois de l'esprit, je rentre dans ma cellule. Les États savent ce qu'ils ont à faire et je ne les empêche pas de pratiquer le mensonge, s'ils le jugent bon. Je les empêche de dire qu'il est la vérité.'

Et si l'État eût ajouté: 'Vous savez bien que le peuple est ainsi fait qu'il n'acceptera le mensonge que présenté comme vérité; qu'il n'admettra la condamnation d'un innocent que si on lui assure qu'il est coupable', j'eusse riposté: 'Eh bien,

---

1. Var. *What rose up in arms in my case, and most enthusiastically*.

3. **History**: the capital letter will give the sense sufficiently: var. *my historical training*.

4. **'writing man'**: var. '*lit'ry gent*'; *littérateur* may not be in itself offensive, but the context adds a note of contempt.

9. Var. *a doctrine for which there is a good deal to be said*.

19. **Now that**: *Dès que = du moment que = puisque*.

21. **cell**: an allusion to Benda's favourite notion of the author as the modern representative of the mediæval order of

53. REFLECTIONS ON THE DREYFUS AFFAIR

The force which mobilized within me, and did so with complete enthusiasm, during that affair, was my respect for Method, as inculcated in me by Mathematics and History, and my dislike of the 'writing man' with his operatic tenor effects which he mistakes for arguments, and his contempt for patient research, of which he is by his very nature utterly incapable. As for those who invoked 'reasons of State', I in no way blamed them for that. *Raison d'État* always did seem to me quite a defensible doctrine and, with the attraction which the idea of authority possesses for another side of my mind, I always did feel a certain amount of sympathy with it. Where I thought they were wrong was in not invoking it frankly, but trying to make us believe they had a respect for truth, whereas they were never done distorting it outrageously.

I believe that—as I was to put it, writing thirty years later—if the State had said to me: 'Dreyfus' conviction was quite unjust; but, for reasons of a social nature, we are letting it stand', I should have replied: 'Now that you have given up proclaiming that two and two make five and violating the laws of thought, I am going back to my cell. States know what their job is and it is not for me to prevent them practising falsehood if they see fit. But I must prevent them saying that falsehood is truth.'

And if the State had added: 'You know well enough that the French public is so constituted that it will not accept falsehood except when put forward as truth—that it will not agree to the conviction of an innocent man, unless it has been

clerks, whose place is the cloister and who should not meddle with secular quarrels, in which truth ceases to have the absolute value it has, or should have, for the scholar.

22. Var. *what action they must take.*

26. **the French public:** *le peuple* means here not so much 'the plebs', 'the lower orders', as 'the mass of the people', 'the man in the street'; *la nation* is the French phrase where we should say 'the country'; *le pays* is coming into use in political circles, possibly as an Anglicism, and still jars a little on French purists.

éduquez le peuple. Obtenez qu'il comprenne la valeur du mensonge. Je fais mon devoir d'intellectuel en défendant les lois de l'esprit. Faites votre devoir de réaliste en lui apprenant à les mépriser.' En bref, ce qui se dressait en moi, c'était l'orgueil de l'intellectuel, qui sait que le social est le plus fort, mais lui aura du moins signifié qu'il n'est pas l'intellectuel; c'était l'orgueil du roseau pensant, qui souffre que la matière l'écrase, mais ne souffre pas qu'elle se dise pensante. JULIEN BENDA, *La Jeunesse d'un Clerc.*

29. **that he is guilty**: var. *of his guilt.*
34. **the social factor**: var. *the social order (fact)*; *le social* is neuter; *l'intellectuel* also—at the end of the sentence, although masculine at the beginning.
35. **pointed out**: var. *intimated, given it to understand, made it clear.*

assured he is guilty', I should have retorted: 'Well, then, educate the country. Get it to understand the value of lying. I do my duty as an intellectual, by defending the laws of thought. Do yours as a realist, by teaching people to despise them.' In short, what rose up in revolt within me was the pride of the intellectual, who knows that the social factor is too strong for him, but who will at least have pointed out that *social* is not *intellectual*—the pride of Pascal's 'thinking reed', which will suffer matter to crush it, but will not suffer matter to call itself 'thinking'.

36. **Pascal's.** The addition may or may not be necessary. Miss Rebecca West published a novel (1936) called *The Thinking Reed*, but some of her public may not have recognized the allusion—to Pascal, *Les Pensées*.

54. BATAILLES DE JADIS

Assis au fond de la salle, les coudes aux genoux et le menton dans les mains, François s'émerveillait des fantaisies chevaleresques qui composaient le répertoire du *Théâtre des Marionnettes*.

Au milieu de simples paysages, flanqués d'architectures anachroniques, les plus terribles preux de l'histoire et de la légende rivalisaient de bravoure et d'éloquence. Casqués et cuirassés, le verbe fier et la moustache en croc, ils portaient la victoire dans leurs yeux. Il fallait les entendre, entre deux estocades, exhaler leurs humeurs homicides contre les Sarrazins! Tandis qu'ils s'éloignaient, ressaisis dans les aventures de la guerre, leurs lointaines amantes, sorties de la coulisse voisine, venaient se plaindre aux fleurs et aux oiseaux, puis se retiraient en des solitudes, les mains tendues vers le ciel, an agitant les cornes de leur hennin.

Mais on n'avait pas le temps de s'attendrir, car les armées ennemies, précipitant l'attaque, jetaient leurs bataillons sur la scène. Toute la salle, trépignant de joie, les excitait avec des jurons et des cris; le tambour battait; l'accordéon faisait rage. C'était un vacarme assourdissant, qui se calmait à grand'peine et reprenait tout à coup lorsqu'on voyait les païens...tournoyer dans l'air et s'abattre sur les planches où leurs bras et leurs jambes se dressaient pêle-mêle, avec des gestes impénitents....

Un homme dominait la bataille: Charlemagne. Il dépassait les plus grands de la hauteur de son casque: sa cuirasse écaillée bombait sur sa poitrine: ses éperons vermeils sonnaient sur le plancher; et il allait d'un bout à l'autre de la

1. Var. *with his chin cupped in his hands.*
10. Var. ? *between sword-thrusts*; for the omission of 'two' cp. No. 17, note 25; *after every mighty thrust.*
11. Var. *breathing fire and slaughter against.*
18. Var. *to indulge their sympathy.*
19. **hastening.** The reference here and in the lines above is probably to the suddenness of exits and entrances in a Puppet Theatre, where the wings are open.
22. **went**: var. *played.*

54. BATTLES LONG AGO

At the back of the hall, elbows on knees and chin in hand, Francis sat lost in wonder at the extravaganzas from the Days of Chivalry which made up the repertory of the Puppet Theatre.

Amid simple landscapes with architectural anachronisms on either side, the most redoubtable knights of history and legend vied with each other in eloquence and deeds of derring-do. In helm and breast-plate, they spoke out loud and bold, mustachios up-curled and the light of victory in their eyes. You should have heard them, between a couple of mighty thrusts, venting their murderous spleen upon the Saracens. As they moved away, caught up again in the hazards of war, their distant lady-loves, appearing from the adjacent wings, came making their moan to the flowers and the birds, and then withdrew into solitary seclusion, their hands uplifted to the heavens, the peaks of their hennins all of a tremble.

But spectators had no time for sentiment, for the opposing hosts were hastening their attack, hurling their battalions on the scene. The whole house, stamping with delight, yelled and cursed them on; the drum was beating; the concertina went fast and furious. It was a deafening din, which was quietened down with great difficulty and suddenly broke out afresh when the paynims... were seen to spin round in the air and crash down on the stage from which their jumbled arms and legs stuck up in attitudes impenitent.

One man dominated the battle—Charlemagne. He stood a helmet's height above the tallest; his scaly breastplate swelled forth upon his chest; his gilt spurs rang out upon the boards; and he strode up and down the stage, draped

---

22. Var. *which took some calming down*; cp. *Calmez-vous*. In a later passage order is restored among the juvenile audience by an attendant armed with a pole.

28. **scaly**: var. *scaled*. N.B. *écaillé* adj. [= qui a des écailles = 'scales' and 'scale-armour', e.g. Les *poissons écaillés* et les *poissons sans écailles*] is to be distinguished from *écaillé* past participle = 'scaled', 'peeled off'.

scène, raide et majestueux dans les draperies de son manteau, le sourcil autoritaire et la voix souveraine. Il était toujours le plus fougueux dans les mêlées, au-dessus desquelles on voyait ses joues écarlates et sa barbe luisant de colle bondir à la façon d'un étendard.

François, immobile dans son coin, s'exaltait à ses prouesses.

EDMOND GLESENER, *Le Théâtre des Marionnettes*,
in *A la Gloire de la Belgique*.

34. **gum**: *colle* is 'paste', and also 'gum', which seems more appropriate here.

fluttering: var.—if the top of the pole is meant rather than

rigid and majestic in the folds of his mantle, authority in his eyebrow and, in his voice, command. He was ever the fiercest in the fray, and above it all his bright red cheeks and his beard shiny with gum could be seen fluttering like a battle-standard. 35

Francis sat spellbound in his corner, thrilled by his feats of valour.

the flag itself—*dancing*; cp. Macaulay, *Battle of Lake Regillus*:
'Ensigns *dancing* wild above,
Blades all in line below.'
36. **feats of valour**: var. *doughty deeds*.

IV. CHARACTERS

55. MADAME DE ROUCY ET SON MARI

C'étoit une personne extrêmement laide, qui avoit de l'esprit, fort glorieuse, pleine d'ambition, folle des moindres distinctions, engouée à l'excès de la cour, basse à proportion de la faveur et des besoins, qui cherchoit à faire des affaires à toutes mains, aigre à merveilles jusqu'aux injures et fréquemment en querelle avec quelqu'un, toujours occupée de ses affaires, que son opiniâtreté, son humeur et sa malhabileté perdoient, et qui vivoit noyée de biens, d'affaires et de créanciers, envieuse, haineuse, par conséquent peu aimée, et qui, pour couronner tout cela, ne manquoit point de grand'messes à la paroisse et rarement à communier tous les huit jours.

Son mari n'avoit qu'une belle mais forte figure: glorieux et bas plus qu'elle, panier percé qui jouoit tout et perdoit tout, toujours en course et à la chasse, dont la sottise lui avoit tourné à mérite, parce qu'il ne faisoit jalousie à personne, et dont la familiarité avec les valets le faisoit aimer. Il avoit aussi les dames pour lui, parce qu'il étoit leur fait, et avec toute sa bêtise un entregent de cour que l'usage du grand monde lui avoit donné. Il étoit de tout avec Monseigneur, et le Roi le traitoit bien à cause de M. de la Rochefoucauld et des maréchaux de Duras et de Lorges, frères de sa mère, qui tous trois avoient fait de lui et de ses frères comme de leurs enfants, depuis que la révocation de

1. **woman**: *une personne* often had this definite meaning; cp. modern French, *une jeune personne* = a young *woman*.
4. **the favour**: perhaps *la faveur* means 'the service asked for' or perhaps it means 'the influence brought to bear'.
5. *à toutes mains = de toute manière, par tous les moyens.* Pierre Adam, *Contribution à l'Étude des Mémoires de Saint-Simon*, 1920, p. 103, quotes: 'leur argent, dont ils s'étoient gorgés *à toutes mains* en Italie'; 'prenant *à toutes mains* et toujours gueux'.
10. **business transactions**: ? *law-suits*.
17. Var. *had told in his favour*; *had turned out to be an advantage*.
19. **with the serving-men.** Elsewhere Saint-Simon says of M. de Roucy: 'Lui et ses frères étaient les rois de la canaille.'

55. MADAME DE ROUCY AND HER HUSBAND

She was an extremely ugly woman, who had some wit, exceeding vainglorious, full of ambition, crazy about the most trifling honours, infatuated beyond all measure with Court life, stooping as low as the favour, and the necessity for it, required, striving to do good business by hook or by crook, uncommon sharp of tongue, to the point of abuse, and often having a quarrel with somebody, always busy with her affairs, which became involved because of her own obstinacy, ill temper and mismanagement, living in a pother of property matters, business transactions and creditors, full of envy, hatred and malice and therefore ill-liked, and to crown all that, missing never a high mass at the parish church and rarely failing to communicate once a week.

Her husband had naught but a handsome, though a stout, figure; he was vainglorious and obsequious—more so than she—a spendthrift who would stake all and lose all, for ever riding and hunting, a man whose foolishness had to advantage turned, because he made nobody jealous of him, and whose familiarity with the serving-men gave him some popularity. He had also the ladies on his side, because he was the very man for them, and he had, with all his dullness, a courtly address acquired from his experience of the great world. He went about everywhere with Monseigneur, and the King used him well for the sake of M. de la Rochefoucauld and Marshals de Duras and de Lorges, his maternal uncles, who had, all three, treated both him and his brothers as their own children, ever since the Revocation of the Edict

---

22. **experience:** cp. Littré, s.v. USAGE, 11° *Usage du monde* = '*expérience* de la société, habitude d'en pratiquer les devoirs, d'en observer les manières'.

23. **went about everywhere:** cp. Littré, s.v. TOUT: 'Être de tout, se mêler de toutes les affaires, aller dans toutes les sociétés, être de toutes les parties.'

Monseigneur: The *Grand Dauphin*, son of Louis XIV.

27. i.e. *comme ils faisaient de [à l'égard de] leurs enfants.*

l'édit de Nantes avoit fait sortir du royaume le comte et la
comtesse de Roye, ses père et mère. Son grand mérite étoit
ses inepties, qu'on répétoit et qui néanmoins se trouvoient
quelquefois exprimer quelque chose.

SAINT-SIMON, *Mémoires*.

28. **Count and Countess de Roye.** The Count went to Holland
and in 1688 to England, where William of Orange made him

of Nantes had driven his parents, Count and Countess de
Roye, out of the kingdom. His chief recommendation lay
in his silly remarks, which went the round and which occasion- 30
ally turned out after all to have something in them.

Earl of Lifford. He died at Bath, June 15, 1690. The Countess,
a sister of Marshal de Lorges, died in London in 1715, aged 82.
M. de Roucy had abjured Protestantism in 1684.

30. Var. *which were bruited abroad* (*about*).

56. MADAME DE CASTRIES

Mme de Castries étoit un quart de femme, une espèce de biscuit manqué, extrêmement petite, mais bien prise, et auroit passé dans un médiocre anneau; ni gorge, ni menton, fort laide, l'air toujours en peine et étonné; avec cela une physionomie qui éclatoit d'esprit et qui tenoit encore plus parole. Elle savoit tout: histoire, philosophie, mathématiques, langues savantes; et jamais il ne paroissoit qu'elle sût mieux que parler françois; mais son parler avoit une justesse, une énergie, une éloquence, une grâce jusque dans les choses les plus communes, avec ce tour unique qui n'est propre qu'aux Mortemart. Aimable, amusante, gaie, sérieuse, toute à tous, charmante quand elle vouloit plaire, plaisante naturellement, avec la dernière finesse, sans la vouloir être, et assénant aussi les ridicules à ne les jamais oublier, glorieuse, choquée de mille choses, avec un ton plaintif qui emportoit la pièce, cruellement méchante quand

1. **little sponge-cake.** We have added 'little' because 'cake' alone might suggest something substantial, for cutting: "sponge finger" would suit the idea of *passer dans un médiocre anneau*, but is a nineteenth-century word. Another meaning of *biscuit* is 'porcelain', as in *biscuit de Sèvres*, which is often taken to be the allusion here. But the point is that Mme de Castries, though well-proportioned, was made on a quarter-size scale. A spongecake gone wrong in the baking is of the same shape, but not the same size, as the successful product.

12. **the Mortemarts.** Mme de Castries, wife of Joseph-François de Castries (1663–1728), was Marie-Élisabeth de Rochechouart-Mortemart. She was the daughter of Marshal de Vivonne and the cousin of Mme de Montespan, whose reputation for wit and culture was shared by her brother and sisters.

13. **all things**, etc. The French phrase is not necessarily depreciatory, any more than the English. Cp. *Journal des Débats*, September 2, 1924: obituary of General de Lacroix: 'Surtout depuis que l'âge l'avait condamné à la retraite, il *était tout à tous*, il écoutait patiemment l'exposé des craintes et des doléances de quiconque s'adressait en lui, au soldat et au patriote.' The sense of *toute à tous* may be that Mme de Castries

56. MADAME DE CASTRIES

Madame de Castries was a mite of a woman, a sort of little sponge-cake which had not 'risen', extremely slight, but shapely, and would have gone through a middle-sized ring— neither bust nor chin, uncommon ugly, and always wore a look of pained astonishment; withal, a face which beamed 5 intelligence and more than redeemed its promise. There was nothing she did not know: history, philosophy, mathematics, the learned tongues; and yet she never let it appear that she knew more than plain French; but her speech had an exactness, a force, an eloquence, a grace of its own even in the 10 commonest matters, with that unique turn of phrase which is peculiar to the Mortemarts. Friendly, entertaining, gay and grave, all things to all men, charming when she wished to please, amusing naturally and with the utmost acuteness of perception, but without making purpose of it, and more- 15 over showing the ridiculous side of people in a way which was never forgotten, vain, taking offence at a host of things in a plaintive tone of voice that went home, cruelly sarcastic

had the useful social gift of appearing to devote her whole attention to the person to whom she happened to be talking; cp. 'Il était *tout* à son ouvrage'=engrossed in his work.

14. **amusing**: *plaisante* might mean 'pleasing' here; but the context on the whole, and the quotation in Note 15 below, suggest rather 'amusing' [in the sense of 'droll', 'funny', etc.] as contrasted with *amusante* above [='keeping people amused', entertaining or interesting their minds].

15. In '*sans la vouloir être*', *la* (Modern French *le*) refers to *plaisante*.

showing, etc.: *asséner* (also *assener*; Saint-Simon spells it *acener*) *un coup*=*porter un coup violent*; *asséner* (Lat. *assignare*) means to distribute, deal, allot; *les ridicules* is the object of *asséner* and means things (not people) which seem ridiculous. Cp. No. 61, line 19: se montrent du doigt votre *ridicule*. Cp. also Saint-Simon, *Mém.* (Chéruel et Régnier), I, p. 341: 'Sa conversation [de Mme de Nangis] étoit charmante, et personne *n'assénoit si* plaisamment *les ridicules* même où il n'y en avoit point, et comme n'y touchant pas.' Var. *pointing out people's absurdities.*

il lui plaisoit, et fort bonne amie, polie, gracieuse, obligeante en général, sans aucune galanterie, mais délicate sur l'esprit, et amoureuse de l'esprit où elle le trouvoit à son gré, avec cela un talent de raconter qui charmoit, et, quand elle vouloit faire un roman sur-le-champ une source de production, de variété et d'agrément qui étonnoit. Avec sa gloire, elle se croyoit bien mariée par l'amitié qu'elle eut pour son mari. Elle l'étendit sur tout ce qui lui appartenoit, et elle étoit aussi glorieuse pour lui que pour elle; elle en recevoit le réciproque et toutes sortes d'égards et respects.

SAINT-SIMON, *Mémoires*.

18. '*qui emportait la pièce*' = took out the bit, i.e. did its work once for all; left a permanent mark. The allusion is to an 'outil d'acier dont plusieurs artisans se servent pour découper *d'un seul coup* les différentes matières qui servent à leurs ouvrages'. Littré; hence applied to *biting* sarcasms.

20. **finely sensible**, etc.: var. *with a nice taste in wit; fastidious in matters of wit.*

22. **story-telling**: a characteristic seventeenth-century accomplishment: cp. Cardinal de Bernis, *Mém.* I, p. 44, 'L'abbé de

when she liked, yet a right good friend, courteous, gracious,
obliging generally, devoid of coquetry, but finely sensible 20
of witty discourse and enamoured of wit wherever she found
it to her taste; moreover, a gift of story-telling which en-
thralled her hearers and, when she was minded to make up
a tale on the spur of the moment, a fount of invention
and variety and delight which was amazing. With her 25
vanity, she believed herself happily married, by reason
of the affection she bore her husband. She extended that
feeling to everything pertaining to him, and she was vain
for his sake as much as for her own; she received the like
from him in return, and all manner of attentions and respect. 30

Fleury...racontait à merveille (qualité qui était assez commune
sous Louis XIV, et qui n'est guère plus à la mode aujourd'hui).'
Louis himself was a master in the art.

24. **fount:** var. *fund.*

28. Var. *she was as proud of him as of herself.*

29. **received the like:** *recevoit le réciproque* appears to be a
phrase coined by Saint-Simon on the analogy of *rendre le
réciproque.*

57. VOLTAIRE

Quoi qu'il en soit, Voltaire, même au début, avant le rire bouffon et le rire décharné, Voltaire dans sa fleur de gaieté et de malice était bien, par tempérament comme par principes, le poète et l'artiste d'une époque dont le but et l'inspiration avouée était le plaisir, avant tout le plaisir.

Mais les cercles les plus agréables ne suffisaient point à Voltaire et ne pouvaient l'enfermer: il en sortait, à tout moment, je l'ai dit, et par des défauts et par des parties plus sérieuses et louables. Il en sortait parce qu'il avait le *diable au corps*, et parce qu'il avait aussi des étincelles du dieu. Se moquer est bien amusant; mais ce n'est qu'un mince plaisir si l'on ne se moque des gens à leur nez et à leur barbe, si les 'sots ennemis' qu'on drape n'en sont pas informés et désolés; de là mille saillies, mille escarmouches imprudentes qui devenaient entre eux et lui des guerres à mort. Le théâtre le livrait au public par un plus noble côté. L'histoire ne le conviait pas moins à devenir un auteur célèbre dans le sens le plus respectable du mot, le peintre de son siècle et du siècle précédent. Voltaire s'intéressait à tout ce qui se passait dans le monde auprès de lui ou loin de lui; il y prenait part, il y prenait feu; il s'occupait des affaires des autres, et, pour peu que sa fibre en fût émue, il en faisait les siennes propres.... Ce *diable d'homme* ne pouvait donc,

1. **Be that as it may.** The preceding sentences were: 'On sent en plus d'un endroit une sorte de parti pris de rire. Il ne rit pas seulement, il ricane; il y a un peu de tic, c'est le défaut. A la longue, on prend toujours la ride de son sourire.'
2. **cackle...grin**: *rire*, qualified by an epithet, is often best translated by a specific word: 'guffaw', 'snigger', 'chuckle', etc.
   emaciated: var. *cadaverous*.
3. Var. *in the flower of his merry mischievous spring-time*. N.B. *la malice* is not "malice", but 'maliciousness', mischievousness, sprightliness, roguishness.
5. **was.** The French text has *était*, not *étaient*, as if *but* and *inspiration* together formed a single idea. Var. *which found its object and inspiration in pleasure*.

57. VOLTAIRE

Be that as it may, Voltaire, even at the outset, before the days of the merry-andrew cackle and the emaciated grin, Voltaire in his gayest, sprightliest hey-day was clearly, as regards both temperament and principles, the poet and the painter of an age whose avowed aim and inspiration was 5 pleasure, pleasure before all else.

But the most congenial circles were not enough for Voltaire and could not contain him; he was constantly *escaping*, as I have said before, by reason both of failings and of more serious and praiseworthy qualities, escaping because he had 10 a bit of the devil in him and because he had also sparks of the divine. To make game of people is quite entertaining, but it is poor sport unless you can do it to their very faces, right under their very noses, unless the 'addle-pated enemies' you are ridiculing are made to know it and feel annoyed; 15 hence, innumerable reckless sallies and skirmishings which developed into wars to the death between him and them. The stage showed the public a nobler side of his character. History was also inviting him to become a famous author, in the worthiest sense of the term, the painter of his own age 20 and the preceding one. Voltaire was interested in everything that was going on in the world, near him or far away; he took his share in it all and caught fire in the process; he looked after other people's affairs and, were his deeper feelings in any way aroused, he made their case his own. 25 This 'astounding creature' could not therefore in any event,

8. **contain him**: var. *keep him in.*
escaping: var. *breaking away, breaking bounds.*
12. **quite entertaining**: var. *highly diverting.*
14. Var. *unless their noses are pulled.*
24. Var. *took up the cudgels for other people.*

Var. *were his inmost being in any way stirred.* N.B. *pour peu que* = if only, if at all, if ever so little. It is roughly equivalent to *pourvu que*, but with an additional limitation: *pour peu que vous connaissiez les femmes...* = if you know women ever so slightly.

dans aucun cas, malgré ses velléités de retraite et de riante sagesse, se confiner à l'existence brillante et douce d'un Horace. SAINTE-BEUVE, *Causeries du Lundi*, t. XIII.

27. **leanings toward**: *velléités* (cp. No. 33) sometimes = half-hearted thoughts, sometimes = hankerings. A preceding passage had: 'Il écrit à Madame de Bernières...il fait des rêves de

for all his leanings toward seclusion and laughing philosophy, restrict himself to the brilliant and placid existence of a Horace.

retraite délicieuse avec elle dans sa maison de La Rivière-Bourdet.' Var. *although he toyed with the idea of retirement and happy pursuit of wisdom.*
   28. **placid**: var. *peaceful, uneventful.*

58. JUGEMENT D'ENSEMBLE SUR VOLTAIRE

Rien n'est plus difficile que de porter un jugement d'ensemble sur Voltaire. Il est tout pétri d'amour-propre; il en a de toutes les sortes: entêtement de ses idées, vanité d'auteur, vanité de bourgeois enrichi et anobli. Il est tout nerfs, irritable, bilieux, rancunier, vindicatif, intéressé, menteur, flagorneur de toutes les puissances, à la fois impudent et servile, familier et plat. Mais ce même homme a aimé ses amis, même ceux qui le trahissaient, qui le volaient, comme ce parasite de Thieriot. La moitié de ses ennemis étaient ses obligés, *ses ingrats*. Intéressé comme il s'est montré souvent, il abandonnait sans cesse à ses amis, à ses libraires, à ses comédiens, à quelque pauvre hère, le produit de ses œuvres. Jamais gueux de lettres ne trouva sa bourse fermée. Il se fit le défenseur de toutes les causes justes, de tous les innocents que les institutions ou les hommes opprimaient. Amour du bruit, réclame de journaliste, je le veux bien: horreur physique du sang et de la souffrance, je le veux bien encore: mais il a aussi un vif sentiment de la justice, un réel instinct d'humanité, de bienfaisance, de générosité. Au fond, il y eut toujours en Voltaire un terrible gamin; il eut

1. **to sum up**: var. *to give a comprehensive (general) estimate of*.
2. Var. *The raw material of his make-up is self-esteem (self-conceit)*; *pétri* means 'kneaded up'; i.e. what is called *la pâte* or *la pâte humaine* was in his case egotism.
3. **obstinate persistence in**: var. *persistent clinging to, infatuation with*.
5. **rancorous**: var. *unforgiving, keeping up spite, spiteful*.
7. **obsequious**: *plat* = too humble, cringing, cp. *un plat personnage*.
familiar: var. *too familiar*.
8. **loved his friends.** The changes of tense (*est* until now, *a aimé* here, *se fit, manqua*, etc., further on) should be noted, though they cannot all be reflected in English. The present = Voltaire's character, summed up, *is* such and such. The perfect (*a aimé, s'est montré*) is more vivid than the past continuous (*aimait*) and contains the notion of 'at different times' = he *loved* the friends he had at different periods of his life, *showed himself*

58. GENERAL ESTIMATE OF VOLTAIRE

Nothing is more difficult to do than to sum up Voltaire. His make-up is all egotism; he has every variety of it (obstinate persistence in his own ideas, author's vanity, vanity of the middle-class man risen to wealth and rank). He is all nerves, irritable, atrabilious, rancorous, vindictive, self-seeking, mendacious, toadying to all the powers that be, at once impudent and servile, obsequious and familiar. But this same man loved his friends, even those who betrayed or robbed him, like the parasite Thieriot. Half his enemies were under some obligation to him ('my ingrates'). Self-seeking though he often showed himself to be, he was continually making over the proceeds of his books to his friends, his publishers, his actors, or else to some starveling. No needy scribbler ever found his purse closed. He constituted himself defender of all just causes, all innocent victims of oppression by institutions or by men. Love of notoriety? A journalist's self-advertisement?—Granted. Physical horror of pain and bloodshed?—That can be granted, too. But he has also a keen sense of justice, a genuine instinctive feeling for humanity, for charity, for generosity. Really there always was in Voltaire something of the unruly urchin, an infinite frivolity and impish-

---

on different occasions self-seeking. Use of the past historic implies that Voltaire's life is considered as something entirely in the past and reviewed as a completed whole.

10. **'my ingrates'**: var. *'his ingrates', as he called them.*
14. Var. *No down-at-heel literary man.*
Var. *He championed all,* etc.
17. Var. *Explain it if you like as...as a journalist's instinct for advertisement or as a loathing for,* etc.
19. **also**: var. *in addition to that.*
20. **charity**: *bienfaisance* includes support of all the public charities usually maintained in this country by subscriptions from private individuals, often in present-day France by the Church or by the State.
22. **unruly urchin**: var. *irrepressible small boy.*
impishness: for *malice* see No. 57, note 3.

infiniment de légèreté, de malice. Il manqua de gravité, de décence, de respect d'autrui et de soi-même : qui donc en ce siècle avait souci d'embellir son être intérieur? qui donc n'était pas prêt à absoudre les actes *qui ne font de mal à personne, et font du bien à quelqu'un,* mensonges ou autres? Rousseau peut-être; et nul autre.

LANSON, *Histoire de la littérature française.*

24. **who**: *donc* in *qui donc* usually expresses impatience = who, I ask you? who then? who indeed? It seems here sufficiently rendered by 'but who'.

Var. *cared anything for (troubled about) improving his soul (inner self).*

ness. He lacked gravity, decency, respect for others and self-respect; but who in that age had a care for improvement of his inward being? Who indeed was not prepared to condone the acts that 'do nobody any harm and somebody some good', whether white lies or anything else? Rousseau, possibly, and no other.

27. **white lies.** We take *les actes...mensonges ou autres* to mean anything which by word or deed helps a friend but is not in accordance with strict morality (political or financial integrity, truthfulness, etc.).

59. LE COMMANDANT GENESTAS

Espèce de Bayard sans faste, M. Pierre-Joseph Genestas n'offrait en lui rien de poétique ni rien de romanesque, tant il paraissait vulgaire. Sa tenue était celle d'un homme cossu. Quoiqu'il n'eût que sa solde pour fortune, et que sa retraite fût tout son avenir, néanmoins, semblable aux vieux loups du commerce auxquels les malheurs ont fait une expérience qui avoisine l'entêtement, le chef d'escadron gardait toujours devant lui deux années de solde et ne dépensait jamais ses appointements. Il était si peu joueur, qu'il regardait sa botte quand en compagnie on demandait un rentrant ou quelque supplément de pari pour l'écarté. Mais, s'il ne se permettait rien d'extraordinaire, il ne manquait à aucune chose d'usage. Ses uniformes lui duraient plus longtemps qu'à tout autre officier du régiment, par suite des soins qu'inspire la médiocrité de fortune, et dont l'habitude était devenue chez lui machinale. Peut-être l'eût-on soupçonné d'avarice sans l'admirable désintéressement, sans la facilité fraternelle avec lesquels il ouvrait sa bourse à quelque jeune étourdi ruiné par un coup de carte ou par toute autre folie. Il semblait avoir perdu jadis de grosses sommes au jeu, tant il mettait de délicatesse à obliger; il ne se croyait point le droit de contrôler les actions de son débiteur et ne lui parlait jamais de sa créance.

Enfant de troupe, seul dans le monde, il s'était fait une patrie de l'armée et de son régiment une famille. Aussi, rarement recherchait-on le motif de sa respectable économie; on se plaisait à l'attribuer au désir assez naturel d'augmenter la somme de son bien-être pendant ses vieux jours. A la veille de devenir lieutenant-colonel de cavalerie, il était présumable que son ambition consistait à se retirer dans

4. Var. *though he had only his pay to live on.*
12. **extravagance**: var. *extras.*
21. **considerate**: var. *tactful.*
23. **the loan**: var. *his claim upon him.*
24. **Born and bred in the barracks.** 'Born' may outrun the evidence but 'bred' is correct: *un enfant de troupe* is a soldier's son or orphan who is brought up at State expense and receives his schooling more or less 'in the barracks'.

59. MAJOR GENESTAS

A sort of unostentatious Bayard, Pierre-Joseph Genestas had apparently nothing poetical or romantic about him, so commonplace was he in appearance. He dressed like a man who was well off. Though he had nothing beyond his pay, and no other prospects than his pension, yet—resembling in this the tough old business men who from unfortunate experiences have learned caution bordering on obstinacy —he always kept two years' pay by him and never lived up to his income. Major Genestas was so little given to gambling that when at any social gathering someone was wanted to take a hand or put down an extra stake at écarté, he would look at his boots. But while he allowed himself no extravagance, he did all the usual things. His uniforms lasted him longer than any other officer's in the regiment, because of the careful treatment which is prompted by limited means and which, from long habit, had to him become second nature. He might perhaps have come under suspicion of meanness but for the admirably disinterested and easy, brotherly way in which he loosened his purse-strings to any harum-scarum young fellow ruined at cards or by any such folly. He seemed to have lost heavily himself at one time, so considerate was he in obliging; nor did he feel entitled to keep a check on his debtor's actions and he never alluded to the loan.

Born and bred in the barracks, alone in the world, he had made the army his fatherland, and the regiment his family. People therefore seldom inquired into the motives for his praiseworthy thriftiness; they liked to ascribe it to the natural enough desire for increased comfort in old age. As he was on the point of attaining the rank of lieutenant-colonel in the cavalry, it was to be presumed that his ambition took the form of retiring to a place in the country,

30. Var. *his ambition presumably was to retire*, etc.
31. place: *une campagne* is a house or small estate in the country (cp. *une propriété*). Cp. A. Bellessort, *Revue de Paris*, November 1937, p. 41: 'un superbe mouton mérinos que le docteur [le père d'Eugène Sue] faisait élever dans *sa campagne* proche de la ville.'

quelque campagne avec la retraite et les épaulettes de colonel. Après la manœuvre, si les jeunes officiers causaient de Genestas, ils le rangeaient dans la classe des hommes qui ont obtenu au collège les prix d'excellence, et qui durant leur vie restent exacts, probes, sans passions, utiles et fades comme le pain blanc; mais les gens sérieux le jugeaient bien différemment. Souvent quelque regard, souvent une expression pleine de sens comme l'est la parole du Sauvage, échappaient à cet homme et attestaient en lui les orages de l'âme. Bien étudié, son front calme accusait le pouvoir d'imposer silence aux passions et de les refouler au fond de son cœur, pouvoir chèrement conquis par l'habitude des dangers et des malheurs imprévus de la guerre.

BALZAC, *Le Médecin de campagne.*

34. **got all the prizes:** we use the stock phrase, but *prix d'excellence* are properly class-prizes.

36. **uninteresting:** var. *unexciting.*

37. **plain bread:** var. *household bread*: it has changed its colour at various periods, from brown in the sixteenth century to white at the present day; *pain blanc* means *ordinary* bread— at a time when it is comparatively refined, and therefore correspondingly *fade* or tasteless.

39–41. **speech:** ? *utterance.* The 'Savage' is brought in un-

with the rank and pension of colonel. When the younger
officers after drill happened to talk about Genestas, they
put him down as one of those men who got all the prizes at
school and who for the rest of their lives go on being exact, 35
conscientious, passionless, as necessary, and as uninteresting,
as plain bread. But thoughtful people judged him quite
differently. Often a look—or often an expression pregnant
with meaning as the speech of the Savage—would escape
him and betray the storms raging in the soul. His calm 40
forehead, when carefully examined, was evidence of his
power to silence the passions and force them back into the
heart, a power dearly bought by familiarity with the dangers
and unforeseen calamities of war.

expectedly, Balzac being interested in the 'sciences' of his day,
whether ethnology or phrenology; hence *étudié* and *front* are
to be translated, not by 'studied' and 'brow', but by the more
'phrenological' terms 'examined' and 'forehead', and *l'âme* not
by 'his soul', but by 'the soul'. *Les orages de l'âme* are mental
states discoverable by 'scientific' observation.

44. **unforeseen**: *imprévus* goes with *malheurs* only, not with
dangers. In war, dangers in general can be easily foreseen, but
the particular form they take when they occur may be unforeseen.

60. M. BERNARD

Sur les voies du triage pesaient les longues rames de wagons non couverts, chargés de charbon, de gueuses de fonte, et ceux aux toits cintrés, vernis de bruine. Le trafic de coton et de laine des ports, de métal vers les aciéries, et les expéditions des houillères donnaient beaucoup. En plus des quatre-vingt-un trains réguliers de marchandises, la gare avait reçu, dans la nuit, onze facultatifs. Cette poussée achevait l'encombrement chronique et total du samedi.

L'humidité souveraine s'alimentait aux flaques crêpées par le vent. M. Bernard, le plus ancien sous-chef, sortait, à l'éclaircie, de son bureau poussiéreux. Il montrait bien son caractère, en osant se risquer avec une situation aussi chargée: trois mille wagons en gare, à s'abriter de la pluie à huit heures du matin.... La tranquillité définitive de cet homme que ne tourmentait aucune espérance, devenait précieuse dans les occasions de désarroi. Le petit personnel se réglait sur la paix contagieuse du sous-chef fixé au calme par le dégoût.

M. Bernard traversa les deux voies nues et regarda la manœuvre débrancher les trains arrivés la nuit. Le surveillant Doucet lui expliqua la situation: 'Tout le travail reste à faire. Le 7205 est entier à trier sur 9.... Le 4320, le 4340 sont annoncés. On ne connaît pas leur composition; je n'ai pas de voies pour les recevoir. Il n'y a plus moyen d'y arriver.' M. Bernard lui imposa le bienfait de sa parole douce comme une bénédiction. 'On y arrivera. Depuis vingt ans je vois le triage plein. Les trains sont toujours entrés.'

D'avoir connu tant de surveillants de manœuvres renoncer à éclaircir des situations qui, cependant, s'éclaircissaient, M. Bernard savait attendre de la Nécessité qu'elle assure que ce qui doit être fait, soit fait. PIERRE HAMP, *Le Rail*.

2. **pig-iron**: will do here. But *gueuse de fonte* is properly 'pig', 'pigs', whereas pig-iron, i.e. cast-iron in pigs or ingots, as first reduced from the ore, is *fer en gueuse* or *gueuse de fer*.

vans: *un wagon* is a carriage (coach), or a truck, or a van, so that *ceux aux toits cintrés* = 'those with the rounded roofs', (or, as *ceux aux* is colloquial, 'the rounded-top ones)', are just the *wagons* which we call 'vans'.

60. M. BERNARD

The sidings were cluttered up with long lines of open trucks carrying coal and pig-iron, and vans with their rounded tops shiny with drizzle. Cotton and wool traffic from the ports, metal traffic for the steel-works and consignments of coal from the mines were at their heaviest, and, in addition to the eighty-one regular goods trains, the shunting yard had taken in eleven specials during the night. This pressure put the finishing touch to the complete block chronic on Saturdays.

The all-pervading damp fed on the puddles rippling in the wind. When the rain stopped, M. Bernard, the senior assistant-inspector, emerged from his dusty office. It was very much in character that he should have ventured, in such congested conditions—three thousand trucks in the yard—to take shelter from the rain at 8 a.m.... The absolute imperturbability of the man, untroubled as he was by any expectations whatsoever, proved invaluable on panic occasions. The employees took example by the infectious coolness of an official who always kept calm because utterly disillusioned.

M. Bernard stepped across the two clear through-lines and watched the trains which had come in during the night being shunted and broken up. Doucet, the man in charge, explained the position: 'We haven't made a start on the job. 7205, the whole of her, has got to be shunted on to 9.... 4320 and 4340 are signalled. We don't know anything about their make-up; I haven't lines for them. The thing just can't be done.' M. Bernard applied the balm of his words which came soothing as a benediction: 'We'll do it all right. Twenty years now I've seen the yard full up. The trains always got in.'

Having known so many men in charge of shunting operations give up trying to straighten out things which nevertheless did straighten themselves out, M. Bernard could trust Necessity to ensure that what has to be done *is* done.

4. **consignments:** var. *deliveries.*
5. **at their heaviest:** *donnaient* is intransitive = were in full swing; cp. *la lampe* **donne** *bien; la machine* **donne** *à plein rendement.*
10. Var. *When it cleared up.*
17. **employees:** *le petit personnel* is the subordinate staff, as distinguished from the higher officials, *le haut personnel.*
30. Var. *liquidate (deal with) situations.*

61. LES CHAMPENOIS

Plus on les regarde, plus on trouve que leurs gestes, les formes de leurs visages annoncent une race à part. Il y a un mois, en Flandre, surtout en Hollande, ce n'étaient que grands traits mal agencés, osseux, trop saillants; à mesure qu'on avançait vers les marécages, le corps devenait plus lymphatique, le teint plus pâle, l'œil plus vitreux, plus engorgé dans la chair blafarde. En Allemagne, je découvrais dans les regards une expression de vague mélancolie ou de résignation inerte; d'autres fois, l'œil bleu gardait jusque dans la vieillesse sa limpidité virginale; et la joue rose des jeunes hommes, la vaillante pousse des corps superbes annonçait l'intégrité et la vigueur de la sève primitive. Ici, et à cinquante lieues à l'entour de Paris, la beauté manque, mais l'intelligence brille, non pas la verve pétulante et la gaieté bavarde des méridionaux, mais l'esprit leste, juste, avisé, malin, prompt à l'ironie, qui trouve son amusement dans les mécomptes d'autrui. Ces bourgeois, sur le pas de leur porte, clignent de l'œil derrière vous; ces apprentis derrière l'établi se montrent du doigt votre ridicule et vont gloser. On n'entre jamais ici dans un atelier sans inquiétude; fussiez-vous prince et brodé d'or, ces gamins en manches sales vous auront pesé en une minute, tout gros monsieur que vous êtes, et il est presque sûr que vous leur servirez de marionnette à la sortie du soir.

TAINE, La Fontaine et ses Fables.

2. **denote:** var. *herald*, since Taine is returning from abroad and coming into contact with the frontier population before the more typically French inhabitants of the interior.
4. **were to be seen:** for *Ce n'étaient que*, see No. 5, note 8.
8. **detect:** var. *discover*.
13. Var. *within a radius of fifty leagues from Paris*.

61. THE INHABITANTS OF CHAMPAGNE

The longer you look at them, the more you become convinced
that their gestures and the shape of their faces denote a race
apart. A month ago, in Flanders, in Holland more particularly, only large features were to be seen, ill-assorted, bony
and unduly prominent; as one went on toward the marsh-
lands, the habit became more lymphatic, the complexion
paler, the eye more glassy, deeper imbedded in the pasty
face. In Germany, I could detect an expression of vague
melancholy or of listless resignation in the glance; in other
cases, the blue eyes preserved their virginal clearness into
old age; and the young men's rosy cheeks and strong,
splendidly developed bodies proclaimed the integrity and
the vigour of the original stock. Here, and for fifty leagues
round Paris, beauty is far to seek, but intelligence shines
out, not the lively verve, the garrulous gaiety of the
southern French, but the type of mind which is sprightly,
well-balanced, shrewd and sharp, turning readily to irony,
and finding food for amusement in other people's misadventures. The worthy townsfolk, on their doorsteps, give
a wink after you go by; these apprentices at the bench draw
each other's attention to your ridiculous side and will be
jeering before long. One never sets foot in a workshop here
without misgivings; were you a prince and all in gold lace,
these dirty-sleeved little rascals will have you sized up in a
minute, important person though you be, and it is practically certain they will be guying you when they leave the
works at closing time.

15. **lively**: *pétulant* is *not* "petulant".
17. **shrewd**: var. *wary*.
18. **misadventures**: var. *mishaps*.
19. **townsfolk**: var. *folk*.
21. For *ridicules* see also No. 56, note 15.
24. **sized**: var. *weighed*.
26. Var. *you will be their Aunt Sally*.

62. LE HOBEREAU

Sur cette frontière indécise où le Limousin se fait moins âpre et le Périgord plus sauvage, on a toujours vu foisonner une petite noblesse terrienne, gourmande, besogneuse et faraude. Quand elle donne sa fleur, elle produit les Mortemart, les Noailles ou les Saint-Chamans; quand elle demeure à l'état fruste, elle continue les Pourceaugnac. Partout vous voyez en passant, derrière nos arbres, sur nos coteaux, une grosse ferme à pigeonnier, une maison flanquée de tourelles. Beaucoup de ces vieilles bâtisses ne servent plus que de greniers ou de granges, quand elles ne sont pas un perchoir pour tous les oiseaux de nuit. Tourmentés d'un désir de fortune, les maîtres ont fait comme les métayers: ils sont partis eux aussi pour la ville, où volontiers ils acceptent ces professions ambulantes—agents de compagnies d'assurances, représentants de maisons d'automobiles—qui tiennent de la

1. **ill-defined**: var. *indeterminate*; for *indécis* cp. No. 13: 'L'Aventin...c'est un lieu indécis', etc., and No. 1, note 18.

the Limousin...Périgord. For 'the' see No. 25, note 6.

2. **inhospitable**: var. *rough, rugged, stern, bleak*.

there have always been: *vu* is not to be translated. Cp. 'le pays qui m'a *vu* naître' = the country which gave me birth. 'Tout le monde était étonné de le *voir* revenir' = everybody was surprised at his return.

3. **small landed gentry**: 'small' may be unnecessary, cp. *la grande noblesse, la petite noblesse* = nobility and gentry.

fond of good living: var. *epicurean, great eaters*.

4. **impecunious**: var. *needy, necessitous*.

uppish: var. *affected, snobbish, pretentious, having a good conceit of themselves, holding their heads high*; *faraud* is used properly of rustics, dressed up in their best and yet appearing ridiculous to sophisticated eyes; here it has a more general sense. Cp. Tharaud, op. cit. p. 34: 'Pourtant je les aime, ces hobereaux. J'aime leur pauvreté altière, leur âme rustique et *faraude*', and Daudet, *Le Nabab*, p. 210: 'Leur mère me fait un peu peur; c'est une grande dame tout à fait....Mais eux, les enfants, je suis sûre qu'ils ne sont pas *farauds* et qu'ils aimeraient bien leur vieille grand'mère.'

5. **Mortemarts**: see No. 56, note 12.
6. **in the rough**: var. *in the unpolished state*; *fruste* denotes

62. THE SQUIREEN

On that ill-defined borderland where the Limousin grows less inhospitable and Périgord wilder, there have always been plenty of small landed gentry, fond of good living, impecunious and uppish. When they give of their best, they produce your Mortemarts, your Noailles or Saint-Chamans; when they remain in the rough, they carry on the line of the Pourceaugnacs. Everywhere, behind our trees, on our hillsides, you can see as you go by a big farmstead with a dovecote, or a house with turrets at the sides. Many of these ramshackle old buildings are now used only as granaries or barns, when they are not just roosting-places for all manner of night-birds. Tormented by an urge for riches, the landlords have gone the way of the tenant-farmers; they have migrated like them to the towns, where they often take up those itinerant callings—insurance agent or traveller for a motor firm—which have a certain affinity to shooting and

properly the worn surface of a coin or a statue. It is used also of a surface which has not been dressed, and figuratively, with the meaning 'rough', 'unpolished', 'uncultivated'; cp. No. 51: *à l'état* de culs-de-sac.

carry on: var. *perpetuate*.

7. **Pourceaugnacs.** M. de Pourceaugnac, in Molière's comedy of that name, is the typical country squire come to town, to be fleeced, a Bob Acres.

8. **dovecote.** The significance of the *pigeonnier* is that in feudal times the owners of the place were entitled to keep pigeons, a privilege reserved to the lord of the manor.

10. **ramshackle**: *une bâtisse* is usually a ramshackle building, or one with no architectural pretensions.

12. **for riches**: var. *to make their fortune*.

landlords: var. *land-owners*.

13. **gone the way of**: var. *followed the example of* (*in the footsteps of*).

tenant-farmers: *métayers* are tenants who pay in kind.

14. **often**: for this sense of *volontiers*, cp. *Le merle fait* **volontiers** *son nid dans les buissons*.

16. **have a certain affinity to**: var. *are akin to, have in them an element of*.

chasse et du jeu et qui les font vivre au café. Ceux qui restent, ceux qui s'attardent entre nos haies plantées de chênes donnent leur marque à ces campagnes et en font un pays à part, archaïque et romanesque. Presque tous, ils mènent entre eux une existence de bohème campagnarde. Quand ils ont vendu leur bétail, leur récolte ou leur bois, ils s'en vont faire la fête à Périgueux ou à Limoges, le temps que dure leur argent; après quoi ils rentrent chez eux, où ils vivent toute l'année de légumes et de volailles, voire de chasse en la saison.

C'est là notre vrai hobereau. Ni l'ambition ni la gêne ne parviennent à l'arracher à ces arpents de terre où il est un personnage. Si quelqu'un de ses amis plus hardi lui raconte sa réussite dans quelque contrée lointaine, à Toulouse ou à Bordeaux, il écoute, rêve un moment; il compare son humble destin à cette large vie qu'on lui vante; il s'exalte, célèbre à l'envi cette existence de Cocagne, que son penchant naturel à l'exagération embellit. Vous croiriez que lui aussi va partir. Mais non, il reste dans son pigeonnier, malcontent et satisfait tout ensemble de sa médiocrité, et s'attarde à songer parfois, dans quelque chemin creux qui mène à sa gentilhommière ou bien en face d'un beau tournant de la Vienne ou de la Dordogne, à une vie chimérique dans un pays fortuné.

J. ET J. THARAUD, *La Maîtresse Servante.*

17. Var. *which let them pass their time in the cafés.*
18. **the oaks in the hedgerows**: *plantées* in *haies plantées de chênes* is not to be translated; cp. *les cours plantées d'arbustes* in No. 51, line 23. The oaks grew in the hedges and formed part of them.
21. **rustic**: var. *countrified.*
22. **cattle**: var. *livestock.*
25. **game**: var. *plus game.* The function of *voire* is to bring into prominence a word following it. The effect may be sufficiently shown by putting a dash before the word so emphasized; "game, if you please" would be rather strong.
27. Var. *There is our real Squireen for you.*
28. Var. *avails (has power) to uproot him.*
29. Var. *a more enterprising friend.*

THE SQUIREEN

gambling and give an opportunity for café life. Those who
stay on, those who linger here by the oaks in the hedgerows,
set their mark on this countryside and make it a region
apart, old-world and romantic. Nearly all of them lead, 20
among themselves, a life of rustic Bohemianism. Once they
have sold their cattle, crops or timber, off they go to have
a good time at Périgueux or Limoges, for as long as their
money lasts; after which, home they come again to live the
whole year round on vegetables and poultry—game in the 25
shooting season.

And there you have our true Squireen. Neither ambition
nor yet penury can tear him away from these acres where he
is somebody. Should one of his more adventurous friends
tell him his tale of success in a far country, Toulouse or 30
Bordeaux, he will listen, and indulge in a brief day-dream;
he compares his humble destiny with the life of affluence
extolled to him; he works himself up, grows louder than any
in his praises of that land of plenty which his natural
tendency to exaggeration leads him to paint in glowing 35
colours. You would think that he, too, was about to take
his departure. Not a bit of it. He stays on in his dovecote,
discontented and at the same time satisfied with his undis-
tinguished lot, and sometimes, as he saunters along some
sunken lane leading to his manor, or looks across at some 40
lovely bend of the Vienne or the Dordogne, he pauses to
dream of a visionary life in a land of heart's desire.

30. Var. *in some distant part of the country*.

32. Var. *ampler (fuller) life*; for *cette* large *vie* cp. Il gagne
largement sa vie. Ses déplacements sont *largement* payés = He
is allowed ample travelling expenses.

33. Var. *he praises, none better, that land*, etc.

36. Var. *he, too, is just off; he is off, too; he is going, too*.

37. **Not a bit of it**: var. *Not at all; O dear, no*.

38. **discontented**: but as *malcontent* is preferred to the usual
mécontent we might prefer the less usual and similar English
term; cp. Stevenson, *Across the Plains* (O.E.D.): 'He has ever
since been *malcontent* with literature.'

40. **sunken lane**: for *chemin creux* see No. 24, note 12.

Var. *manor house*: for *gentilhommière*, cp. *fourmilière, taupinière*.

V. CONVERSATIONAL

63. LA GRÈVE

Philippe. La grève gagne? Nous allons l'avoir ici?

Gaucherond. Oui, et par Langouët....Avant-hier, je n'ai pas voulu lui faire du tort. C'est comme si on était du même sang, quand on a fait donner à quelqu'un ses premiers coups de varlope....Mais c'est lui qui mène la grève, et c'est lui le saboteur.

Philippe. Eh bien, moi, je continue à le croire incapable de cette infamie. La grève, c'est une chose; le sabotage, c'en est une autre. J'admets la première, mais l'autre? Cette lâcheté? La travail des camarades détérioré, gâché?

Gaucherond. Et le travail des camarades empêché? Car, c'est ça, la grève. Non, non, monsieur Philippe. Grève et sabotage, sabotage et grève, ça se vaut et c'est bon pour les propres à rien. Je vais avoir soixante ans, moi, j'en avais seize quand je suis entré chez M. Firmin et trente-cinq lorsqu'il a cédé son fonds à monsieur votre père. Est-ce que j'ai jamais été en grève? J'ai fait mon affaire qui était de travailler mes bouts de bois comme le patron a fait la sienne qui était de me commander ma besogne et de me la payer. Et pour cela, je n'ai pas eu besoin de leurs syndicats. Quand ils en ont fondé un, je n'ai rien voulu savoir. 'Je suis assez grand garçon, que je leur ai dit, pour faire mes affaires tout seul.' Et c'est comme ça qu'on est un homme libre.

Philippe. Il n'y a pas que la liberté au monde, Gaucherond. Il y a la fraternité et la justice.

Gaucherond. Ah çà! est-ce qu'ils vous auraient mis dedans, vous aussi, monsieur Philippe, avec leurs grandes phrases? Faites excuse, mais je vous ai vu haut comme ça. La fraternité? Les quinze mille balles aux députés socialistes

---

Note. **Gaucherond...Langouët...Firmin.** We have altered these names because they are immaterial and because they would be fatal to the British atmosphere which it seems worth while attempting to produce here.

4. Var. *I didn't like to let him down.*
6. **plane**: precisely, *trying plane, jointer*.
22. Var. *I wouldn't hear of it; I had no use for it.*

63. THE STRIKE

PHILIP. The strike's spreading? We're going to get it here, are we?

GARRATT. Yes, and all along of Langton!...The day before yesterday, I didn't want to get him into trouble. Blood's thicker than water, when you've put a young chap up to using his plane. But *he's* the one that's leading the strike; he's doing the sabotage, he is.

PHILIP. Well, for my part I still think he is incapable of such blackguardly conduct. A strike is one thing; sabotage is quite another. I can understand the one, but— that cowardly business? The other fellows' work all damaged and spoiled?

GARRATT. And what about stopping the other lads working? For that's what a strike is. No, no, Mr Philip. Strike and sabotage, says I, sabotage and strike, it's six and half-a-dozen, and all right for the wasters. I'm nigh sixty, I am; I was sixteen when I started for Mr Farmer and thirty-five when your father took over the business. Have I ever been out on strike? I've done my job—working away at my bits o' wood, the same as the master's done his—giving me out my work and paying me for it. I didn't need their Unions for that! When they started one, I'd have nothing to do with it. 'I'm a big enough lad', I says to them, says I, 'to look after myself.' And that's the way a man's a free man.

PHILIP. There are other things in the world besides freedom, Garratt. There's brotherhood and justice.

GARRATT. Crikey! So they've been coming it over you as well, Mr Philip, with their grand words? Begging your pardon, but I knew you when you were that high! Brotherhood? That'll be the six hundred quid for the Socialist

---

31. **the six hundred quid**: *les quinze mille balles* (*balles* is slang for *francs*) was the sum fixed for payment of French members of Parliament (not without considerable criticism) when the rate of exchange was still 25.

qui montent le coup à de pauvres ouvriers! (*Levant les bras au ciel.*) La justice? vous trouvez ça juste, vous, cette unification de salaires qu'ils réclament dans leur grève d'aujourd'hui? La paye égale pour tous, hommes et femmes, capables et incapables? Le travail d'une bonne main, moi, par exemple, qui ai quarante ans de métier dans les pattes, serait payé comme celui d'un sabot? Mais, c'est absurde. Mais tout est inégal dans le monde! Tout! Tout! Tout!

PAUL BOURGET, *La Barricade.*

32. Lifting, etc. We take the phrase from G. Moore, *Ave atque Vale*, p. 269; Blunden, *Undertones of War*, p. 21, says 'flung

M.P.'s, them as stuffs up the poor working-man. (*Lifting his arms above his head.*) Justice? So that's what you call just, this flat rate o' wages they're out for in this 'ere strike of theirs? Equal pay all round, men and women, skilled and 35 unskilled? A good hand, me for one, forty years at the job, getting the same pay for his work as a bungler? Why, it's perfect nonsense. Why, there's nothing equal in the world! Nothing! Nothing! Nothing!

his arms heavenwards'. It may be doubted, however, if the British workman is given to any such gesture.

36. Var. *with forty years' work in the trade gone through my fingers.*

64. QU'EST-CE QUE LA JUSTICE?

Guéret. Vraiment, je ne comprends pas ton attitude vis-à-vis de ces gaillards-là! Pour un peu, tout à l'heure, tu allais me désavouer devant le père Brosse, et ça, comme maladresse, c'eût été du raffinement! D'ailleurs, tu es décidément ce qu'on peut appeler un drôle de pistolet. Ou bien des susceptibilités excessives, des explosions à tout casser, un déchaînement d'autorité, ou bien la faiblesse. Jamais de mesure!... Cependant c'est avec de la mesure et de la fermeté qu'on mène les hommes, mon petit....

Robert. Monsieur Guéret, nous n'allons pas reprendre pour la centième fois cet échange de vues, puisqu'il y a un mot sur lequel nous n'arrivons pas à nous mettre d'accord.

Guéret. Tu vas me sortir encore ta 'Justice'?

Robert. Je ne vois pas de fermeté, je ne vois pas de mesure sans justice. Il y a là trois idées inséparables.

Guéret (*sans violence*). Mais, sacrée tête de mule, quand tu auras dîné vingt ans avec ce beau mot-là, tu ne connaîtras pas encore son sens exact. Pour le connaître, il faudrait qu'il prît à la justice la fantaisie de devenir absolue. Mais tant qu'elle s'obstinera à n'être qu'une manifestation de nos consciences, et tant que nos consciences différeront comme nos moustaches et nos goûts, il sera indispensable, surtout dans la direction d'une industrie comme la nôtre, de faire une moyenne entre *nos* justices qui ont une forme, et *la* justice qui est un fantôme.

Robert (*tranquillement mais avec foi*). Non, non, il y a une justice évidente.

Guéret. Où donc? Les gens qui font profession de l'appliquer ne savent pas comment s'y prendre. Les tribunaux d'appel réforment les jugements des tribunaux de

---

21. **living on it**: the metaphor is not quite that of *dîné avec*, which means rather 'living on familiar terms with'. In both cases, however, the general sense is the same = 'using as a household word'.

64. WHAT IS JUSTICE?

GUÉRET. Really, I can't understand your attitude to these fellows. The least thing more, just now, and you'd have let me down before old Brosse, and that would have been putting your foot in it, beautifully! You know, you really *are* a funny chap! Either you're frightfully touchy, throwing your weight about, the master coming it over the men. Or else you simply truckle under. Never anything in moderation! And yet it's moderation and firmness that's wanted for managing men, my boy...

ROBERT. Monsieur Guéret, we're not going to have this argument all over again, for the hundredth time, because there's one word we never manage to come to any agreement about.

GUÉRET. So you're going to trot out your 'Justice' again, are you?

ROBERT. I can't visualize firmness, or moderation, without justice. These three notions, they're all bound up together.

GUÉRET (*with some restraint*). Well, you *are* pigheaded! 'Justice' is a grand word, but when you've been living on it for twenty years you won't even then know the exact meaning of it. Before you *could* know, justice would need to take a turn at being absolute. But so long as justice persists in being simply a manifestation of our own particular conscience, and so long as our consciences are as different as our moustaches are, or our own private tastes, it will be essential, especially for anybody managing an industry like ours, to strike a balance between *our* sorts of justice, which do have form and substance, and Justice with a capital 'J', which is a disembodied spirit.

ROBERT (*quietly, but with conviction*). No, no, there *is* an outward and visible Justice.

GUÉRET. Well, where is it? The people who have to apply it professionally don't know how to go about it. The

30. **disembodied spirit:** 'spirit' alone seems ambiguous = *état d'âme*.

première instance, et la Cour suprême casse les arrêts d'appel. La justice change avec la couleur des robes de magistrats.... Tu m'agaces à la fin avec ta justice....Crois donc en Dieu, c'est plus simple.

ROBERT. C'est la même chose.

KISTEMAECKERS, *L'Embuscade.*

Courts of Appeal reverse decisions by the Courts of first instance, and the Supreme Court quashes the decisions on appeal. Justice varies according to the colour of Judges' robes.... You're getting on my nerves with your justice... Why can't you believe in God when you're at it? It's much simpler.

ROBERT. It's the same thing.

65. CHOIX D'UN MINISTRE

Le Comte (*devenu très sérieux*). Votre Majesté pense-t-elle avoir un tempérament de joueur?

Le Roi. Non, le jeu m'ennuie.

Le Comte. Parce que moi, qui suis assez joueur, je me vois très bien, si j'étais le roi, choisissant Denis par une impulsion de joueur.

La Reine. Vous croyez à sa chance?

Le Comte. Moins et plus que cela, madame. J'ai l'impression qu'il déplace avec lui une quantité de hasard beaucoup plus grande qu'un homme comme moi. Et mon hasard à moi se sent comme attiré vers cette masse.

Le Roi (*comme à part lui*). Est-ce tellement rassurant?

La Reine (*au comte*). Je disais au roi, tout à l'heure, que cet homme-là m'inspirerait peut-être plus de confiance pour l'avenir que tel de vos politiciens soi-disant de tout repos.... N'est-ce pas un peu le même sentiment que le vôtre?

Le Comte. En quelque sorte. Mais Votre Majesté attire notre attention, je crois, sur une particularité plus intérieure de la nature de Denis. Moi, c'est l'auréole des gens qui me frappe d'abord, leur cortège d'événements possibles.... (*Reprenant.*) Oui, sur ceci donc qu'il est encore plus homme que politicien, plus homme que doctrinaire. Si attaché qu'il pense être à ses idées, il n'est nullement improbable que le pouvoir, l'approche des grandeurs humaines dans ce qu'elles ont de plus noble ou de plus charmant (*il s'est imperceptiblement incliné vers le roi, puis vers la reine*), l'accès à des régions brillantes de la vie, aient sur lui le plus excellent effet.

Le Roi (*égayé par ces euphémismes*). En termes moins académiques, ce serait d'abord un ambitieux?

N.B. The conversation should be that of a 'gentilhomme d'une soixantaine d'années, de très bon ton, un rien avantageux, l'œil spirituel. On le sent dans une vieille familiarité avec le couple royal.'

11. Var. *feels some magnetic attraction to.*

65. CHOOSING A MINISTER

THE COUNT (*very serious now*). Is Your Majesty in any way conscious of possessing a gambler's temperament?

THE KING. No. Gambling bores me.

THE COUNT. Because I am a bit of a gambler and I can quite fancy myself, if I were the King, choosing Denis by gambler's instinct.

THE QUEEN. Do you believe he is lucky?

THE COUNT. More than that, ma'am, and less. I have an impression that when he moves he displaces a much greater quantity of chance than a man like myself. And my chance feels somehow attracted towards the mass of his.

THE KING (*thinking aloud*). Is that so very reassuring?

THE QUEEN (*to the Count*). I was saying to the King just now that that man might possibly inspire me with more confidence for the future than one of your so-called safe politicians. Isn't that rather the sort of feeling you have?

THE COUNT. Up to a point.... But Your Majesty is calling our attention, I think, to a more inward peculiarity of Denis' character. The first thing that strikes *me* about people is their halo, their aura of potentialities.... (*Returning to the point.*) Yes, you *are* drawing our attention to the fact that he is after all more man than politician, more man than doctrinaire. However firmly attached he may think he is to his own views, it is not at all unlikely that being in power, coming into close contact with human greatness in its most noble, or in its most charming, aspects (*this with an imperceptible bow to the King, and then to the Queen*), having access to brilliant spheres of life, might have the most excellent effect on him.

THE KING (*amused by the euphemisms*). In less choice terms, he would appear to be first and foremost a man of ambition?

---

17. **Up to a point**: var. *To some extent*; *In a way.*

30. **choice**: var. *distinguished, select*: not "Academic" (see No. 34, note 17), which is *universitaire*.

Le Comte. Ambitieux, sire... vous pensez bien que tous ces gens-là sont ambitieux. Mais tant que nous n'arrivons pas à nous représenter ce qu'ils ont exactement dans la tête quand leur ambition les travaille, ce qu'ils voient, oui, les visions, les espèces de fulgurations qui les traversent à ce moment-là, c'est comme si nous n'avions rien dit. Ambitieux! Mais votre premier chapelain l'est aussi, et votre troisième marmiton.

(*Le roi, qui a écouté avec un extrême intérêt, reste songeur.*)

La Reine. Et son ambition, à lui, vous arrivez à vous la représenter?

Le Comte (*plus léger, comme pris de remords d'avoir été si lourdement sérieux*). Que Votre Majesté me pardonne! Mais je n'y avais jamais tant pensé qu'aujourd'hui. D'ici à demain je tâcherai d'imaginer quelque chose qui sauve au moins mon amour-propre.

JULES ROMAINS, *Le Dictateur.*

34. Var. *men like him.*
38. Var. *we shall be no further on.*

THE COUNT. Ambition, Sir...you may be sure that people of that sort are all ambitious. But till we are able to form some idea of just what they have in mind when their ambition is at work, of exactly what they see, I mean the visions, or whatever flashes through them at such times, we shall not be getting anywhere. Ambition? Why even your First Chaplain is a man of ambition; so is your Third Assistant-Cook and Bottle-Washer.

(*The King, who has been extremely interested, remains lost in thought.*)

THE QUEEN. And *his* ambition? Can you form any idea of what it is?

THE COUNT (*in lighter vein, as though remorseful for being so ponderously serious*). Your Majesty must pardon me! But I never really thought much about it till to-day. Between now and to-morrow I will try to think out something that will at least save my face.

46. **ponderously**: var. *heavily*.
49. Var. *so as at least to save my face.*

66. DE L'IMPRESSIONNISME

Girard. Vous aimez ça? Vous avez du plaisir à regarder ça? Ces tons criards, ces couleurs grinçantes?

M. Cocatrix. C'est de l'impressionnisme, évidemment.

Girard. C'est de l'impressionnisme pour bourgeois.

M. Cocatrix (*ironique*). Ce n'est pas pommadé, cependant.

Girard. Parbleu! Au contraire, c'est exagéré dans la violence. C'est brutal. Plus audacieux que le vrai. Seulement, ce n'est pas sincère. Comprenez-vous tout ce qu'il veut dire, ce petit mot-là: *sincère*? Il excuse tout, il grandit tout, il rend tout respectable. Mais vos toiles ne sont pas sincères. Elles sont faites pour vous épater, et elles vous épatent et vous les achetez pour épater vos amis qui commencent par rire et qui finissent par en acheter à leur tour pour avoir l'air d'être des connaisseurs....Voilà mon opinion.... (*Il se lève, d'un autre ton.*) Alors, pour la galette, rien à faire?

M. Cocatrix. Tous mes regrets.

Girard (*à la porte*). Ça va bien! Votre socialisme ressemble à votre goût pour la peinture nouvelle. C'est de la pose. Au fond, vous êtes pompier en art et réactionnaire en politique. Adieu!

M. Cocatrix. C'est trop fort! Monsieur, je ne vous permets pas de suspecter ma bonne foi!

Girard. Mais, vous êtes de bonne foi, c'est ce qu'il y a de rigolo. Peut-être vous ne l'avez pas toujours été. Vous ne vous rappelez pas. Vous m'avez avoué un jour que, malgré tous vos efforts, vous n'aviez pas pu tout de suite adopter, en peinture, les opinions à la mode. Alors, au vernissage, avec vos amis avancés, vous aviez trouvé un moyen de ne pas leur paraître ridicule. Lorsqu'un tableau vous plaisait, vous disiez: 'Quelle ordure!' Et vous déclariez admirables ceux qui vous repoussaient. Et vous ne vous trompiez jamais. Je connais un type dans votre genre: il a fini par se convaincre lui-même, et, des toiles impressionnistes, il n'y en a plus d'assez extravagantes pour lui. On

66. IMPRESSIONISM

GIRARD. You like that sort of thing? Enjoy looking at it? These staring tones? jarring colours?

M. COCATRIX. Well, it's Impressionist, of course.

GIRARD. Impressionist for the bourgeois!

M. COCATRIX (*ironically*). It's not what you'd call pretty-pretty, anyway.

GIRARD. I should think it isn't. Quite the reverse: it's far too violent. It's knock-me-down. A lot more daring than the truth! But it's not *sincere*. Do you realize what it means, that little word—'sincere'? It excuses things, gives 'em size and merit. *Your* pictures aren't sincere. They're got up to impress you; and they do it, and you go and buy them just to impress your friends. They think them frightfully funny at first and then end up by buying them, too, so as to look as if they were connoisseurs. That's what *I* think about it. (*Getting up; with a different tone in his voice.*) What about the dough, then? Nothing doing?

M. COCATRIX. So sorry.

GIRARD (*from the door*). That's right! Your socialism's the same sort of thing as your craze for Modern Art. Just window-dressing. At bottom you're a Philistine in art and a dug-out in politics. Good-bye!

M. COCATRIX. That's going a bit too far! I won't have you calling my good faith in question.

GIRARD. Oh, you're in good faith right enough. That's just the funny thing about it. Perhaps you weren't always. You forget you once told me you couldn't, for the life of you, pick up the fashionable ideas about painting, right off. And so when you went to private views with your advanced friends, you hit on a good trick, so as not to look silly. When you rather liked a picture, you used to say: What muck! And anything you couldn't bear the sight of, you used to call first-rate. So you never made a mistake. I know another chap like you; he got himself to believe it in the end. Impressionist pictures?—Why, there aren't any crazy enough for him now. They've to get them specially done for him.

est forcé de lui en confectionner exprès....Allons, adieu.
Ne me gardez pas rancune de vous asticoter comme je viens
de le faire....Je n'oublie pas que nous avons eu des en-
thousiasmes communs....Vous faisiez peut-être semblant
d'être convaincu, mais peu importe: les bourgeois qui
pensent ou agissent comme vous sont tout de même de bons
ouvriers pour leur propre chambardement. Adieu.

     BRIEUX, *Le Bourgeois aux Champs.*

Well, good-bye! Don't be angry with me if I've given you
a bit of a dressing down. I'm not forgetting that once upon
a time we were both keen on the same things. Perhaps you
were only pretending to be convinced; doesn't really matter.
Middle class blighters with your ways of thinking and doing
are pretty handy at driving nails into their own coffin.
Good-bye!

67. LES PLAISIRS DE L'IMAGINATION

Léopold (*comme quelqu'un qui essaierait de raisonner un inconscient*). Chut! monsieur.

M. Ponce. Je me tais.... Cela mord un peu? (*Léopold lance une boulette.*) Avec quoi appâtez-vous?

Léopold (*excédé et poli*). Avec des petits pois.

M. Ponce. Il faut connaître son poisson.... Ce peuplier dans l'eau me donne l'impression d'un peuplier du dix-huitième siècle.... Je ne sais par quel enchaînement d'idées. ...L'imagination.... Je disais tout à l'heure, parlant de cette imagination qui est ma seule richesse, en dépit de ma profession.... Je rectifie; à cause, peut-être, de ma profession.... Les Postes, ce sont les lettres.... Les lettres, ce sont les timbres.... C'est le bout du monde sur deux centimètres carrés.

Léopold (*avec une certaine sympathie*). Ah! il vous intéresse, le bout du monde?

M. Ponce. Monsieur, il m'arrive de rêver sur des timbres: c'est un cocotier qui se balance, un guerrier armé, deux lamas sur un rocher, un lac avec un volcan.... Ah! monsieur, les pays où je n'irai point!

Léopold (*doux*). Moi, j'y suis allé.

M. Ponce. Vraiment? Comme je vous envie!

Léopold. Oui, j'ai traîné mes guêtres sur pas mal de ponts de navires et sous des tas d'arbres à palmes... pour le compte du 'Planteur jamaïquais'.

M. Ponce. Maison de cafés, poivres et épices.

Léopold. Oui.

M. Ponce. Moi, je suis un stationnaire. Je suis sur-

N.B. Stage Direction:
 Un coin de rivière, et le bord de la rivière.
 Six heures du soir, au mois de juillet.
3. Var. *I'll keep quiet.*
4. Var. *makes a cast with a pellet.*
5. **Peas**: are commonly used as bait; var. (if the remark is intended as a snub) *green peas, garden peas*. There had been a discussion with Leopold's brother, an Abbé, about the proper

67. THE PLEASURES OF IMAGINATION

Leopold (*like a man trying to keep some unthinking person quiet*). Sh!

M. Ponce. I won't say a word....Got a nibble? (*Leopold casts a pellet.*) What bait d'you use?

Leopold (*exasperated and polite*). Peas.

M. Ponce. You need to know your fish....That poplar in the water makes me think of an eighteenth-century poplar....I don't know what's the association of ideas.... Imagination....I was saying just now, talking about imagination, which is all I've got in the world, in spite of my calling....It would be more correct to say...because of my calling, perhaps...the Post Office; that means letters.... Letters mean stamps...the ends of the earth on half a square inch of paper.

Leopold (*with some fellow-feeling*). So you take an interest in the ends of the earth, do you?

M. Ponce. I get thinking, you know, over stamps. A coconut tree in the wind, a native in his war-paint, a pair of llamas on a rock, a lake with a volcano....Ah! the countries I'll never go to!

Leopold (*nicely*). *I've* been.

M. Ponce. You don't say so! I *do* envy you!

Leopold. Yes, I've knocked about a bit, on board ship, under no end of palm-trees...travelling for The Jamaica Planter.

M. Ponce. Coffee, pepper and spice merchants.

Leopold. That's it.

M. Ponce. Mine's a 'staying put' sort of a job. Inspector,

bait: 'L'Abbé roule dans sa main des boulettes: "J'appâte." — Léopold. Avec quoi?—Avec ma petite composition habituelle... très étudiée.'

7. Var. *a poplar in an eighteenth-century picture.*
13. Var. *far countries.*
17. Var. *Stamps set me thinking, you know.*
21. **nicely:** ? *gently, softly, modestly, unassumingly.*
22. Var. *Have you really (now)?*
24. Var. *any number.*

veillant du service des lettres en rebut, à Paris. Il n'y a que l'esprit qui voyage...dans tous les domaines....Vous devez être bien heureux, monsieur!

Léopold. De quoi?

M. Ponce. De voyager.

Léopold. Si je vous disais à quoi je pense parfois, quand je me promène sous des magnolias ou dans les plantations de café de la Guadeloupe, ou d'ailleurs, vous ne me croiriez pas!

M. Ponce. A quoi pensez-vous?

Léopold. A des bêtises, monsieur: à la couleur qu'avaient les pommes en septembre, dans la boutique de la mère Douillard, là, près de la mairie, quand j'étais petit, ou à l'odeur du café chaud, l'hiver, dans un petit établissement de la rue des Martyrs où je fréquentais quand j'avais vingt ans. On arrive à se demander s'il est utile d'aller au bout du monde pour penser à cela quand on y est.

M. Ponce. Mon Dieu! Quand je prends ma petite demi-tasse au coin de la rue Réaumur et de la rue d'Aboukir, moi qui pense à l'odeur que doivent avoir les plantations de café, et qui me promène en pensée dans les forêts tropicales quand j'achète un ananas le dimanche....Ça a mordu?

Léopold. Non, non....C'est une herbe.

JEAN SARMENT, *Léopold le Bien-Aimé.*

29. **my mind**: M. Ponce is talking of himself; for *l'esprit* cp. the words of an invalid: **La** *santé n'est pas trop mauvaise* or **La** *jambe ne va pas fort.*

THE PLEASURES OF IMAGINATION 247

Dead-Letter Office, Paris. It's only my mind that travels—
in every field of life.... You must be a very happy man.

LEOPOLD. Happy—what about?

M. PONCE. Being able to travel.

LEOPOLD. If I told you what I think about sometimes, when I am walking around among magnolia trees or in the coffee plantations in Guadeloupe or anywhere else, you wouldn't believe me!

M. PONCE. What do you think about?

LEOPOLD. The silliest things: the colour the apples used to be in September, when I was a small boy, at old mother Douillard's shop, up near the town-hall, or the smell of hot coffee, in the winter-time, at a little place in the Rue des Martyrs I used to go to as a young fellow. I wonder sometimes if it's worth it—going to the ends of the earth only to think about that sort of thing once you've got there.

M. PONCE. Well I never! When I'm having my small coffee, at the corner of the rue Réaumur and the rue d'Aboukir, *I* think about the lovely smell there must be in the coffee plantations and when I buy a pineapple on a Sunday *I* fancy myself wandering about in the tropical forests.... Got a bite?

LEOPOLD. No, no.... Just weeds.

42. **as a young fellow**: *quand j'avais vingt ans* (=just out of my teens) is a more or less stock phrase; cp. Paul Doumer's book entitled *Pour mes fils quand ils auront vingt ans*.

45. **small coffee**: *demi-tasse* (vulgarly "demmy tassy") is the regular American expression for 'black coffee'.

68. POSSIBILITÉS FORMIDABLES

Lamendin. Vous êtes allé en Amérique, monsieur le directeur?

Le Directeur (*peu fier*). Non. Pas encore.

Lamendin (*indulgent*). Vous avez idée de ce que sont des villes comme Pittsburg ou Detroit?

Le Directeur. Oui, par le cinéma.

Lamendin. Eh bien, imaginez juste le contraire. (*Un temps. Le Directeur imagine.*) Je veux dire qu'à mon avis (*d'un ton de rude franchise*), Donogoo est une ville ratée. Pas de plan d'ensemble. Pas d'autorité administrative. Le va-comme-je-te-pousse. Oui. Mais des possibilités formidables, et personne qui nous embête. Les gens ne pensent qu'aux sables. Ils se fichent du reste. C'est un campement pour eux. Vous me voyez venir. Je me jette sur la ville, avec mes millions. J'achète tous les emplacements dont je sais d'avance ce que je veux faire. J'ai ça pour un morceau de pain. Les malins essaient de m'avoir? Je change mes tracés. Vous comprenez la force du monsieur qui peut dire: 'C'est ici que je ferai les grands hôtels, ici l'avenue où je mettrai la poste et la Bourse', et qui peut jouer sur une marge d'un kilomètre? Pendant ce temps-là, les placers travaillent à leurs risques et pour qui, en définitive? Pour moi, qui draine les salaires et qui enregistre tranquillement mes plus-values! Ce qui ne m'empêche pas de cueillir à l'occasion un placer qui périclite ou d'en créer d'autres avec un outillage dernier cri qui me rend maître du marché. (*Il laisse un instant le Directeur sous le coup de cette évocation, puis, d'un ton de calme ironie.*) J'ajoute que si nous laissons aux Américains du Nord le temps de 'réaliser' la situation, comme ils disent,

Context. Premier Tableau. La première Banque, le bureau du directeur. Lamendin, fort correctement vêtu, une serviette sous le bras, pénètre dans le bureau....Bref, je vous apporte une affaire vierge Donogoo-Tonka...un coin où nous sommes allés les premiers, nous autres Français. Nous n'aurions jamais dû laisser personne rôder autour....Si les Américains me laissent tranquille pendant la période où je négocie, etc.

68. TREMENDOUS POSSIBILITIES

LAMENDIN (*to the Director*). Ever been to America?

THE DIRECTOR (*feeling small*). No. Not yet.

LAMENDIN (*not rubbing it in*). You know the sort of town Detroit is, or Pittsburg?

THE DIRECTOR. Yes, from the films.

LAMENDIN. Well, imagine the exact opposite. (*A pause, while the Director imagines.*) I mean that, to my way of thinking (*in a tone of brutal frankness*), Donogoo as a town is a complete frost. No general plan. No administrative authority. Muddling through—that's what it is. But—but —tremendous possibilities. And nobody to get in your way. The people can't think about anything but the sands; they don't care two hoots about the rest. For them it's just a camp. Now d'you see what I'm driving at? I swoop down on the place with my millions, buy up all the sites I know beforehand what to do with, get the whole show for next to nothing. The smart guys try to do me. I alter my lay-out. You see the strong position of the fellow who can say: 'Here's where I'll put up the big hotels. Here's the Avenue for the G.P.O. and the Stock Exchange'—and keep a mile or so in hand to play with. Meanwhile the placers are working at their own risk—and who for, in the long run? Me, tapping the wages and cashing in my increments on the quiet. And that doesn't hinder me picking up an odd placer or two that's feeling the draught, or starting new ones with a plant absolutely the last word, which puts me at the top of the market. (*He leaves the Director for a moment staggered by the vision conjured up, then, in a tone of quiet sarcasm.*) Let me add: if we give the North Americans

---

12. **the sands:** i.e. those washed for gold.
17. **the smart guys:** var. *the cute chaps.*
22. **in the long run:** var. *in the end.*
25. **feeling the draught:** var. *coming to grief, getting into difficulties.*
26. Var. *with the very last word in equipment.*

nous pourrons venir ensuite avec nos 75 millions de francs-papier !

Le Directeur (*beaucoup plus impressionné qu'il ne voudrait le paraître*). Vous estimez qu'actuellement ce capital-là suffirait ?

Lamendin. A condition qu'il soit entièrement versé, oui. 150,000 actions de 500 francs, émises au pair. (*Accommodant.*) Versement en deux tranches, à six mois d'intervalle, à la rigueur.   JULES ROMAINS, *Donogoo*.

30. 'get wise' to. The point is that *réaliser* in the English sense of 'realize'='to grasp' (although now quite common) is

time to 'get wise' to the situation, as they put it, much use it 30
will be our coming in then with our 75 million paper-francs!

THE DIRECTOR (*much more impressed than he would like to appear*). You consider that would be enough capital at present?

LAMENDIN. Fully paid-up, yes. 150,000 five-hundred 35
franc shares, issued at par. (*Considerately.*) Payment in two instalments, six months' interval, if you like.

still felt to be an Americanism or an Anglicism. The normal sense is 'to convert into reality', as in *réaliser un rêve*.
36. **Considerately**: var. *Obligingly, Accommodatingly.*
37. **if you like**: var. *if need be.*

VI. LITERATURE AND ART

69. QUERELLE LITTÉRAIRE

Mais ce qui me choque de ces beaux esprits, c'est qu'ils ne se rendent pas utiles à leur patrie, et qu'ils amusent leurs talents à des choses puériles. Par exemple, lorsque j'arrivai à Paris, je les trouvai échauffés sur une dispute la plus mince qui se puisse imaginer: il s'agissait de la réputation d'un vieux poète grec dont, depuis deux mille ans, on ignore la patrie aussi bien que le temps de sa mort. Les deux partis avouaient que c'était un poète excellent: il n'était question que du plus ou du moins de mérite qu'il fallait lui attribuer. Chacun en voulait donner le taux; mais, parmi ces distributeurs de réputation, les uns faisaient meilleur poids que les autres; voilà la querelle. Elle était bien vive; car on se disait cordialement de part et d'autre des injures si grossières, on faisait des plaisanteries si amères, que je n'admirais pas moins la manière de disputer que le sujet de la dispute. Si quelqu'un, disais-je en moi-même, était assez étourdi pour aller devant l'un de ces défenseurs du poète grec attaquer la réputation de quelque honnête citoyen, il ne serait pas mal relevé; et je crois que ce zèle si délicat sur la réputation des morts s'embraserait bien pour défendre celle des vivants! Mais, quoi qu'il en soit, ajoutais-je, Dieu me garde de m'attirer jamais l'inimitié des censeurs de ce poète, que le séjour de deux mille ans dans le tombeau n'a pu garantir d'une haine si implacable! Ils frappent à présent des coups en l'air: mais que serait-ce, si leur fureur était animée par la présence d'un ennemi?   MONTESQUIEU, *Lettres persanes*.

1. **I mislike**: var. *mislikes me* (preserving the construction of the French, but rather too archaic for the date, 1721, of the *Lettres persanes*); 'mislike' gives closely enough the sense of '*choque*', viz. 'offends', 'jars upon'.

wits: in eighteenth-century English, corresponds to the contemporary '*beaux esprits*'; "scholars" would be too strong, cp. Dr Johnson (O.E.D.): 'Latinity which entitled him to the same height of place among the *scholars* as he possessed before among the *wits*.' Cp. Thibaudet, *Tableau de la litt. fr.* p. 144: 'Racine, répondit Boileau, est un bel esprit à qui j'ai appris à faire difficilement des vers faciles. Entendez, bien entendu, bel esprit au sens du dix-septième siecle, un homme intelligent, cultivé et fin.'

69. A LITERARY QUARREL

But what I mislike in these wits is that they make not themselves of service to their country, but fritter away their talents on childish things. For instance, when I came to Paris, I found them all agog over a dispute, the flimsiest that may be conceived: 'twas about the reputation of an old Greek poet of whom, these two thousand years, men have known neither the place of birth nor yet the time of death. Both sides allowed he was an excellent poet; the only question was the greater, or the less, degree of merit that should be ascribed to him. Every man was for settling the amount; but, amongst those dispensers of reputation, some gave better weight than others; hence the quarrel. 'Twas a very lively one; for such rude abuse was bandied about right heartily, such bitter jests were made, that I marvelled no less at the manner of disputation than at the subject of the dispute. 'Were any man', I said within myself, 'heedless enough to go to one of those champions of the Greek poet and assail the reputation of some honourable citizen, he would be taken sharply to task; and I believe that so nice a zeal for the reputation of the dead would flare up to defend that of the living! But, howe'er it be,' I added, 'God forbid that I should ever incur the enmity of the critics of this poet whom two thousand years in the grave have not availed to preserve from hatred so implacable! At present they do but smite the air; but what should it be, were their fury inflamed by the presence of an adversary?'

2. **fritter away:** the contemporary (1728, Pope, *Dunciad*) expression = 'to spend (energy, time) on trifles'.

4. **flimsiest:** var. *slenderest, pettiest*.

7. **place of birth:** one of the common senses of *patrie*, notably (here) in connexion with Homer, like Lat. *patria*:
   'Smyrna, Chios, Colophon, Salamis, Rhodos, Argos, Athenae,
         Orbis de *patria* certat, Homere, tua.'

16. **subject:** var. *matter*.

17. **to go to:** *aller devant* = *aller trouver quelqu'un* = go and see someone.

21. **flare up:** in *s'embraserait bien* the sense of *bien* is 'really', but this seems hardly required in English.

70. LE STYLE D'ESCHYLE

Le style d'Eschyle est extraordinaire comme son génie; il fait le bruit d'un orage, il a le cours d'un torrent. Ses contours grecs sont tourmentés par l'hyperbole asiatique. Saumaise s'offusquait de le trouver 'pétri d'hébraïsmes', et le savant voyait juste, si le pédant a tort. Eschyle a parfois la voix d'un psalmiste ou d'un prophète d'Israël. Mêmes ellipses énigmatiques, même âpreté de ton et d'accent, mêmes ruissellements de larmes et mêmes éclats d'anathèmes. On dirait l'arc de David tendu par la main d'Apollon. Rien de comparable à ses chants lyriques pour l'emportement de l'allure, l'audace effrénée des tons et des rythmes, le débordement des images. Les métaphores sont prodigieuses, elles ont moins de beauté que d'énormité. Il appelle la poussière, 'sœur altérée de la boue'; la fumée, 'sœur chatoyante du feu'; la mer est 'la marâtre des vaisseaux'. Après les naufrages des Grecs revenant de Troie, il la voit 'toute fleurie de cadavres'. Aristophane raillait Eschyle de ce tonnerre qui détonait dans l'atmosphère athénienne. Cependant l'admiration perce sous ses moqueries. On dirait le satyre du bas-relief, qui mesure avec une grimace effrayée l'orteil de Polyphème endormi.

PAUL DE SAINT-VICTOR, *Les Deux Masques.*

2. **mountain stream**: var. *torrent*, which, however, is a vaguer word than the French *torrent*.

4. **Salmasius**: Claude Saumaise, the French Classical scholar (1588–1653).

14. **Mire's consorting sister**: Headlam's translation; Sidgwick's is: 'thirsty dust, neighbour brother of the clay.'

15. **'many-hued'**, etc.: 'black smoke, flickering sister of flame' (Headlam).

70. THE STYLE OF ÆSCHYLUS

The style of Æschylus is as extraordinary as his genius; it has the crash of a thunderstorm and the rush of a mountain stream. Its Grecian outlines are contorted with Asiatic hyperbole. Salmasius was scandalized to find it 'compounded of Hebraisms', and the scholar in him saw truly, 5 though the pedant is in the wrong. Æschylus sometimes has the voice of a psalmist or a prophet in Israel: the same enigmatic ellipses, the same sternness of tone and accent, the same floods of tears, the same outbursts of anathemas. It is as though the bow of David were bent by Apollo's hand. 10 Nothing can compare with his lyrics for the sweep of the movement, the wild audacity of tones and rhythms, the exuberance of the imagery. The metaphors are tremendous, not so much beautiful as colossal. He calls dust 'Mire's consorting sister, thirsty Dust'; smoke 'many-hued sister 15 of fire'; the sea is the 'step-mother of ships'; after the Greeks were wrecked on the voyage home from Troy, he sees it 'in flower with corpses'. Aristophanes twitted Æschylus with the thunder which reverberated through the Athenian air. Yet admiration peeps out from under his jeers— 20 like the satyr in the bas-relief measuring with a frightened grin the great toe of Polyphemus asleep.

16. **step-mother:** var. *step-dame.*
19. **reverberated:** var. *rang out, pealed*; *détonait* is exactly 'detonated', 'exploded'; *détonnait* would give a better sense: 'was out of place in the Athenian atmosphere' (of light irony).
21. Var. *sickly grin.*
22. **Polyphemus:** the most famous of the Cyclopes—of gigantic stature, with one eye in the middle of his forehead; slain by Odysseus.

71. D'AUBIGNÉ POÈTE

D'Aubigné avait des dons poétiques assez rares. Il avait quelquefois l'idée poétique. Cette idée, au gré de fortune, ou se délayait dans un développement lâche et fastidieux et y demeurait comme noyée, ou se ramassait en un vers vigoureux et éclatant où elle restait fixée à jamais. Il avait le mouvement, sinon la puissance oratoire, et poussait vigoureusement un couplet d'invective.

Mais il manquait d'haleine, et n'a pas écrit toute une bonne page en vers; il manquait de composition, et personne ne s'est répété et ne s'est recommencé plus que lui; il manquait de goût, et le pire dans la platitude touche chez lui et enveloppe des traits qui approchent du sublime, sans qu'on puisse bien savoir s'il a distingué les uns de l'autre. Il était fait pour la pièce courte, rapide et incisive. Il a écrit tout un volume qu'il faudrait réduire à vingt pages. Il ne s'est pas trompé absolument en s'avisant qu'il était poète; mais il s'est formellement abusé sur la manière dont il l'était.

ÉMILE FAGUET, *Le XVIe Siècle*.

4. **fluid**: the metaphor in *noyée* would be wrongly rendered by "submerged" or "swamped"; it is as in the expression 'to drown the miller'=to add too much water to spirits. For 'diluted' cp. *Times Lit. Suppl.* April 10, 1937: 'No poet of his stature has repeated and diluted himself so recklessly' [as Swinburne].

5. Var. *in which it found immortal form.*

7. Var. *could write a stanza of vigorous invective.* N.B. not "couplet"; *couplet* in French is a succession of lines riming together, stanza, etc., and not as in English *a pair* of successive lines.

71. D'AUBIGNÉ AS A POET

D'Aubigné had poetic gifts which are rather unusual. His thought, occasionally, was poetic. That thought, as chance decreed, either became diluted in a sloppy, tedious amplification and remained fluid, or else it collected into one powerful, splendid line, and was crystallized in it for ever. He had the rhythm, if not the power, of the orator, and could turn out slashing invective in verse.

But he lacked staying power, and never wrote one whole page of good verse: he lacked order, and no writer ever repeated himself more or made more false starts; he lacked taste: in him the direst platitude is found close beside, and round about, phrases which approach the sublime, and you can never quite tell whether he knew the one from the other. He was naturally suited for the short, swift, incisive piece. He wrote a whole volume which would require reduction to twenty pages. He was not absolutely wrong in thinking he was a poet; but he was definitely mistaken as to what manner of poet he was.

9. **order:** var. *arrangement.*
11. **direst:** var. *most woeful.*
platitude: var. *insipidity*; not "platitudes". English 'platitude' has two senses: (1) common-placeness of speech or writing; (2) a common-place remark. Sense (1) is the more usual in French.
13. **tell:** cp. '*Sait-on jamais?*'=Shaw's play, '*You never can tell*'.
16. Var. *in taking himself for a poet, but he was under a misapprehension as to,* etc.

72. UN GROTESQUE

Cette audace et cette témérité n'abandonnaient pas Cyrano lorsqu'il quittait l'épée pour la plume; le même caractère de hardiesse extravagante et spirituelle se retrouve dans tous ses ouvrages; chaque phrase est un duel avec la raison; la raison a beau se mettre en garde et se ramasser sous la coquille de sa rapière, la folle du logis a toujours en réserve quelque botte secrète qu'elle lui pousse au ventre et qui la jette sur le pré; comme le capitan Chasteaufort, en moins d'une minute elle a gagné et rompu la mesure, surpris le fort, coupé sous le bras,... porté le coup de dessous, paré, riposté, passé et tué, non pas plus de trente hommes, mais plus de trente belles idées vraiment neuves et philosophiques; les bottes dont elle se sert le plus communément sont les métaphores outrées, les comparaisons alambiquées, les jeux de mots, les équivoques, les rébus, les concetti, les pointes, les turlupinades, les recherches précieuses, les sentiments quintessenciés, tout ce que le mauvais goût espagnol a de démesuré, le mauvais goût italien d'ingénieux et de chatoyant, le mauvais goût français de froid et de maniéré. Vous concevez que cette pauvre raison ne peut pas avoir bien souvent le dessus avec un tel adversaire; cependant elle sort quelquefois victorieuse de ce duel inégal, et fait regretter qu'elle ne remporte pas plus d'avantages sur sa fantasque ennemie.

TITLE. 'A Ruffling Blade' describes only one side of Cyrano's activities. As a term of literary history *un Grotesque* means not a comic personage, but a certain type of seventeenth-century author prior to the Classical School. Thus Faguet, *Histoire de la poésie fr.*, has a section on 'Les Grotesques ou les Romantiques de 1620'.

2. **dropped**: var. *laid aside*.

3. **recurs**: for the value of *re-* in *se retrouve* see No. 2, note 5.

5. **'daft chiel'**: var. *Dame Fancy*; *the madcap of the mind*; *la folle du logis* means the imagination.

6. **at hand**: var. *in reserve, in readiness*. Var. *some hidden thrust to launch at the body*.

7. **on the field**: *pré* = the duelling ground; cp. *aller sur le pré* = to fight a duel.

72. A RUFFLING BLADE

That audacity and foolhardiness did not forsake Cyrano when he dropped the sword for the pen. The like temper of whimsical and sprightly recklessness recurs in all his writings. Every sentence is a bout with Logic. In vain does Logic stand on guard and crouch behind its rapier-hilt. The 'daft chiel' in Cyrano has ever at hand some secret quirk of fence, that runs Logic through and lays it on the field. Like the swashbuckler Chasteaufort, in less than a minute he has engaged and disengaged, surprised the forte, cut below the sword-arm,...thrust beneath the guard, parried, riposted, passed, and killed not 'thirty men or more', but thirty fine ideas or more, which were really new and philosophically sound. The thrusts he most commonly uses are strained metaphors, double-distilled similes, puns, equivocations, rebuses, concetti, witty phrases, buffooneries, euphuistic subtleties, fine-spun supersentiments, whatever in Spanish bad taste is excessive, in Italian bad taste is over-ingenious and florid, in French bad taste is frigid and stilted. You may well imagine that poor Logic cannot very often get the better of such an adversary; sometimes, however, it does come out victorious from the ill-matched duel—and makes one regret that Logic does not win more advantages over its freakish foe.

9. **surprised the forte:** ? *tricked his opponent's guard.* 'Forte' is the strongest part of a sword-blade. *Le fort de l'épée*=le tiers du tranchant qui est à partir du talon, et avec lequel on pare surtout.

11. **passed:** ? *disarmed:* 'to pass' is to bring the left foot in front of the right so as to be in a position to master the opponent's 'forte' and *disarm* him.

14. **double-distilled:** var. *over-subtle.*

15. **witty phrases:** var. *verbal ingenuities; points* [*une pointe* is usually 'conceit' but 'point' is also used].

buffooneries: var. *clownings*; for *turlupinades* cp. Larousse: 'Turlupin (du nom d'un acteur de nos anciennes farces). Homme qui fait des allusions froides et basses, de mauvais jeux de mots.'

19. Var. *have the upper hand with.*

Au reste, Cyrano, sous tous les rapports, est bien de son temps; cette folle audace qu'on lui voit dans la pensée et dans l'action n'était pas rare dans ce siècle; le matamore, type charmant effacé de nos comédies, comme vont l'être ou le sont déjà à l'heure où je parle les types des Scapins et des Lisettes, n'était réellement qu'un portrait légèrement chargé.

THÉOPHILE GAUTIER, *Cyrano de Bergerac* (Fasquelle).

24. Var. *Cyrano is, from every point of view, a true type of his times.*

Moreover, Cyrano, in every respect, is typical of his time. That madcap daring of his in thought and action was not uncommon in that age. The matamore, a delectable character who has dropped out of our comedies, as the Scapins and Lisettes will shortly do or have already done at the time when I write this, was in reality but a portrait slightly overdrawn.

26. **the matamore:** var. *the hectoring blade.*
27. Var. *the Scapin and Lisette characters.*

73. L'ORIGINALITÉ DE LA FONTAINE

Il y a une grandeur, dans La Fontaine, dont nos académiciens ne peuvent trouver la mesure. Car ils voient bien les effets, qui sont pour désespérer tout homme qui tient une plume. Un trait léger, égal et suffisant, qui court d'une fable à l'autre sans se rompre jamais, sans jamais marquer ni forcer, dessine comme une longue frise des choses humaines, où chacun, de la nuque au talon circonscrit, trouve sa place éternelle. Comme en *l'Éthique* de Spinoza, où toutes choses sont fixées en leur vérité, et finalement égales devant le jugement dernier et premier. Car, dans Spinoza aussi, le Loup et l'Agneau, et sans rien à reprendre. Mais le vrai spectateur ne s'est pas montré souvent. Toutes nos pensées, ou presque, sont plaidoyers. L'importance y fait des bosses et contorsions, que le rire, au mieux, tord à rebours: c'est STYLE. 'Alain' was the pseudonym of the philosopher and teacher Émile-Auguste Chartier, who expounded his ideas as informal, unconventional philosophizings under the title *Propos d'Alain*. The semi-conversational tone should be preserved in English so far as possible, but occasionally some expansion may be required to make the train of thought quite clear.

1. **literary critics:** *un académicien* is properly a member of the French Academy, but the term is extended to other authoritative exponents of more or less 'official' literary criticism. Not "academics", which would be *universitaires* (see No. 34, note 17): 'Academicians' would have a clear enough sense in a French context; elsewhere it would be taken as = artists of the Royal Academy.

2. **although:** *Car* is used vaguely, as often in conversation. The word naturally used in opposition to *effects* is *cause* and not, as here, *mesure* = standard of measure. The opposition is perhaps between the whole phrases *trouver la mesure* and *voir les effets*, but it is not a clear-cut antithesis.

4. **outline:** var. *tracing*. La Fontaine's art is compared with that of a draughtsman.

7. **from neck,** etc.: i.e. the figures of the frieze are in follow-my-leader order, each seen from behind. But *de la nuque au talon* is in common use as a stock phrase = from head to foot and may mean nothing more than that here. Chartier is evidently quoting, since the words make an alexandrine line.

73. LA FONTAINE'S ORIGINALITY

There is a greatness in La Fontaine which literary critics never can fathom, although they do see the effects, and these are the despair of any man who wields a pen. A slender, an even, a sufficient outline which runs from Fable to Fable without ever breaking or ever becoming obtrusive or forced, delineates, as it were, the human scene in one long frieze, in which every man is traced right round from neck to heel, and given his proper place for all time. Just as in Spinoza's *Ethics*, where all things are immutable in their true values and ultimately found equal at the last judgment, which is also the first. For in Spinoza, too, you get the Wolf and the Lamb, and done perfectly. But the genuine spectator is a rare occurrence. All our thoughts, or nearly all, are special pleading. Self-conceit gives them contortions and humps, which laughter, at the best, twists t'other way; that

---

9. **immutable**: var. *immobilized*. Spinoza links up his ethics with his theory of knowledge; the mind by intuition apprehends all things in God and God in all things; it identifies itself with cosmic thought and thereby becomes eternal. Hence the last judgment is also the first.

11. **the Wolf**, etc. *Le Loup et l'Agneau*, La Fontaine I, 10, personifying injustice *versus* innocence.

12. **and done perfectly**: *reprendre* means to find fault with; *et sans rien à reprendre* = and with nothing to find fault with. Var. *and could not be improved on* (*bettered*).

13. Var. *has not often been forthcoming*.

14. **special pleading**: this translation may be permissible, though not legally accurate, *un plaidoyer* being the speech of an advocate, especially for the defence. Var. *speeches for the defence*; *forensic arguments*.

self-conceit: see note 19, below.

Var. *humps and deformities*; *protuberances and malformations*. Cp. Larousse: '*La contorsion* de l'épine dorsale constitue ce qu'on appelle vulgairement *une bosse*.'

15. Var. *to which laughter, at most, gives a contrary twist; that is the scoffers' way of righting matters*; *redresser* = to set right, metaphorically or literally; cp. garage hand's instructions to driver: Redressez! = 'Straighten up!'

ainsi que les moqueurs redressent. Par quoi Rabelais, Molière, Voltaire ont leur grandeur aussi; mais ils sont dans le jeu, ce qui se voit au rire. Qui n'est pris du tout à l'importance ne rit point; le diaphragme qui se relâche s'était donc tendu et fatigué au respect. Et y sera pris encore, et le sait. Au lieu qu'il n'y a point de rire dans La Fontaine, ni aucun mouvement de moquerie qui dérange la ligne. Ni aucun cynisme, ni aucun tonneau diogénique. Tous ces renards, fourmis, chats ou chiens, voisins ou voisines, archiprêtres et jardiniers sont à leur affaire, et l'on n'y voit point de ridicule. 'Enterrer ce mort au plus vite.' Mais il faudrait citer tout. L'homme s'est donc, cette fois, retiré du jeu. Quand il prend ainsi le siège du juge, pour un court moment, l'académicien lui-même retrouve la sûreté et souplesse de main; toutefois il la perd bientôt, saisissant sa plume comme un sceptre.

Cette sottise, qui naît aussitôt d'importance, pèse sur le trait; quand la ligne serait juste, le dessin est vulgaire. Or cette faute n'est point en La Fontaine; je n'y en vois aucune trace. L'emphase n'y est jamais admirée, ni seulement pardonnée. ALAIN, *Propos de littérature.*

19. **He who**, etc. The use of *Qui* is that common in proverbial expressions: *Qui dort dîne*, etc.; for *pris* cp. La Fontaine's line: *Celui est pris qui croyait prendre* = the biter bit. Note *l'importance* = *self*-importance, vanity—a good seventeenth-century sense of the noun, but now usually of the adjective.

24. **excursion into humour:** *mouvement* = inclination, feeling, i.e. a movement of the mind: cp. *Un bon mouvement!* = Make yourself agreeable! Var. *intention to ridicule*.

25. **ribaldry:** *cynisme* seems to be used in its popular sense, i.e. disregard for decent behaviour or decent language, which is different from the popular sense of 'cynicism', viz. sneering attitude. The other meaning of both *cynisme* and 'Cynicism' = a system of philosophy (that of Diogenes) seems unlikely here, since the wording of Alain's sentence implies some differentiation between *cynisme* and *le tonneau diogénique*.

LA FONTAINE'S ORIGINALITY

is the scoffers' method of setting things right. By the same
token Rabelais, Molière, Voltaire have also their greatness;
but they are in the game themselves, which is evident from
the laughter. He who is in no wise taken in by self-conceit
does *not* laugh; the diaphragm that relaxes must previously
have been on the stretch and feeling the strain of a defer-
ential attitude. And its possessor will be taken in again by
self-conceit, and knows it. Whereas in La Fontaine there
is no laughter, nor any excursion into humour which might
disturb the line. No ribaldry either, nor any Diogenes'
tub. All these Foxes, Ants, Cats or Dogs, gaffers or gammers,
archpriests and gardeners, are just going about their daily
business, and no one sees anything funny in that: e.g. 'To
get through the funeral in double-quick time'—but there
would be no end to quoting. This time, then, the writer has
come out of the game. Your literary critic himself, when he
takes his seat thus on the judicial bench for one brief
moment, recovers sureness and delicacy of touch, which
however, he soon loses, gripping his pen as though it were
a sceptre.

That foolish proceeding, which is the immediate con-
sequence of self-conceit, makes the outlining heavy-handed;
even though the line be true, the drawing is vulgar. Now,
that fault is not in La Fontaine; I cannot see a trace of it
in him. In La Fontaine pomposity is never admired, nor so
much as condoned.

26. Var. *neighbours* (*gossips*) *of either sex.*
29. The reference is to La Fontaine VII, 11, *Le Curé et le Mort*:
       'Un Curé s'en allait gaiement
       Enterrer ce mort au plus vite.'
Translated by Sir Edward Marsh:
       'A Clergyman with cheerful gait
       Was following along the road,
       In haste to get the funeral over.'
40. **pomposity**: not "emphasis".
Var. *bombast is never shown as admirable, nor even as pardonable.*
Properly *seulement* = so much as.

74. LETTRES DE DIDEROT À
Mlle VOLLAND

Ici Diderot se révèle et s'épanche tout entier. Ses goûts, ses mœurs, la tournure secrète de ses idées et de ses désirs; ce qu'il était dans la maturité de l'âge et de la pensée; sa sensibilité intarissable au sein des plus arides occupations et sous les paquets d'épreuves de l'*Encyclopédie*; ses affectueux retours vers les temps d'autrefois, son amour de la ville natale, de la maison paternelle...son vœu de retraite solitaire, de campagne avec peu d'amis, d'oisiveté entremêlée d'émotions et de lectures; et puis, au milieu de cette société charmante, à laquelle il se laisse aller tout en la jugeant, les figures sans nombre, gracieuses ou grimaçantes, les épisodes tendres ou bouffons qui ressortent et se croisent dans ses récits; Mme d'Épinay, les boucles de cheveux pendantes, un cordon bleu au front, langoureuse en face de Grimm...le baron d'Holbach, au ton moqueur et discordant, près de sa moitié au fin sourire; l'abbé Galiani, 'trésor dans les jours pluvieux', meuble si indispensable que 'tout le monde voudrait en avoir un à la campagne, si on en faisait chez les tabletiers'; l'incomparable portrait d'"Uranie', de cette belle et auguste Mme Legendre, la plus vertueuse des coquettes, la plus désespérante des femmes qui disent: Je vous aime;—un franc parler sur les personnages célèbres; Voltaire, 'ce méchant et extraordinaire enfant des Délices', qui a beau critiquer, railler, se démener, et qui 'verra toujours au-dessus de lui une douzaine d'hommes de sa nation, qui, sans s'élever sur la pointe du pied, le passeront de la tête, car il n'est que le second dans tous les genres';

1. **unlocks his heart**: var. *pours out his whole self*.
2. **hidden**: var. *secret*.
5. **occupations**: var. *pursuits*.
6. Var. *the affectionate way in which he looked back on old times*.
10. **spells of reading**: var. *books*.
12. Var. *though seeing its defects*.
14. Var. *sweet or sour, pleasant or wry*.
15. **descriptions**: var. *story*.

Mme d'Épinay, etc. These are members of the house-party

74. DIDEROT; LETTERS TO Mlle VOLLAND

In these letters Diderot reveals himself, unlocks his heart. Here we have his tastes, his ways, the hidden bent of his ideas and aspirations; Diderot, as he was in the maturity of his age and mental vigour; his sensibility inexhaustible amid the dullest occupations and even when he was submerged under bundles of *Encyclopédie* proofs; his fond remembrances of early days, his love for his native town and the house where he was born... his longing for solitary seclusion, for life in the country with only a few friends, or for a leisured existence varied with emotional experiences and spells of reading. Also we see him in that charming society into which, criticize it though he may, he lets himself drift; the countless faces, gracious or grimacing, the episodes, sentimental or farcical, which stand out and inter-cross in his descriptions; Mme d'Épinay, her ringlets dangling, a blue ribbon round her forehead, looking languishingly at Grimm; Baron d'Holbach, he of the mocking discordant voice, beside his spouse with the subtle smile; the abbé Galiani, 'a godsend on a rainy day', such a useful acquisition that 'everybody would want to have one for his country house, if you could get them in the toy-shops'; the peerless portrait of 'Uranie', handsome, stately Mme Legendre, most virtuous of coquettes, most provoking of women given to exclaiming 'I love you';—plain speaking about celebrities; Voltaire 'that naughty, marvellous boy at Les Délices' who, for all his criticizing and jesting and rampaging, 'will always have a dozen fellow-countrymen head and shoulders above him, and none of your standing on tip-toe, for he is only second in all *genres*'; Rousseau, that incon-

---

at Baron d'Holbach's country seat at Grandval; Grimm, editor of the *Correspondance littéraire*, was the lover of Mme d'Épinay, whose *Mémoires* are a main source of information on Rousseau; Galiani was a witty and diminutive Italian *abbé*. Diderot, staying at Grandval, reports their doings to Sophie Volland.

19. Var. *such an indispensable commodity*.
21. **toy-shops:** var. *fancy goods shops*.
22. '**Uranie**': Sophie Volland's married sister, Mme Legendre.

Rousseau, cet être incohérent, 'excessif, tournant perpétuellement autour d'une capucinière où il se fourrera un beau matin, et sans cesse ballotté de l'athéisme au baptême des cloches';—c'en est assez, je crois, pour indiquer que Diderot, homme, moraliste, peintre et critique, se montre à nu dans cette Correspondance, si heureusement conservée, si à propos offerte à l'admiration empressée de nos contemporains. SAINTE-BEUVE, *Portraits littéraires*.

33. **simple piety**: var. *unquestioning piety*; *the Christening of the Bells* (*Blessing the Bells*), *Le Baptême des Cloches*, is a ceremony peculiar to France, which has no great religious significance, e.g. when a new bell is put in a church steeple. Diderot takes

sistent creature, 'extravagant, for ever hovering round a Capuchin Friary, and likely, one of these days, to find himself inside, and perpetually torn this way and that between atheism and simple piety'. All this will suffice, I think, to show that Diderot, as a man, moralist, portrait-painter and critic, lays his soul bare in this Correspondence which has been so fortunately preserved and so opportunely presented for the interest and admiration of present day readers.

it as an example of touching or child-like, even superstitious, faith which makes no distinction between important matters in religion and unimportant.

36. **presented.** Diderot's *Correspondance* with Sophie Volland had just been published and Sainte-Beuve was reviewing it.

75. ALFRED DE MUSSET

Musset ne s'attarda pas dans le romantisme: les disputes littéraires ne l'intéressaient guère. Il avait fait des niches aux classiques à perruque de 1830; il aimait les grands classiques de 1660, y compris Racine, la bête noire en ce temps-là des esprits larges; il ne se gêna pas pour se moquer des romantiques, du pittoresque plaqué, des désespoirs byroniens, des pleurnicheries lamartiniennes. Affectant un certain mépris de la forme et de l'art, il posa que toute l'œuvre littéraire consiste à ouvrir son cœur, et pénétrer dans le cœur du lecteur: émouvoir en étant ému, voilà toute sa doctrine: et si l'émotion est sincère, communicative, peu importe quelle forme l'exprime et la convoie. 'Vive le mélodrame où Margot a pleuré.' Il n'eut donc souci que de dire les joies et les tristesses de son âme. Il a vécu sa poésie: elle est comme le journal de sa vie. Non qu'elle enregistre les faits, elle note seulement le retentissement des faits dans les profondeurs de sa sensibilité.

Il n'y a rien en somme que de commun dans la vie de Musset: beaucoup de folie, beaucoup de plaisir, beaucoup de passion, à la fin le naufrage dans l'habitude insipide et tenace, avec l'amertume de la désillusion impuissante.

LANSON, *Histoire de la littérature française.*

1. **fold**: var. *tents, camp.*
3. **die-hards.** The tone of the passage is, for Lanson, almost unconventional, and a few modernisms may not come amiss. Var. *the be-wigged Classics.* Cp. Balzac, quoted by Littré: 'Le mot *perruque* était le dernier mot trouvé par le journalisme romantique, qui en avait affublé les classiques.' Littré defines *perruque* as 'personne...attachée à des idées qui ont passé de mode'.
4. **including**: var. *among them.*
5. **the 'Moderns'**: var. *the 'high-brows', the advanced.*
6. **adventitious**: less expressive than *plaqué* = appliqué comme une plaque, i.e. 'stuck on', 'clapped on'.
7. **sob-stuff**: no doubt a slight anachronism: O.E.D. *Suppl.*: S. Vines, 1928: Dickensian sob-stuff. Var. *snivelling.*
8. **maintained**: properly *posited*, laid it down.
9. Var. *in literature the conclusion of the whole matter is to lay*, etc.

75. ALFRED DE MUSSET

Musset did not tarry in the Romantic fold; literary squabbles were not of much interest to him. He had played pranks on the Classical die-hards of 1830; he loved the great Classics of 1660, including Racine, the pet aversion, at that time, of the 'Moderns'; he had no compunction in poking fun at the Romanticists, at the adventitious 'picturesque', the Byronic dark despair, the Lamartinian 'sob-stuff'. Affecting a certain contempt for craftsmanship and form, he maintained that the only aim in literature is to lay one's own heart bare and reach the heart of the reader; to move others by being oneself moved—that was all his doctrine—and if only the emotion be sincere and communicable, it is immaterial by what form it is expressed and conveyed. 'Here's to the melodrama that made Margot cry!' Hence he cared for nothing but telling the joys and sorrows of his own soul. He *lived* his poetry; it is a sort of diary of his life. Not that it records the facts; it notes only the echoing of these facts in the depths of his own sensibility.

There is nothing after all in Musset's life but what is common: much folly, much pleasure-seeking, much passion and, at the end of it all, shipwreck on the shoals of dull tenacious habit, with the added bitterness of helpless disillusionment.

13. **accompanied**: var. *conveyed*.

16. Var. *His poetry is his experience of life—as it were, his diary*, etc.

17. **echoing...in**: var. *re-echoing (repercussion)...through*.

20. **common**: *commun* implies 'vulgar' as well as 'commonplace', the reference being not to wild bouts, but to persistent 'vulgar' drinking.

21. **shipwreck**, etc. The metaphor requires expansion. It is not quite "making a shipwreck of one's life". The allusion in *le naufrage* is not to a ship striking a rock, but to one running aground, e.g. on sands, and being eventually *enlisé*. Var. *coming to grief*.

22. **added**: useful for eking out the sense of 'with', which by itself would scarcely render the full force of *avec*.

76. A LA RECHERCHE DU MOT JUSTE

Tu me parles de tes découragements; si tu pouvais voir les miens! Je ne sais pas comment quelquefois les bras ne me tombent pas de fatigue et ma tête ne s'en va pas en bouillie. Je mène une vie âpre, déserte de toute joie extérieure, et où je n'ai rien pour me soutenir qu'une espèce de rage permanente qui pleure quelquefois d'impuissance, mais qui est continuelle. J'aime mon travail d'un amour frénétique et perverti comme un ascète; le cilice me gratte le ventre. Quelquefois quand je me trouve vide, quand l'expression se refuse, quand, après avoir griffonné de longues pages, je découvre n'avoir pas fait une phrase, je tombe sur mon divan et j'y reste hébété dans un marais intérieur d'ennui.

Je me hais et je m'accuse de cette démence d'orgueil qui me fait palpiter après la chimère. Un quart d'heure après, tout est changé, le cœur me bat de joie. Mercredi dernier, j'ai été obligé de me lever pour aller chercher mon mouchoir de poche; les larmes me coulaient sur la figure. Je m'étais attendri moi-même en écrivant, je jouissais délicieusement, et de l'émotion de mon idée et de la phrase qui la rendait, et de la satisfaction de l'avoir trouvée; du moins je crois qu'il y avait de tout cela dans cette émotion, où les nerfs après tout avaient plus de place que le reste; il y en a dans cet ordre de plus élevées, ce sont celles où l'élément sensible n'est pour rien; elles dépassent alors la vertu en beauté morale, tant elles sont indépendantes de personnalité, de toute relation humaine. J'ai entrevu quelquefois (dans mes grands jours de soleil), à la lueur d'un enthousiasme qui faisait frissonner ma peau du talon à la racine des cheveux, un état de l'âme ainsi supérieur à la vie, pour qui la gloire ne serait rien, et le bonheur même inutile....

FLAUBERT, *Correspondance*.

The letter is addressed '*à Madame X*', and dated '*Croisset, août,* 1852'.

5–6. Var. *which bewails its own impotence.*
8. Var. *the hair-shirt mortifies my flesh.*

76. FINDING THE RIGHT WORD

You talk about your fits of depression. If you could only see mine! I can't think sometimes why my arms don't drop with weariness and my brain is not reduced to pulp. I lead a grim life, with no outward pleasures and nothing to keep me going but a kind of chronic fury which leads to tears of utter impotence, sometimes, but is continuous. I love my work in a frenzied, perverted sort of way, like an ascetic —I can feel the hair shirt rough against my skin. Sometimes, when I find my mind a blank, when the words won't come and, after scribbling pages and pages, I realize I haven't one sentence right, I slump on my couch and lie there stupid, in a mental Slough of Despond.

I loathe myself and take the blame for this insane conceit which sends me fluttering after the unattainable. A quarter of an hour later, things are looking quite different and my heart is beating with delight. Last Wednesday, I had to get up and go for a handkerchief; the tears were running down my face. I had written myself into a sentimental mood, and was revelling in the emotion caused by the idea I had in mind, and the phrase expressing it, and the satisfaction of having hit on the phrase; at least I think there was something of all that in the emotion, though nerves had really more to do with it than anything else. There are emotions in this connection which are nobler, I mean those into which the element of sensibility does not enter. Such emotions rank higher for moral beauty than virtue does, so absolutely independent are they of personality, of all human relationships. I have had the presentiment sometimes (on one of my brighter days) in the illumination of an *enthusiasm* which sent a shiver down my back—the presentiment of a state of the mind which in some such way transcends life and in which fame would be as naught and happiness itself superfluous.

12. Var. *floundering in an internal bog of depression.*
14. Var. *fluttering off in vain imaginings.*
19. Var. *and found an exquisite delight in.*

77. REMBRANDT

A ce moment d'ailleurs, tout tournait mal, fortune, honneur, et quand il quitte le *Breestraat*, sans gîte, sans le sou, mais en règle avec ses créanciers, il n'y a plus talent ni gloire acquise qui tienne. On perd sa trace, on l'oublie, et pour le coup sa personne disparaît dans la petite vie nécessiteuse et obscure d'où il n'était, à dire vrai, jamais sorti.

En tout, comme on le voit, c'était un homme à part, un rêveur, peut-être un taciturne, quoique sa figure dise le contraire; peut-être un caractère anguleux et un peu rude, tendu, tranchant, peu commode à contredire, encore moins à convaincre, ondoyant au fond, roide en ses formes, à coup sûr un original. S'il fut célèbre et choyé et vanté d'abord, en dépit des jaloux, des gens à courte vue, des pédants et des imbéciles, on se vengea bien quand il ne fut plus là.

Dans sa pratique, il ne peignait, ne crayonnait, ne gravait comme personne. Ses œuvres étaient même, en leurs procédés, des énigmes. On admirait non sans quelque inquiétude; on le suivait sans trop le comprendre. C'était surtout à son travail qu'il avait des airs d'alchimiste. A le voir à son chevalet, avec une palette certainement engluée, d'où sortaient tant de matières lourdes, d'où se dégageaient tant d'essences subtiles, ou penché sur ses planches de cuivre et burinant contre toutes les règles—on cherchait, au bout de son burin et de sa brosse, des secrets qui venaient de plus loin. Sa manière était si nouvelle, qu'elle déroutait les esprits forts, passionnait les esprits simples. Tout ce qu'il y avait de jeune, d'entreprenant, d'insubordonné et d'étourdi parmi les écoliers peintres courait à lui. Ses disciples directs furent médiocres; la queue fut détestable.

FROMENTIN, *Les Maîtres d'autrefois*.

1. Var. *honour and emolument*.
9. Var. *a taciturn type*.
24. **subtle essences**: *subtiles* is contrasted with *lourdes* and must have somewhat the sense of 'volatile'; *essences* may have its chemical or its philosophic senses. In translation, the choice lies between, e.g., 'airy creations' and a phrase as cryptic as the French.
25. **scraping**: the technical term in English.

77. REMBRANDT

At this moment, moreover, everything was going wrong, fortune and repute, and when he leaves the Breedstraat, homeless, penniless, but square with his creditors, neither talent nor fame acquired can now avail him. He is lost sight of, forgotten, and this time his personality does vanish into the mean, necessitous, obscure existence from which he had never really emerged.

In all, he was, as we see, a man apart, a dreamer of dreams, perhaps a man of few words, though his face suggests the opposite of that; perhaps a person 'with corners' and somewhat rugged, rigid, dogmatic, not easy to contradict and still less to convince, versatile in reality, unbending in outward forms, assuredly a 'character'. Though he was famous, made much of and lauded at first, in spite of the jealous, the short-sighted, the pedants and the fools, yet people took their vengeance when he was gone.

In the practice of his art, he did not paint, draw or engrave like anybody else. Indeed his works were a puzzle, as regards technique. People admired him not without some uneasiness. They followed him without quite understanding him. Especially at his work did he seem to have something of the alchemist. When they watched him at his easel, with a palette smeared all over, for sure, which produced so much thick pigment and released so many subtle essences, or bending over his copper-plates and scraping in defiance of all the rules, they looked to his graver and his brush for secrets which came from afar. His manner was so novel that it nonplussed the sceptical and moved simple souls to passionate admiration. All the youthful, audacious, rebellious and harum-scarum elements among the apprentice painters flocked round him. His direct disciples proved second-rate, the minor followers among them, beneath contempt.

27. Var. *summoned from afar*; *de loin* suggests some occult source, such as the Evil One.

31. **proved**: note the change of tense to *furent* = 'turned out to be'.

32. **the minor followers**: var. *the tail*; *the stragglers*. They, too, were direct disciples; hence the addition 'among them'.

78. LE SAÜL DE REMBRANDT

Le Saül de Rembrandt nous révèle jusqu'où peut atteindre une détresse humaine. Plus que les éclairs de la tunique jaune à la lumière plus profonde que l'or, les cassures du lourd manteau cramoisi et le turban gonflé de soie, sortent de l'ombre un morceau de nuque sous l'oreille et une pommette dont l'œil cave et la joue ravagée accusent le relief. Avec un geste d'enfant craintif le vieux roi cache l'autre moitié de sa figure dans le pli d'un rideau. A-t-il peur d'une de ces pensées qui battent comme une aile de chouette dans la pénombre de ses veilles, ou bien du jeune homme qui joue de la harpe devant lui, David, petit employé juif qui guette le moment de prendre la place de son patron?

L'histoire n'a pas eu la pitié qu'il fallait de Saül, jouet des caprices d'un dieu. Soldat de fortune trahi par le petit Javeh d'Israël, Rembrandt a pressenti cette version de Renan tout en élargissant sa portée jusqu'à l'universel. Le naïf Saül s'étonne devant la poussière où est réduit son éclatant passé.... Dans le mortel silence qui a suivi les chants qui l'accompagnaient aux sommets héroïques de sa carrière, il a usé ses dernières forces de vivre. Sa vertu s'en est allée dans un tremblement fébrile, et la main aux maigres doigts, allongée sur le bois de la lance qui repose contre son genou, ne pourrait même plus se refermer dans le simulacre d'une menace. Il a peur de l'affront qu'il pressent et dont il est incapable de tirer vengeance. Et le voici qui demeure aux écoutes: caché derrière ce pan de rideau avec lequel il essuie

---

1. Var. *is a revelation to us of how far human (a man's) distress can go.*
3. ?*which in the light is deeper than gold.*
5. Var. *the turban puffed out with silk.*
7. timid: var. *nervous, frightened.*
Var. (more exact) *with a gesture as of a timid child.*
11. youth: var. *stripling.*
12. hireling: var. *menial, underling;* "employee" is too modern.
13. Var. *the chance of supplanting his master.*
16. Yahweh: var. *Jehovah.*

78. REMBRANDT'S SAUL

Rembrandt's Saul reveals to us the very depths of human distress. What stands out from the shadow, more striking than the glitter of the yellow tunic which glows deeper than gold, more striking than the folds of the heavy crimson mantle or the billowing silk turban, is a bit of neck below the ear, and a cheek-bone which the sunken eye and the wasted cheek throw into sharp relief. With the gesture of a timid child, the old King conceals the other side of his face in the fold of a curtain. What is it that he fears? One of those phantasies which throb through the dim watches of his nights like the beating of an owl's wings? Or the youth who plays before him on the harp—David, a Jewish hireling waiting for his chance to step into his master's shoes?

History has not shown the pity it should for Saul, the plaything of a god's caprice. A soldier of fortune betrayed by the petty Yahweh of Israel—Rembrandt anticipates Renan's version and widens it to a universal application. Saul, the simple-minded, marvels to see the dust to which his brilliant past has turned.... In the deathly silence following the hymns which accompanied him on the heroic heights of his career he has spent his last reserves of strength. His natural force has departed and left a fevered trembling, and now the emaciated hand which reaches along the shaft of the javelin resting against his knee could not even close into the semblance of a threat. He dreads the insult which he feels coming and for which he is unable to take vengeance. And so we see him sitting there, all intent; hidden behind that curtain, with which he is wiping away a

17. **version**: var. *interpretation; version of the story.*
18. **simple-minded**: var. *guileless.*
19. **has turned**: var. *is turned (come).*
20. **on**: ? perhaps *to.*
25. **even close**: var. *so much as clench.*
26. **coming**: var. *imminent.*
27. **all intent**: var. *on the watch.*
28. **curtain**: var. *strip of curtain;* but cp. *un pan de mur,* a stretch of wall, often = a wall.

une larme, il tend le cou moins encore pour épier les spectres de sa terreur que pour surprendre les fantômes exilés de sa puissance.

Comme cette peinture aide à découvrir l'amertume qui est au fond de l'apologue du vieux lion et de l'âne! Mais la fable ne fournit en somme que l'exemple d'une goujaterie. Rembrandt, pour émouvoir la détresse du roi caduc au delà de ces limites où chavirent notre raison et notre conscience, a trouvé mieux qu'une brutale insulte: le sourire du jeune joueur de harpe qui prélude à un chant de victoire.

CHARLES BERNARD, *Saül et Rembrandt.*

29. **he cranes**: var. *and craning.*
37. **reel**: var. *founder*, but 'found' follows immediately.

tear, he cranes forward not so much to keep watch on the
spectres born of his terror as to catch a glimpse of the 30
banished phantoms of his power.

How admirably this picture helps us to detect the bitterness underlying the Apologue of the Ass and the Aged Lion!
But the Fable, after all, merely exemplifies an ill-bred action.
Rembrandt, to charge the broken King's distress with 35
emotions passing those bounds where reason and conscience
reel, has found something better than bare-faced insult: the
smile of the youthful harper who is playing the opening chords
of a hymn of victory.

38. Hardly "playing over the prelude to"; "prelude" seems
too formal for *préluder à*, which is not a very technical musical
term.

79. LA DAME AUX BRACELETS

Il y a au musée du Luxembourg un portrait de femme où la sûreté, la puissance et la liberté du métier de Charles Guérin sont plus clairement discernables qu'en aucune autre toile du même artiste. Je veux parler de *la Dame aux bracelets*. C'est par l'opulence et le chatoiement de la matière que cette œuvre commence à se saisir de vous. L'interprétation de la chair y est magnifique. Le carmin diffusé du masque brûle à force de richesse. La carnation du col et des bras nus a l'éclat d'une pesante coulée d'or brun, marbrée par les ombres froides et verdissantes des passages. La couleur des vêtements n'est pas moins splendide. Une admirable audace de coloriste se révèle dans le corsage d'un rouge corallin, martelé de touches orangées et parsemé de motifs blancs. Rien de plus complexe que l'organisation chromatique de *la Dame aux bracelets*. L'analyse du ton y est poussée aussi loin que chez les plus subtils des impressionnistes. Cependant la fermeté des contours est telle, le jeu des valeurs est si sûr, les touches sont si habilement juxtaposées ou fondues que les traces de ce labeur analytique échappent à une rétine peu attentive ou insuffisamment exercée. Charles Guérin tend de plus en plus à dissimuler ce libre et fougueux travail du pinceau que montrent agressivement la plupart des tableaux modernes. Mais sous la netteté de l'exécution, la vigueur des accents demeure. Par la subtilité des combinaisons harmoniques, la riche plénitude du dessin qui, comme chez tous les peintres authentiques, reste toujours 'au service de la pâte', cette effigie féminine est l'œuvre d'un maître. Je veux dire d'un artiste qui, s'étant posé le plus difficile des problèmes, a su 'faire de l'impressionnisme un art solide et durable comme celui des musées'.

FERNAND ROMANET, *L'art de Charles Guérin.*

10. **passes**: '*passage*: Terme de peinture: Succession graduée des nuances d'une couleur, depuis la plus foncée jusqu'à la plus légère: succession des ombres depuis la plus forte jusqu'à la plus claire, jusqu'au clair lui-même. [Dans ce portrait] point

79. THE LADY OF THE BRACELETS

There is in the Luxembourg Gallery a portrait of a woman in which the sureness, the power and the freedom of Charles Guérin's work are more clearly discernible than in any other canvas by the same artist. I refer to 'the Lady of the Bracelets'. It is by the richness and iridescence of the impasto that his work first appeals. The rendering of the flesh-tints is magnificent. The diffused carmine of the face glows, from very sumptuousness. The tints of the bare neck and arms gleam like a massive bar of dark gold, merging into cool green hues where it passes to shadow. The colour of the draperies is no less splendid. An admirable boldness in the use of colour is revealed by the bodice, of coralline red, touched here and there with orange and dappled with a small white pattern. What could be more complex than the colour scheme of 'the Lady of the Bracelets'? Tone analysis is here carried as far as by the subtlest of the impressionists. Yet so firm are the relations of the contours, so sure is the interplay of values, so skilfully juxtaposed and fused are the touches of brushwork, that no trace of laborious analysis is perceived by an unobservant or unpractised retina. Charles Guérin tends more and more to disguise the free and spirited handling which is aggressively apparent in most modern pictures. But under the directness of the execution, a vigour of accentuation persists. In the subtlety of the harmonic combinations, and the absolute fulness of the draughtsmanship which, as with all genuine painters, is always 'obedient to the properties of his medium', this portrayal of a woman is the work of a master—I mean, of an artist who, having set himself the hardest of problems, has succeeded in 'making impressionism an art as strong and as enduring as the art of the galleries'.

de nuances, point de *passages*, nulles teintes dans les chairs.' Littré. Cp. also Diderot, *Salons* (Garnier, p. 344): [Portrait de Mme Greuze] 'Les *passages* du front sont trop jaunes.'
  22. **handling**: var. *brush-work*.
  27. var. '*subservient (subordinate) to the paint*'.
  30. 'making', etc. A quotation from Cézanne.

VII. PHILOSOPHICAL AND REFLECTIVE

80. L'IMMENSITÉ DE L'UNIVERS

Que l'homme contemple donc la nature entière dans sa haute et pleine majesté, qu'il éloigne sa vue des objets bas qui l'environnent. Qu'il regarde cette éclatante lumière, mise comme une lampe éternelle pour éclairer l'univers, que la terre lui paraisse comme un point au prix du vaste tour que cet astre décrit et qu'il s'étonne de ce que ce vaste tour lui-même n'est qu'une pointe très délicate à l'égard de celui que les astres qui roulent dans le firmament embrassent. Mais si notre vue s'arrête là, que l'imagination passe outre; elle se lassera plutôt de concevoir, que la nature de fournir. Tout ce monde visible n'est qu'un trait imperceptible dans l'ample sein de la nature. Nulle idée n'en approche. Nous avons beau enfler nos conceptions, au delà des espaces imaginables, nous n'enfantons que des atomes, au prix de la réalité des choses. C'est une sphère dont le centre est partout, la circonférence nulle part. Enfin c'est le plus grand caractère sensible de la toute-puissance de Dieu, que notre imagination se perde dans cette pensée.

PASCAL, *Pensées*.

1. Var. *in her full and lofty majesty*. But English seems to require the superlative.

3. **which surround**: var. *around*.

5. **appear**: var. *come*.

of dust: 'speck' alone seems insufficient, for sense and for rhythm.

6. **Star**: has the same extended sense (see No. 4, note 1) as *astre*; cp. Day Star, star of noon, etc. (O.E.D.).

7. **how**: avoids the awkward 'that that' and reflects accurately enough *de ce que* + indicative.

80. THE IMMENSITY OF THE UNIVERSE

Let man therefore contemplate Nature as a whole in her highest and fullest majesty, let him turn his gaze far from the lowly objects which surround him. Let him look upon that shining light, set as an everlasting lamp to lighten the universe, let earth appear before him as a speck of dust in comparison with the mighty orbit which that Star describes and let him marvel how that mighty orbit itself is but a very slender pin-point in regard to that which the stars rolling in the firmament embrace. But though our gaze can go no further, let Imagination sweep on; rather shall she weary in conceiving than Nature in providing. All this visible world is only an imperceptible mark on the ample bosom of Nature. No idea can come nigh to her. Increase our conceptions as we may, beyond the realms of imaginable space, we bring forth but atoms, in comparison with the reality of things. The universe is a sphere whereof the centre is everywhere, the circumference nowhere. Nay, it is the greatest apparent attribute to God's omnipotence that our imagination should lose itself in that thought.

10. **sweep on**: *passer* seems at first a colourless word. But cp. 'Ils ne passeront pas'. Sometimes it means 'pass,' but generally it is to be translated by an English word of more 'body', e.g. 'sail'. *Passer* is like a blank cheque to be filled up suitably from the context. Here *passer* is merely part of a phrase *passer outre*=to proceed.

12. **mark**: *trait* (properly=thin line, streak) has probably no very definite sense, except as the last stage in the decrescendo: *un point...une pointe...un trait*.

13. **Increase**: var. *Expand*.

18. **attribute**: cp. *Merchant of Venice*: 'It [Mercy] is an *attribute* to God himself.'

81. LA CRITIQUE DANS LES SCIENCES

Le point essentiel dans l'étude de la nature est de découvrir les milieux des vérités connues, et de les placer dans l'ordre de leur enchaînement. On trouvait des carrières de marbre dans le sein des plus hautes montagnes, on en voyait se former sur les bords de l'Océan par le ciment du sel marin, on connaissait le parallélisme des couches de la terre; mais, répandus dans la physique, ces faits n'y jetaient aucune lumière; ils ont été rapprochés, et l'on y reconnaît les monuments de l'immersion totale ou successive de ce globe. C'est à cet ordre lumineux que le critique devrait surtout contribuer.

Il est pour les découvertes un temps de maturité avant lequel les recherches semblent infructueuses. Une vérité attend, pour éclore, la réunion de ses éléments. Ces germes ne se rencontrent et ne s'arrangent que par une longue suite de combinaisons: ainsi, ce qu'un siècle n'a fait que couver, s'il est permis de le dire, est produit par le siècle qui lui succède. C'est cette espèce de fermentation de l'esprit humain, cette digestion de nos connaissances, que le critique doit observer avec soin. Ce serait à lui de suivre pas à pas la science dans ses progrès, de marquer les obstacles qui l'ont retardée, comment ces obstacles ont été levés, et par quel enchaînement de difficultés et de solutions elle a passé

TITLE: **Science**: Marmontel has in this article, called *Critique*, two subsections, entitled *Critique dans les sciences* and *Critique dans les arts libéraux*. The plural *sciences* is used here as in *Académie des Sciences*, where we should employ the singular.

2. **connexion**: *les milieux* is here used by Marmontel in a peculiar sense, as almost = *chaînons*. In a preceding passage he has said: 'Pour réduire en règles l'investigation des vérités physiques, le critique devrait tenir *le milieu* et les extrémités de la chaîne; un chaînon qui lui échappe est un échelon qui lui manque pour s'élever à la démonstration.'

Var. *ascertained facts*.

3. Var. *marble quarries*, since in Marmontel's time the sense of English 'quarry' = *carrière* = a large mass of stone or rock in its natural state, capable of being quarried, was not yet obsolete.

81. CRITICISM IN SCIENCE

The essential point in the study of nature is to discover the connexion between known truths and set them in their proper sequence. We found deposits of marble in the heart of the loftiest mountains; we observed them forming on the shores of the Ocean from the cement of sea-salt; we knew the parallelism of the earth's strata. But these facts, so long as they lay scattered in physical science, were unilluminating; they have been brought into relation and are now seen to be the monuments of the total or successive submergence of the globe. It is to such luminous ordering as this that the critic should especially contribute.

Discoveries have a maturity period, prior to which research seems unfruitful. A truth must, for its full development, wait till all its elements have been assembled. These *germina* do not come together and fall into order till after a long series of different combinations; thus what one age has, if we may so say, merely incubated, is brought forth by the succeeding age. That sort of fermentation in the human mind, that digesting of our knowledge, is what the critic must observe carefully. It would thus be his function to follow up the advance of science step by step, note the obstacles which have retarded it, how they have been removed, and by what concatenation of difficulties and their

---

8. Var. *brought together*.

9. **monuments**: the older use of the word = French *monument* = evidence, record, still found in scientific writings.

13. Var. *A preliminary condition for the full development of any truth is the assembling of its constituent elements*.

14. **germina**: this eighteenth century scientific term = French *germes* is safer here than 'germs'.

20. **It would thus be:** *Ce serait* means 'It appears to be'. This is the conditional used for tentative statements, e.g. '*D'après* un journal du soir, le ministère l'*aurait* déjà décidé'.

21. **science**: *la science* may mean 'knowledge' or 'learning' or 'science', and it is difficult in an eighteenth-century context to say which English word is best.

du doute à la probabilité, de la probabilité à l'évidence. Par là il imposerait silence à ceux qui ne font que grossir le volume de la science, sans en augmenter le trésor; il marquerait le pas qu'elle aurait fait dans un ouvrage, ou renverrait l'ouvrage au néant, si l'auteur la laissait où il l'aurait prise. Tels seraient dans cette partie l'objet et le fruit de la critique. Combien cette réforme nous restituerait d'espace dans nos bibliothèques!

MARMONTEL, *Éléments de littérature.*

25. Var. *undeniable (incontrovertible) fact; certainty.*
26. **increase**, etc. For the idea, cp. La Bruyère, *Car.* (*De*

solutions science has proceeded from doubt to probability, from probability to proved fact. By that means he would silence those who merely increase the bulk of science and add nothing to its treasures; he would indicate the step forward which it had taken in a particular book, or consign the book to oblivion, should its author have left science where he found it. Such would be, in this branch of knowledge, the object and the fruits of criticism. By that reform how much space would be restored to us in our libraries!

Quelques Usages): 'C'est la paresse des hommes qui a encouragé le pédantisme à *grossir* plutôt qu'à enrichir les bibliothèques.'

82. DÉVOUEMENT A LA SCIENCE

Si, comme je me plais à le croire, l'intérêt de la science est compté au nombre des grands intérêts nationaux, j'ai donné à mon pays tout ce que lui donne le soldat mutilé sur le champ de bataille. Quelle que soit la destinée de mes travaux, cet exemple, je l'espère, ne sera pas perdu. Je voudrais qu'il servît à combattre l'espèce d'affaissement moral qui est la maladie de la génération nouvelle; qu'il pût ramener dans le droit chemin de la vie quelqu'une de ces âmes énervées qui se plaignent de manquer de foi, qui ne savent où se prendre et vont cherchant partout, sans le rencontrer nulle part, un objet de culte et de dévouement. Pourquoi se dire avec tant d'amertume que, dans le monde constitué comme il est, il n'y a pas d'air pour toutes les poitrines, pas d'emploi pour toutes les intelligences? L'étude sérieuse et calme n'est-elle pas là? et n'y a-t-il pas en elle un refuge, une espérance, une carrière à la portée de chacun de nous? Avec elle, on traverse les mauvais jours sans en sentir le poids, on se fait à soi-même sa destinée; on use noblement la vie. Voilà ce que j'ai fait et ce que je ferais encore; si j'avais à recommencer ma route, je prendrais celle qui m'a conduit où je suis. Aveugle, et souffrant sans espoir et presque sans relâche, je puis rendre ce témoignage, qui de ma part ne sera pas suspect: il y a au monde quelque

CONTEXT. The great historian Thierry (1795–1856) had read himself blind by 1826. He wrote this preface in 1834.

1. Var. *If, as I like (love) to think*, etc.

5. **forgotten**: the phrase *Cet exemple ne sera pas perdu* is almost a stock expression = We have noted the fact, the example will not be wasted (lost sight of); e.g. *L'Action française*, April 12, 1922: 'Constantin triomphe silencieusement de nous s'il ne triomphe pas des Turcs. *Cet exemple ne sera pas perdu*', and *Journal des Débats*, December 19, 1923: 'On sent chez M. Paul Bourget l'amour et l'orgueil de sa profession, et l'on voudrait qu'*un pareil exemple ne fût pas perdu*.'

82. DEVOTION TO LEARNING

If the interests of learning are, as I fondly believe, numbered among the great national interests, then I have given my country all that is given her by the soldier maimed upon the battlefield. Whatever the ultimate fate of my own work, the example, I hope, will not be forgotten. Would that it might help to counteract the sort of moral lassitude which is the malady of the rising generation; that it could bring back into the straight path one or other of these enervated beings who complain of lacking faith, who know not what to cling to, and go seeking high and low, yet find nowhere, an object of veneration and devotion! Why say to oneself with such bitterness that in the world as it is constituted there is not air enough for every pair of lungs, not work enough for every kind of intelligence? Is not earnest, quiet study always with us? and is there not in it a haven, a hope, a career, within the reach of everyone among us? With it, we live through evil days without feeling their burden, carve out our own destiny, spend life nobly. That is what I have done and should do again· had I to start once more on life's journey, I should take the road which has brought me where I stand. Blind, and suffering pain without hope and well nigh without respite, I can give this testimony which, coming from me, will not be suspect: there is in the world

---

6. **lassitude**: var. *collapse*.

11. Var. *Why should they say to themselves?*

14. **work**: var. *employment*.

18. **spend life**: distinguish *user de* = to use and *user* = to wear out = to spend.

19–20. **have done...has brought**. Not "did"..."brought". Thierry wrote many works after 1834.

21. **suffering pain**: 'suffering' alone might be either mental or physical; *souffrir* often = 'to be in pain'; e.g. a dentist, entering his waiting room: 'Il y a ici quelqu'un qui *souffre*?'

chose qui vaut mieux que les jouissances matérielles, mieux que la fortune, mieux que la santé elle-même, c'est le dévouement à la science.

THIERRY, *Dix Ans d'Études historiques*
(Preface).

24. **material**: var. *physical*; cp. 'Il est *matériellement* impossible...' = 'It is *physically* impossible....'

a better thing than material pleasures, better than wealth, better even than health, and it is devotion to learning. 25

24–25. Cp. C. Kingsley, *The Heroes*: 'No, children, there is a better thing on earth than wealth, a better thing than life itself; and that is to have done something before you die, for which good men may honour you.'

83. L'INTELLIGENCE EN HISTOIRE

C'est cette qualité, appliquée aux grands objets de l'histoire, qui à mon avis est la qualité essentielle du narrateur, et qui, lorsqu'elle existe, amène bientôt à sa suite toutes les autres, pourvu qu'au don de la nature on joigne l'expérience, née de la pratique. En effet, avec ce que je nomme l'intelligence, on démêle bien le vrai du faux, on ne se laisse pas tromper par les vaines traditions ou les faux bruits de l'histoire, on a de la critique; on saisit bien le caractère des hommes et des temps, on n'exagère rien, on ne fait rien trop grand ou trop petit, on donne à chaque personnage ses traits véritables, on écarte le fard, de tous les ornements le plus malséant en histoire; on peint juste; on entre dans les secrets ressorts des choses, on comprend et on fait comprendre comment elles se sont accomplies; diplomatie, administration, guerre, marine, on met ces objets si divers à la portée de la plupart des esprits, parce qu'on a su les saisir dans leur généralité intelligible à tous; et quand on est arrivé ainsi à s'emparer des nombreux éléments dont un vaste récit doit se composer, l'ordre dans lequel il faut les présenter, on le trouve dans l'enchaînement des événements, car celui qui a su saisir le lien mystérieux qui les unit, la manière dont ils se sont engendrés les uns les autres, a découvert l'ordre de narration le plus beau, parce que c'est le plus naturel; et si, de plus, il n'est pas de glace devant les grandes scènes de la vie des nations, il mêle fortement le tout ensemble, le fait succéder avec aisance et vivacité; il laisse au fleuve du temps sa fluidité, sa puissance, sa grâce même, en ne forçant aucun de ses mouvements, en n'altérant aucun de ses heureux

---

4. **he can add.** Throughout the passage *on* gives trouble. It seems best to make it more precise, e.g. 'he', 'the historian', etc.

8. **baseless:** *vaines* = properly 'empty'; var. *idle*. Cp. No. 104, line 2.

9. **will judge:** the form with 'will' is perhaps clearer than the simple present, here and further on.

13. **colouring:** for *fard* see No. 45, note 28.

83. INTELLIGENCE IN HISTORICAL MATTERS

It is that quality, applied to the great objects of History, which in my opinion is the essential quality of the narrator and which, when forthcoming, soon brings all the others in its train, provided that he can add to a natural gift the experience born of practice. In fact the historian, if only he possesses what I term 'intelligence', really does disentangle truth from falsehood, and is not deceived by the baseless traditions or the false rumours with which History abounds; he is *critical*. Possessing intelligence, he will judge correctly the character of men and the nature of their times, exaggerate nothing, neither magnify nor minimize, give to every personage his true features, avoid the meretricious colouring which is of all embellishments the most unseemly in historical writing, and paint accurately; he will enter into the hidden causes of things, understand and explain how these things came about. Diplomacy, administration, war, naval affairs—he will bring those very diverse subjects within the reach of most minds, because he has had vision to see them in their general aspect, which is intelligible to all. And when he has thus fully mastered the numerous elements of which a large-scale History must be composed, the proper order in which to present them will be found in the sequence of events, for he who has succeeded in discovering the mysterious link between events, the way in which one gave rise to another, has discovered the order of narration which is the best because it is the most natural. If, moreover, the historian does not himself remain unmoved when he surveys the great scenes in the life of nations, he will weld his material into a complete whole, carry on the story in an easy, vivacious way; he will leave to the river of time its natural flow, its power, we might even say its grace, forcing none of its movements, spoiling none of its pleasing

22. Var. *he will find the proper order of their presentation in the sequence*, etc.

contours; enfin, dernière et suprême condition, il est équitable, parce que rien ne calme, n'abat les passions comme la connaissance profonde des hommes.

THIERS, *Histoire du Consulat et de l'Empire.*

33. **possessing intelligence.** The passage being lengthy, it may be useful to recall the original phrase at this point.

curves. Last and chief requirement—possessing intelligence, he will be just, because nothing soothes, nothing allays the passions so much as a profound knowledge of human nature.[35]

35. **human nature:** var. *mankind.*

84. LE TÉMOIGNAGE DES CONTEMPORAINS

L'histoire ne doit pas dire seulement les choses vraies, mais les dire dans la vraie mesure, ne pas les mettre toutes à la fois sur le premier plan, ne pas subordonner les grandes en exagérant les petites. Appréciation difficile, en ce que les contemporains l'aident fort peu. Au contraire, ils travaillent tous à nous tromper en cela. Chacun, dans ses Mémoires, ne manque pas de mettre en saillie sa petite importance, telle chose secondaire, qu'il a vue, sue, ou faite. Nous-mêmes, élevés tous dans la littérature et l'histoire de ce temps, les ayant connues de bonne heure, avant toute critique, nous gardons des préjugés de sentiment sur telle œuvre ou tel acte dont la première impression s'est liée à nos souvenirs d'enfance....

C'est une œuvre virile d'historien de résister ainsi à ses propres préjugés d'enfance, à ceux de ses lecteurs, et enfin aux illusions que les contemporains eux-mêmes ont consacrées. Il lui faut une certaine force pour marcher ferme à travers tout cela, en écartant les vaines ombres, en fondant, ou rejetant même, nombre de vérités minimes qui encombreraient la voie. Mais s'il se garde ainsi, il a pour récompense de voir surgir de l'océan confus la chaîne des grandes causes vivantes. Connaissance généralement refusée aux contemporains qui ont vu jour par jour, et qui, trop près des choses, se sont souvent aveuglés du détail. Ils ont vu les victoires, les fêtes, les événements officiels, fort rarement senti la sourde circulation de la vie, certain travail latent qui pourtant un matin éclate avec la force souveraine des révolutions et change le monde.

MICHELET, *Histoire de France*.

84. CONTEMPORARY EVIDENCE

History must not merely present the things which are true, but must present them in their true proportion—not put all of them indiscriminately in the foreground, not depreciate the major facts by over-stressing the minor. This discrimination is difficult, in that contemporaries are of very little assistance. Rather do they tend to lead us astray in the matter. Everybody, in his Memoirs, unfailingly gives prominence to his own precious importance, to such or such a thing of secondary interest which he saw, he heard of, or he did. We ourselves—brought up, as we have all of us been, on the literature and history of our own time and having become acquainted with them at an early stage, before we had developed any critical faculty—retain sentimental preconceptions about such and such a work, this action or that, the first impression which it made on us being bound up with our own childhood memories....

It is a man's job for an historian to fight thus against childish preconceptions, his own and those of his readers, and also against the illusions which contemporaries themselves have sanctioned. He requires some strength of mind to proceed on his way through all this confusion, neglecting vain shadows, fusing together or, it may be, discarding large numbers of unimportant facts which would cumber the path. But if he so safeguards himself, he is rewarded by seeing the links in the chain of great living causes emerge from the ocean of chaos. Knowledge of that kind is generally denied to contemporaries. They were day-to-day spectators; placed too near the events, they often failed to see the wood for the trees. They saw the victories, the ceremonies, the official happenings, but very seldom felt the obscure pulsing of life —certain processes which are latent and yet one day break forth with the all-compelling force of revolutions and alter the face of the world.

85. L'*ANGELUS*

Un soir que la fenêtre était ouverte, et que, assise au bord, elle venait de regarder Lestiboudois, le bedeau, qui taillait le buis, elle entendit tout à coup sonner l'*Angelus*.

On était au commencement d'avril, quand les primevères sont écloses; un vent tiède se roule sur les plates-bandes labourées, et les jardins, comme des femmes, semblent faire leur toilette pour les fêtes de l'été. Par les barreaux de la tonnelle et au delà tout alentour, on voyait la rivière dans la prairie, où elle dessinait sur l'herbe des sinuosités vagabondes. La vapeur du soir passait entre les peupliers sans feuilles, estompant leurs contours d'une teinte violette, plus pâle et plus transparente qu'une gaze subtile arrêtée sur leurs branchages. Au loin, des bestiaux marchaient; on n'entendait ni leurs pas, ni leurs mugissements; et la cloche, sonnant toujours, continuait dans les airs sa lamentation pacifique.

A ce tintement répété, la pensée de la jeune femme s'égarait dans ses vieux souvenirs de jeunesse et de pension. Elle se rappela les grands chandeliers, qui dépassaient sur l'autel les vases pleins de fleurs et le tabernacle à colonnettes. Elle aurait voulu, comme autrefois, être encore confondue dans la longue ligne des voiles blancs, que marquaient de noir çà et là les capuchons raides des bonnes sœurs inclinées sur leur prie-Dieu; le dimanche, à la messe, quand elle relevait sa tête, elle apercevait le doux visage de la Vierge, parmi les tourbillons bleuâtres de l'encens qui montait. Alors un attendrissement la saisit: elle se sentit molle et

6. **dug**: var. *turned*.
7. **girls**: *femmes* is not always = women.
  beautiful: var. *smart*.
13. **fine gauze**, etc. Flaubert's simile seems open to the objection that *gaze* does not necessarily imply colour.
18. **ringing**: not of course "tinkling"; *tinter* means properly the slow ringing of a bell, with the clapper striking only one side, and generally the notes of a more or less distant bell. Cp. Larousse s.v. CLOCHE: 'L'étroitesse de ces beffrois est une preuve

85. THE ANGELUS

One evening when the window was open and, sitting by it, just a moment before, she had been watching Lestiboudois the verger clipping the hedge, she suddenly heard the Angelus ringing.

It was early April, when the primroses are out and a warm wind goes rollicking over the freshly dug flower-beds and the gardens seem like girls making themselves beautiful for the summer season. Through the lattice of the arbour, and beyond it and round about, the river could be seen in the meadows, marking out its truant windings upon the grass. The evening mist was stealing through between the leafless poplars, softening their outlines with a tinge of purple which was paler and more transparent than fine gauze clinging to their branches. In the distance, cattle were on the move; no sound of hooves or lowing could be heard; and the bell, never ceasing, rang out upon the air in peaceful lamentation.

To the sound of this insistent ringing, the young woman's thoughts were wandering away to far-off memories of school and girlhood days. Her mind went back to the tall candlesticks on the altar, standing high above the flower-filled vases and the pillared tabernacle. She could have wished to be, as of old, still lost in the long line of white veils broken here and there by the black of the stiff hoods worn by the nuns bending over their praying-desks; on Sundays, at Mass, when she raised her head, she could see the sweet face of the Virgin through the faint blue coils of the rising incense. At that remembrance she was overcome by tender emotion;

---

que dans le principe, on ne sonnait pas les cloches à toute volée; on se contentait de les *tinter*.'

20. Var. *She recollected*—perhaps more exact because *se rappela* is active, as opposed to *se souvint de*, which is said rather of passive, involuntary remembering.

25. **praying-desks:** *prie-dieu* is also in common English use; its plural in English (*prie-dieu* in French) is not given in O.E.D.

tout abandonnée comme un duvet d'oiseau qui tournoie dans la tempête; et ce fut sans en avoir conscience qu'elle s'achemina vers l'église, disposée à n'importe quelle dévotion, pourvu qu'elle y courbât son âme et que son existence entière y disparût.

Elle rencontra, sur la place, Lestiboudois, qui s'en revenait; car, pour ne pas rogner la journée, il préférait interrompre sa besogne, puis la reprendre, si bien qu'il tintait l'*Angelus* selon sa commodité. D'ailleurs, la sonnerie, faite plus tôt, avertissait les gamins de l'heure du catéchisme.

FLAUBERT, *Madame Bovary*.

29. **limp**: for *molle* cp. No. 36, note 10.
35. **reduce**: var. *cut into, encroach on*; *rogner* = to nibble into.

she felt limp and utterly forsaken, like a bit of down swirling
in the tempest; and without consciousness of what she was
doing she went on her way to the Church, prepared for no
matter what devotion, so might she incline to it her heart
and sink in it her whole existence.

On the Square she met Lestiboudois coming away, for,
so as not to reduce his working-day, he preferred to break
off and begin again, and used to ring the Angelus to suit his
own convenience. Besides, earlier ringing gave the village
boys warning that it was time for Catechism.

The verger seems to have arranged his time-table so as to allow
for an extra half-hour's work in the daylight either before or
after the Angelus, according to the season.

86. RETOURS

Le plus douloureux, à mesure que l'on vieillit, mon amie, c'est qu'on connaît les lendemains, ce qui fait qu'on n'a plus de confiance dans les journées. On sait d'avance que le voyage a ses retours et que l'amour a ses retours et on désire surtout ne pas partir ni pour l'un ni pour l'autre. Pourtant je m'excite encore à l'idée d'un voyage quand revient la belle saison, mais, dérision! je sens que je voudrais surtout revivre le passé, mettre mes pas dans les vieux vestiges, mes regards dans les paysages d'autrefois, mon corps dans la mer connue et familière. Alors peu à peu le rêve tourne à l'ironie, et après lui avoir ri, j'en ris. A quoi bon? Si encore on se retrouvait au même point! Mais il semble à chaque retour que la route se soit déplacée. C'est à peine si l'on retrouve sa maison. Il faut renouer difficilement sa vie, tant qu'il semble qu'elle en vaille encore la peine. Vraiment, je déteste cette période des voyages. Je n'y eus jamais depuis longtemps que des ennuis, que des surprises mauvaises, dont la dernière me hante encore. Il me semble que la vie va de travers, dès que je cesse de la regarder. Mais l'attention se lasse, il faut savoir un instant fermer les yeux.

Alors, je m'en irai tout comme un autre par les routes et par les hôtelleries vers le bout du monde, qui est le rivage le plus proche. Quand il y avait encore des grèves solitaires, quelles belles journées j'ai vécu près de toi, mer aux vagues monotones! Je savais marcher pieds nus comme les pêcheurs

---

1. Var. *What hurts most as age steals on.*
5. **return journeys:** *retours* is used here in two senses: (1) return, (2) revulsion, change of feeling.
6. **summer days:** for *la belle saison*, see No. 1, note 19.
9. Var. *gaze on.*
10. Var. *the old familiar sea.*
12. **indulging in it:** var. *greeting (welcoming) it with a smile.*
16. **so long as:** *tant que* is used as in '*Tant qu*'il y a de la vie, il y a de l'espoir'.

86. RETURNINGS

The most painful thing as a man grows old, dear friend, is that he knows what To-morrows are like and has therefore no confidence in To-days. He knows beforehand that travelling means return journeys—and that love means return journeys, too—and his chief desire is to avoid travels of either sort. Yet when summer days come round again, I still get excited at the thought of going away, but (Oh, the irony of it!) I feel that what I most want to do is to live the past over again, set my feet in the old tracks, my eyes on the scenes of long ago, take a dip in the known and friendly sea. Then gradually the fond dream becomes ironical and after indulging in it I laugh at it. What is the use of travelling? If one could even get back to the same point! But every time we turn homewards it seems as if the road had changed its place. One can hardly find one's own house. The threads of life have to be laboriously picked up again, so long as life still seems worth that much trouble. Frankly I loathe this travelling season. I never got anything from it, in recent years, but worry and unpleasant surprises, of which the latest is still on my mind. It seems to me that life goes all awry the moment I take my eyes off it. But attention flags; one must learn the art of closing one's eyes for a moment.

So off I'll go, just like anybody else, by high-road and hostelry, off to the world's end, that is, the nearest bit of coast. When there were still lonely beaches to be found, what glorious days I lived beside thee, O ever-beating Sea! I could walk bare-foot like the fishermen on the coast and

---

18. **in recent years:** var. *for a long time past. J'eus* = 'I came into possession of', 'I obtained'. *Je n'y eus jamais depuis long-temps* is idiomatic, but illogical and hardly bears grammatical analysis.

26. **lonely:** var. *unspoilt, unfrequented.*

28. **the fishermen on the coast:** as distinguished from deep-sea fishermen: var. *the local fisher-folk.*

de la côte et vivre comme eux dans un sac de molleton. On s'en allait très loin dans l'eau, porté comme une épave par le flot descendant et on revenait amené par le montant. Les pêcheurs avaient pêché et je m'étais assis sur une pointe de rocher, heureux d'être un îlot parmi les autres, puis j'errais par les dunes en déclamant des vers de Byron. Que ce tableau doit vous sembler ridicule! Il est encore émouvant pour moi.

REMY DE GOURMONT, *Lettres à l'Amazone.*

29. **go:** var. *wade. On* includes the speaker and the fishermen. He was probably wading out for shrimps, cockles, etc., although *porté comme une épave* seems at first to suggest that he was in a boat. Taken in conjunction with *près de toi* and *marcher pieds nus*, the sentence seems to mean that he waded out at low tide and came back with the incoming tide. The fishermen, however, being in search of marketable fish, probably used a boat.

31. **fished:** var. *made their catch (drawn their net).*

live like them in a sack of duffel. We used to go far out
in the water, borne like a bit of wreckage by the ebb, 30
and come home on the flood. When the fishers had fished,
and I had sat on the top of a rock, happy to be one islet
among the others, I would roam among the sand-hills,
reciting Byron. How silly the picture must seem to you!
It is still deeply moving to me. 35

32. **on the top of a rock**: *une pointe de rocher* means a more or less conspicuous rock or part of a rock. Cp. Chateaubriand's striking evocation of Napoleon at St Helena: 'On lui a donné un rocher, à *la pointe* duquel il est demeuré au soleil jusqu'à sa mort et d'où il était vu de toute la terre.' V. Hugo said of himself in Guernsey that he lived 'comme perché à *la pointe* d'un rocher'.

islet: although 'rock' is debarred, as having just been used, *un îlot* is often what we should rather call a 'rock', e.g. in No. 109.

87. L'INDUSTRIALISME ET LA POÉSIE

La lande de Lessay est une des plus considérables de cette portion de la Normandie qu'on appelle la presqu'île du Cotentin. Pays de culture, de vallées fertiles, d'herbages verdoyants, de rivières poissonneuses, le Cotentin, cette terre grasse et remuée, a pourtant, comme la Bretagne, sa voisine, la Pauvresse-aux-Genêts, de ces parties stériles et nues où l'homme passe et où rien ne vient, sinon une herbe rare et quelques bruyères, bientôt desséchées. Ces lacunes de culture, ces places vides de végétation jettent dans ces paysages frais, riants et féconds, de soudaines interruptions de mélancolie, des airs soucieux, des aspects sévères. Elles les ombrent d'une estompe plus noire....

Les landes sont comme les lambeaux, laissés sur le sol, d'une poésie primitive et sauvage que la main et la herse de l'homme ont déchirée. Haillons sacrés qui disparaîtront au premier jour sous le souffle de l'industrialisme moderne; car notre époque, grossièrement matérialiste et utilitaire, a pour prétention de faire disparaître toute espèce de friche et de broussailles aussi bien du globe que de l'âme humaine. Asservie aux idées de rapport, la société, cette vieille ménagère qui n'a plus de jeune que ses besoins et qui radote de ses lumières, ne comprend pas plus les divines ignorances de l'esprit, cette poésie de l'âme, qu'elle veut échanger contre de malheureuses connaissances toujours incomplètes, qu'elle n'admet la poésie des yeux, cachée et invisible sous

---

6. **some of those**: var. *those sorts of*.
7. **will not settle**: var. *passes on*.
8. **heather**: the plural *bruyères* is normal French for 'heather' [cp. 'ferns' in English], e.g. Giraudoux, *La Pharmacienne*: 'Elle passa..., les bras chargés de *bruyères*.'
   thin grass: cp. No. 7, note 5.
15. **poem**: *une poésie* may be = either 'poetry' or a (short) 'poem'—as opposed to *un poème*, which is usually longer and more ambitious.
   torn up: var. *torn in pieces*; *rent*.

87. INDUSTRIALISM AND POETRY

Lessay Moor is one of the most extensive in that portion of Normandy known as the Cotentin peninsula. An agricultural district, with fertile valleys, verdant pastures and rivers abounding in fish, the Cotentin, with its rich and well-tilled soil, nevertheless contains (like its neighbour Brittany, 'the Beggar Maid decked out in broom') some of those bare, barren areas where man will not settle and nothing will grow but thin grass and a little heather which is soon withered. These gaps in the farm-land, these patches where there is no vegetation, suddenly break in upon the fresh, smiling, bounteous landscape with a note of gloom, of foreboding, of bleakness. They bring a darker shading into the picture....

The moors are like the tattered remnants, strewn on the soil, of some wild, primitive poem torn up by the hand of man—and by the harrow. Sacred shreds they are, which will be blown away by the first blast of modern industrialism, for our blatantly materialistic and utilitarian age prides itself on removing all manner of scrub and fallow land whether from the surface of the earth or from the human soul. A slave to the idea of profit-making, Society—that ancient housewife who has no remaining traces of youth about her but her exigencies and is for ever prating about her own enlightened notions—can no more understand the divine ignorances of the mind (which are the poetry of the soul and which she nevertheless insists on bartering away for miserable knowledge inevitably incomplete) than she can believe in the poetry of the eye, lying hidden from view

---

22. Var. *whose exigencies are all that now remain to her of youth* (*alone remain youthful*).

27. **miserable**: var. *sorry, worthless*; but *malheureuses* may = *qui portent malheur* = 'ill-starred' and refer to the evils which this sort of knowledge brings, viz. destruction of spiritual values.

inevitably incomplete: var. *doomed to incompleteness*.

28. **believe in**: var. *admit the existence of, recognize*.

Var. *in poetry for the eye* (*which the eye can see*).

l'apparente inutilité des choses. Pour peu que cet effroyable mouvement de la pensée moderne continue, nous n'aurons plus, dans quelques années, un pauvre bout de lande où l'imagination puisse poser son pied pour rêver, comme le héron sur une de ses pattes.

J. BARBEY D'AUREVILLY, *L'Ensorcelée.*

29. **Let**, etc.: for *pour peu que*, see No. 57, note 24.
32. **Imagination**, etc.: var. *a man with imagination.*

in things whose utility is not apparent. Let this disastrous trend of modern thought continue but a little longer and in a few years we shall not have one poor bit of moorland left where Imagination can 'stand and stare'—stand like the heron on one leg.

    'stand and stare': W. H. Davies:
> 'What is this life if, full of care,
> We have no time to stand and stare?'

    the heron: cp. La Fontaine, *Fables* VII, iv: *Le Héron*: 'Un jour, sur ses longs pieds', etc.

88. L'ESPRIT FRANÇAIS

La forme dégradée du type français, c'est l'esprit gaulois, fait de basse jalousie, d'insouciante polissonnerie et d'une inintelligence absolue de tous les intérêts supérieurs de la vie; ou le bon sens bourgeois, terre à terre, indifférent à tout, hors les intérêts matériels, plus jouisseur que sensuel, et plus attaché au gain qu'au plaisir. Sa forme frivole, c'est l'esprit mondain, creux et brillant, mousse légère d'idées qui ne nourrit ni ne grise. Sa forme exquise, c'est cet esprit sans épithète, fine expression de rapports difficiles à démêler, qui surprend, charme, et parfois confond par l'absolue justesse, où l'expression d'abord fait goûter l'idée, où l'idée ensuite entretient la fraîcheur de l'expression. Enfin, la forme grave et supérieure de notre intelligence, c'est l'esprit d'analyse, subtil et fort, et la logique, aiguë et serrée: le don de représenter par une simplification lumineuse les éléments essentiels de la réalité, et celui de suivre à l'infini sans l'embrouiller ni le rompre jamais le fil des raisonnements abstraits; c'est le génie de l'invention psychologique et de la construction mathématique.

LANSON, *Histoire de la littérature française.*

1. **lower**: *dégradée* means at a lower grade, often of colour; "baser" or "debased" would be too strong.

the French type. Lanson has just been discussing *le caractère de la race*.

Var. *arrives at self-expression*.

2. **mean**: var. *unworthy*.

4. **the higher**: 'all' can be omitted.

88. THE FRENCH MIND

The lower form in which the French type finds expression is the so-called 'esprit gaulois', a compound of mean jealousy, light-hearted impropriety and utter inability to understand the higher things of life; or middle-class common sense which is matter-of-fact, indifferent to anything beyond material interests, more self-indulgent than sensual and more set on money-making than on pleasure-seeking. The frivolous form is the 'esprit mondain', empty and showy, an airy froth of ideas which is neither nutritive nor exhilarating. The exquisite form is 'esprit', without further qualification, a delicate expression of relationships difficult to disentangle, which surprises and delights and sometimes astonishes by its absolute rightness, the form first giving a relish to the thought, the thought maintaining the freshness of the expression. Lastly, the grave, the higher form of our French intelligence: the analytical spirit, subtle and strong; our logic, keen and closely reasoned; the gift of showing by some luminous simplification the essential elements of reality, and that of following out the thread of abstract reasoning to infinity without ever ravelling or breaking it—the genius for psychological discovery and mathematical constructiveness.

8. **'esprit mondain'**: var. *the social turn of mind.*
13. Var. *and in which the form first lends savour to (whets our appetite for) the thought and the thought keeps the expression fresh.*
20. Var. *without any confusion or break of continuity.*
21. **constructiveness**: not "construction". Some lines before Lanson had said: 'Notre nation est...logicienne, constructive, et généralisatrice.'

89. LA DÉMOCRATIE ET L'ESPRIT

On dit que la démocratie fait le lit de la tyrannie. Je crois assez que cela vient de ce que la démocratie manque d'esprit, ou, ce qui revient au même, de ce que la justice y est conquise comme une faveur, chacun bousculant le voisin; or, il s'en faut bien que l'égalité consiste dans un droit égal à se pousser; et l'esprit de parti fait voir cet étrange désordre à tous les degrés, de courtisans sans roi. On entend mal le suffrage si ce n'est qu'une loterie ouverte à tout ambitieux. A ce compte la tyrannie serait la perfection de la démocratie; car c'est le parti le plus fort qui élève le tyran. Le fait est que cette démocratie plébiscitaire est à peu près la seule qu'on ait vue. L'Angleterre s'en est gardée, par des combinaisons de prudence qui semblent étranges aux autres peuples. Il se peut bien aussi que la France s'organise selon les mêmes fins, mais selon une autre prudence et d'autres ruses, qui ne sont point non plus des articles d'exportation.

Ce qui est à l'œuvre dans les deux pays, c'est, je suppose, une certaine monnaie d'esprit; et l'esprit se reconnaît à ceci qu'il parle de sa place. Un marchand qui prétend raisonner de politique ne prétend pas pour cela changer de métier et se faire ministre. De tels hommes, qui commencent à ne point nous manquer trop, sont le sel des démocraties. J'en connais même qui voudraient bien désirer un tyran, mais qui ne peuvent, parce qu'ils n'abandonnent rien de leur jugement, et, sur toute opinion, de qui qu'elle vienne, frappent sans pitié; ce sont des chasseurs de sottise.

The difficulty of the passage is the same as in No. 73—extreme condensation of thought and elliptical expressions.

1. **paves the way for**: for *faire le lit de* cp. Jules Romains, *Visite aux Américains* (1936), p. 199: 'Les républicains affirment que l'expérience Roosevelt *fait le lit du* communisme.'

3. **intelligence**: *esprit* evidently requires a single English equivalent throughout the passage and 'intelligence' seems the least unsatisfactory; 'judgment' and 'understanding' are possible also.

9. **taken**: var. *thought*.

11. Var. *On that showing*.

89. DEMOCRACY AND INTELLIGENCE

People say that democracy paves the way for tyranny. I rather think that is because democracy suffers from a shortage of intelligence or, what comes to the same thing, because in a democracy justice is to be obtained as a favour, with every man jostling his neighbour; now, equality does not consist, far from it, in equal rights to self-assertion; and party spirit shows at all levels that strange lack of order when there are courtiers without a King. The franchise is wrongly understood if it is taken to be merely a lottery open to everybody who has ambitions. At that rate, tyranny would be the perfection of democracy, for it is the strongest party that sets up the tyrant. The fact is that such plebiscitary democracy is about the only sort which has been tried. England has avoided it, by means of elaborate safeguards which to other nations seem odd. It may well be, too, that France is setting her house in order with the same ends in view, but with different safeguards and different devices, which also are unsuitable for export.

What is operating in both countries is, I take it, a certain circulating currency of intelligence, and the sign of intelligence is the fact that it speaks from its place of work. A tradesman who wants to discuss politics is not, for that reason, asking for a change of job and a seat in the Cabinet. Such men—and they are beginning to be not so very uncommon in France—are the salt of democracies. I even know some who would be willing to consider a tyrant desirable, but cannot, because they will not make any surrender of their own judgment and mercilessly attack any opinion, no matter who originated it; they are out to destroy fallacies.

17. Var. *with a different sort of caution and different tricks*. 'Alain' is fond of the idea that nature can, and often must, be 'cheated'.

18. **for export**: var. *for foreign consumption; for use abroad*.

21. **place of work**: *place* has this sense (cp. *bureau de placement*), but also means 'proper place'.

28. Var. *any opinion, no matter whose*.

Je dis marchand, je dis administrateur; mais l'ouvrier jugeur, le paysan jugeur, dont nous avons quantité, ont encore une meilleure position, parlant très fort de leur place, et aussitôt écoutés, la main sur l'outil. Et ce que l'esprit sait, partout où il poursuit son examen, c'est que la tyrannie n'est jamais à demi tyrannique; et que le dogmatisme est nécessairement fanatique. Il n'en peut être autrement, puisque les vérités acquises sont de terribles faits, et, pour tout dire, des forces, avec les attributs des forces, et violence qui n'est jamais loin. L'expérience dira si l'on ne vit pas mieux par une active révision de toutes les vérités acquises; mais ce n'est pas premièrement une question de bonheur, car l'esprit dit qu'il le faut. De toute façon écrivons sur nos tablettes qu'une démocratie sans esprit ne peut pas durer longtemps.   ALAIN, *Propos de politique.*

30. **managing director**: var. *director*, if this makes it clear that someone in business is meant; not "administrator", since he is contrasted with the politician.

Though I said 'tradesman' and might have said 'managing director', yet the critically-minded working-man, the critically-minded small farmer—and of these we have plenty—are in a still better position; speaking up from their place of work, leaning on their tools, they command an instant hearing. And what intelligence realizes, wherever it carries out its investigations, is that tyranny is never tyrannical by halves, and that dogmatism is of necessity fanatical. It cannot be otherwise, for established truths are formidable facts; to put it plainly, they are forces—with the attributes of forces, and violence which is never very far away. Experience will show whether we do not get more out of life by active reconsideration of all established truths; but this is not primarily a question of happiness, for intelligence says it is a necessity. In any case, let us jot down this: a democracy without intelligence cannot last long.

34. Var. *they are sure of a hearing.*
41. **reconsideration**: var. *revaluation, re-examination.*
44. Var. *make a note of this.*

90. PRIÈRE QUE JE FIS SUR L'ACROPOLE QUAND JE FUS ARRIVÉ A EN COMPRENDRE LA PARFAITE BEAUTÉ

'Je suis né, déesse aux yeux bleus, de parents barbares, chez les Cimmériens bons et vertueux qui habitent au bord d'une mer sombre, hérissée de rochers, toujours battue par les orages. On y connaît à peine le soleil; les fleurs sont les mousses marines, les algues et les coquillages coloriés qu'on trouve au fond des baies solitaires. Les nuages y paraissent sans couleur, et la joie même y est un peu triste; mais des fontaines d'eau froide y sortent du rocher, et les yeux des jeunes filles y sont comme ces vertes fontaines où, sur des fonds d'herbes ondulées, se mire le ciel.

'Mes pères, aussi loin que nous pouvons remonter, étaient voués aux navigations lointaines, dans des mers que tes Argonautes ne connurent pas. J'entendis, quand j'étais jeune, les chansons des voyages polaires; je fus bercé au souvenir des glaces flottantes, des mers brumeuses semblables à du lait, des îles peuplées d'oiseaux qui chantent à leurs heures et qui, prenant leur volée tous ensemble, obscurcissent le ciel.

N.B. The passage is introduced by the words: 'Un vieux papier que je retrouve parmi mes notes de voyage contint ceci.'

1. **I was born**: Renan was born in 1823, at Tréguier (Côtes-du-Nord) which is at some little distance from the sea. His father, the captain of a small cutter, lived there.

blue-eyed Goddess: γλαυκῶπις 'Αθήνη: Pallas Athene, whose chief temple, the Parthenon, is on the Acropolis and whom Renan addresses as the goddess of Reason.

2. **Cimmerii**: the people who 'In dark Cimmerian desert ever dwell' (*L'Allegro*). They lived 'on the shores' of the Black Sea, between the Danube and the Don.

5. **painted**: var. *brightly coloured*.

6. **head**: not "bed"; the sea-weed, etc., would be found at the highwater mark.

9. **green pools**: these must be the same *fontaines* as in the preceding line; otherwise the repetition would be a blemish. But French uses *fontaine* for both 'spring' and 'well'. The first use here is a 'spring'; the second suggests rock-spring water falling into an eddying pool, where there are *herbes ondulées*; in ordinary use little distinction is made between *ondulé* and

90. THE PRAYER I SAID UPON THE ACRO-POLIS WHEN I HAD COME TO COMPRE-HENSION OF ITS PERFECT BEAUTY

'...I was born, O blue-eyed Goddess, of Barbarian parents, among the kindly, virtuous Cimmerii who dwell by the shore of a dark sea, bristling with rocks and ever beaten upon by storms. There men hardly know the sun; the flowers are the mosses of the sea, the wrack and the painted shells at the head of the lonely bays. The clouds seem to have no colour in them, and joy itself is tinged with sadness; but cool water-springs gush from the rock, and the eyes of the maidens in the land are as those green pools which on a ground of swaying grasses mirror the sky.

'My forefathers, as far back as we can go, gave their lives to distant faring, on seas thy Argonauts never knew. In childhood's days I heard the songs of Polar voyages; I was rocked to sleep with stories of the ice-floes, the misty seas like milk, the islands peopled with birds which utter their cry when the spirit moves them and all rise into flight together, darkening the sky.

ondulant. On the French admiration for 'green' eyes, cp. É-douard Rod, Tr. No. XXXIX: 'les yeux, d'un vert de mer profond'.

11. Another version has: Mes *ancêtres*, aussi loin que *l'on peut* remonter; *pères* is more Biblical and less pretentious.

14. **with stories**: var. *amid memories*. These were evidently reminiscences of mariners, told by them or by their women-folk when the child was falling asleep—possibly in the living-room.

16. Var. *at times*; for the sense of *à leurs heures*, cp. Jules Vallès, *Le Bachelier*, p. 106: 'Les Grecs étaient simples *à leurs heures*, les Conventionnels aussi'; M. van der Meersch, *Invasion* 14, p. 2: 'Samuel était gai, optimiste, poète *à ses heures*, prompt à l'enthousiasme.'

There is a curiously similar passage in Thomson's *Seasons* (*Autumn*):

> 'Or where the Northern ocean in vast whirls
> Boils round the naked melancholy isles
> Of farthest Thule...
> And how the living clouds on clouds arise,
> Infinite wings! till all the plume-dark air
> And rude-resounding shore are one wild cry.'

'Des prêtres d'un culte étranger, venu des Syriens de Palestine, prirent soin de m'élever. Ces prêtres étaient sages et saints. Ils m'apprirent les longues histoires de Cronos qui a créé le monde, et de son fils, qui a, dit-on, accompli un voyage sur la terre. Leurs temples sont trois fois hauts comme le tien, ô Eurhythmie, et semblables à des forêts; seulement ils ne sont pas solides; ils tombent en ruine au bout de cinq ou six cents ans; ce sont des fantaisies de barbares, qui s'imaginent qu'on peut faire quelque chose de bien en dehors des règles que tu as tracées à tes inspirés,

Raison. Mais ces temples me plaisaient; je n'avais pas étudié ton art divin; j'y trouvais Dieu. On y chantait des cantiques dont je me souviens encore: "Salut, étoile de la mer...reine de ceux qui gémissent en cette vallée de larmes"; ou bien: "Rose mystique, Tour d'ivoire, Maison d'or, Étoile du matin...." Tiens, déesse, quand je me rappelle ces chants, mon cœur se fond, je deviens presque apostat. Pardonne-moi ce ridicule; tu ne peux te figurer le charme que les magiciens barbares ont mis dans ces vers, et combien il m'en coûte de suivre la raison toute nue.'

ERNEST RENAN, *Prière sur l'Acropole*.

20. **Cronos:** father of Zeus; he ruled the world in the Golden Age.

23. **Eurhythmia** = beauty of rhythm in architecture, etc.; here apparently = beauty of proportion.

26. **outside:** var. *without*: cp. Kipling: 'the lesser breeds *without* the law.'

29–32. Cp. 'The Office of the Blessed Virgin Mary for the Three Seasons', etc.: during Advent, *Ave, maris stella*; before

'Priests of an alien cult, which came to us from the Syrians of Palestine, cared for my upbringing. These priests were wise men and holy. They taught me the long tales of Cronos, who made the world, and of his son, who is said to have sojourned upon the earth. Their temples are three times as high as thine, O Eurhythmia, and like unto forests; but they are not stable and fall to ruin in five hundred years or six— phantasies of Barbarians who fondly think that men may fashion some goodly thing outside the rules thou hast traced, O Reason, for those whose inspiration is in thee! Yet I loved those temples—I had not studied thy divine art—and in them I found God. Canticles were sung in them that I remember still: "Hail, Star of the Sea... Queen of them that mourn in this vale of tears"; or, again: "Mystical Rose, Tower of Ivory, House of Gold, Morning Star...." Yea, Goddess, when I recall those hymns, my heart melts within me, almost I become an apostate. Bear with me in this folly; thou canst not conceive the spell which the wizards of the Barbarians have laid upon those lines, and how hardly I may follow after Reason unadorned.'

Advent, *Salve, Regina, mater misericordiae*....Ad te clamamus exsules filii Hevæ. Ad te suspiramus, gementes et flentes in hac lacrymarum valle ['Hail, holy Queen, Mother of mercy, hail']... 'To thee we cry, poor banished sons of Eve; to thee we cry, mourning and weeping in this vale of tears'], *Rosa mystica* [Mystical Rose]...*Turris eburnea* [Tower of Ivory]...*Domus aurea* [House of gold]...*Stella matutina* [Morning Star].

34. Cp. *Acts*, xxvi, 28: 'Almost thou persuadest me to be a Christian.'

91. LOUIS JOUE AU CERCEAU

Quand on a joué longtemps au cerceau, comme Louis Bastide, et qu'on a eu la chance d'en trouver un qu'on aime bien, on s'aperçoit en effet que les choses sont tout autres que dans une course ordinaire. Essayez de trotter seul; vous serez fatigué au bout de quelques minutes. Avec un cerceau, la fatigue se fait attendre indéfiniment. Vous avez l'impression de vous appuyer, presque d'être porté. Quand vous éprouvez un instant de lassitude, il semble que le cerceau amicalement vous passe de la force.

D'ailleurs, on n'a pas toujours besoin de courir à grande allure. Avec du savoir-faire, on arrive à marcher presque au pas. La difficulté est que le cerceau n'aille pas se jeter à droite ou à gauche; ou s'accrocher aux jambes d'un passant, qui se débat comme un rat pris au piège; ou s'aplatir sur le sol après d'extraordinaires contorsions. Il faut savoir se servir du bâton, donner des coups très légers, qui sont presque des frôlements, et qui accompagnent le cerceau. Il faut surtout, entre les coups, rester maître des moindres écarts du cerceau, grâce au bâton qui ne cesse, d'un côté ou de l'autre, d'en caresser la tranche, qui en soutient ou en corrige la marche, et dont la pointe intervient vivement à tout endroit où menace de naître une embardée.

Louis Bastide aurait pu ne plus penser à ces détails, car il jouait au cerceau depuis longtemps, et il était devenu assez habile pour n'avoir plus besoin de calculer tous ses gestes. Mais il avait un fond de scrupule et d'inquiétude qui l'empêchait de rien faire d'un peu important avec distraction. Et il ne savait pas non plus être distrait pour prendre un plaisir. Dès qu'une occupation ne l'ennuyait pas, il s'y appliquait passionnément, et les moindres incidents lui en apparaissaient avec une netteté vibrante, avec une acuité qui faisait de chacun d'eux quelque chose d'inoubliable. Il était né pour une présence très grande de l'esprit. Mais son attention ne l'empêchait pas de s'exalter. Et si la conduite même du cerceau ne cessait à aucun moment d'être pour lui une opération précise, effectuée dans une zone de lumière sans complaisance, la course à travers les rues devenait une

91. LOUIS BOWLS A HOOP

When you are an old hand at bowling a hoop, as Louis Bastide was, and have been lucky enough to get one you really like, you do in fact realize that things are quite different from what they are in ordinary running. Try taking a run without a hoop, and you will tire in a few minutes, whereas with one, fatigue can be staved off indefinitely; you have a sense of leaning on something, almost of being carried. When you feel a momentary weariness, it seems as if the hoop is giving you a friendly loan of a little energy.

Nor need you always be running fast. Once you have the knack, you can keep almost to walking pace. The difficulty is to prevent the hoop going off at a tangent; or getting mixed up in the feet of some passer-by who wriggles like a rat in a trap; or else falling down flat after a series of extraordinary contortions. You must know how to use your stick, giving the hoop very slight taps, just flicks, and following it up all the time. The main thing is, in between the taps, to control the slightest swerve, by using the stick so as to be continually patting the tread on one side or the other, steadying up the hoop or adjusting the running, and intervening smartly with the end of the stick wherever a wobble seems likely to develop.

Louis Bastide could have stopped thinking of such details, for he had been bowling hoops for a long time now and become expert enough not to have to think out all his movements. But he had a deep sense of anxious scruple which made it impossible for him to do anything at all important without giving his whole mind to it. Nor had he the faculty, either, of letting his thoughts idle, for recreation purposes. Provided an occupation did not actually bore him, he threw himself into it whole-heartedly and its smallest details came up before him with a tense clearness, a sharpness, which made every one of them something quite unforgettable. Nature had given him very great powers of concentration. But attention in his case was not incompatible with enthusiasm. And while the actual guiding of the hoop never for a moment seemed to him anything but a work of pre-

aventure touffue et mystérieuse, dont l'enchaînement ressemblait à celui des rêves, et dont les péripéties inexplicables l'amenaient peu à peu, et tour à tour, à des moments d'enthousiasme, ou d'ivresse, ou de soulevante mélancolie.

JULES ROMAINS, *Les Hommes de bonne Volonté*.

43. melancholy: for *mélancolie*, cp. Lamartine, *Confessions*: 'Les chevaux mêmes, que j'ai tant aimés, ne donnent pas au

cision carried out in a medium of matter-of-fact daylight, a run through the streets would turn into an eventful and mysterious adventure, which, with its dream-like sequence of happenings and its unaccountable ups-and-downs, gave him gradually and by turns moments of exhilaration, wild delight or uplifting melancholy.

cavalier ce délire *mélancolique* que les grands lacs glacés donnent au patineur.'

92. VITESSE

A Montlhéry, en regardant passer hier les voitures de course, j'admirais cet état pathétique où le sport automobile a su amener la machine. Là, gagner, c'est comme toujours vouloir, vouloir de toutes ses forces; mais autrefois les hommes seuls—ou à la rigueur les pur-sang—savaient gagner avec leur intelligence, leur fierté: or, aujourd'hui le métal inerte a pris vie; il est devenu l'un de nous et paie de sa personne; il se dilate au delà de ce qui est permis; on voit la matière faire l'impossible, tout comme si elle était esprit; les moteurs crient de douleur; l'huile paresseuse prend l'activité courageuse du sang; des mains du vainqueur, impassible et assis droit, des mains des conducteurs enfermés sous l'auvent courbe de leur monoplace, une sensibilité animale semblait se répandre jusqu'aux roues. L'état d'exaltation où l'effort amène l'âme s'était communiqué aux constructions les plus sûres des ingénieurs, à ces bolides coloriés, que je voyais, après la ligne droite, se jeter sur l'horizon comme le projectile se jette sur le but; mais l'horizon élastique, sans s'émouvoir, les renvoyait aux virages et les virages absorbaient leur élan furieux comme les falaises absorbent celui des tempêtes....

Je goûtais cette léthargie poétique où nous plongent les spectacles sportifs d'aujourd'hui, état second, peut-être plus

1. **Montlhéry.** The first motor-racing track in France was opened there in 1924.
flash past: for the force of *passer*, see No. 80, note 10.
2. **sentient state:** var. *sentience, capacity for feeling*; "pathetic state" would suggest *état pitoyable*.
6. Var. *thoroughbreds*.
7. **spirit:** var. *reluctance to be beaten*; *mettle* is the best word, but debarred by 'metal' following.
8. Var. *is doing its bit*.
19. **cars:** *bolide* is probably not to be taken very strictly as a metaphor, being now in common use as a familiar term for a fast high-powered car; "meteor" would be an unfortunate name for a car as suggesting a meteoric and short-lived career.
21. **slung:** var. *catapulted*.

92. SPEED

Yesterday at Montlhéry, as I watched the racing-cars flash past, I marvelled at the *sentient* state into which motor-racing has managed to bring machines. On the track, to win means, as always, to will, and to will with all one's might. But whereas in former times only men, or at the most race-horses, had the power of winning by their intelligence or spirit, to-day inanimate metal has sprung to life; it has become one of us and is in the struggle too; it expands beyond the permitted limits; it shows us matter achieving the impossible, just as though it were mind; the engines scream with pain; the sluggish oil begins to course as actively and vigorously as the blood in our veins; from the hands of the winner who sat upright and unmoved, of the drivers boxed up in the curving scuttle of their single-seaters, some kind of animal sensitivity seemed to spread through to the wheels. The excitement of soul which is induced by strain and effort had communicated itself to the most reliable products of engineering skill, these brightly coloured cars which I could see, once they got away from the straight, hurtling on to the horizon, like a projectile on to its mark; but the elastic horizon slung them nonchalantly back on to the bends and the bends absorbed their rushing fury, as cliffs absorb the fury of the storm....

I rejoiced in the poetic lethargy which we sink into nowadays when watching sporting events—a hypnotic con-

---

Var. *unconcernedly.*
25. **hypnotic condition**: *état second* is a modern psychological term which has passed into the vocabulary of writers in France, though apparently not in England; cp. *Nouvelles litt.* 1939: 'Le lecteur [des romans de Simenon] a l'impression d'y pénétrer, de les appréhender, même de s'y mouvoir, mais comme dans un *état second*'; Albert Moll, *Hypnotism* (1909 ed.), p. 192: 'Régis, etc....lay special stress on the toxic origin of many forms of delirium. Régis, for example, considers the delirium of infectious diseases the delirium of a dream caused by toxic action; for him it is a kind of *état second*, analogous to the hypnotic state.'

propice au rêve que le calme des lacs 1830 ou la pénombre des parcs de Watteau. Certes, l'homme s'adaptera un jour à cette force brutale; nos descendants, vivant dans l'amitié de la foudre, riront de nos infimes vitesses; mais pour le moment ces jouets neufs sont encore pour nous pleins de surprises; ils nous transforment et nous grandissent; des luttes acharnées comme celles d'hier nous purifient; le spectacle merveilleux de ces coureurs dont aucun n'a connu, pendant quelques heures, la bêtise, l'inertie ou la peur, nous arrachent au resquillage et à la combine où Paris vit, là-bas, sous ses fumées rousses; une épreuve comme ce Grand Prix doit rendre désormais impossible la mortelle lenteur, lenteur des instructions judiciaires, lenteur de la gendarmerie, lenteur de nos lois par rapport aux mœurs, lenteur du pays légal par rapport au pays réel, lenteur voluptueuse des partis d'ordre sous les coups droits de la révolution. Sera-ce cette fée nouvelle, la vitesse, qui va administrer à la France la purge dont elle a besoin?

PAUL MORAND, *Rond-point des Champs-Élysées*.

27. **the 1830 Lakes**: *Wordsworthian lakes* might convey more to the English reader.

29. **brute force**: for *brutal* see No. 37, note 22.

Var. *on terms of intimacy with*.

32. Var. *keen contests*.

36. Var. *takes us right away from*.

37. **graft and racketeering**: *resquillage* means originally 'gate-crashing'; *la combine* = 'wangling', scheming, especially in business.

dition which is perhaps more conducive to reverie than was
the quiet of the 1830 Lakes or the half-light of Watteau's
parks. We may be sure that some day man will adapt himself
to this brute force; our descendants, living on familiar terms
with the thunderbolt, will laugh at our petty speeds. But,
for the time being, these new toys are still, for us, full of
surprises; they transform us, and add to our stature; sharply
contested struggles, like yesterday's, purify our emotions;
the wonderful sight of these racing-drivers, not one of whom,
for the space of a few short hours, has known stupidity,
inertia or fear, lifts us forcibly out of the atmosphere of
graft and racketeering in which Paris lives—there in the
distance, under its veil of russet smoke. A test like this
Grand-Prix must surely make deadly slowness henceforth
impossible—be it the slowness of judicial enquiries, the slowness of the country police, the slowness of our laws in comparison with our social habits, the slowness of legal France,
as compared with the real France, or the luxurious slowness
of the parties of law and order, when exposed to the direct
onslaught of revolution. Is Speed to be that fairy god-mother
of a new kind who will administer the purge which France
requires?

39. **deadly**: *mortelle* in *mortelle lenteur* may mean human slowness (dilatoriness), as opposed to the speed of machines.
43. **luxurious**: var. *complacent*.
44. Var. *direct action*.

VIII. VERSE

93. PAYSAGE POLAIRE

Un monde mort, immense écume de la mer,
Gouffre d'ombre stérile et de lueurs spectrales,
Jets de pics convulsifs étirés en spirales
Qui vont éperdument dans le brouillard amer.

Un ciel rugueux roulant par blocs, un âpre enfer
Où passent à plein vol les clameurs sépulcrales,
Les rires, les sanglots, les cris aigus, les râles
Qu'un vent sinistre arrache à son clairon de fer.

Sur les hauts caps branlants, rongés des flots voraces,
Se roidissent les Dieux brumeux des vieilles races,
Congelés dans leur rêve et leur lividité;

Et les grands ours, blanchis par les neiges antiques,
Çà et là, balançant leurs cous épileptiques,
Ivres et monstrueux, bavent de volupté.

LECONTE DE LISLE, *Poèmes barbares*.

1. Var. *sea-foam immeasurable* (*unending*), the white tracts of the Polar landscape being compared with vast stretches of foam. Cp. Leconte de Lisle, *L'Épée d'Angantyr*: 'O Chef, qui labourais *l'écume de la mer*.'

2. **A waste**: var. *Vortex*.

spectral. In French as in English *spectral* may mean either 'ghostly' or 'prismatic', cp. *spectre* = both 'spectre' and 'spectrum'. Some of the latter meaning is probably intended. So careful a writer as Leconte de Lisle would not miss the prismatic nature of Polar light; cp. P. Loti, *Pêcheur d'Islande*, p. 27: 'Et pourtant, autour d'eux, c'étaient des aspects de non-vie, de monde fini ou pas encore créé; la lumière n'avait aucune chaleur; les choses se tenaient immobiles et comme refroidies à jamais, sous le regard de cette espèce de grand œil *spectral* qu'était le soleil.'

3. **up-cast**. *Jet* indicates the 'spring', e.g. of an arch from the ground.

4. **wildly**: for *éperdument* cp. No. 8: 'les vents...sonnant dans leur trompe *éperdue*.'

bitter: var. *salty*.

93. A POLAR LANDSCAPE

A lifeless world, vast drift of ocean foam,
A waste of barren gloom and spectral lights,
And peaks convulsively up-cast, that wreathe
Wildly away into the bitter fog.

A furrowed sky, all swirling rack, a hell
Of ice, winged over by the graveyard shrieks,
The laughter, sobs, sharp screams and dying groans
A dismal wind tears from his iron trump.

On tottering cliffs gnawed by the ravening waves,
Stark stand the mist-born Gods of olden tribes,
Fast frozen in their brooding ghastliness,

And the great bears, blanched by the ancient snows,
One here, one there, lolling their palsied necks,
Drunken and monstrous, slaver in ecstasy.

5. **furrowed**: var. *wrinkled*.
all swirling rack: var. *in swirling (wheeling) masses*. We take the allusion to be to massive clouds.
a hell of ice: *âpre* commonly applies to winter, e.g. V. Hugo, *L'Expiation*: 'L'*âpre* hiver fondait en avalanche'; '*un âpre enfer*' may not be altogether oxymoron; missionaries among the Esquimaux are said to have presented Hell as a place of extreme cold.
6. Var. *where on full wing (borne upon the blast) come sweeping by*.
7. **dying groans**: cp. *râler*, No. 95, note 3.
12. **blanched**: var. *bleached*.
13. **palsied**: var. *writhing*. The allusion in *cous épileptiques* may, however, be to spasmodic jerky movement.
14. **Drunken**: var. *Reeling*, with reference to the shambling gait of bears. The line is reminiscent of Musset's Pelican: '*Ivre de volupté, de tendresse et d'horreur.*'
monstrous: *monstrueux* has generally a notion of portentous, supernatural; cp. Latin *monstrum, monstruosus*; var. *uncanny, uncouth*.

94. LÉVIATHAN

L'œil distingue, au milieu du gouffre où l'air sanglote,
Quelque chose d'informe et de hideux qui flotte,
Un grand cachalot mort à carcasse de fer,
On ne sait quel cadavre à vau-l'eau dans la mer,
Œuf de titan dont l'homme aurait fait un navire.
Cela vogue, cela nage, cela chavire;
Cela fut un vaisseau; l'écume aux blancs amas
Cache et montre à grand bruit les tronçons de sept mâts.
Le colosse, échoué sur le ventre, fuit, plonge,
S'engloutit, reparaît, se meut comme le songe,
Chaos d'agrès rompus, de poutres, de haubans;
Le grand mât vaincu semble un spectre aux bras tombants.
L'onde passe à travers ce débris; l'eau s'engage
Et déferle en hurlant le long du bastingage,

1. **the wind:** *l'air* often means air in motion, as sometimes English 'air': cp. White, *Natural History of Selborne* (Froude), p. 168: 'It (the spider) went off with considerable velocity in a place where no *air* was stirring... these little crawlers seem to move in the air faster than *the air* itself.'

the waste of seas. Cp. *Canadian Boat-Song*:
'From the lone shieling on the misty island
   Mountains divide us and *the waste of seas.*'
Var. *the deep*: *gouffre* = a void, an abyss; "gulf" might be taken as a geographical expression (= le *golfe* de Mexique, etc.).

2. **formless:** var. *shapeless*; *informe* is not "*mis*shapen", which is *difforme*. Cp. No. 13, note 8.

grisly: *hideux*, like its Latin forerunner *hispidus*, generally suggests something which is unsightly, and horrible because of its rugged or 'prickly' character; such as, here, the wreckage, *agrès rompus*, etc.

awash: more exact than "floating (which floats)". Cf. Conrad, *Mirror of the Sea*, p. 72: 'At first I saw nothing. The sea was one empty wilderness of black and white hills. Suddenly, half-concealed in the tumult of the foaming rollers I made out *awash, something enormous, rising and falling*' [a piece of ice-floe].

3. **sea-monster:** var. *cachalot* [the common cachalot or sperm whale which grows to the length of 70 feet and has a head nearly one-half the length of the body]. Cp. next passage, No. 95: 'le front massif des cachalots.'

94. LEVIATHAN

Here where the wind sobs through the waste of seas,
We sight a formless, grisly thing awash,
A great sea-monster dead, huge iron ribs,
Some nameless carrion drifting on the deep,
A roc's egg, wrought by man into a craft.   5
It sails, it swims, pitches and overturns.
And this was once a Ship! White mantling surf
Roars, and reveals the stumps of seven masts.
Colossus fallen flat—it flees and dives,
Plunges and rises, moves as in a dream,   10
Welter of riven yards and booms and shrouds;
The mainmast beaten to a huddling ghost.
The wave sweeps through the wreckage; seas come in
And break along the bulwarks with a shriek,

dead. The position of *mort* should be retained in English: cp. 'Home they brought her warrior *dead*'; Ruskin, *Unto This Last*: 'A camp-follower's bundle of rags unwrapped from the breasts of goodly soldiers *dead*.'

huge iron ribs: var. *iron-ribbed*; for *carcasse*, see No. 14, note 26.

5. **wrought**: var. *fashioned*. N.B. *aurait* is the conditional used in similes: see No. 27, note 7.

craft: to avoid repetition of 'ship'; *navire* here is less 'noble' than *vaisseau* in line 7.

7. **was once**: the past historic is used, as often, of something that has ended for ever, cp. Latin *fuit* in *fuit Troja*. Var. *a smother of white foam*.

9. **fallen flat**: not "stranded": the ship may have run aground and afterwards floated off, but we are not told so; *échoué* may either continue the idea expressed in *cela chavire* or mean little more than 'come to grief'.

12. Cp. Conrad, op. cit. p. 76: 'the pathos of a ship vanquished in a battle with the elements...to look at a sailing-vessel with her lofty spars gone is to look upon a defeated but indomitable warrior. There is defiance in the remaining stumps of her masts.' We have been unable to reproduce Hugo's image (of rigging, spars, etc., 'dangling' from the mainmast).

13. **come in**: *s'engager* means to go from a larger into a smaller space; its opposite is *déboucher*.

Et tourmente des bouts de corde à des crampons
Dans le ruissellement formidable des ponts;
La houle éperdument furieuse saccage
Aux deux flancs du vaisseau les cintres d'une cage
Où jadis une roue effrayante a tourné.
Personne: le néant, froid, muet, étonné.

VICTOR HUGO, *La Légende des Siècles*.

15. **bitts**: var. *hooks, ring-bolts*, etc.; probably *crampons* is not used in a very technical sense.

16. **maelstrom**: var. *torrent, flooding*; *ruissellement* which now seems to have lost some of its original force (see No. 20, note 19) has here its full value.

And harry rope-ends streaming from the bitts 15
In the stupendous maelstrom of the decks;
The swell in headlong fury ravages
On either beam the arches of the box
Where once a fearful wheel went churning round.
No living soul: the void, chill, mute, aghast. 20

17. **headlong**: for *éperdument*, see No. 93, note 4.
18. **box**: *la cage* refers to the paddlebox: cp. *la cage de l'escalier, de l'ascenseur*, etc. Hugo had in mind a ship like the mixed paddle and screw leviathan, the *Great Eastern*, built in the late 'fifties of last century.

95. L'ALBATROS

Dans l'immense largeur du Capricorne au Pôle
Le vent beugle, rugit, siffle, râle et miaule,
Et bondit à travers l'Atlantique tout blanc
De bave furieuse. Il se rue, éraflant
L'eau blême qu'il pourchasse et dissipe en buées;
Il mord, déchire, arrache et tranche les nuées
Par tronçons convulsifs où saigne un brusque éclair;
Il saisit, enveloppe et culbute dans l'air
Un tournoiement confus d'aigres cris et de plumes
Qu'il secoue et qu'il traîne aux crêtes des écumes,
Et martelant le front massif des cachalots,
Mêle à ses hurlements leurs monstrueux sanglots.
Seul, le Roi de l'espace et des mers sans rivages
Vole contre l'assaut des rafales sauvages,
D'un trait puissant et sûr, sans hâte ni retard;
L'œil dardé par-delà le livide brouillard,
De ses ailes de fer rigidement tendues
Il fend le tourbillon des rauques étendues,
Et, tranquille au milieu de l'épouvantement,
Vient, passe, et disparaît majestueusement.

LECONTE DE LISLE, *Poèmes tragiques*.

1. Var. *Through the vast zones 'twixt Capricorn and Pole*; for *immense* "boundless" is debarred, because there are bounds specified.

3. **gasp and screech**: *râler* is said properly of the death-rattle, but cp. Leconte de Lisle, *Le Sommeil du Condor*: 'il râle de plaisir' = croaks; *miauler* is exactly 'caterwauling'.

4. **angry spume**: var. *frenzied foam*.

flays: is exact; "ruffling" is weak for *éraflant*: *érafler* = écorcher légèrement: 'Le coup d'épée lui a éraflé la peau.' Littré. Var. *Upcatching in its flight*.

5. **blenching**: var. *pallid*.

8. **and tosses**: var. *turns over*. Cp. Tennyson, *In Memoriam*, xv:
'The last red leaf is whirl'd away,
  The rooks are blown about the skies.'

9. Var. *A flurry of feathers* (*A heap of fluttering feathers*) *and shrill screams*.

95. THE ALBATROSS

Through wastes of seas from Capricorn to Pole
The wind goes roaring, bellowing, and, with hiss
And gasp and screech, scours the Atlantic, white
With angry spume. Onward it sweeps; it flays
The blenching wave, and hounds the scattered spray;   5
It bites, rives, rips the storm-clouds, which it tears
To quivering shreds lit by a blood-red flash;
It seizes, rolls and tosses in the air
A swirl of fluttering feathers and shrill cries,
Trailed, buffeted, across the crested foam,   10
And, beating on the cachalots' great heads,
Roars louder as the gasping monsters groan.
Only the King of Space and shoreless seas
Bears up against the wild assailing blasts
In strong sure flight, unhastening, unstayed;   15
His glance flung far above the sea-fog pale,
His iron wings unswerving, starkly braced,
He cleaves the whirlwind on the echoing deep,
And, calm where all is dread, comes sailing by
And vanishes in majesty away.   20

11. Var. *And, battering the great heads of cachalots.* For *cachalot* see preceding passage, No. 94, note 3.

12. **Roars**: var. *Shrieks.*

gasping: *leurs sanglots* means that the monsters of the deep are, if we may so say, 'winded'; the tempest takes their breath away; they have been hunted down and the pursuer hears them gasping, and exults. For *monstrueux* see No. 93, note 14.

14. **Bears up**: var. *Holds on his way.*

16. Var. *Shooting his glance athwart.*

18. **cleaves**: var. *stems.*

whirlwind: var. *vortex.*

echoing: for *rauque* as used here cp. André Gide, *Si le grain ne meurt*: *la* rauque *garrigue; les* rauques *étendues* = Homer's '*many-sounding* sea'.

19. Var. *comes, passes by.*

20. **in majesty away**: "majestically" would be inadequate; *majestueusement* fills the whole of the last hemistich; for the rhetorical effect of this, cp. Le Cardonnel, *Invocations d'automne*: 'Prends mon front dans tes mains | *miséricordieuses.*'

96. RÉSIDENCE ROYALE

Les jardins réguliers aux belles ordonnances
Et que peuple le chœur des dieux de marbre blanc,
S'étendent, disposés correctement, mêlant
Pelouses et massifs en douces alternances;

Au soleil reluit la grille à fers de lances
Qui forme tout autour un cercle vigilant;
Et le cri répété d'un ramier roucoulant
Rompt le calme établi des éternels silences;

Le Palais, avec ses façades au cordeau,
Qui dans sa majesté solennelle s'étale
Garde encor sa splendeur imposante et royale:

On rêve en ces jardins le long des pièces d'eau
Où se croisent des cygnes aux ailes de neige,
Le défilé pompeux de quelque lent cortège.
    HENRI DE RÉGNIER, *Premiers Poèmes*.

1. For *jardins réguliers* see the quotation from Jusserand in No. 28, note 8.

96. ROYAL ABODE

In fair and ordered lines the gardens, graced
With galaxies of gods in marble white,
Lie formal, trim, proportioned all aright,
With trees and grass in pleasing sequence placed;

The spear-head railing, in the sunshine traced,   5
Sets round the park a ring of watchful light;
A turtle cooing stirs without respite
The settled calm of scenes silent and waste;

With front severely straight, the Palace breaks
In far-flung majesty upon the view,   10
Bearing itself right royally, and through

Our waking dreams still, down along the lakes,
Where swans are gliding, snow-winged, to and fro,
Passes in pomp some stately train and slow.

  5. **railing**: *une grille* (see No. 28, note 9) is a railing as well as a gate. *reluit* is trisyllabic.
  13. Var. *Where swans with snowy wings wind to and fro.*

97. PAN DE MUR

De la maison momie enterrée au Marais
Où, du monde cloîtré, jadis je demeurais,
L'on a pour perspective une muraille sombre
Où des pignons voisins tombe, à grands angles, l'ombre.
—A ses flancs dégradés par la pluie et les ans,
Pousse dans les gravois l'ortie aux feux cuisants,
Et sur ses pieds moisis, comme un tapis verdâtre,
La mousse se déploie et fait gercer le plâtre.
—Une treille stérile avec ses bras grimpants
Jusqu'au premier étage en festonne les pans;
Le bleu volubilis dans les fentes s'accroche,
La capucine rouge épanouit sa cloche,
—Et, mariant en l'air leurs tranchantes couleurs,
A sa fenêtre font comme un cadre de fleurs:

Car elle n'en a qu'une, et sans cesse vous lorgne
De son regard unique ainsi que fait un borgne,
Allumant aux brasiers du soir, comme autant d'yeux,
Dans leurs mailles de plomb ses carreaux chassieux.
—Une caisse d'œillets, un pot de giroflée
Qui laisse choir au vent sa feuille étiolée....
C'est un tableau tout fait qui vaut qu'on l'étudie;
Mais il faut pour le rendre une touche hardie.

THÉOPHILE GAUTIER, *Poésies*.

1. **Marais**: the once fashionable quarter of Paris where the houses of Mme de Sévigné, Victor Hugo and other illustrious residents are still to be seen. The house was 'like a mummy', because still comparatively well preserved and buried deep in the *Marais*.

97. BLANK WALL

From the house like a mummy entombed in the Marais,
Where once I lived cloistered, in days that are past,
You have for perspective a wall dark in shadow
Which neighbouring gables at wide angles cast.
At the sides, which the rain and the years, too, have ravaged, 5
The sharp-stinging nettle takes rubble for bed;
On its mildewy base, making cracks in the mortar,
The moss like a green-growing carpet is spread.
—A barren vine climbing and wreathing her branches
As high as the first floor, festoons the expanse. 10
The blue Morning Glory clings fast in the fissures,
Nasturtiums with full-blowing trumpets advance,
—And, uniting their bright red and blue in the open,
They set round the window a frame-work of flowers:

For it has but one window, and fixes you always 15
Like a man with one eye, and it glimmers and glowers,
And it lights at the fire of the sunset its lattice,
Bleared panes in lead sockets, like so many eyes.
—A box of carnations; a gillyflower, potted,
That drops its wan leaves on the wind ere it dies.... 20
There's a ready-made picture which promises much,
But it needs, for the painting, a vigorous touch.

6. Cp. Crabbe, *Borough*: 'At the wall's base the fiery nettle springs.'

12. **trumpets**: *cloche* (of the *capucine* = nasturtium) is in English rather 'trumpet' than 'bell'.

21. Cp. R. Browning, *Andrea del Sarto*:
'You smile? Why there's my picture ready made,
That length of convent-wall across the way.'

98. CHÂTEAU DE CABIDOS, PRÈS D'ARZACQ

Le lourd château rêvait dans l'épaisse moisson,
Sous le ciel de lit bleu d'un beau temps sans frisson.
Dans la cuisine l'eau jaillissait d'une pompe.
Quelques aïeux, encor qu'avec assez de pompe
Trônant dans le salon, étaient assez mal faits,
Dont les dames portaient sur le sein des bouquets.
Des fauteuils recouverts, d'un goût Louis-Philippe,
Aux souples fleurs des champs mélangeaient les tulipes.
La maîtresse du lieu faisait sonner ses clefs,
Ouvrant tout grands, de chambre en chambre, les volets;
Des rideaux de brocart y criaient comme crient
Les grillons au plus fort des flammes des prairies:
On n'avait pu parquer la campagne au dehors,
Ici continuant ses mille boutons d'or.
On aurait beau donner deux tours à la serrure
Lorsque l'on s'en irait, que toujours la nature
Aux cheveux de soleil s'étendrait là-dedans,
Pareille à toi dans l'ombre, ô Belle-au-bois-dormant.

FRANCIS JAMMES, *Ma France poétique.*

2. *ciel de lit* = tester; *sans frisson* = calm, untroubled. Cp.
E. B. Browning, *Aurora Leigh*:

'the straight
Small bed was curtained greenly, and the folds
Hung green about the window which let in
The outdoor world with all its greenery.'

98. CHÂTEAU DE CABIDOS

Drowsy the château in the thick corn lay,
Blue curtained by a cloudless summer's day.
Sounds from the kitchen of a pump in spate:
Some ancestors, although they sat in state
Around the drawing-room walls, deserved small praise;   5
The ladies on their bosoms wore bouquets;
And arm-chairs tapestried, style Louis-Philip,
Twined supple wild flowers round the stately tulip.
The Châtelaine, keys jingling at her side,
From room to room went opening shutters wide;   10
Curtains of stiff brocade cried out as cry
Crickets in fields when fiercest flames the sky;
The country, banished out of doors in vain,
Its myriad buttercups spilled in again.
'Twere labour lost to double-lock the door   15
On leaving here, for Nature, as before,
Would come and lie down, sunny-haired—the way
You in the shade, O Sleeping Beauty, lay.

15. *On aurait beau donner...que...s'étendrait*: for this double conditional, see No. 28, note 1. The sense remains the same when *que* is added, viz. 'Even though'. Cp. 'Je dirais le contraire *que* vous ne me croiriez pas'.

17. **come**, etc.: *s'étendre* means to 'lie down' in the afternoon, 'take a nap'; it also means 'to extend' and carries on the idea of *continuant* (l. 14).

99. MINUETTO

La Vierge, au piano, rêve dans l'ombre exquise;
Un rayon rose et bleu tremble à ses doigts fluets;
Et sa langueur se berce au chant des menuets,
Qui ressuscite en elle une âme de marquise.

Dans le boudoir, où traîne un charme suranné,
Dont le regret confus peuple sa solitude,
Elle sourit, sans trouble et sans inquiétude,
Au rêve que ses doigts câlins ont égrené.

Puis, voici qu'à genoux, sans effrayer ses lèvres,
De beaux seigneurs musqués l'effleurent galamment
D'un hommage, discret comme un chuchotement—
Et sa candeur s'effeuille en des sourires mièvres.

ANDRÉ RIVOIRE, *Les Vierges*.

5. **drifts with**: in *berce* there is a notion of following the music physically, as in No. 36.

minuet's: for the slow stately measure of the minuet cp. Bagehot *Lit. Stud.* (O.E.D.): 'You should do everything', said Lord Chesterfield, 'in minuet time. It was in that time that Gibbon wrote his history.'

7. **again**: the force of *re-* in *ressuscite* is a *re-*awakening of hereditary feeling.

13. **untroubled**: French *trouble* generally implies emotional disturbance, an idea present in the English adjective or participle, though not in the English noun.

15. **fondly**: *câlins*, coming after the caesura goes more closely with *ont égrené* than with *doigts*, and thus acquires some adverbial force.

99. MINUETTO

The Maiden at the piano sits a-dreaming
    In the sweet shade;
A ray of rose and blue along her slender
    Fingers strayed:
Her listless mood drifts with the minuet's
    Slow melodies,
Which bring to life again in her the soul
    Of some Marquise,

And in the boudoir, with a lingering charm
    Of days gone by,
And dim remembrances her solitude
    To occupy,
She smiles, untroubled and from all misgiving
    Still remote,
Over the dream her fingers fondly wove,
    Note after note.

Behold! on bended knee, giving her lips
    Small cause for fears,
Fine lords, perfumed with musk, obeisance make—
    True cavaliers,
Whose homage, distant, seems a murmured prayer—
    And betweenwhiles
Her sweet simplicity its blossom sheds
    In simpering smiles.

16. **note after note**: for *égrener* see No. 14, note 2; for a somewhat similar, if less poetical, description, see *picorer*, No. 26, note 27.

19. **fine lords**: normally, 'gay lords' would represent *beaux seigneurs*, but in this context "gay" seems less appropriate.

23. **sweet simplicity**: the collocation of *candeur* and *mièvres* gives a touch of irony.

24. **simpering**: var. *dainty*.

100. HÉRAKLÈS

Ils franchissent le seuil et son double pilier,
Et dardent leur œil glauque au fond du bouclier.
Iphiklès, en sursaut, à l'aspect des deux bêtes,
De la langue qui siffle et des dents toutes prêtes,
Tremble, et son jeune cœur se glace, et pâlissant,
Dans sa terreur soudaine il jette un cri perçant,
Se débat, et veut fuir le danger qui le presse;
Mais Héraklès, debout, dans ses langes se dresse,
S'attache aux deux serpents, rive à leurs cous visqueux
Ses doigts divins, et fait, en jouant avec eux,
Leurs globes élargis sous l'étreinte subite
Jaillir comme une braise au delà de l'orbite.
Ils fouettent en vain l'air, musculeux et gonflés,
L'Enfant sacré les tient, les secoue étranglés,
Et rit en les voyant, pleins de rage et de bave,
Se tordre tout autour du bouclier concave,
Puis, il les jette morts le long des marbres blancs,
Et croise pour dormir ses petits bras sanglants.

LECONTE DE LISLE, *L'Enfance d'Héraklès.*

CONTEXT. Héraklès and his twin brother Iphiklès have been placed by their mother, Alkmenè, in their cradle which is a shield. During the night Héra sends two serpents to destroy Héraklès. Iphiklès is an ordinary child, destined for no great career. But Héraklès is the son of Zeus and strangles both the serpents. See H. J. Rose, *Handbook to Greek Mythology*, p. 206.

4. teeth: var. *fangs.*

100. HÉRAKLÈS

They cross the threshold, pass the pillars twain,
And flash their sea-green eyes into the shield.
Iphiklès starts, sees the two monsters plain,
The tongues that hiss, the ravening teeth revealed,
And trembles; his young blood runs cold; he pales 5
With sudden fear, he shrieks and, in the throes
Of terror, from the instant peril quails.
But Héraklès stands in his swaddling clothes,
Clutches both snakes; his god-like fingers clasp
Their slimy throats, and, all in play, he makes 10
Their eyeballs, bulging with his sudden grasp,
Start from their spheres like coals of fire. The snakes
Lash out in vain—their swelling coils unrolled—
Fast in the sacred Infant's strangle-hold;
He shakes them, laughs to see them venom yield 15
And writhe in fury round the hollow shield,
Along the marble white then flings them dead,
And folds his little hands to sleep, all red.

17–18. Cp. Bible, *Proverbs*, VI, 10: Yet a little sleep, a little slumber, a little folding of the hands to sleep.

The last couplet seems to defy exact or adequate translation in verse. Variants such as

Then flings them dead along the marble floor,
And folds his little arms to sleep once more.

or *Along the marble white then flings them slain,*
And folds his blood-stained arms to sleep again.

omit essential elements like *blancs* or *sanglants* or *petits* (the first two, rime-words), and add the notion of 'again' which is not explicit in the text.

101. LA TREBBIA

L'aube d'un jour sinistre a blanchi les hauteurs.
Le camp s'éveille. En bas roule et gronde le fleuve
Où l'escadron léger des Numides s'abreuve.
Partout sonne l'appel clair des buccinateurs.

Car malgré Scipion, les augures menteurs,
La Trebbia débordée, et qu'il vente et qu'il pleuve,
Sempronius Consul, fier de sa gloire neuve,
A fait lever la hache et marcher les licteurs.

Rougissant le ciel noir de flamboîments lugubres,
A l'horizon, brûlaient les villages Insubres;
On entendait au loin barrir un éléphant,

CONTEXT. The historical circumstances, Hannibal's victory on the Trebia, 218 B.C., are given thus by E. Cavaignac, *Histoire de l'Antiquité* (Fontemoing, 1914), p. 286: 'Hannibal avait pris la ville des Taurins; ceux-ci...étaient en guerre avec les Insubres. ...Il n'avait plus alors que 26,000 hommes (et 21 éléphants).... Scipion, battu et blessé, dut se retirer sous Plaisance pour attendre Sempronius....La Trébie séparait les deux armées. Hannibal s'avança jusqu'au bord du fleuve, et y embusqua son jeune frère Magon. Lui-même vint se replacer à la tête de son infanterie et attendit le choc. Au petit matin, les Romains, provoqués par les Numides, se mirent en route sans avoir mangé, traversèrent la rivière glacée, et, défilant devant Magon, attaquèrent....'

The above account follows Polybius (III, 61–67). The other authorities are Livy (XXI, chap. 54) and the poet Silius Italicus, who confines himself to depicting the slaughter. While some of Heredia's details are imaginary, e.g. 'sous le pont', others are taken from Livy.

TITLE: **Trebia**: *Trebbia*, adopted by Heredia, is the modern Italian form; French *Trébie*.

101. TREBIA

The hills have whitened with a dawn of woe.
The camp awakes. Down by the roaring tide
Numidian light-horse water; on every side
The war-horns ring out clear, the trumpets blow.

For—scorning augurs false and Scipio, 5
Trebia in flood, storm, rain, whate'er betide—
Sempronius Consul, puffed with new-made pride,
Has bid the lictors raise the Axe and go.

Red flares leaped on the black horizon, these,
The burning hamlets of the Insubres; 10
Afar, a sound of elephants. Apart,

1. **hills**: var. *heights*: *les hauteurs* = the summits of the snow-clad Alps or Apennines. The line may be construed as = 'Dawn (Daybreak) has whitened the heights (blanched the hill-tops) with dismal day' or as = 'The dawn (dawning) of an evil day has whitened the heights'; *sinistre* suggests both the ghastly light and the gruesome carnage of the day: cp. Leconte de Lisle, *Le Soir d'une bataille*: 'Le ciel *d'un soir sinistre* estompe au loin leurs masses.'

4. **horns...trumpets**: for *buccins* see No. 8, note 14. Var. *The war-horns of the buccinators blow.*

7. **Sempronius Consul**: Heredia prefers this (Latin) order of words, as he also prefers *buccinateurs* and the Latin title *Imperator* in No. 102.

9–10. Var.
> '*Flushing the murky sky with flames of doom,*
> *The Insubrian hamlets burning lit the gloom.*'

For Heredia's description, cp. Macaulay, *Horatius*:
> 'Now from the rock Tarpeian
> Could the wan burghers spy
> The line of blazing villages
> Red in the midnight sky.'

> Et là-bas, sous le pont, adossé contre une arche,
> Hannibal écoutait, pensif et triomphant,
> Le piétinement sourd des légions en marche.
>
> JOSÉ-MARIA DE HEREDIA, *Les Trophées:
> Rome et les Barbares*.

13. *pensif*: is used more freely than 'pensive'; cp. Banville, *Les Exilés*: 'Haletants, ils ouvraient leurs bouches *pensives*', and may mean 'eager'. With Heredia's line cp. Vigny's *Moïse*:
> '...Marchant vers la terre promise,
> Josué s'avançait pensif et pâlissant.'

Beneath the bridge, his back against an arch,
Hannibal heard, with triumph in his heart,
The muffled tramp—the Legions on the march!

triomphant means not "triumphant", but 'triumphing', 'exultant'. Hannibal is not yet victorious; his 'triumph' is still only a matter of probability.

14. Cp. M. Arnold, *Obermann Once More*:

'The East bow'd low before the blast
In patient deep disdain;
She let the legions thunder past,
And plunged in thought again.'

102. SOIR DE BATAILLE

Le choc avait été très rude. Les tribuns
Et les centurions, ralliant les cohortes,
Humaient encor dans l'air où vibraient leurs voix fortes
La chaleur du carnage et ses âcres parfums.

D'un œil morne, comptant leurs compagnons défunts,
Les soldats regardaient, comme des feuilles mortes,
Au loin, tourbillonner les archers de Phraortes;
Et la sueur coulait de leurs visages bruns.

C'est alors qu'apparut, tout hérissé de flèches,
Rouge du flux vermeil de ses blessures fraîches,
Sous la pourpre flottante et l'airain rutilant,

Au fracas des buccins qui sonnaient leur fanfare,
Superbe, maîtrisant son cheval qui s'effare,
Sur le ciel enflammé, l'Imperator sanglant.

HEREDIA.

N.B. The circumstances evidently are that a Roman column on the march has been attacked by cavalry which retires discharging 'Parthian shots'. Heredia has probably no very definite historical personage in view when he mentions 'Phraortes'. There were five Parthian Kings called Phraates.

1. **The attack:** *Le choc* = 'the shock' (cp. 'shock-troops'); var. *The charge, The clash.* Var. *It was a sharp attack;* for 'was' = *avait été* see No. 14, note 18.

2. **The tribunes:** we found it necessary to omit either *les tribuns* or *les cohortes.* Both give local colour. The tribunes being officers of high rank, the fact that their *voix fortes* are heard is a sign of grave emergency.

102. EVENING AFTER BATTLE

The attack had been severe. Rallying their men,
The tribunes and centurions still could feel
Upon the air rent by their hoarse appeal
The strong, warm reek of slaughter rise again.

Counting the comrades dead within their ken, 5
The soldiers, sullen, watched afar, as reel
Wild autumn leaves, Phraortes' bowmen wheel,
And sweat streamed from their faces swart. 'Twas then

That burst in view—with arrows bristled o'er,
Red with the crimson flow of gashes sore, 10
In gleaming brass and pallium's purple flood,

Proud, while the trumpets flung their fanfare high,
Mastering his startled steed—on flaming sky,
The Roman Imperator, man of blood.

feel: *humer* has no exact English equivalent; it includes both to 'inhale' and to 'sniff' and implies conscious effort; cp. No. 37: 'Les narines mobiles *humaient* l'air.'

9. **arrows:** var. (if 'arrows' is not clear enough) *Loomed forth—with clinging arrows bristled o'er.*

11. **purple:** for *la pourpre* = the Roman purple see No. 19, note 7.

12. **Proud:** *Superbe* retains its Latin sense; see No. 12, note 16.
trumpets: for *buccins* see No. 8, note 14.

103. MURDOC'H

Au revers reluisant des avirons de frêne
L'écume se suspend en frange, et la carène
Coupe l'eau qui frémit tout le long de la nef.
Là, cinquante guerriers sont debout près du chef.
L'ardent désir du meurtre élargit leurs narines
Et gonfle les réseaux d'acier sur leurs poitrines.
Le carquois de cuir brut au dos et l'arc en main,
Portant au ceinturon le court glaive romain,
Tous, quand la nef gravit la houle encore haute,
Regardent les lueurs qui flambent à la côte.
Sur la proue, au long col de dragon rouge et noir,
Murdoc'h le Kambrien se dresse pour mieux voir.
Appuyé des deux mains sur la massive épée,
L'épaule des longs plis d'un manteau blanc drapée,
Un étroit cercle d'or sur ses épais cheveux
Et de lourds bracelets à ses poignets nerveux,

CONTEXT. 'C'est au temps où le christianisme commence à conquérir les pays du Nord. Autour de Mona, l'Île sainte... autel central du monde, tous les Dieux Kymris se sont assemblés. Les Bardes sont aussi venus là....L'innombrable essaim des Dieux...disparaît dans la nuit. Alors s'avance une nef.... Murdoc'h, en changeant de foi, n'a pas changé de cœur....Le voilà devant les Bardes, le Persécuteur. Impassible à leurs chants sacrés, il rit et blasphème....Murdoc'h fait signe à ses guerriers...! A l'aube,
"Un long vol de corbeaux tourbillonnait dans l'air."'
J. Vianey, *Les Sources de Leconte de Lisle*, Montpellier, 1907, pp. 186–8.

TITLE. **Murdoc'h.** Leconte de Lisle, who had fads in matters of spelling, e.g. *Qaïn*, *Kambrien*, wrote *Murdoc'h*, no doubt on the analogy of Breton names like *Penmarc'h*, *Ronarc'h* (pronounced *-sh*).

103. MURDOC'H

The oars of ash gleam as they turn, and drip
With fringing foam, while, cleft on either hand,
The water shivers all along the ship.
There, fifty warriors by their chieftain stand.
The lust of slaughter fills their nostrils wide 5
And swells the chain-mail out upon their chests,
With bow in hand, on back the quiver of hide,
Short Roman sword which at the girdle rests,
All, on the inshore billows lifted now,
Stare at the flames that light the beach. Long-necked, 10
And black and red, a dragon forms the prow;
Murdoc'h the Cambrian, intent, erect,
Resting upon his massy sword, stands there,
A long white mantle round his shoulders flung,
A thin gold circlet on his matted hair, 15
His sinewy wrists with heavy bracelets hung—

10. **flames...beach.** The allusion is to the torches borne by nine priestesses; cp. the subsequent lines:
'Or la sinistre nef court au sommet des lames
Vers la plage fatale où luisent les neuf flammes.'

12. *pour mieux voir* means 'in order to get a better view', or merely 'so as to see': cp. Zola, *Bête humaine*, p. 206: 'Et debout sur la plaque de tôle qui reliait la machine au tender....Jacques, malgré la neige, se penchait à droite, *pour mieux voir*'; *se dresse* is exactly = drawing himself to his full height.

13. **Resting**: accounts sufficiently for *appuyé des deux mains*; cp. *Times*, January 1936: 'King Edward and his brothers took their places between the Guards already on duty and for a quarter of an hour remained motionless, *resting on their swords.*'

massy: cp. Shakespeare, *Tempest*, III, iii: 'Your swords are now too *massy* for your strength.'

16. Cp. 'two massive gold armlets...extremely heavy and of pure gold....The boat was adapted for riding the waves' (*Manchester Guardian*, August 18, 1939, à propos of the discoveries at Woodbridge, Suffolk, Ship-Burial of a Saxon King).

Murdoc'h, fléau des fils de Math, traître à sa race,
Dans les bois, sur la mer, la poursuit à la trace,
Et prêche par le fer, en son aveuglement,
La loi du jeune Dieu qui fut doux et clément.
LECONTE DE LISLE, *Poèmes barbares*.

17. **the Druids' Scourge:** *fils de Math* = Druids. 'Math (la Nature). Leconte de Lisle appelle plusieurs fois les Kimris "les fils de Math", d'après Henri Martin. Mais d'après les Triades,

Murdoc'h the Druids' Scourge, the apostate lord,
Who tracks his kinsmen down by sea and wild,
And in his blindness preaches by the sword
The young God's law Who gentle was and mild.   20

Math est un des trois grands magiciens de la Grande-Bretagne.'
Vianey, *op. cit.* p. 190.

20. **law**: for *La loi* cp. Chateaubriand, *Les Martyrs*, IV, 168: 'Ma famille fut la première dans la Grèce à embrasser *la loi* de Jésus-Christ.'

104. LA FUITE DE POMPÉE

Seigneur, quand par le fer les choses sont vidées,
La justice et le droit sont de vaines idées;
Et qui veut être juste en de telles saisons
Balance le pouvoir, et non pas les raisons.
Voyez donc votre force, et regardez Pompée,
Sa fortune abattue, et sa valeur trompée.
César n'est pas le seul qu'il fuie en cet état:
Il fuit et le reproche et les yeux du sénat,
Dont plus de la moitié piteusement étale
Une indigne curée aux vautours de Pharsale;
Il fuit Rome perdue, il fuit tous les Romains,
A qui par sa défaite il met les fers aux mains;
Il fuit le désespoir des peuples et des princes
Qui vengeraient sur lui le sang de leurs provinces,
Leurs États et d'argent et d'hommes épuisés,
Leurs trônes mis en cendre, et leurs sceptres brisés:
Auteur des maux de tous, il est à tous en butte,
Et fuit le monde entier écrasé sous sa chute.

CORNEILLE, *Pompée*.

CONTEXT. Ptolemy is warned by his Minister against receiving Pompey in Egypt after his defeat at Pharsalus in Thessaly, 48 B.C.

104. THE FLIGHT OF POMPEY

Sire, when disputes are settled by the sword,
Justice or right is but an empty word,
And he who would be just in such events,
Must judge the power, and not the arguments.
Look at your own strength, then—and Pompey see: 5
His fortunes fallen, baulked his bravery.
He flees not only Cæsar in his plight,
He flees the Senate's anger and their sight,
Of whom full half most piteously expose
A sorry prey to the Pharsalian crows; 10
He flees Rome lost—the Romans all, whom he,
By his defeat, consigns to slavery;
Flees the despair of peoples, potentates
Who would avenge on him their ruined States,
Their gold, their men, a martyred country's groans, 15
Their broken sceptres and their shattered thrones:
Author of all men's ills, assailed by all,
He flees the universe, crushed in his fall.

1. *Seigneur*: the earlier editions have *Sire*.
2. **empty**: this is often the exact sense of *vain* = Lat. *vanus*; cp. No. 113, line 4, *son eau vaine*.

105. PROPOS FRANCS

Je t'ai fait comte, grand de Castille, et marquis;
Vil tas de dignités, bien gagné, mal acquis.
Agir par ruse, ou bien par force, t'est facile;
Tu te prendrais de bec avec tout un concile
Ou tu le chasserais, le démon en fût-il.
Tu sais être hardi tout en restant subtil.
Quoique fait pour ramper, tu braves la tempête.
Tu saurais, s'il le faut, pour quelque coup de tête
Te risquer, et, toi vieux, mettre l'épée au poing.
Tu conseilles le mal, mais tu ne le fais point.
N'être innocent de rien, n'être de rien coupable,
C'est ta propreté, comte, et je te crois capable
De tout, même d'aimer quelqu'un. A ce qu'on dit,
Tu t'es fait de valet brigand, et de bandit
Courtisan. Moi, j'observe en riant tes manœuvres.
J'ai du plaisir à voir serpenter les couleuvres.
Tes projets que, pensif, tu dévides sans bruit,
Sorte de fil flottant qui se perd dans la nuit,
Tes talents, ton esprit, ta fortune, ta fange,
Tout cela fait de toi quelque chose d'étrange,
De sinistre et d'ingrat dont j'aime à me servir....

VICTOR HUGO, *Torquemada*.

CONTEXT. The King of Spain addresses a shady courtier.

105. PLAIN SPEAKING

I made you Count, Marquis, Grandee—poor lot
Of dignities well worked for and ill got!
You act by guile, or force, with equal ease;
You'd fight the Synod of a Diocese
Or break it up, though Satan with it sits. 5
You can be rash, yet keep your crafty wits.
Though made for cringing, you can face a storm,
And could, at need, some folly to perform,
Risk your old bones and draw the sword anew.
You counsel evil, but no evil do. 10
Think every sin, and never a crime commit—
Your form of honour, Count! I hold you fit
For anything—fit even to love! I'm told
You rose from valet, bandit, brigand bold,
To courtier. *I* observe your tricks, and smile; 15
Snakes in the grass I like to watch awhile.
The schemes you weave in silence, recondite,
A floating web that trails into the night,
Your talents and your wit, your slime, your star,
All go to make the strange thing that you are: 20
A graceless, evil thing I'm pleased to use....

1. **poor:** *vil* = not "vile", but cheap, worthless; cp. Latin *vile damnum*.
9. Var. *Defy old age*.
17. **in silence:** for *pensif*, see No. 101, note 13.

106. LA PENSÉE

La pensée est une eau sans cesse jaillissante.
Elle surgit d'un jet puissant du cœur des mots,
Retombe, s'éparpille en perles, jase, chante,
Forme une aile neigeuse ou de neigeux rameaux,
Se rompt, sursaute, imite un saule au clair de lune,
S'écroule, décroît, cesse. Elle est sœur d'Ariel
Et ceint l'écharpe aux tons changeants de la Fortune
Où l'on voit par instants se jouer tout le ciel.
Et si, pour reposer leurs yeux du jour, des femmes,
Le soir, rêvent devant le jet mobile et vain
Qui pleut avec la nuit dans l'azur du bassin,
L'eau pure les caresse et rafraîchit leurs âmes
Et fait battre leurs cils et palpiter leur sein,
Tandis que la pensée en rejetant ses voiles,
Dans un nouvel essor jongle avec les étoiles.

CHARLES GUÉRIN, *Le Semeur de Cendres*.

1. **a fountain**: *les eaux jaillissantes* (de Versailles, Fontainebleau, etc.) are 'the fountains'. Var. *Thought is as water which unceasing (for ever) springs*.
3. Var. *scatters in pearls*.
6. Var. *Then breaks, dwindles and dies*.

106. THOUGHT

Thought is a fountain that for ever springs.
It shoots its column from the heart of words,
Falls back, breaks into pearls; it gurgles, sings,
And shapes out snowy boughs or snow-winged birds,
Dissolves, leaps up, a moonlit willow seems, 5
Crumbles and dies away. 'Tis Ariel's sister
And wears the Scarf with Fortune's changing gleams
Shot through, and bright with all the heaven's glister.
When women come, day-wearied eyes to rest,
And dream at evening by the idle spray 10
Which rains with night on the blue water, they
Are by that pure, soul-soothing shower caressed,
And bosoms throb, eyes falter, and away
Thought flings her veils, to take a further flight
And toss the starry baubles of the night. 15

7. **the Scarf**, etc.: cp. *Tempest*, IV, i (loq. Ceres):
'Hail, *many-coloured* messenger (Iris...)
Who with thy saffron wings, upon my flowers
Diffusest honey drops, refreshing showers;
And with each end of thy blue bow dost crown
My bosky acres, and my unshrubb'd down,
Rich *scarf* to my proud earth....'

107. HÉLÈNE

Adieu, belle Cassandre, et vous, belle Marie,
Pour qui je fu trois ans en servage à Bourgueil;
L'une vit, l'autre est morte, et ores de son œil
Le ciel se réjouit, dont la terre est marrie.

Sur mon premier avril, d'une amoureuse envie
J'adoray vos beautez, mais vostre fier orgueil
Ne s'amollit jamais pour larmes ny pour dueil,
Tant d'une gauche main la Parque ourdit ma vie.

Maintenant, en automne encores malheureux,
Je vy comme au printemps, de nature amoureux,
Afin que tout mon age aille au gré de la peine,

Et, ore que je deusse estre exempt du harnois,
Mon colonnel m'envoye à grands coups de carquois,
Rassieger Ilion pour conquerir Heleine.

                RONSARD, *Sonnets pour Hélène*.

N.B. Ronsard (then twenty) saw Cassandra Salviati (then thirteen) when he went with the Court to Tours (April 21, 1545). The Court left Tours three days later: 'Il n'eut moyen que de la voir, de l'aimer et de la laisser à même instant', says Brantôme. The date has the same significance, mostly literary, as that of April 6, 1327, when Petrarch saw Laura at Avignon. Marie was probably Marie Dupin, daughter of an innkeeper at Bourgueil, in Touraine, whom Ronsard met in April 1555. He was by then a very famous person and *en servage* does not imply either three years' residence at Bourgueil or 'serving', as Jacob for

107. HELAYNE

Adieu, Cassandra fair, fair Marie, too,
For whom I toiled at Bourgueil three long years!
One lives, the other died whose bright eye cheers
The heavens now, and leaves the earth to rue.

I in my early spring-tide, fain to woo, 5
Adored your charms, but your proud hearts, my dears,
Would ne'er relent, for sorrow nor for tears,
So clumsily the Fate had spun my clew.

Now, in my autumn unrequited still,
Love-lorn I go as in mine Averil, 10
That all my days be spent in toil and pain,

And, when I should from bearing arms be free,
My Colonel with his darts is driving me
Back to the siege of Troy, to win Helayne.

Rachel. The play on *Marie* and *marrie* = 'sad', which we have been unable to render, is the only internal evidence to show which of the ladies had died.

   11. Var. *Doomed all days of my life to toil and pain.*

   13. **darts**: It is doubtful whether 'grands coups de carquois' is to be taken as = beating a reluctant lover's back or as = discharging a shower of arrows.

   14. Var. *Back to the siege of Ilion. for Helayne.*

108. SONNET POUR HÉLÈNE

Quand vous serez bien vieille, au soir, à la chandelle,
Assise auprès du feu, dévidant et filant,
Direz, chantant mes vers, en vous émerveillant:
'Ronsard me célébroit, du temps que j'étois belle!'

Lors vous n'aurez servante, oyant telle nouvelle,
Déjà sous le labeur à demy sommeillant,
Qui au bruit de mon nom ne s'aille réveillant,
Bénissant votre nom de louange immortelle.

Je seray sous la terre et, fantôme sans os,
Par les ombres myrteux je prendray mon repos;
Vous serez au foyer une vieille accroupie,

Regrettant mon amour et votre fier dédain.
Vivez, si m'en croyez, n'attendez à demain,
Cueillez dès aujourd'huy les roses de la vie.

RONSARD.

N.B. There are numerous verse renderings of this sonnet, e.g. by Dean Carrington, *Anthology of French Poetry*; Andrew Lang, *Ballads and Lyrics of Old France*; Humbert Wolfe, *Sonnets à Hélène*; F. L. Lucas, *Poems*; J. G. Legge, *Chanticleer*. With all their felicities, they seem to overstress the tragic note (*sans os* is at the least flippant and *repos* is certainly not the Christian idea of rest after labour), and to over-polish the form (*-ant*

108. SONNET FOR HÉLÈNE

When you are old, at candlelight maybe,
Spinning and winding by the fire, you'll sing
Some verse of mine and say, a-wondering:
'I once was fair and Ronsard sang of me!'

No serving maid that hears the like—were she 5
Over the weary work nigh slumbering—
But at my name will start and, wakening,
Bless yours with praise of immortality.

I'll be below the earth, taking mine ease,
An airy spirit, by the myrtle trees; 10
You by the hearth, a bent old crone, shall stay,

My love lamenting and your own proud scorn.
Live now—trust me in this—wait not till morn!
Gather the roses of this life to-day!

occurs nine times, four times in the rime-word). The circumstances in which the startling revelation is made, the reasons why it has been so long deferred and the number of persons informed, are not clear. The tone of the poem is not so very much more serious than that of the preceding sonnet (No. 107).

4. **sang**: var. *wrote*.
10. **the myrtle trees**: cp. O.E.D., s.v. MYRTLE, 2.
14. **life**: var. *world*.

109. LES RÊVES MORTS

Vois! cette mer si calme a comme un lourd bélier
Effondré tout un jour le flanc des promontoires,
Escaladé par bonds leur fumant escalier,
Et versé sur les rocs, qui hurlent sans plier,
Le frisson écumeux des longues houles noires.
Un vent frais, aujourd'hui, palpite sur les eaux;
La beauté du soleil monte et les illumine,
Et vers l'horizon pur où nagent les vaisseaux,
De la côte azurée, un tourbillon d'oiseaux
S'échappe, en arpentant l'immensité divine.
Mais, parmi les varechs, aux pointes des îlots,
Ceux qu'a brisés l'assaut sans frein de la tourmente,
Livides et sanglants sous la lourdeur des flots,
La bouche ouverte et pleine encore de sanglots,
Dardent leurs yeux hagards à travers l'eau dormante.
Ami, ton cœur profond est tel que cette mer
Qui sur le sable fin déroule ses volutes:
Il a pleuré, rugi comme l'abîme amer,
Il s'est rué cent fois contre des rocs de fer,
Tout un long jour d'ivresse et d'effroyables luttes.
Maintenant il reflue, il s'apaise, il s'abat.
Sans peur et sans désir que l'ouragan renaisse,
Sous l'immortel soleil c'est à peine s'il bat,
Mais génie, espérance, amour, force et jeunesse
Sont là, morts, dans l'écume et le sang du combat.

LECONTE DE LISLE, *Poèmes barbares.*

5. **shuddering foam**: the suggestion in *versé le frisson écumeux* is not that the rocks quiver under the shock.

6. **a light wind**: "a fresh wind (breeze)" implies too much velocity, and "a cool wind" too low a temperature, to form a sufficient contrast with the preceding tempest.

10. **wings across**: *arpenter* = (1) to measure, (2) to stride; cp. 'striding the blast'.

11. **off the rocks**: for *îlots* = 'rocks' rather than 'islets' see No. 86, note 31.

109. DEAD DREAMS

Look now! This quiet sea through one whole day
Battered the headlands like some ponderous ram,
Leaped up their smoking terraces and flung
Over the shrieking and unyielding rocks
The black long-rolling breakers' shuddering foam. 5
To-day, a light wind shakes along the waves
Lit with the beauty of the climbing sun,
And toward the clear horizon, bright with sail,
From the blue coast a cloud of wheeling birds
Rises, and wings across the boundless heaven. 10
But in the floating sea-weed, off the rocks,
Those that the storm's unbridled fury broke,
Ghastly and bleeding from the heavy waves,
Their mouths agape still full of bitter cry,
Up through the sleeping water wildly stare. 15
Friend, your deep heart is as the sea to-day
Whose curling wavelets lap on finest sand:
It wept, it raved as did the bitter sea;
It dashed on iron rocks a hundred times
All one long day of frenzied, dreadful strife. 20
And now it ebbs away, is stilled—at rest.
It neither fears nor seeks the storm's return,
And in the immortal sunlight scarcely beats;
But hope and love, strength, youth and genius lie
There in the blood and foam of battle, dead. 25

12. **Those that**: a neutral translation, leaving open the question whether *Ceux que* refers to seamen or sea-birds. The latter view finds support in these facts: grammatically, *Ceux que* can mean only *Les oiseaux que*; the use of *livide* and *bouche* is not restricted to human beings, and *bec* is of course impossible; the victims are victims of the storm-wind, not of the waves, and dead sea-birds are a common sight after a storm.

13. **from**: the force of *sous* is as in another line of Leconte de Lisle's: 'La cervelle a jailli *sous* la lourdeur des crosses.'

14. **bitter cry**: var. *choking sobs*.

19. **rocks**: var. *coasts*.

110. 'UNE TEMPÊTE SOUFFLE...'

Une Tempête souffle, et sur l'immense plage
S'appesantit un ciel presque noir et cruel,
Où s'obstine le vol grisâtre d'un pétrel,
Qui le rend plus funèbre encore et plus sauvage;

Un tourbillon de sable éperdu se propage
Vers un horizon blême où tout semble irréel;
Il traîne sur la dune un lamentable appel
Fait du courroux des vents et de cris de naufrage;

Les joncs verts frissonnants sont pâles dans la brume;
Sous le morne brouillard qui roule sur la mer,
Bondit, hurle et s'écroule un tumulte d'écume;

Et dans ce vaste deuil qu'étreint ce ciel de fer,
Nous sentons dans nos cœurs l'indicible amertume
De nos baisers d'adieu flagellés par l'hiver.

AUGUSTE ANGELLIER, *A l'Amie perdue.*

3. Var. *A petrel flying grey against the wrack.*
4. **gloom**, etc.: *funèbre* = 'funereal', 'dismal', 'gloomy' (cp. No. 111, line 9 *chrysalides funèbres*, and No. 112, line 18); *sauvage* = 'desolate' rather than 'wild'. The presence of one living thing accentuates the emptiness of the scene, and the pathetic persistence of the flying makes the sky seem yet more cruel, more inhospitable.

110. 'A STORM-WIND BLOWS...'

A storm-wind blows; over the wide shore lies
A brooding sky, forbidding, all but black,
Where one lone petrel's grey persistent track
The gloom and solitude intensifies.

Sand wildly whirling toward the horizon flies— 5
Wan, eerie realm where form and substance lack;
Across the dunes a call comes wailing back,
Whoop of the winds, and shipwrecked seamen's cries.

The green bent shivers in the mist to grey;
Lost in the wreathing sea-fog drear, the surge 10
Leaps, roars and crashes in tumultuous spray,

And iron sky and universal dirge
Deep in our hearts the untold sadness say
Of parting kisses lashed by winter's scourge.

7. **Across,** etc. *Il* might be taken as = *tourbillon*; *traîne* would then be transitive, and the *lamentable appel* would follow in the wake of the sand-storm. But it seems better to consider *Il* as impersonal and *traîne* as intransitive. On that interpretation, the *tourbillon* is heading for the horizon and the *appel* is continued over the dunes. This idea of 'lingering' or 'haunting' accords best with the vagueness of the sounds.

14. **parting:** var. *farewell.*

111. LE FLACON

Il est de forts parfums pour qui toute matière
Est poreuse. On dirait qu'ils pénètrent le verre.
En ouvrant un coffret venu de l'Orient
Dont la serrure grince et rechigne en criant,

Ou dans une maison déserte quelque armoire
Pleine de l'âcre odeur des temps, poudreuse et noire,
Parfois on trouve un vieux flacon qui se souvient,
D'où jaillit toute vive une âme qui revient.

Mille pensers dormaient, chrysalides funèbres,
Frémissant doucement dans les lourdes ténèbres,
Qui dégagent leur aile et prennent leur essor,
Teintés d'azur, glacés de rose, lamés d'or.

Voilà le souvenir enivrant qui voltige
Dans l'air troublé; les yeux se ferment; le Vertige
Saisit l'âme vaincue et la pousse à deux mains
Vers un gouffre obscurci de miasmes humains.

Il la terrasse au bord d'un gouffre séculaire,
Où, Lazare odorant déchirant son suaire,
Se meut dans son réveil le cadavre spectral
D'un vieil amour ranci, charmant et sépulcral.

Ainsi, quand je serai perdu dans la mémoire
Des hommes, dans le coin d'une sinistre armoire
Quand on m'aura jeté, vieux flacon désolé,
Décrépit, poudreux, sale, abject, visqueux, fêlé,

3-7. **You unlock...You'll find**: var. (if 'you' seems too direct) *One unlocks...Or opens...One finds.*

4. Var. *rasping clasp*: some onomatopoetic harshness seems required, as in the French.

12. Cp. Shelley, *A Dream of the Unknown*:
    'And flowers azure, black and streaked with gold.'

111. THE PHIAL

Perfumes there are, intense, for which all matter
Is porous. They will go through glass, it seems.
Sometimes, when you unlock some Eastern casket
Whose clasp rasps and in shrill remonstrance screams,

Or open in an empty house an aumbry 5
Filled with time's bitter odour, dusty, black,
You'll find an ancient phial that remembers,
From whence springs, vital still, a soul come back.

Thoughts that were sleeping, death-like chrysalids,
Scarce pulsing in the heavy gloom, unfold 10
Their wings, and rise in myriads, azure-tinted,
And glazed with sheeny rose and streaked with gold.

And lo! delirious memory is swirling
In the thick air; eyes close; the senses sway;
It takes the vanquished soul, and sweeps her onward, 15
Down to a gulf dark-reeking with decay.

It lays her by an age-old bourne whereunder,
Like odoured Lazarus rending his sheet,
Stirs and awakes the pallid corpse and spectral
Of some old love, sepulchral, rank, yet sweet. 20

So, too, when I am lost from men's remembrance,
Away into some dismal aumbry packed,
When I'm an old, forlorn, discarded phial,
Decrepit, dusty, foul, vile, viscous, cracked,

18. **odoured**: *odorant* may mean odorous or malodorous, or,
in Baudelaire's idea, both; cp. St John xi, 39; Ostervald version:
'il sent déjà mauvais'.
20. **sweet**: cp. in No. 14: 'la cité des tombes *charmantes*.'
23. Var. *Like some old desolate discarded phial.*

Je serai ton cercueil, aimable pestilence!
Le témoin de ta force et de ta virulence,
Cher poison préparé par les anges! liqueur
Qui me ronge, ô la vie et la mort de mon cœur.

CHARLES BAUDELAIRE, *Les Fleurs du Mal*.

O! lovely Pestilence! I'll be thy coffin, 25
Which to thy power and pungence witnesseth!
O! poison dear, by angel hand compounded,
Wine that corrodes me, my heart's life, heart's death!

112. LES PAONS

Les paons blancs qu'on a vus errer dans mes jardins
N'aimaient que l'aube pâle et la lune voilée
Et plus blancs que le marbre pur des blancs gradins
Étalaient largement leur roue immaculée.

Ils aimaient mon visage et mes longs voiles blancs;
Mais leur cri détesté troublait le doux silence...
Et mes mains ont rougi les plumes de leurs flancs;
J'ai tué les oiseaux de joie et d'innocence.

Et j'eus des paons d'orgueil dont les pas étoilés
Suivaient le reflet vert de mes écharpes bleues
En faisant rayonner par les soirs ocellés
Les astres éclatants qui constellaient leurs queues,

Mais le semblable cri, leur cri rauque et discors,
Déchirait le ciel clair d'aube et de lune où rôde
L'âme des oiseaux blancs, fidèle aux blancs décors;
Et j'ai tué les paons aux plumes d'émeraude.

Et maintenant, hélas! j'ai des paons inconnus,
Qui noirs, silencieux, splendides et funèbres,
Sont muets comme l'ombre, et qui semblent venus
De l'Érèbe, en rouant des gloires de ténèbres,

1-2. Var.
'*When the white peacocks through my gardens strayed,
They loved but moonlight veiled (the shrouded moon), the dawn's
pale light.*'
3. Var. *And on my pure white marble steps displayed.*
4. Var. *Their fans*; *Trains of.*

immaculate: cp. O.E.D., s.v. sense 3*b*: Without coloured spots or marks; unspotted': 1797 Bewick, *Brit. Birds*: 'He describes the male bird to be *of an immaculate white.*'

6. **dear**: var. *sweet.*
9. **took**. The past historic *j'eus* is more precise than 'I had'.
10. **veils**: *écharpes* are scarves—admittedly not the same

112. THE PEACOCKS

The peacocks white that through my gardens strayed
Loved but the hooded moon and dawn's pale light,
And whiter than the marble steps, displayed
Fans of immaculate and purer white.

They loved my face, my long white veils, yet sped   5
With their detested cry dear silence hence—
And my hands stained their feathered sides with red:
I killed the birds of joy and innocence.

Peacocks I took which, star-like in their pride,
Strutting behind my blue green-glimmering veils,   10
Flashed through the many-twinkling eventide
The glory of their constellated tails,

But the same cry, their harsh, discordant cry,
Rent the clear skies where moon or dawn illumes
White haunts, by white birds' souls beloved, and I—   15
I slew the peacocks with the emerald plumes.

Ah! I have others now, mysterious,—
Black silent birds of rich funereal plume,
Mute as the shades and come from Erebus
With spreading trains like aureoles of gloom.   20

---

thing, cp. O. Onions, *Widdershins*: 'her *veils* and *scarves* fluttered and spun.' A possible variant is 'To strut behind my scarves of green and blue', but it is difficult to work this in with line 12.

11. **many-twinkling**: var. *ocellated* = ornamented with ocelli; having eye-like spots, cp. the Ocellated Turkey, Lizard, etc.; but 'ocellated' is in form too like 'constellated' in the next line, and sounds more 'scientific' than *ocellé*, which springs to a French mind readily enough, e.g. 'the great trout with their yellow sides and peacock backs' is translated by M. Las Vergnas, N.M., p. 273: *les belles truites aux flancs dorés et au dos ocellé*.

17. **others**: var. *peacocks*, but the word is more obtrusive than the monosyllabic *paons* and need not be repeated here.

Et je voudrais t'entendre, ô cri des grands paons noirs
Qui marchent aux côtés de ma robe aux plis tristes,
Et que je sens frôler mes obscurs désespoirs
De leur plumage sombre ocellé d'améthystes.

GÉRARD D'HOUVILLE (MME HENRI DE RÉGNIER).

THE PEACOCKS

I fain would hear your cry, O great black brood
Of peacocks stalking by my weeds of woe,
Obtruding on my dark despairing mood
Your sombre plumes with amethysts a-glow.

113. L'OUBLI SUPRÊME

Que m'importe le soir puisque mon âme est pleine
De la vaste rumeur du jour où j'ai vécu!
Que d'autres en pleurant maudissent la fontaine
D'avoir entre leurs doigts écoulé son eau vaine
Où brille au fond l'argent de quelque anneau perdu.

Tous les bruits de ma vie emplissent mes oreilles
De leur écho lointain déjà et proche encor;
Une rouge saveur aux grappes de ma treille
Bourdonne sourdement son ivresse d'abeilles
Et du pampre de pourpre éclate un raisin d'or.

Le souvenir unit en ma longue mémoire
La volupté rieuse au souriant amour,
Et le Passé debout me chante, blanche ou noire,
Sur sa flûte d'ébène ou sa flûte d'ivoire,
Sa tristesse ou sa joie, au pas léger ou lourd.

Toute ma vie en moi toujours chante ou bourdonne;
Ma grappe a son abeille et ma source a son eau;
Que m'importe le soir, que m'importe l'automne,
Si l'été fut fécond et si l'aube fut bonne,
Si le désir fut fort et si l'amour fut beau!

TITLE: var. *Final (Supreme) Oblivion*; not "Perfect (Utter) Forgetfulness".

1. **eve**: var. *night*.

4. **empty**: for *vain* in this sense, see No. 83, note 8 and No. 104, line 2.

trickling: *écouler*, except in technical or commercial language, is generally intransitive.

5. Var. *While, silver in the depths, gleamed some lost ring*: cp. Paul Valéry, *Étude pour Narcisse*:
'Fontaine, ma fontaine,
O présence pensive, eau calme qui recueilles
Tout un sombre trésor de fables et de feuilles,
L'oiseau mort, le fruit mûr, lentement descendus,
Et les rares lueurs des clairs anneaux perdus.'

8. **vine**: var. *vineyard*: cp. 'under my own vine and fig-tree'.

113. THE LAST FORGETTING

What matters eve to me! My soul is teeming
With the vast murmur of my day of living!
Let others weep, let others curse the spring
That trickles, through their fingers, empty water
While in the depths gleams some lost silver ring.   5

With all sounds of my life my ears are ringing,
Their echoes, distant now, are yet beside me;
My clustered vine has flavour red and bold,
And drunken drone of bees still softly humming,
And from the scarlet bough shine grapes of gold.   10

Remembrance in my memory's long annals
Links with the Love that smiles Joy's merry laughter;
The Past before me pipes, or black or white,
On flute of ivory, or flute of ebon,
Its mirth or sadness, measures grave or light.   15

Still all my life within me pipes or murmurs,
Still has my vine its bees, my spring its water;
What matters eve to me, what, autumn cool,
So dawn was bright and summer brought the harvest,
Desire was strong and love was beautiful!   20

10. **scarlet**: for *pourpre* = red, see No. 19, note 7; cp. Shelley:
>"'Tis the noon of autumn's glow...
>And the *red* and golden vines
>Piercing with their trellised lines,' etc.

grapes: *Un raisin* (cp. for the singular *son abeille*, below) = one variety of white grapes (*d'or*); *rouge* describes their taste, not their colour—a transposed sense impression; cp. Baudelaire:
>'Il est des *parfums*...*verts* comme les prairies.'

11. **Remembrance...memory**: *Le souvenir* is active = the power to recall, *ma mémoire* is passive = the storehouse of the mind.

13. The carefully arranged chiasmus (*blanche...noire*; *ébène...ivoire*; *tristesse...joie*; *léger...lourd*) we have endeavoured to keep, in inverse order.

19. **Since.** *Si* introduces a fact here (*fut*), not an hypothesis.

Ce ne sera pas trop du Temps sans jours ni nombre
Et de tout le silence et de toute la nuit
Qui sur l'homme à jamais pèse au sépulcre sombre,
Ce ne sera pas trop, vois-tu, de toute l'ombre
Pour lui faire oublier ce qui vécut en lui.
                HENRI DE RÉGNIER, *La Cité des eaux*.

21. **that Time**: *le Temps* is contrasted with *le Passé* and is further qualified by *sans jours*, etc.

number: var. *reckoning*.

Var. *Scarce in that Time...In all the silence...In all the shade ...Shall man forget*, etc.

THE LAST FORGETTING

Scarce shall that Time which knows not days or number,
And all the silence, all the dark which ever
Weighs down on man in his last dwelling dim,
And all the shade there is and all the shadow
Make man forget that which had life in him. 25

24. **shade...shadow.** For *toute l'ombre* cp. the conclusion of *Tristesse d'Olympio*: 'C'est toi qui dors dans l'ombre, ô sacré souvenir.'

25. **man:** var. *him*.

had life: var. *was life, once lived, did live*; for the force of the past historic *fut* see No. 94, note 7.

114. CÉSAR

César, calme César, le pied sur toute chose,
Les poings durs dans la barbe, et l'œil sombre peuplé
D'aigles et des combats du couchant contemplé,
Ton cœur s'enfle, et se sent toute-puissante Cause.

Le lac en vain palpite et lèche son lit rose;
En vain d'or précieux brille le jeune blé;
Tu durcis dans les nœuds de ton corps rassemblé
L'ordre, qui doit enfin fendre ta bouche close.

L'ample monde, au-delà de l'immense horizon,
L'Empire attend l'éclair, le décret, le tison
Qui changeront le soir en furieuse aurore.

Heureux là-bas sur l'onde, et bercé du hasard,
Un pêcheur indolent qui flotte et chante, ignore
Quelle foudre s'amasse au centre de César.
    PAUL VALÉRY, *Album de vers anciens.*

2. **Chin on hard fists:** the resemblance to Rodin's *Penseur* is marked; *barbe* is not necessarily a full beard; often=stubble.
Var. *and glint in sombre eye.*

114. CÆSAR

Cæsar, calm Cæsar, foot upon the laws,
Chin on hard fists, gleam in the sombre eye,
Of eagles and the sunset's warring sky—
Now swells thy heart, and feels all-powerful Cause.

Unheeded go the Lake that frets and gnaws   5
Her rosy bed, the gold of harvest nigh;
In thy tense, knotted frame the orders lie
Hardening, which shall at last part thy closed jaws.

Beyond the wide horizon waits the land,
The Empire, for the flash, the word, the brand   10
Turning to frenzied dawn the evening glow.

Out on the Lake, a fisher, oars at rest,
Drifts idly singing, happy not to know
The thunderbolt that forms in Cæsar's breast.

3. Var. *the warring sunset sky*; *le couchant*, although occasionally = the setting sun, is properly = the western sky. Even when *soleil* is added, e.g. in No. 2: 'le couchant du soleil en fusion', the translation is 'sunset' rather than 'setting sun'.

4. Var. *Thy swelling heart feels now all-powerful Cause; Thy heart swells, feels itself All-powerful Cause.*

TABLE OF PASSAGES

FOUND ALSO IN *TRANSLATION FROM FRENCH* AND IN *FRENCH PASSAGES FOR TRANSLATION*

The following are contained also in *Translation from French*, where they have the numbering indicated in Roman numerals.

1	I	28	XIII	71	LXXXVIII
2	VI	29	XXIX	72	LXXXIX
3	III	30	XLI	75	XCI
5	IX	32	XLII	80	XCIX
6	IV	39	LV	82	XCVIII
7	XIV	42	LXVI	88	CXIII
11	XVIII	55	LVIII	90	CXIX
12	XXIV	56	LIX	93	X
14	XXII	61	LXIX	94	XII
15	XXVI	63	LXXXI	101	XLVII
16	XVII	69	XCVI	103	XLIV
22	XXXVI	70	LXXXVI	111	CXII

I	1	XXIV	12	LXIX	61
III	3	XXVI	15	LXXXI	63
IV	6	XXIX	29	LXXXVI	70
VI	2	XXXVI	22	LXXXVIII	71
IX	5	XLI	30	LXXXIX	72
X	93	XLII	32	XCI	75
XII	94	XLIV	103	XCVI	69
XIII	28	XLVII	101	XCVIII	82
XIV	7	LV	39	XCIX	80
XVII	16	LVIII	55	CXII	111
XVIII	11	LIX	56	CXIII	88
XXII	14	LXVI	42	CXIX	90

The following are contained also (with the same numbering) in *French Passages for Translation*.

4	26	45	60	81	99
8	27	46	62	83	100
9	31	47	64	84	102
10	33	48	65	85	104
13	34	49	66	86	105
17	35	50	67	87	106
18	36	51	68	89	107
19	37	52	73	91	108
20	38	53	74	92	109
21	40	54	76	95	110
23	41	57	77	96	112
24	43	58	78	97	113
25	44	59	79	98	114

INDEX OF AUTHORS OF PASSAGES

The numbers refer to passages, not pages

'Alain' [Émile-Auguste Chartier], 73, 89
Angellier, Auguste, 110

Bainville, Jacques, 38, 41, 43
Balzac, 31, 32, 59
Barbey d'Aurevilly, 87
Barrès, Maurice, 34
Baudelaire, 111
Benda, Julien, 53
Bernard, Charles, 78
Bertrand, Louis, 20
Bonnard, Abel, 13
Bourget, Paul, 63
Brieux, 66

Cals, Jeanne Ramel, 26
Chartier, Émile-Auguste ['Alain'], 73, 89
Chateaubriand, 5, 6
Châteaubriant, A. de, 24
Corneille, 104

Daudet, Alphonse, 47, 48

Faguet, Émile, 71
Flaubert, 7, 11, 35, 76, 85
France, Anatole, 15
Fromentin, 28, 77

Gallotti, Jean, 23
Gautier, Théophile, 33, 72, 97
Giraudoux, Jean, 4, 25
Glesener, Edmond, 54
Goncourt, Edmond et Jules de, 2, 3, 12, 36
Gourmont, Remy de, 86
Guérin, Charles, 106

Hamp, Pierre, 18, 60
Heredia, José-Maria de, 101, 102
Herriot, Édouard, 19
Houville, Gérard d', [Mme Henri de Régnier], 112
Hugo, Victor, 8, 94, 105
Huysmans, 29

Jammes, Francis, 98

Kistemaeckers, 64

Lanson, 58, 75, 88
Leconte de Lisle, 93, 95, 100, 103, 109
Loti, Pierre, 9, 10

Marmontel, 81
Michelet, 30, 84
Montesquieu, 69
Morand, Paul, 92

Pascal, 80
Proust, Marcel, 27

Régnier, Henri de, 96, 113
Régnier, Mme Henri de, [Gérard d'Houville], 112
Renan, Ernest, 90
Rivoire, André, 99
Rod, Édouard, 22
Rolland, Romain, 16
Romains, Jules, 51, 52, 65, 68, 91
Romanet, Fernand, 79
Ronsard, 107, 108

Sainte-Beuve, 44, 57, 74
Saint-Simon, 55, 56
Saint-Victor, Paul de, 70
Sarment, Jean, 67
Sorel, Albert, 40, 42

Taine, 21, 61
Tharaud, J. et J., 62
Theuriet, 39
Thierry, 82
Thiers, 83

Valéry, Paul, 17, 45, 114
Van der Meersch, Maxence, 37
Vogüé, E.-M. de, 1, 14

Zola, Émile, 46, 49, 50

INDEX OF TITLES OF PASSAGES

The numbers refer to passages, not pages

A Amsterdam, 17
A la recherche du mot juste, 76
Agence d'espionnage sous le Consulat, Une, 42
Albatros, L', 95
Alfred de Musset, 75
Angelus, L', 85
Aventin, L', 13

Balzac, 33
Batailles de jadis, 54
Boulogne, 18

Camp des émigrés, Le, 39
Campo Vaccino, Le, 12
Carthage, 11
César, 114
Champenois, Les, 61
Château de Cabidos, 98
Chefs des puissances coalisées, Les, 40
Choix d'un ministre, 65
Clair de lune, 4
Coucher de soleil en Amérique, 5
Coucher de soleil sur la Jungfrau, 22
Cousin Pons, Le, 32
Crime de Napoléon, Le, 41
Critique dans les sciences, La, 81

Dame aux bracelets, La, 79
Dans la forêt, 24
Dans la cathédrale de Chartres, 29
D'Aubigné poète, 71
De l'Impressionnisme, 66
Demi-tour, 25
Démocratie et l'esprit, La, 89
Départ de la 'Lison', 49
Dévouement à la science, 82

Esprit français, L', 88
Expansion de Paris, L' (i), 51
Expansion de Paris, L' (ii), 52

Falaise, 19
Flacon, Le, 111
France de 1820, La, 44

France sous Louis-Philippe, La, 45
Fuite de Pompée, 104

Genestas, Le Commandant, 59
Gorge de Pierrefitte, La, 21
Grève, La, 63
Grotesque, Un, 72

Hélène, 107
Héraklès, 100
Hobereau, Le, 62

Immensité de l'univers, L', 80
Industrialisme et la poésie, L', 87
Intelligence en histoire, L', 83

Jardin des Trembles, Le, 28

La Fontaine, Originalité de, 73
La 'Lison' bloquée dans les neiges, 50
Lettres de Diderot à Mlle Volland, 74
Léviathan, 94
Louis joue au cerceau, 91

Madame de Castries, 56
Madame de Roucy et son mari, 55
Médecin de Campagne, Le, 31
Minuetto, 99
M. Bernard, 60
Murdoc'h, 103

Nuit dans le Nouveau-Monde, Une, 6

Odeurs, 27
Oubli suprême, L', 113

Pan de mur, 97
Paons, Les, 112
Paris brûlant, 46
Paris: sur les quais, 15
Parlements, Les, 38
Paysage d'automne, 1
Paysage du soir, 2
Paysage polaire, 93

TITLES OF PASSAGES

Pensée, La, 106
Per amica silentia lunae, 3
Petite ville, La, 26
Plaisirs de l'imagination, Les, 67
Polka, La, 36
Port de Marseille, Le, 20
Possibilités formidables, 68
Prière que je fis sur l'Acropole, etc., 90
Propos francs, 105

Querelle littéraire, 69
Qu'est-ce que la Justice? 64
Quinquagénaire, Un, 37

Réflexions sur l'Affaire Dreyfus, 53
Rembrandt, 77
Résidence royale, 96
Retours, 86
Rêves morts, Les, 109
Rhin, Le, 16

Sa dernière espérance, 48
Saint-Just, 30
Saül de Rembrandt, Le, 78
Servante, La vieille, 35
Soir de bataille, 102
Sonnet pour Hélène, 108
Sous l'Équateur, 10
Style d'Éschyle, Le, 70

Taine, 34
Témoignage des contemporains, Le, 84
Tempête, La, 9
Tombe de Chateaubriand, La, 7
Tombeaux des Khalifes, Les, 14
Trajet sans arrêt, 47
Trebbia, La, 101

'Une Tempête souffle...', 110

Vents du large, Les, 8
Vitesse, 92
Voix de la campagne, Les, 23
Voltaire, 57
Voltaire, Jugement d'ensemble sur, 58

Waterloo, 43

INDEX OF FIRST WORDS IN PASSAGES

The numbers refer to passages, not pages
[N.B. The 36 passages marked * are given also in *Translation from French*. Their number in that book is added in Roman numerals.]

A ce moment d'ailleurs, tout tournait mal..., 77
*A cet admirable roman—*Une ténébreuse affaire*... [lxvi], 42
A Montlhéry, en regardant passer..., 92
Adieu, belle Cassandre..., 107
Afin de ne pas être bloqués..., 20
Ainsi l'enceinte de 1846..., 51
Alors on vit s'avancer sur l'estrade..., 35
*Après être tombée toute la nuit... [lv], 39
*Assemblage unique des plus gracieux bijoux... [xxii], 14
Assis au fond de la salle..., 54
Au commencement de cette étude..., 33
Au jour où je l'ai vue, Falaise..., 19
Au milieu de terrains vagues..., 26
*Au revers reluisant... [xliv], 103

Benassis était un homme..., 31
Boulogne-sur-Mer, en novembre..., 18

Ce qui m'a frappé le plus..., 44
Ce qui se mobilisait chez moi..., 53
César, calme César..., 114
C'est cette qualité..., 83
Cet homme pouvait avoir cinquante ans..., 37
*C'était le *Campo Vaccino*... [xxiv], 12
*C'étoit une personne extrêmement laide... [lviii], 55
*Cette audace et cette témérité... [lxxxix], 72
*Cette basilique, elle était... [xxix], 29
Chut! monsieur.—Je me tais..., 67

Dans le couloir, Jansoulet..., 48
Dans l'immense largeur du Capricorne..., 95

*D'Aubigné avait des dons poétiques... [lxxxviii], 71
De la hune où Yves habitait..., 10
De la maison momie..., 97
De lourds nuages montaient..., 21
De toutes les batailles que Napoléon a livrées..., 43
Déjà, sous la halle couverte..., 49
Depuis deux jours, la grande voix..., 9
Depuis les temps de la Fronde..., 38

*En face des remparts... [xiv], 7
Espèce de Bayard sans faste..., 59

Frédéric-Guillaume et François..., 40

Ici Diderot se révèle..., 74
*Il est de forts parfums... [cxii], 111
Il y a au musée du Luxembourg..., 79
Il y a une grandeur, dans La Fontaine..., 73
Ils franchissent le seuil..., 100

Jacques remarquait que la cause..., 50
*J'aime à regarder de ma fenêtre la Seine... [xxvi], 15
J'aime le mélancolique..., 13
Jamais conjonctures plus propices..., 45
J'avais dix-huit ans. J'étais heureuse..., 25
Je couchais dans une salle paysanne..., 23
*Je suis né, déesse aux yeux bleus... [cxix], 90
Je t'ai fait comte..., 105
Jean, plein d'angoisse, se retourna..., 46

*L'aube d'un jour sinistre... [xlvii], 101

INDEX OF FIRST WORDS IN PASSAGES

L'histoire ne doit pas dire seulement..., 84
*L'œil distingue, au milieu du gouffre... [xii], 94

*La forme dégradée du type français... [cxiii], 88
*La grève gagne?... [lxxxi], 63
La lande de Lessay..., 87
La lune était à son plein..., 4
*La lune pleine, rayonnante... [iii], 3
La pensée est une eau..., 106
La Vierge, au piano..., 99
Le choc avait été très rude..., 102
Le lourd château rêvait..., 98
Le philosophe avait alors cinquante-six ans..., 34
Le plus douloureux, à mesure que l'on vieillit..., 86
Le point essentiel dans l'étude..., 81
Le Saül de Rembrandt..., 78
*Le soleil tomba derrière le rideau d'arbres... [ix], 5
*Le style d'Eschyle... [lxxxvi], 70
Le vaste trouble des solitudes..., 8
Les conjurés ayant tous déclaré..., 41
Les jardins réguliers..., 96
Les paons blancs..., 112
*Les paroles de Saint-Just... [xli], 30

*Mme de Castries... [lix], 56
*Mais ce qui me choque... [xcvi], 69
*Mais une barre lumineuse... [xviii], 11
*Musset ne s'attarda pas... [xci], 75

On dit que la démocratie..., 89

*Plus on les regarde... [lxix], 61
*Puis, il longeait la petite mare... [vi], 2

Quand on a joué longtemps au cerceau..., 91
Quand vous serez bien vieille..., 108

Quant aux Villages..., 52
*Que l'homme contemple... [xcix], 80
Que m'importe le soir...! 113
Quoi qu'il en soit, Voltaire..., 57

Reprenant vivement sa polka..., 36
Rien n'est plus difficile...Voltaire..., 58

Seigneur, quand par le fer..., 104
*Si, comme je me plais à le croire... [xcviii], 82
Son appartement particulier..., 27
*Son seul ami, le confident... [xvii], 16
*Sous ce chapeau, qui paraissait... [xlii], 32
Sur cette frontière indécise..., 62
Sur les voies du triage..., 60

*Tournoël ne se fit pas répéter l'ordre... [i], 1
Tout en rêvant mille choses de lui..., 17
Tu me parles de tes découragements..., 76

Un grand nuage de pluie..., 24
*Un monde mort... [x], 93
*Un nuage allongé... [xxxvi], 22
Un sifflet strident retentit..., 47
Un soir que la fenêtre..., 85
*Une heure après le coucher du soleil... [iv], 6
Une Tempête souffle..., 110

Vois! cette mer si calme..., 109
Votre Majesté pense-t-elle avoir...? 65
Vous aimez ça? Vous avez du plaisir à...? 66
*Vous auriez beau connaître... [xiii], 28
Vous êtes allé en Amérique...? 68
Vraiment, je ne comprends pas..., 64

INDEX OF WORDS MENTIONED OR DISCUSSED

acacia, beignets d', No. 25, *n.* 22
académicien, No. 73, *n.* 1
accroché, No. 49, *n.* 21
acener, see *asséner*
à cent pas, No. 7, *n.* 1
à chaque pas, No. 21, *n.* 18
achever de, No. 46, *n.* 23
Addition of words, No. 25, *n.* 12; No. 41, *n.* 17
à demi, No. 25, *n.* 33
adieu, No. 110, *n.* 14
air, No. 94, *n.* 1
'Alain', No. 73, STYLE
Alkmenè, No. 100, CONTEXT
alleluia, more usually *alléluia*, No. 29, *n.* 18
alliteration, No. 3, *n.* 2
amadou, No. 29, *n.* 21
amalgamé, No. 8, *n.* 14
Amaury, No. 44, *n.* 1
à même, No. 7, *n.* 9; No. 27, *n.* 6
l'ami de Paris, No. 42, CONTEXT
amusant, No. 17, *n.* 2; No. 56, *n.* 14
angoisse, No. 46, *n.* 1
angulaire, No. 24, *n.* 14
animé, No. 15, *n.* 5
anneau clair...argent, No. 113, *n.* 5
d'Antraigues, No. 42, CONTEXT
apointi, appointi, No. 22, *n.* 1
appel, No. 110, *n.* 7
appuyé des deux mains, No. 103, *n.* 13
âpre, No. 93, *n.* 5
arbres de coupe, No. 24, *n.* 13
arête, No. 1, *n.* 13
arpenter, No. 109, *n.* 10
arrêté, No. 34, *n.* 11
assemblage, No. 14, *n.* 1
asséner, also *assener*, No. 56, *n.* 15

assises = foundations of a mountain, No. 22, *n.* 4
assurer, No. 41, *n.* 33
astre, No. 4, *n.* 1; No. 6, *n.* 5
-âtre; *grisâtre*, No. 27, *n.* 4; *verdâtre*, No. 28, *n.* 15
aube, No. 19, *n.* 14
aurait in similes, No. 27, *n.* 7; No. 94, *n.* 5
aurore, No. 19, *n.* 14
avait été = was, No. 102, *n.* 1
avoir beau: on aurait beau...que, No. 28, *n.* 1; No. 98, *n.* 15
avoir: = make, *eut un geste*, No. 36, *n.* 17; *eut un grognement*, etc., No. 49, *n.* 5; No. 50, *n.* 34; = 'get', No. 50, *n.* 16

baigner, No. 1, *n.* 6
'*balles*' = francs, No. 63, *n.* 31
baptême des cloches, No. 74, *n.* 33
barbe, No. 114, *n.* 2.
la barre = tiller: *l'homme à la —, l'homme de la —*, No. 17, *n.* 15
la base, No. 22, *n.* 4
basilique, No. 12, *n.* 7; No. 29, *n.* 1
une bâtisse, No. 62, *n.* 10
bâtisseurs, No. 51, *n.* 21
battue, faire la, No. 8, *n.* 18
beau, avoir, see *avoir beau*
beaux esprits, No. 69, *n.* 1
beaux jours, les derniers, No. 1, *n.* 19
beaux seigneurs, No. 99, *n.* 19
béguin, No. 35, *n.* 14
beignets d'acacia, No. 25, *n.* 22
bêlement, No. 25, *n.* 18
la belle saison, No. 86, *n.* **6**
bergère, No. 25, *n.* 29

INDEX OF WORDS MENTIONED OR DISCUSSED 397

beuglement, No. 25, *n.* 18
bien, omitted in translation, No. 69, *n.* 21
bienfaisance, No. 58, *n.* 20
biscuit, No. 56, *n.* 1
blessure, No. 21, *n.* 12; — *en séton*, No. 25, *n.* 33
bloc erratique, No. 32, *n.* 14
bonhomme, No. 42, *n.* 13
bosse, No. 73, *n.* 14
le bouquet, No. 46, *n.* 10
Bourgueil, No. 107, N.B.
bourrasque, No. 8, *n.* 2
bousculade, No. 49, *n.* 16
bras: levant les — au ciel, No. 63, *n.* 33
brodé, No. 26, *n.* 12
Brummel = Brummell, No. 33, *n.* 8
brutal, No. 37, *n.* 22; No. 38, *n.* 35; No. 92, *n.* 29
bruyère, No. 87, *n.* 8
buccin, No. 8, *n.* 14; No. 101, *n.* 4; No. 102, *n.* 12

cachalot, No. 94, *n.* 3; No. 95, *n.* 11
cage, No. 94, *n.* 18
caisson, No. 12, *n.* 7
câlin, No. 99, *n.* 15
se calmer, No. 54, *n.* 22
Calonne, No. 38, *n.* 14
une campagne = small estate, No. 59, *n.* 31
candeur, No. 99, *n.* 23
canetille, cannetille, No. 23, *n.* 27
capter, No. 42, *n.* 14
capucine, No. 97, *n.* 12
car, No. 73, *n.* 2
la carcasse, No. 14, *n.* 26; No. 24, *n.* 3
carquois, coups de, No. 107, *n.* 13
carré: pieds carrés, No. 7, *n.* 10; *tête carrée*, No. 31, *n.* 22
carrière, No. 81, *n.* 3
caserne Lobau, No. 46, *n.* 16
Cassandre, No. 107, N.B.

Castries, Mme de, No. 56, *n.* 12
catastrophe, No. 43, *n.* 3
ce = this or that, No. 7, *n.* 3
c'est que, No. 25, *n.* 27
c'étaient)(*il y avait*, No. 9, *n.* 10
cellule, No. 53, *n.* 21
celui = one who, No. 27, *n.* 29
cercle, No. 4, *n.* 23
chaînon, No. 81, *n.* 2
char, chariot, No. 11, *n.* 26
Chartier, M., see also 'Alain', No. 73, STYLE
charmant, No. 14, *n.* 11
château, No. 19, *n.* 29
chevaliers de Saint-Louis, No. 39, *n.* 12
chiasmus, No. 113, *n.* 13
choc, No. 102, *n.* 1
choquer, No. 69, *n.* 1
ciel: levant les bras au —, No. 63, *n.* 33; *ciel de lit*, No. 98, *n.* 2
Cimmériens, No. 90, *n.* 2
cintré, No. 60, *n.* 2
cipolin, No. 12, *n.* 14
clef anglaise, No. 50, *n.* 13
cloche: of *une capucine* (nasturtium), No. 97, *n.* 12; *baptême des cloches*, No. 74, *n.* 33
cocarde, No. 45, *n.* 9
cocasse, No. 32, *n.* 2
cohortes, No. 102, *n.* 2
colle = paste, No. 54, *n.* 34
colorié, No. 90, *n.* 5
la combine, No. 92, *n.* 37
comme, avoiding 'as it were', No. 3, *n.* 4 and *n.* 6; — = as it were, No. 20, *n.* 11
commencement, No. 43, *n.* 32
la Commune, No. 46, CONTEXT
compagnie, No. 35, *n.* 17
complot, No. 41, *n.* 1
Conditional: in similes, No. 27, *n.* 7; No. 94, *n.* 5; in tentative statements, No. 81, *n.* 20; double conditional, No. 28, *n.* 1; No. 98, *n.* 15
confidents, No. 40, *n.* 21

congestionné, No. 42, *n*. 23
conjugué, No. 14, *n*. 10
conjuré, No. 41, *n*. 1
conspirateur, No. 41, *n*. 1
conspiration, No. 41, *n*. 1
construction, No. 88, *n*. 21
contorsion, No. 73, *n*. 14
la coque, No. 17, *n*. 12
corde, No. 33, *n*. 14
côté: du — de, No. 11, *n*. 1
le couchant, No. 114, *n*. 3
couleur du temps, No. 27, *n*. 18
couplet, No. 71, *n*. 7
coutume, No. 38, *n*. 27
crampon, No. 94, *n*. 15
crêpe = crape, No. 16, *n*. 11
crêpelé, No. 20, *n*. 8
crocher, No. 9, *n*. 32
Cronos, No. 90, *n*. 20
cuistre, No. 42, *n*. 12
cuivré, No. 1, *n*. 7
curé: '*Le Curé et le Mort*', No. 73, *n*. 30
cynisme, No. 73, *n*. 25

dalle, No. 7, *n*. 11; No. 12, *n*. 9
déboucher, No. 94, *n*. 13
de ces = such...as, No. 27, *n*. 10
déchaussé, No. 24, *n*. 19
déesse aux yeux bleus, No. 90, *n*. 1
Def. art., generic or specific, No. 27, *n*. 15
défilé, No. 27, *n*. 6
dégradé, No. 88, *n*. 1
déjà, No. 9, *n*. 25; No. 31, *n*. 16; No. 33, *n*. 30
déjeuner, No. 25, *n*. 21
demi-siècle, No. 35, *n*. 24; No. 45, *n*. 29
demi-tour, No. 25, *n*. 9
dépaysé, No. 52, *n*. 30
déployer, No. 6, *n*. 8
dépoli, No. 12, *n*. 14
dernières, les vérités, No. 45, *n*. 28
des, translated 'the', No. 3, *n*. 16; No. 9, *n*. 21; No. 12, *n*. 4
dès que, No. 53, *n*. 19

détoner, No. 70, *n*. 19
deux, omitted in *entre deux trains*, etc., No. 17, *n*. 25; No. 54, *n*. 10
devant; aller — qqn = aller trouver qqn, No. 69, *n*. 17
Diderot, No. 74, *n*. 15
difforme, No. 94, *n*. 2
dîner, sb., No. 25, *n*. 21; vb., No. 64, *n*. 21
diogénique, le tonneau, No. 73, *n*. 25
disparaître: — dans le brouillard, etc., No. 13, *n*. 9; No. 20, *n*. 10; = die, No. 41, *n*. 1
donc: in *qui donc?* No. 58, *n*. 24
donner, No. 60, *n*. 5
doucement, No. 24, *n*. 15
douceur, No. 15, *n*. 2
doux, No. 6, *n*. 11; No. 34, *n*. 12
droit, avoir — à, No. 24, *n*. 25
dû: avait dû)(*a dû*, No. 32, *n*. 15
du moment que, No. 53, *n*. 19
Dupin, Marie, No. 107, N.B.

eau; — claire, No. 35, *n*. 11; *— de perles*, No. 3, *n*. 4; *—x jaillissantes*, No. 106, *n*. 1
écaille, écaillé, No. 54, *n*. 28
échalas, No. 52, *n*. 17
écharpe, No. 106, *n*. 7
échoué, No. 94, *n*. 9
éclairer, intrans., No. 10, *n*. 31
écorces, No. 3, *n*. 16
écouler, trans., No. 113, *n*. 4
écouter, No. 8, *n*. 15
écume, No. 11, *n*. 6; No. 93, *n*. 1
effectif, effectivement, No. 27, *n*. 8
effleurer, No. 17, *n*. 25
égaré, No. 45, *n*. 12
égrener, No. 14, *n*. 2; No. 99, *n*. 16
électrique, d'une pâleur, No. 2, *n*. 15
s'élever, No. 7, *n*. 2
elle-même, lui-même, translated 'own', No. 39, *n*. 12
éminence grise, No. 42, *n*. 11

INDEX OF WORDS MENTIONED OR DISCUSSED

emphase, No. 73, *n.* 40
emporter la pièce, No. 56, *n.* 18
encombré, No. 13, *n.* 6
en face de, No. 7, *n.* 1
enfant de troupe, No. 59, *n.* 24
enfermé, No. 26, *n.* 21
engager, No. 1, *n.* 1; No. 94, *n.* 13
Enghien, duc d', No. 41, CONTEXT
engluer, No. 77, *n.* 23
s'enlever, No. 24, *n.* 1
enlisé, No. 75, *n.* 21
enserrer, No. 23, *n.* 3
entendre, No. 8, *n.* 15
entonnoir, No. 47, *n.* 2
entre, in *entre deux trains*, etc., No. 17, *n.* 25
éperdu, éperdument, No. 93, *n.* 4
épiderme, No. 29, *n.* 5
épileptique, No. 93, *n.* 13
Épinay, Mme d', No. 74, *n.* 15
épouse, No. 52, *n.* 30
érafler, No. 95, *n.* 4
éraillé, No. 35, *n.* 9
essence, No. 77, *n.* 24
erratique, bloc, No. 32, *n.* 14
esprit, No. 89, *n.* 3
état : à l'— de, No. 51, *n.* 8; No. 62, *n.* 6; *— second*, No. 92, *n.* 25
s'étendre, No. 98, *n.* 17
Ettenheim, No. 41, *n.* 1
étudier, No. 59, *n.* 39–41
Eurhythmia, No. 90, *n.* 23
eut, No. 86, *n.* 18
eût = *aurait* in similes, No. 27, *n.* 7
exemple...perdu, No. 82, *n.* 5
exostose, No. 24, *n.* 21
exploits, No. 43, *n.* 5

face, No. 32, *n.* 4; No. 37, *n.* 5–6
faire un bond, No. 24, *n.* 24
falot, No. 32, *n.* 2
fanal, No. 49, *n.* 21
fantasmagorie, No. 45, *n.* 9
faraud, No. 62, *n.* 4
fascine, No. 46, *n.* 12
femme, No. 52, *n.* 30; No. 85, *n.* 7

figure, No. 32, *n.* 4
fine fleur, No. 27, *n.* 31
flamme, retour de, No. 45, *n.* 19
fleur, fine, No. 27, *n.* 31
Fleurus, No. 43, *n.* 16
flotter, No. 94, *n.* 2
foire, No. 25, *n.* 6
la folle du logis, No. 72, *n.* 5
fond = background, No. 20, *n.* 15; No. 90, *n.* 6
fontaine, No. 19, *n.* 26; No. 39, *n.* 16; No. 90, *n.* 9
fort, sb.: *le — de l'épée*, No. 72, *n.* 9
fouine, No. 25, *n.* 32
foulées, No. 23, *n.* 5
fourmilière, No. 62, *n.* 40
foyer (d'un incendie), No. 29, *n.* 19
Franchart, No. 2, *n.* 1–4
François = François II, empereur d'Allemagne, No. 40, *n.* 1
Frédéric-Guillaume, No. 40, *n.* 1
frisson, No. 109, *n.* 5; *sans —*, No. 98, *n.* 2
front, No. 59, *n.* 39
fruste, No. 62, *n.* 6
fuir, fuite, No. 52, *n.* 22
fumant, No. 47, *n.* 4
funèbre, No. 110, *n.* 4
fut, No. 94, *n.* 7; No. 113, *n.* 25; introduced by *si*, No. 113, *n.* 19
futaie, No. 5, *n.* 4; No. 23, *n.* 11
Future tense, *see* Tense

Galiani, No. 74, *n.* 15
gamme, No. 8, *n.* 1–3
gelée, No. 27, *n.* 21 and *n.* 24
généreux, générosité, No. 44, *n.* 31
gentilhommière, No. 62, *n.* 40
Georges, *conspiration de*, No. 41, *n.* 18
gerbe, No. 46, *n.* 10
germe, No. 81, *n.* 14
gibbosité, No. 24, *n.* 20
glabre, No. 33, *n.* 14; No. 37, *n.* 5
la glu, No. 77, *n.* 23
Gobseck, No. 42, *n.* 5
golfe, gouffre, No. 94, *n.* 1

grain (of wind), No. 8, *n.* 2
Grand-Bay, No. 7, *n.* 1
Grandval, No. 74, *n.* 15
grenier, No. 23, *n.* 2
Greuze, No. 23, *n.* 2
grille, No. 28, *n.* 9
gris, No. 22, *n.* 9
grisâtre, No. 27, *n.* 4
gros, of *souliers*, No. 33, *n.* 13
grossir, No. 81, *n.* 26
grotesque, sb., No. 72, TITLE
gueuse de fonte, etc., No. 60, *n.* 2

l'habit noir, No. 35, *n.* 19
hallali, No. 29, *n.* 16
Hamon (Port-Royal), No. 44, *n.* 17
hauteurs, No. 101, *n.* 1
Héra, No. 100, CONTEXT
Héraklès, No. 100, CONTEXT
héron, No. 87, *n.* 32
hésiter à, No. 18, *n.* 36
hêtre pourpre, — rouge, No. 19, *n.* 4
heures, à ses, No. 90, *n.* 16
heureux, No. 46, *n.* 18
hideux, No. 94, *n.* 2
d'Holbach, Baron, No. 74, *n.* 15
hosanna, No. 29, *n.* 18
humer, No. 102, *n.* 2

îlots, No. 86, *n.* 31; No. 109, *n.* 11
imagier, No. 27, *n.* 6
immense, No. 95, *n.* 1
Imperfect tense; translated by 'could', No. 50, *n.* 3; vivid imperf. *continuait = aurait continué*, No. 43, *n.* 16
importance, No. 73, *n.* 14 and *n.* 19
Impressionist style, No. 3, *n.* 9
incendie, No. 46, *n.* 13; No. 49, *n.* 23
indécis, No. 1, *n.* 18; No. 13, *n.* 1; No. 62, *n.* 1
indication, No. 36, *n.* 10
infernale: loge —, No. 33, *n.* 5; *machine —*, No. 41, *n.* 16
informe, No. 13, *n.* 8; No. 94, *n.* 2

ingrat, No. 58, *n.* 10
l'intellectuel, No. 53, *n.* 34
Iphiklès, No. 100, CONTEXT
ivoire, Tour d', No. 90, *n.* 29
ivre de volupté, No. 93, *n.* 14

jaillissantes, eaux, No. 106, *n.* 1
Jansoulet, No. 47, CONTEXT; No. 48, *n.* 2
jardin anglais, No. 28, *n.* 8
Jemmapes, No. 43, *n.* 16
jet, No. 93, *n.* 3
jeu de l'ombre et de l'éclat, No. 4, *n.* 7
jeune; of *la lumière*, No. 21, *n.* 35; of *la lune*, No. 4, *n.* 5
Joliette, La, No. 20, *n.* 9
jour de la lune, — de la nuit, No. 3, *n.* 15
jurer, No. 44, *n.* 30
la justice = police, etc., No. 19, *n.* 11

Kambrien, No. 103, TITLE

la 'Lison', No. 49, TITLE
lanterne, No. 49, *n.* 21
large, No. 7, *n.* 22; No. 62, *n.* 32
largement, No. 62, *n.* 32
Laura, No. 107, N.B.
le, la, translated by 'a', No. 46, *n.* 18; see also under Def. art.
Legendre, Mme ['Uranie'], No. 74, *n.* 22
lessives, No. 35, *n.* 8
se lever, No. 7, *n.* 2
Lifford, Earl of, No. 55, *n.* 28
le Limousin, No. 25, *n.* 6
lit, faire le — de, No. 89, *n.* 1
littérateur, No. 53, *n.* 4
livide, No. 109, *n.* 12
Lobau, *caserne*, No. 46, *n.* 16
loge infernale, No. 33, *n.* 5
logement, No. 51, *n.* 14
se loger, No. 28, *n.* 7
logis, folle du, No. 72, *n.* 5
loi = religion, No. 103, *n.* 20

INDEX OF WORDS MENTIONED OR DISCUSSED 401

de loin, No. 77, *n.* 27
longueur, tout en, No. 25, *n.* 2
Lorges, M de, No. 55, *n.* 28
"*Le Loup et l'Agneau*", No. 73, *n.* 11
lui, omitted in *Je lui ai répondu*, etc., No. 14, *n.* 18
lune, la jeune, No. 4, *n.* 5
lustre, No. 2, *n.* 12
lyre, No. 8, *n.* 1–3

machine infernale, No. 41, *n.* 16
magistrat, No. 45, *n.* 22
magot, No. 32, *n.* 3
maigre, No. 3, *n.* 7; No. 21, *n.* 3
à toutes mains, No. 55, *n.* 5; *appuyé des deux mains*, No. 103, *n.* 13
mais, No. 49, *n.* 24
Maison d'or, No. 90, *n.* 29
majestueusement, No. 95, *n.* 20
Majeure, Sainte-Marie, No. 20, *n.* 13
malcontent, No. 62, *n.* 38
malheureux, No. 87, *n.* 27
malice, No. 57, *n.* 3; No. 58, *n.* 22
manœuvres = workers, No. 40, *n.* 19
Marais, No. 97, *n.* 1
marché, No. 25, *n.* 7
Marie [Dupin], No. 107, N.B.
marri, No. 107, N.B.
masque, No. 32, *n.* 6
massifs, No. 2, *n.* 7
mât: le grand — vaincu, No. 94, *n.* 12; *mâts*, No. 20, *n.* 12
matériel, adj., No. 82, *n.* 24
matériellement, No. 82, *n.* 24
Math, fils de, No. 103, *n.* 17
mâture, No. 20, *n.* 12
mécontent, No. 62, *n.* 38
mélancolique, No. 13, *n.* 1
mémoire, No. 113, *n.* 11
menuet, No. 99, *n.* 5
méplat, No. 32, *n.* 8
merci, No. 25, *n.* 38
messieurs, No. 35, *n.* 17

mesure = cran, No. 18, *n.* 13
métayers, No. 62, *n.* 13
meuglement, No. 25, *n.* 18
mieux: pour — voir, No. 103, *n.* 12
mièvre, No. 99, *n.* 23
milieu, No. 81, *n.* 2
mille, No. 43, *n.* 11
moderne, rendre = *moderniser*, No. 38, *n.* 11
mollesse, No. 6, *n.* 11
monacal, No. 35, *n.* 14
mondain, No. 88, *n.* 8
monstrueux, No. 93, *n.* 14; No. 95, *n.* 12
montagne, translated by plural, No. 25, *n.* 18
Montespan, Mme de, No. 56, *n.* 12
monument, No. 81, *n.* 9
Mora, Duc de, No. 48, *n.* 2
morio, No. 23, *n.* 27
mort, adj., position of, No. 94, *n.* 3
mortel, No. 92, *n.* 39
Mortemart, No. 56, *n.* 12; No. 62, *n.* 5
mou, No. 36, *n.* 10
mouvant, No. 16, *n.* 11
mouvement, No. 73, *n.* 24
mue, sb., No. 45, *n.* 6
muraille, No. 21, *n.* 9
Murdoc'h, No. 103, TITLE

nacre, No. 3, *n.* 2; No. 22, *n.* 21
nappe, No. 1, *n.* 9; No. 3, *n.* 26
nation, No. 53, *n.* 26
naufrage, No. 75, *n.* 21
noblesse, la petite, No. 62, *n.* 3
noir, sb., No. 24, *n.* 19
Notre-Dame de la Garde, No. 20, *n.* 14
noyer, No. 71, *n.* 4
nuque, No. 73, *n.* 7

odorant, No. 111, *n.* 18
ombre, No. 113, *n.* 24
Omission (of French past participle), No. 15, *n.* 11; No. 18, *n.* 10; No. 51, *n.* 23; No. 62,

402 INDEX OF WORDS MENTIONED OR DISCUSSED

Omission (*cont.*)
   n. 18; (of other words), No. 14, *n*. 18; No. 16, *n*. 20; No. 69, *n*. 21
on, No. 7, *n*. 9; No. 83, *n*. 4; vaguely used, No. 9, *n*. 18
ondulant, ondulé, No. 90, *n*. 9
ongulaire, No. 24, *n*. 14
opacité, No. 29, *n*. 4
opaque, No. 16, *n*. 9; No. 29, *n*. 4
organiser, No. 38, *n*. 11
orné, No. 18, *n*. 10
oubli, No. 113, TITLE
outremer, No. 1, *n*. 15
ovale, No. 24, *n*. 29

pain blanc, No. 59, *n*. 37
pâle, pâli, No. 21, *n*. 1; *yeux pâles*, No. 32, *n*. 19
pan de mur, No. 78, *n*. 28
parfums, No. 113, *n*. 10
Parlement, No. 38, *n*. 7
Participle, see Past participle
passage (painting), No. 79, *n*. 10
passer, No. 80, *n*. 10; No. 92, *n*. 1; (fencing), No. 72, *n*. 11
Past historic, see *fut*
Past participle, omitted in English, see Omission; *pâli*)(*pâle; terni*)(*terne*, No. 21, *n*. 1
pâte, No. 58, *n*. 2
pathétique, No. 92, *n*. 2
patrie, No. 69, *n*. 7
pavé, No. 12, *n*. 10
pays, No. 52, *n*. 10; No. 53, *n*. 26
peau, of serpent, No. 29, *n*. 5
Penmarc'h, No. 103, TITLE
pensant, un roseau, No. 53, *n*. 36
pensif, No. 101, *n*. 13; No. 105, *n*. 17
perdu, exemple, No. 82, *n*. 5
perles, eau de, No. 3, *n*. 4
perron, No. 28, *n*. 9
perruque, No. 75, *n*. 3
Personal pronoun to be omitted, see Omission
personne, No. 55, *n*. 1

personnel, sb.: *le petit* —, No. 60, *n*. 17
la petite noblesse, No. 62, *n*. 3
Petrarch, No. 107, N.B.
pétri, No. 58, *n*. 2
pétulant, No. 61, *n*. 15
Phraortes, No. 102, N.B.
picorer, No. 26, *n*. 27
pièce, emporter la, No. 56, *n*. 18
pierre d'attente, No. 26, *n*. 3
pigeonnier, No. 62, *n*. 8
place, No. 89, *n*. 21
plaidoyer, No. 73, *n*. 14
plaie, No. 21, *n*. 12
plaire, No. 32, *n*. 25
plaisant, No. 56, *n*. 14
planté (omitted), No. 51, *n*. 23; No. 62, *n*. 18
plaqué, No. 75, *n*. 6
plat, No. 58, *n*. 7
platitude, No. 71, *n*. 11
à pleins rayons, à pleines mains, No. 11, *n*. 22
pliant, lit, No. 51, *n*. 18
plié, No. 39, *n*. 13
se plier, No. 33, *n*. 46
Pluperfect translated by simple past, No. 14, *n*. 18; No. 102, n. 1
Plural; of sb., No. 3, *n*. 16; of abstract nouns, *vapeurs*, etc., No. 20, *n*. 28
poème, poésie, No. 87, *n*. 15
point, sb., No. 7, *n*. 3
pointe, No. 7, *n*. 3; *une — de rocher*, No. 86, *n*. 31
pointu, No. 22, *n*. 1
poitrail, No. 47, *n*. 5; No. 50, *n*. 42
Polyphème, No. 49, *n*. 21; No. 70, *n*. 22
ponctuel, ponctuellement, No. 27, *n*. 25
posé, No. 15, *n*. 11
positif, No. 45, *n*. 26
la potasse, No. 35, *n*. 8
pour peu que, No. 57, *n*. 24; No. 87, *n*. 29

Pourceaugnac, No. 62, *n*. 7
pourpre, adj. = red, No. 19, *n*. 7; No. 113, *n*. 10; sb., No. 102, *n*. 11
poursuites, No. 23, *n*. 10
pousser au large, No. 1, *n*. 2
poussière, No. 4, *n*. 10; No. 20, *n*. 28
pratiquer, No. 27, *n*. 6
pré, No. 72, *n*. 7
précieux, No. 26, *n*. 24
précipice, No. 21, *n*. 9
préluder à, No. 78, *n*. 38
prendre, see *pris*
presque devant, No. 27, *n*. 5
prie-Dieu, No. 85, *n*. 25
principe = beginning, No. 43, *n*. 32
pris = caught, No. 73, *n*. 19
prix d'excellence, No. 59, *n*. 34; — *de sagesse*, No. 27, *n*. 15
prométhéen, No. 8, *n*. 15
Pronoun; personal, omitted, see Omission; relative, turned by a preposition, No. 1, *n*. 6
propriété, No. 59, *n*. 31
provenir, No. 50, *n*. 2
pur (of brow), No. 17, *n*. 19; (of voice), No. 33, *n*. 45

Qaïn, No. 103, TITLE
qui, as in *Qui dort dîne*, No. 73, *n*. 19

raconter, No. 56, *n*. 22
rafale, No. 8, *n*. 2
raisin, No. 113, *n*. 10
râler, No. 95, *n*. 3
rapide, adj. and sb., No. 47, *n*. 3
rapiéçages, No. 25, *n*. 4
se rappeler, No. 85, *n*. 20
rapprocher, No. 51, *n*. 25
rare, herbe, No. 7, *n*. 5
rauque, No. 95, *n*. 18
re-, in *ressuscite*, No. 99, *n*. 7; see also *retrouver*
réaliser, No. 68, *n*. 30
réciproque, sb., No. 56, *n*. 29

redresser, No. 73, *n*. 15
réduit, sb., No. 51, *n*. 20
Régence, La, No. 38, *n*. 7
religieux (= Latin *religiosus*), No. 12, *n*. 16
Rembrandt, No. 2, *n*. 20; No. 34, *n*. 3
rempart, No. 7, *n*. 1
renflement, No. 20, *n*. 16
reprendre, No. 73, *n*. 12
resquillage, No. 92, *n*. 37
Restauration, La, No. 45, *n*. 18
retour de flamme, No. 45, *n*. 19
retrouver, No. 2, *n*. 5; No. 14, *n*. 16; No. 72, *n*. 3
rire, sb., No. 57, *n*. 2
rocher, une pointe de, No. 86, *n*. 31
rogner, No. 85, *n*. 35
Ronarc'h, No. 103, TITLE
rond (soleil), No. 2, *n*. 18
Rose mystique, No. 90, *n*. 29; *rose sèche*, No. 19, *n*. 13
roseau pensant, No. 53, *n*. 36
rouler, not "roll", No. 21, *n*. 9
roux, sb., No. 29, *n*. 20
Roye, Comte de, No. 55, *n*. 28
ruissellement, No. 20, *n*. 19; No. 94, *n*. 16
rusé, No. 33, *n*. 45

sabot, No. 23, *n*. 5
sagesse, prix de, No. 27, *n*. 15
Saint-Just, No. 30, *n*. 1
Saint-Louis, Chevaliers de, No. 39, *n*. 12
Saint-Nicaise, rue, No. 41, *n*. 16
Sainte-Marie-Majeure, No. 20, *n*. 13
saison, la belle, No. 86, *n*. 6
salle, No. 23, *n*. 1; — *à manger*, No. 51, *n*. 19
Salmasius, see Saumaise
Salviati, Cassandra, No. 107, N.B.
sanglot, No. 95, *n*. 12
sarde, sardonique: sourire —, No. 33, *n*. 39

Saumaise, No. 70, *n.* 4
sauvage, adj., No. 110, *n.* 4; sb., No. 59, *n.* 39–41
savoir, vb., No. 71, *n.* 13
science, No. 81, TITLE and *n.* 21
seigneurs, beaux, No. 99, *n.* 19
sérieux, No. 33, *n.* 24
serré, adj. = close set, No. 3, *n.* 7
serrer, No. 51, *n.* 25
servage, en, No. 107, N.B.
séton, No. 25, *n.* 33
seulement, No. 73, *n.* 40
si, introducing a fact, not a hypothesis, No. 113, *n.* 19
sinistre, No. 101, *n.* 1
sinueux, No. 31, *n.* 11
social, sb., No. 53, *n.* 34
souffrir, No. 82, *n.* 21
souliers, No. 33, *n.* 13; No. 39, *n.* 16
souvenir, No. 113, *n.* 11; *se —*, No. 85, *n.* 20
Spinoza, No. 73, *n.* 9
spirituel, No. 15, *n.* 6
subtil, No. 15, *n.* 6; No. 77, *n.* 24
suie, No. 24, *n.* 19
superbe = Latin *superbus*, No. 12, *n.* 16; No. 102, *n.* 12
supporter, No. 26, *n.* 7
sympathique, encre, No. 42, *n.* 25

tailler, No. 7, *n.* 3
talon, No. 73 *n.* 7
tant que, No. 86, *n.* 16
taupinière, No. 62, *n.* 40
Tauride, la vierge de, No. 30, *n.* 7
teint, sans, No. 34, *n.* 5
tendre, No. 15, *n.* 2
ténébreuse: Une — Affaire, No. 42, *n.* 1
Tense, No. 83, *n.* 9; abrupt change of, No. 1, *n.* 3; No. 4, *n.* 15; No. 7, *n.* 20; No. 11, *n.* 21; No. 25, *n.* 23; No. 58, *n.* 8; No. 77, *n.* 31; future translated by English past, No. 43, *n.* 9; past historic, see *fut*

Tense, see also Imperfect, Pluperfect, Conditional and Past participle
terne, terni, No. 21, *n.* 1
terrain vague, No. 26, *n.* 1
tête, No. 7, *n.* 14; No. 36, *n.* 3; *— carrée*, No. 31, *n.* 22
Thomson, *Seasons*, No. 90, *n.* 16
tintement, No. 20, *n.* 34
tinter, No. 85, *n.* 18
Titania, No. 2, *n.* 21
tolets, No. 1, *n.* 1
tombe, tombeau, No. 7, *n.* 2
tonneau diogénique, No. 73, *n.* 25
torrent, = mountain stream, No. 5, *n.* 9; No. 70, *n.* 2
toucher à, No. 50, *n.* 9
Tour d'ivoire, No. 90, *n.* 29
tourbillon, No. 110, *n.* 7
tourmente, No. 8, *n.* 2
tournevis, No. 50, *n.* 13
tout: — à tous, No. 56, *n.* 13; *— en longueur*, No. 25, *n.* 2; *être de —*, No. 55, *n.* 23; *à toutes mains*, No. 55, *n.* 5
traîner, No. 110, *n.* 7
tranchée, formant, No. 19, *n.* 18
Trebia, *Trebbia, Trébie*, No. 101, *n.* 1, TITLE
tribun, No. 102, *n.* 2
triomphant, No. 101, *n.* 13
trompe des journaux, No. 25, *n.* 15
tronc, No. 12, *n.* 13
trouble, No. 99, *n.* 13
troupe, enfant de, No. 59, *n.* 24
troupeau, No. 25, *n.* 8
turquoises, No. 33, *n.* 4

uni, No. 27, *n.* 4
universitaire, l'Université, No. 34, *n.* 17
'Uranie', No. 74, *n.* 22
l'usage, No. 55, *n.* 22
user, user de, No. 82, *n.* 18

vain = empty, No. 83, *n.* 8; No. 104, *n.* 2; No. 113, *n.* 4

INDEX OF WORDS MENTIONED OR DISCUSSED

velléité, No. 57, *n.* 27
vérité dernière, les vérités dernières, No. 45, *n.* 28
vert, No. 26, *n.* 21; No. 113, *n.* 10
vierge : La — de Tauride, No. 30, *n.* 7
vil, No. 105, *n.* 1
visage, No. 32, *n.* 4; No. 37, *n.* 5–6
vivement, No. 36, *n.* 1
Vivonne, Maréchal de, No. 56, *n.* 12
voir, untranslated, No. 62, *n.* 2; *pour mieux —*, No. 103, *n.* 12; *se —*, No. 35, *n.* 17; *on voyait*, No. 39, *n.* 24
voire, No. 62, *n.* 25
Volland, Sophie, No. 74, *n.* 15
volontiers, No. 62, *n.* 14
volupté, No. 7, *n.* 21; No. 93, *n.* 14
vouloir, a voulu, No. 9, *n.* 3

wagon, No. 60, *n.* 2

y, omitted, No. 51, *n.* 17